Henry William Pullen

The World of Cant

Henry William Pullen

The World of Cant

ISBN/EAN: 9783744731034

Printed in Europe, USA, Canada, Australia, Japan

Cover: Foto ©ninafisch / pixelio.de

More available books at **www.hansebooks.com**

THE
WORLD OF CANT.

Envy.—My Lord, this man . . . neither regardeth prince nor people, law nor custom; but doth all that he can to possess all men with certain of his disloyal notions, which he, in the general, calls principles of faith and holiness. And, in particular, I heard him once myself affirm that Christianity and the customs of our Town of Vanity were diametrically opposite, and could not be reconciled. By which saying, my lord, he doth at once, not only condemn all our laudable doings, but us in the doing of them.

Superstition.—My lord, I have no great acquaintance with this man, nor do I desire to have further knowledge of him. . . . I heard him say that our religion was naught; and such by which a man could by no means please God. Which saying of his, my lord, your lordship very well knows what necessarily thence will follow, to wit, that we still do worship in vain, are yet in our sins.

Pickthank.—I have heard him speak things that ought not to be spoke; for he hath railed on our noble prince Beelzebub, and hath spoken contemptibly of his honourable friends, whose names are the Lord Old Man, the Lord Cardinal Delight, the Lord Luxurious, the Lord Desire of Vain Glory, my old Lord Lechery, Sir Having Greedy, with all the rest of our nobility.

Judge.—(To the prisoner) Sirrah, sirrah, thou deservest to live no longer, but to be slain immediately upon the place; yet, that all men may see our gentleness towards thee, let us hear what thou, vile runagate, hast to say.—[*The trial of Faithful, reported in Bunyan's "Pilgrim's Progress."*]

"May the Lord deliver us from all Cant: may the Lord, whatever else he do or forbear, teach us to look facts honestly in the face, and to beware (with a kind of shudder) of smearing them over with our despicable and damnable palaver into irrecognisability, and so falsifying the Lord's own Gospels to his unhappy blockheads of Children, all staggering down to Gehenna and the everlasting Swine's-trough, for want of Gospels.

"O Heaven! it is the most accursed sin of man: and done everywhere at present, on the streets and high places at noonday! Verily, seriously I say and pray as my chief orison, May the Lord deliver us from it."—*Letter from Carlyle to Emerson.*

LONDON:

WALTER SCOTT, 24 WARWICK LANE,

PATERNOSTER ROW.

PROLOGUE.

THE writer's aim has been to deal with systems, and not with individuals; with a whole genus, and not with isolated members of a particular fraternity.

A writer of Natural History in treating of bears, lions, or serpents, would not, when he speaks of *the* bear, *the* lion, or *the* serpent, imply any exceptional individual animal, but would intend by those terms to indicate generally the particular type of creature the habits of which he might be delineating.

In like manner the present writer, when speaking of Hardcastle, of Golding, of Everton, of Beeswax, or of the other inhabitants of the World of Cant, does not refer to any individual whatsoever, but to the class generally for which the several names stand, for the time being, as descriptive

CONTENTS.

CHAPTER I.

The mechanism of pageantry. Fashionable prayer and fashionable shows. Cant in combination with worldliness. Extremes of social conditions. Tom 1

CHAPTER II.

Civilized heathenism. Claptrap *versus* Christianity. Pietistic pandering to popular inanities. The Worship of semblances. Snobbery in pew and pulpit. Tom puzzled. The Rev. Falcon Small, Mr. Hardcastle, Mr. Blooster, and Mr. Lorraine 6

CHAPTER III.

Wreck of the *Rasselas*. Melville and the deserted children, Katie and Annie. Cant in combination with cowardice . 4i

CHAPTER IV.

Tom obtains a situation. History of Blooster. The incalculable commercial value of Cant. Gullibility the unfailing friend of Cant. Churches and Chapels degraded by adventurers. Psychological and moral effects of Cant . . . 26

CHAPTER V.

Cant: its cruelty, meanness, and stupidity. The Church as a political machine. Sir Nicol Giltspur, the Conservative Churchman . . . . 3¦

CHAPTER VI.

Melville at Sir Nicol Giltspur's garden party. Art Cant. Lord Everton. Miss Victoria Hardcastle. Cant and flunkeyism. Idolatry 36

CHAPTER VII.

Mr. Tremlin. Mrs. Tremlin, the woman who cants. Cant a debaser of childhood 47

CHAPTER VIII.

Cant and husband-catching. Lord Everton's engagement. Mrs. and Miss Anastatia Hardcastle. Miss Isabel Landor . 57

CHAPTER IX.

Cant the enemy of true teachers. More about Mrs. Tremlin's theology. Mr. Caleb Faithful 65

CHAPTER X.

Cant on the missionary platform. Sir Harry Grapeshot and Mr. Caleb Faithful. War and Christianity. Tom decides to enlist 72

CHAPTER XI.

Cant about newspapers. Hardcastle's party. Mr. Golding, M.P. 79

CHAPTER XII.

Cant, baptism, and game preserving. Tom in trouble. The Rev. Ezekiel Smallweed, Baptist Minister. Katie and Annie 89

CHAPTER XIII.

Cant, conjugal nagging, bill discounting, and heresy hunting Mr. Caleb Faithful's perplexity. Mr. Agnew Mumm . . 96

CHAPTER XIV.

Cant and ignorance. Mr. Beeswax and Mr. Treacles. "The deacon" despotism. Rev. Mr. Rainford, Congregational Minister 10

CHAPTER XV.

Cant, priesthood, and advowsons. The Rev. Mr. Gilmour, the Rector 114

CHAPTER XVI.

Cant and blackguardism. The "We" of religious newspapers. Rev. Jabez Blaze. Boss the Fiddler, and Joyful Ginger . 126

CHAPTER XVII.

Cant the destroyer of domestic peace. Mr. Oscar Crayford, Plymouth Brother. Mrs. Milard, Mr. and Mrs. Lorraine . 133

CHAPTER XVIII.

Cant and fraud. The Plymouth Brother. The dispute between Mr. Lorraine and Mr. Oscar Crayford 149

CHAPTER XIX.

Cant "heevangelical" respecting "the blood." A heroine— Mrs. Rainford. More about "the deacon" despotism. Visit of Beeswax and Treacles to Mr. Rainford. Mr. Rainford's illness 154

CHAPTER XX.

Cant and persecution. John Blunt on dogma divorced from duty. A Church meeting without Beeswax. The tale of the teeth 165

CHAPTER XXI.

Cant usurping the Churchyard. Death of Katie. Scene between the Rev. Tancred Lawson and the High Church Vicar . 171

CHAPTER XXII.

Cant barking according to law. Mr. Ferrett Smuggle, attorney, threatens Mr. Melville. The tale of the teeth concluded. Manœuvres and success of "heevangelical" intolerance. Mr. Melville attends the Chenley tea-meeting. Dr. Sound . 177

CHAPTER XXIII.

Cant the promoter of a spurious matrimony, the destroyer of modesty, and the debaser of woman. Mrs. Hardcastle and Miss Isabel Landor 186

CHAPTER XXIV.

Cant, fashion, and frivolity. Mr. Adolphus Bumpus. Current reasons for Churchmanship 195

CHAPTER XXV.

Cant, confessional, and ritual. Rev. Demetrius Muriel, the High Church Rector. The almighty "She". 202

CHAPTER XXVI.

Cant and inquisitorial effrontery. The Soppet and Larby grand revivalistic exhibition explained. The story of Dandy Filch . . . 210

CHAPTER XXVII.

Cant and callousness. Mr. Tremlin is made ill. The canting wife as nurse. Mr. Melville appeals to Mr. Agnew Mumm. The God of one man is another man's Devil . . . 218

CHAPTER XXVIII.

Cant straining at a gnat and swallowing a camel. Warriors at an anti-vivisection meeting. The assassinators of men proclaiming the inviolability of the black-beetle. . . . 231

CHAPTER XXIX.

Cant gloating over moral putrescence. Pendango—the christian prize champion. A revivalistic festival. Mr. Tremlin dies . 236

CHAPTER XXX.

Cant the debaser of childhood. The Misses Haghard's school—the nursery of Cant. Mrs. Rose's school—the home of truth 241

CHAPTER XXXI.

Cant and wiliness. Rev. Hamilton Carney. Rev. Mr. Rainford removes to London. A missionary working party. A prayer-meeting. An entire day with Rev. Falcon Small—an account of the invaluable and unostentatious work done therein by this popular preacher "to extend his Master's kingdom" 250

CHAPTER XXXII.

Cant as a remunerative profession. The blasphemy of popular theology. Rev. Jehosophat Danks 260

CHAPTER XXXIII.

Cant and colleges. Overcrowded state of denominational harvestfields. Mr. Darnley's protest. Mr. Melville and Mr. Rainford meet 267

CHAPTER XXXIV.

Cant and shuffling. Mr. Melville's visit to the Rev. Falcon Small. The value of a popular preacher as a help in trouble 273

Contents.

CHAPTER XXXV.
Cant and crime. Golding's gamekeeper dies in a scuffle with Tom. Newspaper marvels 278

CHAPTER XXXVI.
Cant and electoral tactics. A drawing-room prayer-meeting. Colonel Sammey's "great work at the Barracks." Miss Irene Graham betrothed to Mr. Oscar Crayford . . . 281

CHAPTER XXXVII.
Cant, persecution, and sly slander. Mr. Melville visits Tom in prison 292

CHAPTER XXXVIII.
Cant neglects the waif, and protects the felon. Tom in prison. The jail Chaplain's theology 298

CHAPTER XXXIX.
Cant the consecrator of monstrous marriages. Mr. and Mrs. Oscar Crayford. The Plymouth Brother in his home. Hannah 302

CHAPTER XL.
Cant and indecorous ceremonies. A baptism at Mr. Crayford's house. Mrs. Christabel Darnley. Mr. Crayford unmasked by Mr. Lorraine. Mrs. Crayford's intercession . . . 311

CHAPTER XLI.
Cant, peculation, and inhumanity. The sanctified rascality which eludes the law. Blooster defrauds Carter the cripple: drives him mad; and prays for him 322

CHAPTER XLII.
Cant committing larcenies on the charitable. The begging circular imposture. Miss Scampion's "Home" investigated in court. Mr. Melville rescues Carter's children . . . 329

CHAPTER XLIII.
Cant and self-deception. Religious coddling, quackery, and silliness. Rev. Mr. Mawksley, Arminian Methodist. Rev. Mr. Howling, Calvinist. Mrs. Tremlin becomes Mrs. Charlesworthy 337

CHAPTER XLIV.

Cant and intrigue. Mr. Lorraine's magnanimity. Mr. Crayford is confronted by Mr. Darnley 348

CHAPTER XLV.

Cant a ladder by which the unscrupulous ascend to power. The Rev. Dandy Filch is exalted. Mr. Blooster is trusted . 359

CHAPTER XLVI.

Cant and perfidiousness. Mr. Hardcastle's unjust will. Lord Everton and Mr. Bumpus harassed by Blooster after Mr. Hardcastle's decease. Blooster dies 362

CHAPTER XLVII.

Cant, blasphemy, profanation, and knavishness. A pair of lawyers. Mr. Falcon Small as a time-server . . . 368

CHAPTER XLVIII.

Cant protected by conventional opinion. Mr. Caleb Faithful's onslaught. Mr. Scorpion and Mr. Krimes baffled. Lord Everton's epistolary castigation of Mr. Falcon Small . . 372

CHAPTER XLIX.

Cant and remunerative philanthropy-mongering. How a religious society is incubated. Mr. Tonkin Sappey and "The Salvation Mission to the Grades." Mr. Adams, the great subscription-list maker 378

CHAPTER L.

Cant and clerical obsequiousness. The Rev. Smallman Petty's assize sermon. Mr. Justice Humpleby. Tom's trial and sentence . . . .

CHAPTER LI.

Cant, ostentation, and counterfeit liberality. Mr. Melville's discovery. Mr. Golding at bay. Tom is hanged . 393

CHAPTER LII.

Cant a curse to mankind. Retrospect. Summary. The crusade against Cant 399

THE WORLD OF CANT.

CHAPTER I.

The Mechanism of Pageantry.—Fashionable Prayer and Fashionable Shows.—Cant in Combination with Worldliness.—Extremes of Social Conditions.—Tom.

IT was a dull morning in the early spring. The clouds lowered gloomily, and the wind, blowing from the north-east, swept coldly and cheerlessly through the London streets. But, notwithstanding the threatening weather and early hour, the citizens of our vast metropolis were already astir, and it needed but a glance at the decorated streets to tell that it was the dawn of a festive day. A court procession was to pass, and this fact was quite enough to bring British subjects from all parts to obtain a glimpse at royalty. No expense had been spared to make this "gracious entry" a consummate success. Decorations were gorgeous. Flags and banners of every colour, interspersed with brilliant pennants, embellished the streets. Numerous devices worked on crimson and yellow cloth were suspended from the windows. Festoons of flowers spanned the thoroughfares; and wherever four roads met pavilions were erected in their centres, resplendent with gildings, groups of statuary, and elaborate ornamentations It was a loyal display, but the loyalty had been organized. Committees of householders had held numerous meetings, when large sums of money were subscribed to raise the necessary funds required for the stupendous panorama. For example, in Regent Street there were two committees, the chairmen of which stimulated the inhabitants "loyally to do their best to make this an important occasion;" and the results of the excitement were, an infectious fever for decorations, and subscriptions amounting to two thousand pounds. Ludgate Hill householders, after several important conferences, and an unanimous resolve "for uniformity of display," raised one thousand pounds. The smaller streets were overcome by the condescension of royalty in deigning to pass through their humble thoroughfares, and, in a frenzy of devoted loyalty, vied with their more aristocratic neighbours in costly and brilliant array.

Most of the shops along the route were closed for ordinary business; the goods which the windows usually contained having been withdrawn in favour of reserved seats to view the procession, the large profits of which were another gratifying indication, especially to the tradesmen, of the popular enthusiasm. Grand stands were erected on all unoccupied plots of ground, the costs of which, and of suitable luncheons to favoured guests, were munificently defrayed by Boards of Works, Metropolitan Vestries, and other local bodies, who were thus able to indulge their personal loyalty at the expense of the ratepayers.

The moments fly by, and the crowd is beginning to assemble; and, notwithstanding the drizzling rain, the people increase at a rapid rate. Locomotion begins to quicken. The long man lengthens his long strides; the short man runs and puffs; the fat man waddles and wheezes. Boys holloo and duck in and out of the crowd. Women clasp their infants closer to them, and fathers raise little urchins on their shoulders. "They come! They come!" Eager forms press forward to catch the first glimpse; the mounted police, with licensed cruelty, backing their horses meanwhile upon the most advanced. The upper spheres now smile upon the scene. "A special correspondent," alert at the exact moment of time to

heavens, has placed the phenomenon upon permanent record in a daily paper. He, with loyal rapture, now beheld that, according to the requirements of the procession, the "sleet crystallized into hail, the hail melted into rain, the rain was reduced to mist, the mist was pierced with light, and ultimately the sunbeams burst through the clouds, realizing the good old adage, 'Royal folks bring royal weather.'" Nor was anything more auspicious than the coincidence by which "the sun shone out in all his welcome splendour at that very moment when the royal pageant alighted at the doors of the holy Cathedral which was its destination." Those whose sentimental susceptibilities were acute saw a kind of spiritual significance in that fact. Its impressiveness seemed greater still when they watched the Bishops and Archbishops leave their prancing horses, gilded equipages, and powdered flunkeys, and walk in state through the decorated approach to the place of prayer. For then the lights of civilization and of nature seemed together to proclaim that the religion of The Galilean had achieved most wondrous progress in the world. And amidst the clanging of bells, and the hurrahs of the multitude, it was made manifest that the stale old command was abrogated which enjoined "praying in secret to a Father who seeth in secret."

The public prayers being ended, the procession was again formed, and returned by nearly the same route, amidst the acclamations of the sight-seers. The sunlight declines with the last of the show. The drizzling rain sets in once more, and the crowd disperses quickly through the damp, dirty streets. Many are hastening to their comfortable homes, and some are seeking the wretched shelter of the miserable haunts which lie hidden at the back of the gaily-dressed streets. Into one of these homes of the poor our business now requires us to turn—into a damp and cellar-like room, where no fire brightens the empty grate, and the furniture consists of one chair and a three-legged table. To the solitary occupant of the place its wretchedness matters little now. Only a few hours more and the poor sufferer will be unconscious of the miseries of a straw-bed and a dark, damp room. "Tom, Tom," she murmurs. "Oh, I wish he would come." She has hardly uttered these words when the door softly opens and a ragged youth of about sixteen years enters. We saw him with the crowd just now trying to sell his fusees. No wonder he begged so earnestly, with a dying mother at home. The woman eagerly beckons him to her.

"Tom, I am near the end, and I have so much to say. You must listen at once."

"I have got a loaf, mother. I bought it coming along. Have some before you talk."

"No, no. Put it down and listen. Thank God, I have done with hunger now."

With a look of disappointment on his somewhat unintelligent face, Tom places the bread on the table, and seats himself on the ground to listen.

"I wish you could have seen the streets, mother. They was jist fine, and all them r'yal folks they was grand. I climbed up a post and see'd 'em. When you're better, perhaps there'll be anither show. I'd fight for a good place for you."

"Tom, I shall never be better. To-night you will be motherless. And oh, Tom, if all the fine folks you have seen to-day did but know the misery that lies near them, their hearts would surely ache with sympathy for the unfortunate and obscure of the earth. I was not always as I am now, Tom. My circumstances were comfortable and my future bright. But, sad as my life has been ever since your recollection of it, I should have been more miserable still if I had not always endeavoured to be honest and upright. Tom, be honest, whatever you do. We have had a hard struggle, but we have *earned* what we got, and you must be honest still when I am gone. There is a little

have kept it. Get it and the letters which are tied in the small packet near it. They are all I have to give you. The letters are from those who should have been more merciful."

Incoherent mutterings now followed, and Tom strove in vain to catch her words, but the mind was wandering, and the frightened boy's entreaties were unheeded. Darkness was coming on. There were few candles in that court. Tom's last look had been taken of his mother; he now could only feel her hand. How cold it was, as the bleak night wind howled through the court! The boy shivered as he grasped the woman's icy fingers. Her breathing grew slower and slower; Tom could hear how laboured was each respiration, and he guessed that the end was near.

"Tom!"

"I am here, mother, close by."

"That is right, my boy. I can feel you now. Tom, try to be brave and honest."

She spoke no more. One long-drawn sigh, and the fingers that clasped Tom's hand relaxed their hold. He could not see, but, alas! he *felt* she was dead. It was sad that not one ray from the illumined streets entered the little room; and, therefore, these two, who were all in all to one another, parted in utter darkness. But we must not linger on a tragedy like this. Society cannot permit its movements to be chilled and depressed by unpleasant sights. Therefore, ride on, my ladies, lords and gentlemen, Bishops and Archbishops, mistress of the robes, ladies of the bedchamber-in-waiting, maids of honour-in-waiting, groom of the robes, pages of honour, master of the buckhounds, gentlemen ushers, gold stick-in-waiting, silver stick-in-waiting, and all the rest of you! It were ill-bred to intrude on your luxurious pageantry to show you that distracted, ill-starred boy, who, motherless and homeless, now emerges from the awful gloom, and trembles along the gaily-dressed streets over which your processions roll.

CHAPTER II.

CIVILIZED HEATHENISM. — CLAPTRAP *versus* CHRISTIANITY. — PIETISTIC PANDERING TO POPULAR INANITIES.—THE WORSHIP OF SEMBLANCES.—SNOBBERY IN PEW AND PULPIT.—TOM PUZZLED.—MR. HARDCASTLE, MR. BLOOSTER, AND MR. LORRAINE.

SUNDAY morning! The air is resonant with the melody of tuneful bells; and in all parts of London people are flocking to different houses of worship.

In a densely populated third-rate neighbourhood in London rises the stupendous edifice of the Rev. Falcon Small. The congregation is assembling; and the tide of chapel-goers sets strongly in this direction. Tom wanders wearily amidst them, leaving it to chance or caprice to direct his steps. It has been announced during the week on numerous placards and hand-bills, and in every metropolitan paper, that the Rev. Falcon Small would preach this morning on "The Week's Great Event!" Many persons besides the general congregation were drawn by this, which was intended to be a startling announcement. Tom was one of them. The choral service interested him very much, and roused his inquiring faculties. It puzzled him to understand why the six conspicuously healthy, happy-looking maidens in an adjoining pew should sing, "My days are consumed like smoke. My bones are burned as an hearth. My heart is smitten and withered like grass, so that I forget to eat my bread." And also, why a stout, jolly-looking man who stood near him should lustily sing, "By reason of the voice of my groaning, my bones cleave to my skin, and I am withered like grass." Nor was his astonishment less, when some vigorous boys and girls behind him, not over twelve years of age, protested, "Many bulls have compassed me: strong bulls of Bashan have beset me around. My strength is dried up like a potsherd, and my tongue cleaveth to my jaws; and thou hast brought me into the dust of death." It appeared to him that these singers gave the Lord a somewhat fanciful account of their experiences.

The preliminary services having been gone through, a hymn is sung, during which Mr. Falcon Small ascends the pulpit stairs. He is tall, thin, and pale; one of those men who scarcely ever having had a day's illness, yet give you the idea that they are in the last stage of a consumption. His restless, observant eye, hawk-like in acuteness, reads well the changes of expression in his listeners' faces. His thin lips, when they smile, resemble not so much the genial glow of summer's sun as the glitter of the ice under a winter moonbeam. If his forehead is small, the baldness of his head so adds to its dimensions as to give to it quite the appearance of respectable mediocrity; and the extreme diminutiveness of his cranium would not be so observable but for the scantness of his dark hair, which, however, is carefully arranged to do as much service as possible. An aquiline nose of good proportions, indicates at once the shrewdness of its possessor, and gives a character and force to the countenance. A dignified figure, imposing mannerism, some grace of diction, and a good voice, render him effective as a speaker. He joined with eager ostentation the chorus of voices; and directly the hymn was ended he commenced his discourse with a fervour and rapidity of movement intended to suggest that there was not one moment to spare.

"Some of you," said he, "during the past week have mingled in the rejoicings that celebrated the Royal Entry through our metropolis for the purpose of prayer. As I stood at one of the windows in this grand city, and watched the vast concourse of expectant faces, all eager to shout their welcome; as I gazed on the beautified and embellished streets, for whose rich adornings thousands of pounds had been readily and gladly subscribed ; and as I contemplated the celerity with which those streets had been transformed into a fairyland of architectural and floral beauty, my intense wonder and admiration suggested to me the following thoughts on the 'Great Event' which we have recently beheld in this the mightiest city in the world. In unison with these remarks it will not be out of place to direct your attention to the words, 'Render unto Cæsar the things that are Cæsar's.'" The first head of this discourse then followed. "Rendering unto Cæsar is a Divine command," said the preacher as he proceeded to show the fitness of reverencing those who are set in authority over us. Then, comparing the present times with past centuries, he pointed out that this was the age in which religion and fashion were fused together. Passing on to the power of the British nation, he wound up the first part of his sermon in theatrical tones by asking, "And what is it that makes us, as a nation, the first in all the earth? One reason, and to my mind an all-important one, is our intolerance of popery. No Jesuitism saps the splendid fabric of our English court, or is permitted long to lurk in our baronial halls. For, when Rome attempts any new design, these powers join in the sentiment which the working men of this vast country embody in their short, telling, emphatic vernacular, 'No Popery.' But chiefly we occupy this proud position because we are a christian people. The nobles feel that their nobility is safe in the hands of our less fortunate christians who have learnt the great lesson not to be envious of fashion which they must admire, but to render unto Cæsar the things that are his. Our millionaires with their banks and palaces have no misgiving that their splendid treasures will be touched by the working classes who are taught by the pulpit to submit to wealth. Nor do the votaries of fashion, the epicures of

delight those gay and brilliant scenes into which the christian rarely enters, even fear that cynicism will ferment into vindictiveness, or censure take the form of attack. They know full well that the christian pulpits of the land ceaselessly proclaim, 'Render unto Cæsar the things that are Cæsar's!'" The rev. gentleman then passed on to show the excellent effects upon the hearts and consciences of men of this habit of rendering unto Cæsar the things that are Cæsar's. "And this," he said, "led him to consider the position which the mind should assume towards superior authority. The habit of bowing loyally to those in authority was one most salutary and beneficent for the human mind, and was the only one which enabled man to receive the truth. No disloyal crotchets, none of the deterrent influences which warp the soul and blind the judgment, were to be found in the man who undoubtingly had accepted once for all, and in its fullest meaning, the import of the words, 'Render unto Cæsar the things that are Cæsar's.' Such a man, by the very constitution of his mental and moral nature, would be led from reverencing the great to admiring the greater, and worshipping the Greatest, until he was at last ready to be bathed in the atoning blood. He naturally and irresistibly would look up ever afterwards from the worship of the earthly throne to the heavenly palace, from lords and dukes to angels and archangels, from the crowns of time to the diadems of eternity, and from the potentialities of the earth to the powers and principalities and dominions of the sky. Obedient as a subject, he naturally becomes obedient as a Christian; and rendering unto Cæsar the things that are Cæsar's, it follows as certainly as the day follows the dawn, that he will consummate our text and render unto the Higher Authority the obedience that is His."

The reverend gentleman of course made his usual remarks on "simple faith being alone necessary to salvation," assuring all who had accepted the objective fact of the crucifixion, that they had nothing else to trouble about. For there were many in his Church who had a great repugnance to what they called "moral works," and it was always necessary that they should have a doctrine of inactivity placed before them. They required to be informed every Sunday that they had "not to work out their own salvation" by striving to live an ideal life. It was their creed that everything had been done for them 1800 years ago; and in order to get to heaven they had only to believe it was so.

The sermon having ended amidst a chorus of liberated coughs, which sounded like the suppressed applause of those who had, hitherto, sat sedately torpid and devoutly dumb, the Rev. Falcon Small, with elevated eyeballs and in a snuffling whine, gave out the following hymn :—

> "Oh, the Lamb, the Lamb, the bleeding Lamb,
> The Lamb that was slain for me,
> The Lamb that was slain, and that yet rose again,
> That bleeding Lamb for me."

After the effective singing of this by the whole congregation, led by an able choir sustained by a majestic organ, the reverend gentleman made the following statement: "I am requested to announce that collections will be made to-day from pew to pew for the 'Memorial Window.' For the benefit of those who are not usual attendants here, it will be well to give a few words of explanation. Not long since, the late Lord Cakesbury was persuaded by a worshipper here to attend one of our services. The sermon which I then had the honour to preach before that noble lord, by the especial blessing of God, led to his conversion to our views, and from being a strict adherent to the Church of England forms, he became, during the remaining four months of his life, an occasional attendant here. Most generously and nobly he aided our eight schools, by allowing his name to appear as a patron of them ; and his lamented death robbed our cause of the influential support of a noble name. It is proposed that a memorial window be raised to his memory in the south aisle. Five hundred pounds have already been subscribed. There remain but one hundred more to be obtained. If ten of you were to give five pounds, only fifty would be required. May I ask you all to subscribe heartily and liberally this morning to this grand work."

The benediction was then pronounced, and the congregation dispersed. Amongst the crowd walked Tom. As the sermon had not been intended for the sorrowful, of course it was not within its scope to soothe his stricken heart. So far as it affected his dull brains at all, it was to suggest to him that his duty lay in a career of subservience to the classes whom the reverend gentleman extolled.

From that vague impression came another, namely, that in the army, whose officers shone in the late procession, he could serve at once his God, and his country, and carry out his mother's last injunction as to honesty. Revolving these things in his mind, and wondering whether it might ever be his lot to stand among the grand personages whom he had seen at the show, and whose virtues Mr. Small magnified, he pursued his unobserved course.

Meanwhile, other actors are coming on the scene.

"What a splendid sermon!" exclaimed Mr. Hardcastle, in attendant at Mr. Falcon Small's Church for many years, to his friend Mr. Blooster, one of the deacons.

"Magnificent!" assented Blooster in his pompous tones. "I must get him to print that."

Blooster was a tall, stout, consequential man, of a bloated countenance, and with a gross, bull neck. His thick black beard was plentifully streaked with white, and his nose had that upward turn at the extremity which befitted his self-assertive and bombastic character. The man seemed to be a concretion into fleshly form of his oft-repeated phrase, "I know a trick or two."

"Let me introduce you to Mr. Lorraine," continued

Blooster, and the customary salutations having been exchanged, the three gentlemen left the Chapel.

The preliminary topics usually introduced by Englishmen into their conversation having been exhausted, it naturally turned upon the discourse they had just listened to, Mr. Blooster remarking to Mr. Hardcastle, "My friend here has been trying to prove to me that our preacher's logic was at fault, but it won't do."

"What!" exclaimed Mr. Hardcastle, "didn't you like our pastor?"

Mr. Lorraine smiled as this question was put to him. "Your preacher was right in saying that 'rendering to Cæsar' was a Divine command; but cringing to Cæsar's littleness and pandering to his luxury and extravagance, in fact, rendering Cæsar more than is due to him, is *not* a Divine command; and Mr. Small, in his vindication of grandeur and pomp, strayed far away from the meaning of his text. With regard to his logic, one of his chief fallacies lay in the assumption that an idolatry of temporal power and false grandeur was likely to prepare the mind for the proper worship of God. If such an inference could be drawn the greatest admirer of worldly pomp would be the best Christian, which we know is not, and never will be, the case. Fancy Hampden or Milton subscribing to such servility."

Whether Mr. Hardcastle reflected on this it would be difficult to say; he contented himself with remarking—

"Well, the thing was wonderfully clear to me, and I can see better than I ever did before how right it is to reverence those above us."

Mr. Blooster evasively remarked,—

"In these matters we must not allow the intellect to become a stumbling-block."

"Certainly not," responded Lorraine; "but I often observe that there is in some circles a tendency to fetter all intellectual criticism when it ventures within the pulpit region. In your offices you value a clerk according to his capacity for forming sound judgments. In your pews you condemn the clerk for using his brains at all. Why should not a composition by the Rev. Falcon Small be subjected to examination or analysis like any other literary effort?"

"Why?" exclaimed the amazed Mr. Hardcastle; "because, being a minister, he ought to know what's right."

"He ought to know what is right," rejoined Mr. Lorraine; "but is it denied to any one to inquire whether he does or not?"

"But look what he does!" exclaimed Blooster. "Perhaps you have not heard of our eight Sunday-schools, of our Midnight Meeting Movement, of our Ginger-beer and Chestnut Brigade, Shoeblacks' Debating Society, etc. Why, we raise hundreds of pounds, we do, for these sort of things, and Small is at the head of them all. What did one of the Liberal leaders think of him the other day?— why, he had him to tea; and Dean Candles walks arm-in-arm with him, and he can get *any* noble lords to his meetings. I should think *they* might be trusted to judge."

"Judge for whom?" retorted Mr. Lorraine, the fire beginning to flash from his dark eye and redden his cheek. "Judge for those who are carried away by titles and tinsel, and who prefer to have their thinking done for them instead of doing it themselves. I cannot accept Mr. Small's gospel just because he happens to have other people's patronage, and it matters not at all to me whether they have handles to their names or not. Every thinker should shrink from mere traditional authority. This bowing to friendly or fashionable opinion in spiritual matters seems strangely incongruous with the attack made on popery this morning."

"Oh, come," cried Mr. Hardcastle, "this won't do. If there's one thing our pastor is more sound on than another, it is the Roman Catholic question No idolatry, or heathenism, or ritualism for him. Never has been, has there, Blooster?"

"Sound as a rock, sir," asseverated that pompous authority.

"Surely that must depend on what you mean by the terms idolatry and heathenism," was the rejoinder; "for the spirit of them was the moving force in the machinery of that pageant which Mr. Small eulogized as the 'great event.' It is true the wheels of Juggernaut did not pass over the *bodies* of victims; but the poor and starving must have felt their souls crushed by the apparition of your colossal forms of waste and extravagance. And the money offerings that the people cast on the shrine of worthless wealth and barbaric display do not compare favourably with the superstitious sacrifices made by devotees and fanatics to propitiate their idols. All this bowing to pomp and power seems to me nothing but civilized heathenism. Even the hymn which your congregation sang to-day was more suited for the cannibals than an English assembly."

"Indeed," protested Mr. Hardcastle, "you mistake Mr. Small if you think he bows to pomp and power. There is no civilized heathenism in him, sir. All he did was to improve the opportunity, that was all."

"Improve the opportunity!" returned Mr. Lorraine. "Forgive me, that was precisely what he did *not* do. It was an opportunity, a glorious one, to denounce shallowness and empty grandeur, and contrast it with the truly great."

"Surely," said Blooster very suavely, "you would not expect a public man to make invidious remarks on a great christian country."

"I should expect a christian minister," said Mr. Lorraine, "to proclaim Christianity regardless of every one. In my opinion the spirit of that sermon was the very opposite of Christianity. Mr. Small's standard of greatness is false. He had nothing to say about real nobility. He was always on the outside of things. His mind dwells upon externals. He

and glare, and trumpetings, and he has no eye for the silent forces which move the whole. His amazement is expended on the clothing, the armour, the paraphernalia which he sees before him. He does not trouble himself about the mystic entity which stirs behind these dead semblances."

"But did you observe," asked Mr. Hardcastle, "how he urged 'saving faith?' That looks as if he knew the value of the soul."

"Yes, I noticed that," said Mr. Lorraine; "but you will be surprised when I say that even there he showed again that his mind was constructed simply for superficial views of things. His gospel is that man's salvation depends only on his belief that a certain historical event, the crucifixion, was arranged for his redemption."

"Well," urged Mr. Hardcastle, "and what would you have? If there is anything which Mr. Small is more sound on than another, it is on the subject of 'our purchased righteousness.'"

"I have often heard so," returned Lorraine; "but I think even that phrase has in it the sound of the market. Indeed, I fear the religiosity of these times is in its phrases and its phases, much corroded by worldliness."

"Ah," said Blooster—with the view of keeping Hardcastle from making an irritable rejoinder, which he was prone to do when the doctrine of "purchase" was demurred to—"Ah, Mr. Lorraine, that is a large subject. But, as regards our place to-day, I am sure no one can say we are worldly. Could you?"

"Your question," answered Lorraine, "compels an answer which I fear is not what you expect. In my opinion, there was not a little worldliness observable. Is it not rather shrewd, for instance, for the minister to make his pulpit echo the dominant sentiments of the pew? Mr. Small did nothing this morning but put into language the crudities and vanities which have been filling the heads of the people during the past giddy week."

"Certainly," retorted Hardcastle with some asperity, "we would not have a man there who defied our views."

"In Mr. Small's recognition of that fact," continued Lorraine, "I see a good deal of worldly wisdom. It is a weakness of the voluntary system that a minister, unless he is prepared to starve, must not lead or teach his people, but humour them, and perform the part of spokesman of their notions for the time being. To keep the pews filled he must keep himself popular. To keep himself popular he must study whims and pander to prejudices."

"No doubt," commented Blooster, "there is a tendency in some men to do so, but Mr. Small takes a proper course; he does not offend public opinion. His popularity is a great testimony to his worth. If he were not popular, what would become of our collections?"

"There again," resumed Lorraine, "we have the worldly view. And your collection of this morning, what did it imply of tender interest for such as the Church should care for? It was, in fact, an arrangement whereby to get a piece of unnecessary decoration for your already well-decorated Church, and for advertising the fact that a peer had once actually worshipped in it. Lord Cakesbury first came to you about four months before he died, I think, and attended altogether only about eight or nine times."

"However that may be," replied Hardcastle, "he was a useful man to us."

"Oh, you can't tell me anything about Cakesbury I don't know," asserted Lorraine. "Cakesbury and I knew each other behind the scenes. He was a poor, inoffensive fellow who had not enough nature to be either a great saint or sinner. What did he do for you? Nothing to justify a window to his memory. I suppose there have been men at your Chapel, as at others, who have stuck to the place for forty years, and given in that time a little fortune in the way of contributions. Yet you would never think of putting up a window to their memory. You like the idea of associating the place with a peer. One might think it gave Christianity a certain respectability: hence this appreciation of the memory of Cakesbury."

The face of Hardcastle wore a most puzzled expression. For it was a shock to this cringing deacon to hear the man whose name had always been pronounced in his Chapel with almost reverential tones, thus familiarly spoken of.

"It is quite true," affirmed Blooster, "that Lord Cakesbury didn't drop much money at our Chapel, but it meant a great deal with the people in a neighbourhood like this when they knew a noble lord patronized the place."

"What a fearfully low ebb must the tide of thought be at, when people accept a religion or creed because a noble lord supports it," rejoined Lorraine.

"Well," said Hardcastle, "all I know is, that if many reasoned like you, Mr. Lorraine, the popular preachers of to-day would be nowhere. And then, what would become of the people?"

"They would be far better without your popular preachers," returned Lorraine. "If popularity-hunters were suppressed there would be no fear of Christianity being publicly misrepresented in order to make it palatable and paying. Christianity is a glorious proclamation, but some of your popular men have degraded it into an ignoble trade. The ideal of a christian's life was not even referred to in Mr. Small's sermon to-day. In order to give prominence to the dogma about "substituted righteousness" he dared not hold up the ideal life of the founder of Christianity, lest fanatics should charge him with being an Unitarian and preaching Christ as an example. I find not one distinctive truth of Christ asserted in such sermons as this, and not one thing condemned which Christ would condemn."

"Ah, well," observed Blooster, "if you did not like our minister's style this morning, you could not find fault with his writings. I daresay you have not read his little work 'How!' of which ten thousand have been sold. The style in that is simple in the extreme, and very different from this morning's oratory."

"Sort of 'rock-me-to-sleep' platitudes, I presume," remarked Lorraine. "What a title for a book!"

"It is those simple titles that take with the multitude," remarked Hardcastle.

"Query, Mr. Hardcastle, simple or silly?" inquired Lorraine.

"My good fellow," said Blooster, with a patronizing grandeur that seemed intended to settle the whole question, "what does it matter whether it be simple or silly so long as it does the required work?"

"All depends on what your required work is," declared Lorraine.

"Why, sir," returned Hardcastle, "to bring wanderers into the fold."

"Well, I must say," answered Lorraine, "as to many 'folds,' they are too full of sheep's heads already. As to others, the beauty of the pastures is spoilt by the nasty nature of many who have 'gathered themselves in'; and for others, the wretched contracted mean nature of the 'folds' themselves would render it very undesirable that any intelligent existence should be hampered and penned up in them."

"Do you object to measures being taken to add communicants to the Church?" asked Hardcastle, determined not to let the debate end.

"With regard to many Churches," responded Lorraine, "I answer, yes. And as to some, no. Take such a Church as Mr. Caleb Faithful's. I am delighted when a man like Mr. Faithful has a large number under his influence. I consider him to be a true illustration of the Eastern shepherd, who goes before the sheep, finding out what seems to him the

But the English theological shepherd drives the sheep over the road of barren dogma, pens them up in his own narrow sect, and finally destroys their mental independence in the shambles of his conventicle,—a process in which he is often helped by the importunate barking of his Church officials."

"Mr. Caleb Faithful a true shepherd to his flock?" exclaimed Hardcastle. "Why, he is considered a most heterodox man; in fact, I believe, by some he is put down as a Rationalist. Is HE your model pastor, sir?"

"I know of no man whose opinion I respect more," returned Lorraine. "He is my model preacher. I have read most of his works, and generally hear him preach when I am in London. Have you ever heard him, Mr. Blooster?"

"No, I have not," answered Blooster. "I have been told about some queer things he has said though, and I am sincerely sorry that he should be better suited to your taste than Mr. Small. A dangerous man, depend upon it. Indeed, I have heard Small hint as much, not once or twice."

"Mr. Small's plan, of injuring the reputation of the absent, by hints, is not new to the Church," retorted Lorraine. "Whenever orthodoxy wants to be most murderous it always whispers. But let me at least say this of Mr. Faithful, that he possesses the four chief characteristics of the true teacher: the eye to see; the heart to feel; the courage to brave opposition; and an intellectual and moral sympathy which qualifies him to enter into and expound those two marvellous books, Nature and the Bible."

By this time the disputatious trio had arrived at their place of parting, as Lorraine's course lay in an opposite direction to the road which his companions had to follow So, after a suitable leave-taking, Hardcastle and Blooster continued both their walk and conversation together.

"Who is he?" was the first question Hardcastle asked of Blooster, when Lorraine was out of hearing.

good deal abroad at one time. Has purchased a large estate in Norfolk quite lately, but lives in town best part of the year. He is a nephew of Justice Shallow, and a great friend of Melville: *the* Melville you know. I was obliged to let him criticise pretty freely this morning, because he came to hear Small at my particular request—to oblige me, I may say."

"Ah, well," observed Hardcastle, instantly mollified "there is some excuse for a man of property like that having peculiar views. He couldn't do any harm at my house, they are all too 'sound.' I might have asked him to dinner. But you might bring him up some evening, and Mrs. Hardcastle and my daughters could give him a little music. Perhaps you could induce him, Blooster. I wish I had known before who he was."

"All right. I'll see what I can do. It's a good connection."

After this reply, by Blooster, these worthies shook hands and parted.

CHAPTER III.

WRECK OF THE *RASSELAS.*—MELVILLE AND THE DESERTED CHILDREN KATE AND ANNIE.—CANT IN COMBINATION WITH COWARDICE.

THE day was declining, and a gentle breeze which had sprung up towards afternoon filled the sails of the good ship *Rasselas*, as she glided through the blue deeps of the Irish Sea.

"Land ahead! Land ahead!" cried the jolly tars, and a rush was made to the starboard side of the ship for the first glimpse of Great Britain's shores. Telescopes were raised and eager eyes strained for a sight of the wished-for land.

"We shall have some rough weather before we are there," spoke a young American to an English gentleman by his side.

"Do you think so? The wind is only just enough to help us at present."

"Look where the sun is going down," rejoined his companion. "I never saw a sunset like that, so intensely yellow and weird, without making sure of a squall. I have made a few voyages too."

"I trust it will not hinder us much. I am tired of this endless sailing. I believe no heart hailed that cry, 'Land ahead!' like mine."

"It is a long voyage, but especially to those who are anticipating re-unions with loved ones."

Very long and very tedious the succeeding hours seemed to all. For not only did the ship make but little progress, but the gloom of the sky continued to increase; and the feeling of listlessness and impatience which had taken possession of the passengers prevented them from finding those happy diversions in reading, conversation, and games by which time on board ship is generally beguiled.

"Oh, Mr. Melville," exclaimed a young and beautiful woman, stopping on her way to the cabin to eagerly interrogate the Englishman, "do you think we shall have a storm?"

"I fear we shall, Mrs. Sinclaire. At any rate the captain is making preparations for one, and he ought to know."

"In sight of land," she murmured mournfully, "and perhaps never to reach it."

"My dear lady, that is rather a gloomy view. The *Rasselas* has weathered many gales, as you and I know. Why should you fancy she is to be beaten by this particular storm?"

"Because just on that point of land which is now coming into view I have three dear children, and a presentiment has haunted me all through this voyage that I shall never see them again. This horrible presentiment takes a new form of terror in the storm which must be overcome before home is reached. It is nearly two years since I saw my children, Mr. Melville; but they do not forget; and I know at this moment they are eagerly anticipating our arrival."

"You will soon meet them, Mrs. Sinclaire. But a few hours now and all the ocean-tossing will be ended."

"I shall never meet them, Mr. Melville. *Never;* till they come to me in that other world."

Tears filled her eyes as she slowly pronounced these words; and Melville felt deeply affected by her earnestness. Tenderly and gently he remarked,—

"We must trust in God that all will be well."

She smiled gratefully at his consolation, and retired to the cabin with her husband and others who were seeking

The heavens soon became black. The wind moaned and shrieked. How suddenly the ocean's roar fell upon the ear! The storm had broken in all its fury. Melville shuddered when with a glance at the distant land he thought of the three little children waiting in the English home for the longed-for moment when they should be clasped in their mother's embrace. The night drew on, and with it the blackest darkness. The sea was running mountains high, and the *Rasselas* met with her first misfortune—two of her boats being swept off by the waves. Downstairs in the cabin were terror and confusion. The passengers were crying and praying. Melville, the captain, and a few of the ship's officers were the only ones who were calm and collected. Melville incessantly endeavoured to cheer and sustain his fellow-passengers, and by his own composure comfort those who were in despair. "Will the ship get through it?" "Is there much danger?" "Shall we go to the bottom?" were the questions addressed to him on every side. How eagerly, in moments of danger, we credit the calm souls with superior knowledge! For all his questioners Melville had a kind and brave answer. Once only did he offer reproof, and that was to the Rev. Jabez Blaze D.D., a tall, powerful man, who during all the voyage hitherto had pestered the crew with mawkish tracts and vapid pietism. Assistance being urgently wanted on deck, this fellow would not stir; but, bellowing with horror and white with fear, concerned himself solely with his own personal safety. To him Melville said with almost sternness, "Cannot you, who talk so much about God, face death like a man?"

Amidst the shriekings of the wind and the dashing of the sea, "Man overboard!" was heard; and the passengers gazed in mute agony on one another, not knowing how soon their turn might follow. The awful hours wore on, and affairs grew more and more hopeless. The engineer reported that the water was pouring through the bunker slides, and in a couple of hours the fires would be out. The steam-pump was promptly got to work, and water was brought up from the hold by the ton. Bravely they laboured, the good captain and his courageous men, determined not to give up while there was any hope. But the water was gaining on the pumps, and the last device was failing. The morning now was dawning; a ray of light was visible in the east. Still the storm raged, still the water gained on the hold. Another hour and the wind was abating—the storm was dying, but not before it had conquered the *Rasselas*. The fires were out, and the vessel lay like a huge, helpless log in the hissing ocean, whose foam washed over her. The last hope was the boats, of which three only remained, and the order was passed to prepare them. Then a heart-rending scene ensued. Only a very limited number of persons could be taken on board. Brave and unselfish natures conquered their love of life, and sacrificed themselves that others might be saved. Among husbands and wives, parents and children, brothers, sisters, and friends, there were a few who loved each other better than life, and refused safety at the price of separation. But the majority, of course, rushed in all directions, eager to avail of the rescue, so that the seats in the boats were soon all crowded. The passengers who were left behind knew that the end had come.

Among the deserted ones were two little children who had been in the custody of a young man named Dandy Filch, who was the travelling companion of that Reverend Jabez Blaze, D.D., whom Melville had reproved for his cowardice. These little ones were not in sight when the last boat pushed away, and so Blaze and Filch left them behind to share the fate of the abandoned. Melville rushed to their aid; and before the billows which would have swept them from the deck had broken over the vessel, he held them securely in his arms. His failing strength warned him, and the rapidly sinking ship made it apparent that the children's safety must be his final task. There was neither time nor opportunity for one other act of mercy now. With that swiftness, and renewed energy, which are given only to the desperate, he made his plan ; and before the *Rasselas* heaved over on her side, he, with the children, floated off upon a raft which his prompt ingenuity had lashed together for their transport. The winds still moaned loudly, and the ocean's foam hissed around him, but above these voices of the storm, and the cries of drowning men and women in the surrounding sea, he heard one tone more tragic than them all. It was the last wild wail of her who, a short time since, had told him of the loving children who were waiting for her in that old home which she never more would see.

CHAPTER IV.

Tom obtains a Situation.—The History of Blooster.—The Incalculable Commercial Value of Cant.—Gullibility the Unfailing Friend of Cant.—Churches and Chapels Degraded by Adventurers.—The Psychological and Moral Effects of Cant.

TOM was an inoffensive kind of lad, and the more he considered the project of becoming a soldier, the more his natural, uneducated feelings, revolted against the idea of wounding, or murdering, for payment, fellow-creatures who had given him no offence. So, instead of enlisting, he occupied the fortnight which succeeded the Sunday when we parted from him at Mr. Small's, in endeavouring to procure a situation as porter and office messenger. After the usual bitter experiences which attend such attempts in an over-crowded city, he at last succeeded in obtaining a situation in the offices of Agnew Mumm, Blooster & Co., to whom his circumstances were well known. The junior partner was that same Blooster whom we saw at Falcon Small's. Of him it is necessary that we should say something. Apart from the interest which centres in him in this history because he is Blooster, he derives an additional importance by reason of his being a specimen of a class of men who are sometimes found in the activities of The World of Cant.

The history of Blooster is a representative history. Who, then, was Blooster? Twenty years ago he came to London an inexperienced, penniless country youth; but, though he then of course lacked knowledge of life, he possessed the seeds of cunning and worldly wisdom :—that sort of wisdom which teaches the fox where to go to steal the goose, and the rats the right time to desert the ship which they have gnawed and plundered. A kind old friend, for his poor father's sake, gave Blooster a letter of introduction to a worthy but weak deacon at Falcon Small's. The deacon, for the writer's sake, was kind to Blooster, and accompanied him to various tea-drinkings, lectures, and meetings, for he felt that his *protégé* ought not to wander in London all alone. Blooster was not long in perceiving that he was in the midst of elements which he could turn to his personal advantage. He had need of society; he obtained it in the Chapel. He had need of a situation; he obtained it in the office of a member of the Chapel. There was no humility in his constitution; therefore, when once started in Falcon Small's world, he diligently introduced himself into every domestic circle of respectability where he could find the slightest pretext for entering. In six months a happy accident enabled him to become a superintendent of a small Sunday-school in connection with the Church. Availing himself of this official position, he perpetually invented excuses for still further increasing his social connections in a variety of directions. A few years passed on, and he began to feel that the hour was ripe for the acquisition of something more than even his welcome notoriety at Small's. He determined that these social relationships which he had now formed should constitute the nucleus of a good business connection. Accordingly he launched out into a new mercantile career, and proudly pointed inquiring strangers, to his standing and reputation in the Church as evidences of the uprightness of his character, and as reasons for the extension to him of a commercial credit.

A wag was once asked what Blooster's business was at this date. He replied, " Everybody's." There could be no better description of it. In the columns of the "London

Directory" he was dignified as a "financial agent;" an elastic term, which, as applied to him, would have sounded ironical but that it had been so frequently used by penniless adventurers before. The sources whence his increased income were now derived will easily be understood by a reference to his private ledger, where we see such entries as "*bonus*," "promotion money," "douceur," "discount of various bills," "fees for procuring loans," "fees for amalgamation of companies," "share of liquidators' profits," etc. Blooster was not backward in giving his friends most exaggerated ideas of the magnitude of his operations; and by throwing a veil of mystery around himself he prevented inquirers from attempting to grasp anything more definite respecting his business than that it was "something in the city." Soon entangled in all kinds of speculations, he necessarily realized that his operations could no more be carried on without some money than bricks could be made without straw. To consolidate his financial position was, therefore, his next exploit; and to this end he thought of that old plan of marriage for money. He knew that at Falcon Small's he had made a favourable impression upon the somewhat *passé*, and altogether plain, eldest daughter of a prosperous old tradesman. He had taken care, long before, to ingratiate himself with the lady's father and the ill-favoured family circle, by the caustic observations which he made on the conduct of persons who married for beauty, and by the appropriate encomiums which he had pronounced upon "goodness" as being the only thing which should be sought after in a wife. So pleasingly did he uphold the paramount claims of "goodness," and so skilfully insinuate his disparagements of beauty as a quality necessarily divorced from "goodness," that, when his marriage was solemnized, there was scarcely a person to be found in his set at Small's who did not believe that the ground which Blooster had taken in selecting his wife was evidence of his fidelity to pious principles. Nothing was more useful to Blooster than this unfailing gullibility of Falcon Small's circle. Without that at his back he would have come to sad disgrace. His feverish passion to get rich rapidly, led him into very questionable courses. Even men of the world spoke more than once in terms of strong reprobation of the means which he adopted to make money. His league with one of the most disreputable solicitors in town, and his share in his plunder, wreckings, and manœuvres, whereby in one particular enterprise relating to an investment company, grievous ill was done on an extensive scale, came to be notorious. Blooster's part in the execrated transaction was undoubted; all the facts were undenied, because undeniable. There was a scandal and a hubbub, and an inquiry into his conduct was suggested. But the unfailing gullibility of The World of Cant came to his rescue.

He was at this time a keen, experienced, unscrupulous man of the world; yet the Smallites, in deacon's meeting assembled, passed a resolution that he was the injured, *not* the injurer, and that he, in the exuberance of his christian charity, had been misled and imposed upon by others, who had made a dupe of him! Commercial morality branded him as a rogue: the unfailing gullibility claimed him as a martyr. After this adventure he stood higher than ever, as being a man whom even calumny had assailed in vain. One family who had been greatly impoverished by his financial conduct, and who entertained proper suspicions as to his dishonesty, were so affected on noticing the high position which he still occupied on Sundays at Mr. Small's, that they positively felt ashamed of their misgivings; and when on Sacrament Sunday he, with marvellous effrontery, marched from the Communion table to convey the elements to the congregation, their nervousness suggested to them that their recent thoughts about so holy a man amounted almost to a sin.

Blooster was one of a numerous class of persons who

deliberately utilize Chapels and Churches for their own private personal ends. When, for his own benefit, an advertiser uses the columns of a newspaper, or a passenger uses a railway, or an actor uses the wardrobe of a *costumier*, there is, of course, a sense of fitness in the proceeding; these things are intended for the uses to which they are thus put, and only exist for the purpose of being so used. But when, in order to advance their fortunes in the world, men of the Blooster type turn the Sanctuary to their own private advantage, the case is different. They prostitute a holy place, and their conduct ought to arouse loathing and execration.

In estimating Blooster's character, it would be too vague and indefinite to describe him simply as a hypocrite. Undoubtedly he was one, but he was one of a peculiar kind; and an analysis of his component parts revealed, moreover, that he was also intimately related to the whole family of social pests. Slander, vulgarity, falsehood, avarice, affectation, and fraud were found to be among the normal elements of his very protoplasm. Cant had so corrupted his life-blood as to make him no less a monster than a curiosity. Besides hardening his heart it had completely clogged his brain cells. The man had, in consequence, become the ridiculous victim of a chronic delusion, which cheated him into the belief that he was a christian. His memory was also affected, so that he completely forgot the fact of his having deliberately planned for himself a life of selfishness. His moral eyesight—always poor—completely deserted him, so that he could not distinguish things of real worth from things of meretricious value. The original terrible taint of egotism which pervaded his entire constitution, was stimulated into pestilent development by the introduction, into his system, of Calvinistic poison. The result was, that he asserted himself to be one of "God's Elect," one of "the dear people," one of a "chosen band" whom the infinite Father had selected for eternal companionship from amongst the millions whom He intended to torture everlastingly in burning lakes of undying flame. As Blooster never had any tender sensibilities, and as the reflective faculty died in him as soon as it was born, he never once turned a scrutinizing glance inwards upon himself, nor ever thought of the pain which his odious life gave to other people. Coarse, hard, rapacious, ignorant, and gluttonous, he was naturally exempt from the sort of sorrows which are felt by men of a higher type. And this immunity from suffering he ostentatiously attributed to his own goodness, whilst he charged the sadness of his superiors to their own unworthiness. It is questionable whether anything less than a miracle could have caused this man one moment's moral self-distrust. When he attended sermons, he heard, not for himself, but for other people, and he applied to their cases the very appeals and denunciations which were most applicable to his own. This habit had so encrusted him with callousness that no arrow of oratory or sarcasm could penetrate to his understanding. His worldly successes had increased his natural swagger, and he audaciously proclaimed himself as a man who was "right for both worlds." At the period of this history he had just entered into a new commercial venture. He had become junior partner in the firm of Agnew Mumm & Co., in which connection we shall again meet with him.

CHAPTER V.

CANT . ITS CRUELTY, MEANNESS, AND STUPIDITY.—THE CHURCH AS A POLITICAL MACHINE.—SIR NICOL GILTSPUR, THE CONSERVATIVE CHURCHMAN.

IT will have suggested itself to any one acquainted with human nature that such a man as Blooster would take no more interest in Tom's welfare than any cannibal would have done. As a Church official, of course he nominally accepted the teaching of a Redeemer whose characteristic it was to seek and to save the lost. But, like men who are under the debilitating influence of such superficial, sentimental preachers as Small, Blooster acted as if dogma were eternally divorced from the affairs of business. In the Sanctuary a man of his type will vaunt a theory which in the market he will not practise for a moment. If Blooster's daily life and creed were set to doggerel, it would be expressed by the lines—

"Of all the human family
I love myself the best :
Kind Providence take care of me,
And Sambo take the rest."

Acting up to this creed, when Blooster found one morning that he could get Tom's work done at less cost, he invented a pretext for a quarrel ; and the poor fellow was discharged without a kind word, without a shilling, without a friend. Tom had again a hard time of it, but eventually obtained employment in the wine stores of Sir Nicol Giltspur & Company in East Cheap. It would be profitless to linger over a description of his monotonous drudgery in that

we must learn something about Sir Nicol Giltspur himself.

Sir Nicol was a good-looking, gentlemanly man. He had been very successful in the wine trade, and he was conspicuous in civic politics. He had the good fortune to hold the office of Sheriff of London during a year when Royalty happened to pass through the city, *en route* for the London Bridge railway station ; and, as a result of that coincidence, his claims to distinction were suddenly discovered by the Court, and he was, according to solemn precedent, raised to the honour of knighthood. He was a Churchman and a Conservative. Accustomed to attend the Church of England from his boyhood, the political teaching of the Church service had influenced him at an early age; and its effects, upon his understanding and career, had been all that even those time-servers who invented a State Church for Henry VIII. could possibly have intended or desired. If they had been alive to see the present working of their experiment, they would have applauded as perfection those subtle processes by which the machinery of the State Church had inseparably amalgamated in Sir Nicol's mind, and in the minds of many men like him, the two generically distinct ideas of loyalty and religion.

For the administration of the criminal law, and for certain constitutional purposes, it has been found convenient to invent the axiom, "The sovereign can do no wrong"; just as in old days it was the custom, in certain judicial and other proceedings relating to land, to make solemn use of an imaginary John Doe and Richard Roe, for the technical requirements of the law. But, like many other persons, Sir Nicol never comprehended this fact. The holy associations with which the State Church always invests the sovereign, had so obfuscated his understanding that he actually accepted this legal fiction about the immaculateness of the Crown as a palpable verity. In

disbelieved the existence of moral goodness if unallied with his kind of loyalty. Indeed, if he had lived in the times of the Stuarts he would have felt it to have been his pious duty to have maintained, in opposition to all the liberties of England, the despot who, for the time being, claimed the throne and the headship of the Church. His churchmanship taught him that the Crown, under all circumstances, was to be supported in every pretension which it might put forward; so that if any court-minion advised the sovereign to strain the prerogative, he was ready with his sycophantic approbation. He had always heard that the Crown was the fountain of honour; and, misled by the metaphor, he supposed, in opposition to all the teaching of history, that moral and religious truth moved downwards from the throne to the people, instead of upwards from the people to the throne. As a consequence of these views he belonged to a party which considers that the Free Churches of England are a nuisance. He was opposed to Dissenters enjoying any of the privileges of the Universities, and he regarded their claim to burial in the national churchyards as a monstrous piece of impudence. The fact that Dissenters had borne their share of the cost of providing and maintaining churchyards did not affect his judgment. And it seemed to him more righteous that bereaved relatives should have the painful and expensive task of conveying the corpse of the most holy Dissenter, or an innocent baby, fifty miles away from home for interment, than that its burial should be permitted in the parish churchyards. He knew that Nature's law had decreed "ashes to ashes and dust to dust," but his Church had taught him that the decree was to be understood as meaning "Churchmen's ashes to Churchmen's ashes only, and Churchmen's dust to Churchmen's dust only." Fifteen thousand Clergymen of the Established Church had, he truly said, signed a statement to that effect.

It is, however, only doing justice to Sir Nicol to say that

his opinions were not the result of any excogitations of his own. Of a kindly nature, and endowed with a fair share of natural ability, if he had manufactured his own opinions they would have been of a different character. But he did not do so. In all departments of life he was a staunch advocate of what he called the "departmental system." Accordingly, when he found that the State had organized a system of religion, and paid princely revenues to Bishops and Archbishops to proclaim ecclesiastical truth, it seemed to him to be his simple duty to accept the teaching. He did so, and the free growth of his mind was, in consequence, an impossibility. A traditional faith enclosed it, as in a box, for evermore. He was deprived of the power to search for truth. He did not even realize that it needed looking for. Beyond what the Church had to tell him, he only cared to know that his father had been a Churchman and a Conservative; and it seemed to him as natural to inherit his father's opinions as it was to inherit his father's gout. Fifty years of constant attendance at Church had given him no higher conception of the spirit and aims of Jesus Christ than that it was his duty to be a Conservative Churchman. But of course his social popularity did not depend upon his creed. He owed that to the fact that he was a rich man, always ready to offer sumptuous hospitality, with geniality and courtesy, to his superiors and equals, and willing to give donations to respectable and well-known institutions which had received approved patronage. Besides, he took care never to struggle against any popular whims, but always to swim with the stream of conventional opinion; and he was ready to sacrifice both personal predilections and religious prejudice in order to secure high social companionship. He therefore found it an easy task to surround himself with visitors whenever his love of ostentation craved for them, and that was very often.

CHAPTER VI.

Mr. Melville at Sir Nicol Giltspur's Garden Party.—Art Cant.—Lord Everton, Mr. and Miss Hardcastle.—Cant and Flunkeyism.—Idolatry.

AT the time to which this narrative relates Sir Nicol Giltspur possessed an elegant villa on the banks of the Thames, near Hampton Court. It was his ambition during all the season to have as many festive gatherings at his house as any of his neighbours. On a certain brilliant Friday afternoon a fashionable garden party gathered there. The company having participated in the outdoor enjoyments, Sir Nicol conducted a group of his friends to view his pictures, of which he was excessively proud. He was surrounded by Mr. Hardcastle, Miss Hardcastle, Lord Everton, and the last arrival, Mr. Melville. Here, as on board the ship *Rasselas*, Melville was the most noteworthy person of all the company. He was graceful and easy, and had the manners of a man who had not been cramped by a class or a locality, but had associated extensively with all varieties of men. His dress would not have satisfied the sloven or the fop, for it was neither conspicuous for its carelessness nor its punctiliousness, but was just the apparel that attracted no particular notice, because so easily suiting the wearer. You could not be occupied in scanning the surroundings of the man, being involuntarily impelled to gaze upon his face. You were attracted not alone by the regular features, beautiful and refined as they were, nor the flowing wavy hair, nor the singular bloom of the countenance, but by the bright intelligence and tender pity which passed like lights over his face, telling of earnest sincerity of purpose, purity of soul, and that pathos and melancholy which are the life companions of the brave and true. You felt you were in the presence of a man, philosophical in intellect and royal in nature, possessing that *seeing* eye which pierces through the shadows and forms of things, deep down to the things themselves; and who was fearless enough to denounce the mere semblances and shams of life by whomsoever promoted and patronized.

"You must indeed be a judge of pictures," said Hardcastle to Mr. Melville, as the group stood before Sir Nicol's latest art treasure. "Sir Nicol tells me you have visited most of the art galleries in the world."

"I certainly have seen very many pictures," replied Melville, "and am much impressed by the fact that even art is often dominated by fashion. Many of the neglected pictures of the world are quite as beautiful as some of those about which society goes into raptures."

"Very likely," said Sir Nicol, "still I must own that the old masters are my delight, though I patronize many of the modern artists."

"I like the old masters," affirmed Hardcastle, anxious to be on safe ground. "Most of my own pictures are very old."

The usual empty talk and simulated ecstasies, current amongst the vain and the pretentious when in the presence of art, were indulged in by Mr. and Miss Hardcastle. There was, however, one unvarying metallic standard which regulated the judgment of these people, for their admiration of every picture visibly increased if Sir Nicol intimated that its money value was great. But as none of them, except Melville, really understood art, or had even the eye to appreciate the beautiful for its own sake, the criticism took such instructive form as could be expressed by the

"What a fine man he was!" "How touching!" "Really marvellous!"—and so on, and so on. The company might have stalked through the whole picture gallery in this way, but that Hardcastle, happening to espy Herring's picture of the "Three horses' heads," conceived that his opportunity had clearly come to distinguish himself by displaying a little of his special knowledge, and with an air of great wisdom observed, "Ah, fine thing that! Falcon Small has got one in his study. Come here, Victoria. Do you remember Falcon Small's picture like this?"

Miss Hardcastle, thus addressed by her father, swept forward in her best style for Lord Everton's edification, and scrutinised the picture. This gave Sir Nicol the opportunity to remark, aside to Melville, that it was a strange fact that Hardcastle never felt himself so wise as when able, by even most roundabout methods, to connect any object or incident with his everlasting "Falcon Small:" the reverend gentleman having succeeded in convincing him that he was the phenomenon of the age. Sir Nicol had scarcely concluded this observation when Hardcastle, evidently exuberant at the prospect of bringing his pet hobby before a new man, turned round to Melville, and in tones suggesting that a negative answer must imply gross ignorance, and cover any one with confusion, inquired, "Of course, Mr. Melville, you know Falcon Small?"

"Know him," said Melville, "in the way which many others know him, by seeing his name perpetually printed in newspaper paragraphs, whereby he contrives to connect it with all events, from the eruption of Vesuvius to a royal entry into London; the scenery of North Wales; a cold winter, or a hot summer."

Sir Nicol was amused, it may be pleased, at the reply, for he was nearly weary of Hardcastle's constant intrusion of this evangelical prodigy. But Hardcastle, never able to detect irony in connection with such a subject, rejoined,

popular man. You should hear him, Mr. Melville. He draws a good number, I can tell you."

"I have read him," returned Melville, "and must be permitted to remark that this has been almost enough for me."

"Which of his books, may I ask?" said Hardcastle. "His best works are 'How!' 'Come here!' 'Sobs and Stars.'"

"And 'Washed Lambs,' papa," chimed in Miss Hardcastle.

"I have not perused those," replied Melville, "but I read his sermon on the 'Vast Calamity!' and with some interest. Unfortunately I knew more about the subject than he did. The *Rasselas* was wrecked on a Friday; tidings reached London late on Friday night; and Mr. Small advertised a sermon on the wreck to be preached by him on the Sunday. He attracted, I dare say, a congregation, on the expectation of details which he well knew he could not give, because even Lloyd's people and the newspapers could not then furnish them. Afterwards he published this discourse under the heading of the 'Vast Calamity!'"

"Pray, did you read it?" inquired Hardcastle.

"Yes," replied Melville, "and I think I have been able also to read the man. After that sermon on the 'Vast Calamity!' a collection was made for the further ornamentation of the Church, which I have no doubt is ornamented enough, and it struck me that a collection for the poor survivors of the wrecked sailors would have been preferable."

"I cannot understand your not liking his sermon if you read it," said Hardcastle. "He preaches the 'simple gospel,' and what can we want more than that?"

"If you put that question to me, Mr. Hardcastle," said Melville, "I reply, I want unobtrusiveness, independence, sense, consistency, and refinement."

"Do you not remember, Mr. Hardcastle," said Sir Nicol by way of explanation, "I told you Mr. Melville had a mission?"

"To be sure," replied Mr. Hardcastle. "May I ask what it is, Mr. Melville?"

"My mission is to quarrel," answered Melville courteously."

"To quarrel!" ejaculated Miss Hardcastle. "Oh, how very dreadful! Do you mean to quarrel with everybody?"

"No," returned Mr. Melville. "I am anxious not to quarrel with any individual, but to quarrel with, and if possible to kill, the progeny of Cant wherever they exist."

"How extraordinary! How very extraordinary!" said Miss Hardcastle, Mr. Hardcastle, and Lord Everton in chorus.

At this point of the conversation it struck Sir Nicol that his cabinet of curiosities would give a better idea of his own importance than a theological argument, and he accordingly led the party to it. Lord Everton followed Miss Hardcastle, and assured her that, of the books referred to a few minutes before, she had mentioned that work of Falcon Small's which he would care most to see.

"Particularly," said his lordship, "I am concerned—that question. Had no end—pretty lambs die off—my place this spring. Cold east winds—May. Precious loss—my tenants. Suppose your book has more—do with training pet lambs —all that sort—thing. But if—has hints—cottagers and about—protection young lambs generally, I'd get half-dozen copies—distribute—rural population."

The quick jerk with which Lord Everton talked had prevented Miss Hardcastle, till he had finished, from explaining to him, as she then did with all proper precision, that the work in question did not refer to the rural farm but to the spiritual "fold." It was not a treatise on natural history, but on Church members. Often assured by her excellent mother that she owed her conversion to "Washed Lambs," which had completed its work in her soul, she was better able to forgive the profane mistake of his lordship. Her charitable view of the error was also assisted by her remembrance of another truth which her mother had impressed on her—namely, that Lord Everton was a most eligible acquaintance. As for his lordship, a stripling who had not attained his majority, he really possessed no eye for the ludicrous side of things, though doing a little trade of his own in old jokes, so the topic dropped without embarrassment to either.

Sir Nicol's curiosities embraced varieties of all sorts, amongst other things some idols from Siam, Japan, China, and Tahiti; and connected with all he had a long tale to tell of the circumstances by which they had come into his possession.

"What a grotesque shape is this Japanese idol!" said Miss Hardcastle; and then turning to Melville, and pointing with disdain to a small squat figure on a cabinet, she exclaimed, "Is it not remarkable, Mr. Melville, that even in our own dear christian England idolatry still exists? The doll which represents the Virgin in Roman Catholic Churches is an exhibition of idolatry as revolting and as far from *true* worship as these abominable idols."

"It would be well," replied Melville, "if the worship of the Virgin and such gods as these was the only idolatry practised in England, Miss Hardcastle. I find idolatry even more revolting than the worship of heathen gods in many of our Protestant Churches and Chapels."

"You, of course, refer," returned the lady, "to the Ritualists: they are indeed strangely deluded."

"I do not speak of them particularly," said Melville. "I speak of all places where semblances, and not *God*, are worshipped. Empty forms and ceremonies are the gods of some places; and shams, gross superstition, and wealth, those of others. There are many Chapels and Churches in England in which different kinds of idolatry are as rife as in places filled with painted images, and there is plenty of coarse superstition everywhere."

"You astonish me, Mr. Melville," said Miss Hardcastle.

"I know there are numerous sects in this Christian country, but all believe in and worship the same God."

"I think not," rejoined Melville. "The God of one man is the devil of another. The Being which a slavish fanatic professes to adore, is often one from which generous souls would recoil with loathing. In many of the Churches it is a condition of membership that you assent to dogmas which ought to be repulsive to our conceptions of a God. It is not enough that you believe in God. You are required to believe in what some man has asserted about him in the form of a dogma."

"Do you mean to say, sir," exclaimed Hardcastle, coming to the rescue of his astonished daughter, "that a person can be idolatrous who joins a Protestant Church?"

"We must first understand what idolatry means," replied Melville. "Idol is *eidolon*, which means a symbol. All your creeds and sects, all confessions of faith, are symbols, and if a man really worships God by means of his symbols he is not to be condemned. We all have some symbol or *eidolon* by which we worship. The Dissenters find fault with the Ritualists, and condemn their forms ; but what is baptism but a form ; what is sprinkling but a form ? What are all the Dissenter's sacraments but forms? All you can say against Ritualists is that you prefer your symbols to theirs."

"Really, Mr. Melville," said Sir Nicol, "I cannot agree with you in your remarks. I am a good Churchman, and believe in the Church."

"Do you not believe in any worship at all? And do you not hate these idols?" asked Hardcastle.

"I believe in all worship that is sincere," replied Melville. "The poor heathen praying to his idols with his whole soul and with sincerity, worships in a way which does not fill me with intolerance even though I pity his darkness. What I find fault with is *insincere* worship ;

and the censurable people are those who, as Coleridge says, do not believe, but 'only *believe* that they believe.'"

"Do I understand you to say, Mr. Melville," said Hardcastle, rather excitedly, "that you believe more in the worship of idols than in the Christian form of worship?"

"No; I did not say that," answered Melville. "But I mean to imply that my first test of worship is sincerity. And I am of opinion, that the unenlightened heathen who believes in his idols is to be preferred to persons who affect a worship which they only believe they believe in—which is Cant."

"Then," rejoined Hardcastle, "you suppose that the worshippers of idols will be saved?"

"I abstain from going into a matter that I consider beyond my comprehension, Mr. Hardcastle," returned Melville; "but, I certainly see no reason for supposing that God intends limiting His mercy to the Anglo-Saxon races."

"But, my dear sir," ejaculated Hardcastle, "do you really believe that the heathen will be allowed to enter the same Heaven as ourselves?"

"By way of answer," replied Melville with courtesy and calmness, "let me put a case to you. I presume you consider the only true believers to be the followers of Falcon Small. Well, supposing his Church to hold fifteen hundred persons, do you suppose that of the millions who tenant the globe, those who have been accommodated in that and similar Chapels are the only ones who will enjoy future happiness?"

"I can't say," replied Hardcastle; "I only know there must be some one right, and Falcon Small seems to me right."

"You affirm that there must be *one* right," replied Melville; "and I believe that *many* are right. You say there is one road to heaven, and I think there are many roads."

"Well," returned Hardcastle, "at all events I am glad

the people of England are evangelical, and don't believe in idols."

"I think they believe in many idols," said Melville; "and one of them is wealth. Out of their devotion to that god they will even manufacture bronze images like those in this cabinet, and sell them to the very tribes we denounce as heathenish. In Africa, India, and in islands of the southern sea, I learned that many of their little gods had been manufactured in Sheffield and Birmingham. We are so good, we hate idols, but do not object to make a little profit by selling them."

"Ah, very bad, very bad," said Sir Nicol, taking up the conversation; "but passing from the bronzes in the cabinet there, let me show you an old cup which I have here. I think it worth calling your attention to. You must know that George III. stopped his carriage one day at a certain inn near my seat at Rawden Ho! He called for some beer, and from this cup," said Sir Nicol, holding up a quartern mug, "he drank. My ancestor, who stood by at the time, obtained the cup, and it has been handed down in our family as an heirloom, and I have no doubt that many loyal people would give as much gold as it would hold to possess it."

The historian might have added that the inn in question had been kept by Sir Nicol's humble great-grandfather, who had brewed the beer that the king drank. But this, of course, would have been too vulgar. As it was, Mr. Hardcastle appeared wonderfully impressed, and held the cup in his hand almost reverentially.

"What a precious relic!" he observed; whilst Melville's sneer could scarcely be concealed. "Civilized heathenism," he murmured. "I wonder who is the most to be pitied, the flunkey or the idolator."

"And King George's royal lips really touched this cup!" exclaimed Miss Hardcastle with loyal enthusiasm. "No wonder you prize it, Sir Nicol. Fancy, Lord Everton, how truly condescending it was of him to drink from such a cup as that."

"Depends whether he was thirsty," returned Lord Everton.

"But we are not all born with royal blood in our veins," exclaimed Miss Hardcastle.

"No, some of us are born flunkeys," observed Melville, *sotto voce*.

"This," said Sir Nicol, taking up a curious necklace, "is a little relic of a barbarian island. It belonged to Queen Edna of the Sandwich Isles. I got it in a strange way, too long to repeat now; but like most things one is eager to possess, I paid dearly for it."

"You are a happy man, Sir Nicol," said Hardcastle with sincere fervour, "to possess two such trophies of royalty. Falcon Small would appreciate them."

This was a true observation, for Falcon Small was an arrant toady.

It was time now to return to the garden, and as Miss Hardcastle, Lord Everton, and Melville went off in company, Sir Nicol seized the opportunity of saying to Mr. Hardcastle,—

"My friend Mr. Melville holds very extraordinary views, Mr. Hardcastle. He is a good fellow for all that, however —a first class man. He has taken one of my houses in Park Lane, and keeps up a splendid establishment. A little peculiar, it is true, but high bred, and a man of ample means."

"Ah, well," returned the propitiated Hardcastle, "as he has got a stake in the country his notions are not so dangerous. Daresay he could be put right. Should like him to know Falcon Small. Falcon Small would soon convince him."

Whether or not Hardcastle's proselytising zeal was suddenly kindled when he reflected on Melville's social position, and the opportunity for evangelistic work which might be secured for his wife and unmarried daughters, is unknown; but it is certain that shortly after Sir Nicol's last remarks his horror of the unorthodox gentleman began to vanish—just as it had done before, when Mr. Blooster vouched for the wealth of Mr. Lorraine. To extort from Mr. Melville the promise of an early visit was the task to which Hardcastle assiduously addressed himself forthwith.

CHAPTER VII.

Mr. Tremlin.—Mrs. Tremlin, the Woman who Cants—
Cant a Debaser of Childhood.

"DRIVE me to Barkham Terrace," said a well-dressed gentleman, as he stepped into his elegant brougham; and it is not difficult to recognise that he is our friend Melville. Tom, who was looking about for a job, stepped forward and closed the carriage door, for which act of attention he received the first kind word he had heard since his mother's death; and a silver coin glittered in his hand. Melville was at this time on his way to visit the little girls whom he had rescued from the *Rasselas*. Their history was full of painful interest. By the death of their father and mother they were left in Melbourne without any one to care for them but a servant who had attended their parents in their last illness. Communication having been opened up by that good woman with their uncle in London, they were given, as we stated in our third chapter, into the charge of Mr. Dandy Filch for escort to England. Fortunately, the captain of the *Rasselas* knew their story, and had informed Melville of their destination. Though Dandy Filch had deserted them, and the captain had perished in the *Rasselas*, Melville had taken them to their uncle This gentleman, Mr. Maurice Tremlin, was a kind, generous-hearted man. Though battling against impecuniosity, to keep in honest respectability his wife and three children, he eagerly invited and lovingly welcomed his little nieces to his home. As the orphans of his departed brother he loved them for his sake, and would increase his labours that food and raiment should be provided for the adopted ones. Self-sacrificing and anti-sectarian, he was depreciated by his wife because, as she put it, "he was not a decided character." There was one thing that Mrs. Tremlin was certainly decided in, and that was in considering herself an invalid, and in acting the resigned martyr very constantly. Her poor husband, taken in by her Cant, became a victim to her perpetual exactions; and, really believing in her piety, also came to believe in her ill-health. His business hours occupied him from nine in the morning till eight in the evening. During that time Mrs. Tremlin occupied herself with her own enjoyments, and with talking about her ailments and her piety to any gossip who visited her. When poor Maurice came home, tired and fagged, from the office of Messrs. Mumm, Blooster & Co., where he held a clerkship, he was assailed by a list of complaints, followed by sly side hints which were intended to convey Mrs. Tremlin's christian resignation to the lot which Maurice had brought on her. What he had done, however, except load her with every kindness and endeavour to make her life happy, it is hard to know; but at the times when Mrs. Tremlin acted the christian martyr Maurice felt himself to be, without in the least knowing why, the cruellest and most neglectful of husbands. She was, in fact, a lean-natured, hungry woman, always craving for something. When they moved from a smaller to their present house, she still pined for a better one; and when Maurice procured for her, perhaps at the cost of his own dinner, some small luxury which she fancied, it usually caused her a pious lament that "such things were not common with them." Her complaints being made in a resigned tone, and generally commencing with an expression of thanksgiving for what they had, it was not easy, for an impressionable man like Maurice, to detect the leech-like selfishness of the discontented sinner under the whining tones of the enduring saint. But, as in her religion she protested that she was hungering and thirsting after Heaven, so in everything else she was hungering for something better than she possessed; and if she really pined for Heaven at all, it was chiefly because, this world not being good enough for her, she desired better arrangements for her self-indulgence, and a place where she could be more admirably petted and pampered elsewhere.

"And how are Kate and Annie?" asked Melville, as he seated himself in Maurice Tremlin's parlour.

"In excellent health, I am thankful to say," replied Maurice, smiling with pleasure at Melville's visit. "It is most kind of you to come and inquire for them."

On his former visit Melville had not seen Mrs. Tremlin. She was lying on the sofa this time when he entered, it being, as she would have described it, "one of her *bad* days." She languidly assumed the sitting posture during Melville's stay, but took care to inform him of her indifferent health before many minutes had elapsed.

"I am indeed a perfect sufferer, Mr. Melville," she murmured; "and from day to day no one knows what I endure."

"Yes, I am sorry to say my poor wife has very bad health," echoed Maurice.

"The little change of Kate and Annie being with you one might have thought would have proved some diversion for you," spoke Melville, who fancied by the lady's robust appearance that if she suffered from anything it must be from moody self-indulgence.

"Indeed," replied Mrs. Tremlin, "I cannot *bear* them in the room for long together; I can *really* only give my orders to the servant for all the children. It is a great trial to me being always thus; but I trust I take up my cross cheerfully, and feel sure, as I tell my dear Maurice, that *all* is for the best."

"My wife has wonderful faith, Mr. Melville: I often think I might take a lesson from her," observed Tremlin.

Melville's inward conviction was that it would be far

better if he kept to his own course of acting, and left his wife's ways alone.

"I fear," continued Maurice "all the enjoyment of my dear brother's little ones falls to my share. It is indeed a pleasure to me to have under my roof the children of him who was the loved companion of my boyish days."

"And," declared Mrs. Tremlin, "we must not only consider our pleasure in them, but we must also remember our responsibility. I fear that I have not so much pleasure as anxiety; for in bringing them up they must be made to feel the necessity of being washed in the Fountain filled with blood; and I believe I shall have strength given me for this duty, weak as I am. It was only last Sunday, Mr. Melville—in the afternoon—being eager to instruct our dear nieces in the ways of the Lord, that, ill as I was, I resolved to put out all my strength, and warn these dear children of the fearful end of wickedness, and tell them about those who are 'accepted in the Beloved.' Soon after I commenced talking I seemed like one with new strength; and as I told them of the fearful doom of the unbeliever,—more agonizing than even the horrors of a shipwreck,—a new, a strange vigour came over me, and I was enabled, much to the astonishment of my husband, to talk for an hour. Now who could have inspired me with that strength but the Lord? How true it is that strength shall be given as our day, if only we trust!"

Now the facts out of which Mrs. Tremlin constructed this fiction were, very briefly, these: On the Sunday in question Mrs. Tremlin inaugurated the day by condoling with herself on the terrible trial of having these children added to her household, until Tremlin almost felt himself the wickedest man in the world for daring to expend a fraction of his hard-earned income upon any one but his wife. Mrs. Tremlin having affected tears, her husband was compelled to supplicate her forgiveness if he had unconsciously done wrong in giving shelter to the orphans. Having reduced Mr. Tremlin to the most abject humility, Mrs. Tremlin placed her new bonnet on her head, and, at an expense which would have sufficed to keep either of the children for a week, intimated her desire to be conveyed to the Baptist Chapel, where the Rev. Jabez Blaze, D.D., preached. After hearing that reverend person discourse on Hell and torments she returned home, laying the flattering unction to her soul that she was one of Heaven's chosen band, being, to wit, a "particular" Baptist. Elated with this notion, she was enabled once more to assist Tremlin to feel as he always did, poor fellow, how immeasurably inferior he was to his holy wife. Having partaken of a hearty dinner she relapsed into her lounging posture on the sofa, petulant and irritable at the addition of " so many more children," as she described the presence of the two orphans. Unwilling that Tremlin should take the little dears for a ramble, because she was too selfish to do without his incessant attentions, too pious to let them play, too selfish to amuse them, she planned nothing for their happiness. She was solicitous only to gratify her own inordinate love of talk. Intent upon this, she seized the opportunity, as much for her husband's edification as the children's, of impressing on the orphans how grateful they should be for the dinner they had eaten, and the shelter which was being given to them. By a process quite easy to her she then slid into the most horrid parts of Jabez Blaze's sermon, telling the children of Hell and torment, of God keeping a book in which He wrote down everything they did, and of His being ready at any moment to punish them unless they were very good—which she took care to inform them they could always know how to be by consulting her. With other terrible discourse of the like kind she continued, until the children's little lips were almost white and their eyes dilated. Then she taught the orphans a hateful rhyme called a hymn,—

> "There is a dreadful Hell,
>   With never ending flames,
>   Where sinners will with devils dwell,
>   Bound in eternal chains."

Afterwards she sent them to help one another to bed, where they lay sobbing with fright, till Maurice happening to hear them, went and consoled them with childlike gentle talk, some sweets, and a promise of buttercups and daisies on bright days to come.

Melville could not know exactly this history of Sunday, but he could read character, and he saw in the fat, lazy, pretentious woman before him, something so akin to his notion of a hypocrite, that he was not slow in replying to her when again she minced out, "We must at the earliest stage convince them of sin."

"And pray why?" asked Melville, almost testily.

"In order," returned Mrs. Tremlin, evidently disconcerted, "that they may see the need of being washed white in Jesu's blood."

"But childish innocence is already white: you have nothing more pure in this world than the unsophisticated heart of a child," returned Melville.

"But, surely, Mr. Melville," said Mrs. Tremlin, "in teaching a child you would recognise the doctrine of original sin?"

"I recognise," replied Melville, "a mystery when you speak of 'original sin.' But there is a sin which is horridly free from mystery. It is that crime of darkening the joyous days of childhood, which is chiefly done in this country by means of what is called 'spiritual instruction.' By this process persons whose perceptions may have become warped, and whose affections may have become chilled by contact with the grossness of the earth, arrogantly enter into the blissful, sunny, angelic world of child-life, and blacken it with their frowns, jar its harmonies by their

sublime confidence in love and goodness, which is its especial glory and most lovely characteristic."

"Well, I have always been taught," rejoined Mrs. Tremlin, "that as soon as children are old enough to know anything, they ought to be told what evil natures they have, and that they must 'put off the old man.' This, you know, is the object of most of our children's hymns, which are taught in the Sunday-schools."

"Really, my dear," remarked Tremlin, modestly, "I have sometimes thought when I have happened to take the little ones a walk, that the children and flowers are the purest things I have met with in the world."

"I am not at all surprised," said Mrs. Tremlin, with some asperity in her tone, "to hear you make such a remark, for really your religious views are often so loose as to add to the many causes of depression from which I daily suffer."

"For my part," exclaimed Melville, "I think Mr. Tremlin's remark singularly appropriate. And as to the hymns, Mrs. Tremlin, I say at once that the word to write in big black letters across most of the children's hymns would be —'scandalous.' What right have we to make a child parrot words which it does not understand? To make it sing about matters fit only to be groaned about? To frighten it with an awful Hell which it has done nothing to deserve? And when the little thing is absolutely happy with its toys, worry it to hunger after greater bliss, which is represented as being 'far far away?' You teach it to be frightened, to be discontented with its lot, and to pine for some greater enjoyment, and to hypocritically declare that it wishes to 'become an angel.' What is the necessity for all this?"

"To make them see," answered Mrs. Tremlin, "that there is neither enjoyment nor safety for them in this world of sin, and they must struggle all their lives to get to Heaven where there are both."

exclaimed Melville. "Why they will never reach any Heaven if such selfishness engrosses them."

"It is astonishing after all," Tremlin meekly suggested, "how little we know of Heaven."

"Those who have not faith of course know little," observed Mrs. Tremlin, with ineffable sanctity. "I am thankful it is in part revealed to me."

"Madam," said Melville solemnly, "you are now beyond the limits of the finite mind. Speculation may combine with credulity, and their joint assertions may be termed faith, or revelation, or what not. But the fact remains that we are dealing with The Unknowable."

"But surely," persisted Mrs. Tremlin, "it is perfectly known to us that we shall have complete repose in Heaven."

"Forgive me," replied Melville, "if I say that even that is debatable ground. Indeed, a state of repose would be anything but Heaven to many constitutions. The intelligent mind craves for constant activity, and for an adequate sphere for its development."

"And would you not have the children you saved from the wreck trained to seek a better land?" questioned Mrs. Tremlin.

"No," responded Melville. "I would have them trained to do the things which are godly, irrespective of a better or worse land."

"But," remonstrated Mrs. Tremlin, "would you put no reward before the christian mind to induce it to secure eternal happiness?"

"Not in the sense you mean," replied Melville. "I think it is unphilosophical to do so. The man who seeks happiness for its own sake, runs after a shadow which he never overtakes. The selfish man by his very nature is debarred from enjoying what he aims at securing, whether it is a fortune here, or a Heaven yonder. Experience shows us

man. Christianity assures us that in an after-life the mind still survives, and are we to believe that all the laws that governed it here will be reversed? If not, how is it possible that those who have scrambled through earth selfishly anxious during long years to secure a Heaven to themselves, can by any possibility be happy? Such persons, even here, are out of their element when in the society of the generous and the brave: how will they be able to enjoy the company of such in another world? And pray, are these people to be blessed with Heaven on account of their merit in always hungering for it, whilst the others, because they would not be so self-seeking, are to be set aside?"

"I sometimes think," said Tremlin, "that the unselfish performance of duty is the only thing which religion makes absolutely clear to us. All other matters seem speculations, whose solution we have to leave."

"Yes, I know you are contented to leave a great deal," responded Mrs. Tremlin, "but those who 'walk by faith' can see the future that is prepared for them. I am thankful to know myself that I am 'a partaker according to the promises.' It depends on faith, Mr. Melville. We can possess everything if we *only believe*. I refer not only to heavenly enjoyments, but to the things of time. I have seen 'the reward of faith' even in pecuniary matters."

"Indeed!" said Melville, with genuine interest.

"Yes," responded Mrs. Tremlin. "I can refer to one incident in my own family. My cousin, Miss Scampion, founded the St. Gravestone Home, for friendless little girls, entirely on faith. She threw her anxieties absolutely on the Lord. She incurred debts well knowing He would see them paid. Her faith and prayers were rewarded. In answer to her appeals and circulars, money flowed into the home, and she has done a great work."

"To provide a refuge for the friendless is always a great and good work," remarked Melville. "I must remember

I shall also be glad to assist the Institution if it be a good one and in need of funds."

"My cousin would be very grateful, and glad to see you," returned Mrs. Tremlin. "But to prevent your having at any time a fruitless journey, I must tell you that Miss Scampion, like myself, is a thorough disciplinarian; and one of her rules is that visitors are only admitted at stated times and by prearrangement."

"I will remember your cousin's home," said Melville. "And now I must take my leave, begging you, however, to let me know if there should ever be any way in which I can be of service to Kate and Annie."

CHAPTER VIII.

CANT AND HUSBAND-CATCHING.—LORD EVERTON'S ENGAGEMENT.
—MRS. AND ANASTATIA HARDCASTLE.—ISABELLA LANDOR.

THERE are many people in The World of Cant who think that a sin against fashion is almost as heinous as a sin against virtue. The Hardcastles were people of this stamp. At the period to which our history has now to refer, Parliament had just risen. Whether Parliament were in session or not, the personal and business arrangements of the Hardcastles could have pursued their usual course very well. But it was the fashion for such of the middle classes as possessed wealth, to make their annual departure from town simultaneously with the departure of the Court and Parliament. For this reason the Hardcastles were in a fever of fuss to join the great fashionable exodus of some bodies and nobodies which autumnally sets out from London as soon as the mighty Babel of St. Stephen's relapses into merciful silence.

The season which had just terminated had been one of much anxiety to the Hardcastle family. They had been engaged during its continuance in a matrimonial adventure. To understand the transaction we must strip it of all the Cant phrases with which they glossed and concealed its real nature and mechanism, and we must state the simple fact. They had been angling to catch Lord Everton as a husband for Victoria. Of course they would have denied the imputation with superb indignation, and they had played their parts so well that many people would have credited their denial. Even on the morning before their departure eagerly anticipating a farewell call from Lord Everton, which would settle whether or not their manœuvres had been successful, they managed to keep up their appearance of artless innocence.

In The World of Cant people by practice learn to combine the maximum of sanctimoniousness with the maximum of duplicity. As a simple matter of history it is necessary to be recorded that during the preceding weeks Miss Hardcastle had used every means in her power to inspire his lordship's admiration and to bring it to the test. And it is fair to say that nothing had been left undone by the mother or daughter to secure a declaration of love from him. In preparation for this present visit "dear Victoria" had "got herself up" to the best possible advantage; and as her maid gave the last touch to the curls of false hair, the fair enchantress smiled triumphantly at the reflection of herself in the mirror.

"That will do very well, Harrison," she exclaimed to her attendant. "There is just a little too much powder on this side of the face, and I want this eyebrow a little darker. That is better," she concluded, as the maid obeyed her requests. "Now I think I shall do. This morning robe is very charming, is it not?"

"Yes, miss, and suits you wonderfully well."

"I think it is becoming," returned the lady, as she stood putting to proper proportions the cerise bow at her chest, and giving the final close investigations of her complexion in the glass. "I fancy I could bear that bow in my hair now, Harrison. Just get it."

While the effect was being tried his lordship arrived, and Miss Hardcastle in a perfect flurry threw aside the bow that she might have one more moment to examine herself in the cheval glass. Then with a smile of approbation the innocent darling hastened downstairs in accordance with a plan arranged between her and her excellent mother.

in my *deshabille*. We are leaving town to-morrow, you know, and I was busy sorting books, and music, etc. It takes quite a time to make all one's little arrangements."

Lord Everton gazed at her with admiring eyes, and begged her not to apologise. There was something very earnest in his lordship's face this morning. He looked thoughtful and rather solemn, as if some important crisis were at hand. Although he was a man whose mental capacity was not yet well developed, he was strictly a man of honour. He had been brooding over some well directed hints of the Hardcastles as to what society would say if it happened that his attentions to "dear Victoria" had not been seriously intended. Besides, the clever actress herself had in a cunning way given him to understand that her destiny was in his keeping. When a woman who is really elegant and can be fascinating gives a soft-hearted man notice that non-reciprocation of affection on his part means probable suicide on hers, what is her victim to do? "Dear Victoria" knew what he was to do. She knew that it was his duty to make Miss Hardcastle Lady Everton. She knew that this was the morning to settle it; and she made him settle it. Of course, a strong-minded man could not have been caught by such a bait. But where are the men who are strong-minded where women are concerned?

The conversation that took place during the visit of his lordship it is needless to relate. It is sufficient to say that no sooner had Lord Everton left the house than Miss Hardcastle rushed to her mother's apartment, and falling on the maternal neck, exclaimed, "I fear, mamma, you must soon lose your daughter."

"It is settled then?" eagerly rejoined Mrs. Hardcastle. "Your papa will be rejoiced. He thought it would be managed to-day. Well, my dear, I think you have to thank me a little for your success. The hints I have given

an issue; and Lord Everton has heard enough in your praise from me."

"Oh, yes, mamma, you have been most kind and useful in the affair, I am sure. I cannot tell you how tremendously he admires me though. I believe he completely worships me," added Victoria, as she gave a glance of extreme approbation at her reflection in the mirror.

"That is as it should be," proclaimed the fond mother. "There is some hope of a man if he worships his wife."

"Well, it is all settled, mamma," continued Victoria excitedly; "and he is coming to see papa to-night."

"Very good," pronounced Mrs. Hardcastle. "All I wish now is that Mr. Melville would take more to Anastatia; it would be a good match for her. However, your papa has invited him to spend a few days at Broadcray with us, and perhaps that will advance matters a little."

There is no greater error than that of assuming that a person who is absolutely a dullard in the department of religious truth is, in some corresponding degree, a dullard in business or strategic transactions. The bitter experience of life teaches that the ignorant, unctuous, namby-pamby, sentimental character has, for its obverse side, intense cunning, gross cruelty, and insatiable cupidity. It ought to occasion no surprise that Mrs. Hardcastle, after reflecting on what "dear Victoria" had told her, should manifest the depths of worldliness which lay even under her sanctimoniousness. She was in some trepidation lest Lord Everton, who after all was only an inexperienced youth, should repent in the evening the step which he had taken in the morning. She was determined to prearrange for that contingency. She decided that it would be a wise manœuvre at once to place the greatest number of difficulties in the way of his withdrawal from his engagement, if after consultation with his friends he should be induced

best preventive to that calamity would be to make the engagement as public as possible in all directions, without waiting for Mr. Hardcastle's return, or risking even a moment's unnecessary delay. Accordingly she sat down, and wrote the following letter, which she sent with slight variations to every one whom she had the slightest pretext for addressing on family matters :—

"MY DEAREST ———,

"I feel that I really ought not to be guilty of any longer delay in writing to tell you of an event for which no doubt rumour has already somewhat prepared you. I allude to the engagement of our dear Victoria to Lord Everton. Of course we have the very highest regard for Lord Everton; and the knowledge that his long cherished admiration for dear Victoria is at last responded to by her love for him, compels us to feel that in the future happiness of the betrothed ones it is our christian duty to sink that deep sorrow which shadows our unresigned hearts at the idea of being called on to part with our darling daughter. However, it would be wrong of me to repine, for so far my God has supported me wonderfully. I am sure that your prayers will join with ours in asking a blessing on the union."

Whilst Mrs. Hardcastle was occupying herself with this epistolary performance, "dear Victoria" retired to her boudoir to imagine at leisure the splendid commotion which the news would cause among the gossips at Falcon Small's.

All this time there sat in the drawing-room two ladies, very dissimilar from each other. One was Anastatia Hardcastle, of whom it is enough now to say that she was the sister of "dear Victoria," and was an embodiment of fashion, insincerity, and Cant.

The other young lady was her cousin, Miss Isabel Landor. She was a daughter of Mr. Hardcastle's sister, and since the death of her father, which had taken place a year ago, had lived with the Hardcastles. She was a beautiful, intellectual, thoroughly accomplished and noble girl. Her father, who was a barrister, having lost his wife a few years after his marriage, had made Isabel his constant companion, and almost his idol. The daughter loved to dwell on the memory of that father. He was great and good, braver than a lion, and tender with a tenderness which is only possible to a true man. Though he had attained eminence in his profession, he had not been contaminated by either the servility or the artifices of the bar. His independence of mere conventional opinions enabled him to take his stand in the Temple as an advocate who would not hire his tongue to the highest bidder; and solicitors who had a vile cause to maintain well knew that no money would enable them to retain on their side his splendid abilities. His courage was long remembered in Westminster Hall, where no court minion or hectoring judge had ever either by intimidation or cajolery succeeded in inducing him to abandon the cause of the injured or the oppressed. A man of the highest culture and refinement, he took care that his daughter should have, in England and on the Continent, every educational advantage which his ample purse could supply. When he passed into spirit life his daughter felt that the greatest man on earth was dead. For she, who for twenty-one years had lived in closest communion with him, had observed perpetually the true glory of his grand life—the life of a royal soul whose highest ambition was to exemplify bravely all day long and everywhere the spirit of Jesus Christ. It was no wonder that a deep depression fell on the gentle nature of Isabel Landor when she was left in the world alone. Her uncle Hardcastle professed at once for her such distant, respectful, avuncular sympathy as society could demand. After the funeral, however, his sympathy expanded rapidly. **Three** things aided that expansion very much. In the first place, to Hardcastle's great astonishment, the leading newspapers published eulogistic memoirs of Mr. Landor; in the second place, society spoke of him as a great man; and in the third place, his last will and testament disclosed that he had left the whole of his great wealth to Miss Landor absolutely. By degrees Hardcastle assured himself that he felt most generous pity for his niece; and as his wife and daughters, mindful of the three facts which had influenced him, managed to suppress the outward manifestation of that annoyance which half-bred vulgar persons always feel in the presence of a highly cultivated woman of sincere character, it was decided that Miss Landor should become a resident at the Hardcastles' house. It was "most considerate, most self-sacrificing of the Hardcastles." All Falcon Small's people said so; and many an outside asinego repeated the bray, in ignorance of the munificent payment which the niece had to make to the uncle for the enjoyment of the "charms of his christian home."

By the arrangements entered into, Miss Landor, however, was mistress of her own plans; and it happened that she, on the day of Lord Everton's visit, returned to the house immediately after his lordship's departure. During the time that Mrs. Hardcastle and "dear Victoria" were respectively engaged in the ways already described, she had been endeavouring to interest the selfish and vapid Anastatia in a charitable institution for which help was needed. The theme was still being pursued when "dear Victoria," having finished the enjoyment of her boudoir contemplations, swept into the dining-room with an air of newly-acquired magnificence. She lost not a moment in announcing the great event of the morning, but was not altogether elated by the impression it created. Her sister, though for many reasons pleased, was at heart excessively jealous Her cousin looked on the success of "dear Victoria's" manœuvre with all the disdain which it would necessarily inspire in a refined and virtuous mind. Most of the household were half afraid of " dear Victoria ": Miss Landor was not. So when the bride-elect demanded of her cousin, with some asperity, why she did not more cordially congratulate her, Miss Landor replied with perfect composure and sincerity.

"Pray," said Victoria, "tell me what is in your mind about this matter."

"Well," answered Isabel, "I was wondering whether you knew enough of Lord Everton to be certain that you love him; and whether you know enough of your own heart to be sure that you can add to his happiness. A few weeks ago you were scarcely acquainted with him."

"Really, Isabel," retorted Victoria, "you talk most absurdly. 'Few weeks!' Why many engagements and marriages take place in that time."

"I think she is all the more lucky for securing him so quickly," observed Anastatia.

"Securing him!" exclaimed Isabel, scornfully. "What a way to speak of marriage!"

"Well, and a very proper way," said Anastatia. "I am sure all our friends at Mr. Small's will look at it in that light."

"Yes," chimed in Victoria, "and I have no doubt I shall be able to make Lord Everton go a great deal amongst our friends there. I am confident Falcon Small will treat him with the respect due to his position in society."

CHAPTER IX.

CANT THE ENEMY OF TRUE TEACHERS.—MORE ABOUT MRS. TREMLIN'S THEOLOGY.—MR. CALEB FAITHFUL.

ON the Sunday after his visit to Tremlin, Melville decided to go and hear Tremlin's minister, the Rev. Caleb Faithful.

On entering the Church he was saddened to see so few people present. A glance, however, at the minister in the pulpit suggested to him that the scantiness of the congregation might be accounted for on physical grounds. The preacher was a man of noble presence and grand craniological conformation. The face was highly intellectual, yet full of benevolence. In the splendid dark eyes there played the light of genius. He was a teacher of the highest order; Nature evidently intended him to be so. But a man of this stamp can only teach beings of a similar genus. It would be impossible for thoughts which reside in such a brain as his to find a lodgment in the men of puny forehead and stunted soul. You might as well expect a little wren to be thankful for having an eagle's egg placed in her nest, as expect a pigmy soul to be grateful to a man who gives it a great idea for incubation. To a rabble of grossly organized fanatical religionists such a man as Mr. Faithful, by reason of his Divine superiority of mental, moral, and physical constitution, must necessarily be an enigma, if not an annoyance; and they will keep away from his pews. But apart from this physical explanation, there were a variety of reasons why Mr Faithful was not a popular preacher. In the first place, he was not a favourite with that coarse sentimental class of females who abound in metropolitan congregations. He did not know how to flatter them, and would not have stooped to if he had. Nor did his affairs furnish them with topics for spicy scandal. Their popular pets kept their interest alive by stirring up their curiosity, imagination, prurience, and morbid love of horror. One of them in early life had been arrested for stealing books. Another, on the appearance of his millionth sermon, was brought before his presbytery on a charge of shameless lying. Another was tried for criminal liberties with the wife of one of his deacons. A fourth was charged with prostituting his chapel to secular purposes, and using his congregation as advertising agents for his latest publications. A fifth had married four wives, and was reported to be looking out for another. A sixth, the most popular of all, very properly appeared, disappeared, and reappeared; disappeared and reappeared again, to punish vice in the divorce court. How could Mr. Faithful, with his prosaic pure life, compete for a place in the heart or conversation of those scandal-mongers, who from day to day enjoyed the luxury of associating their minister's lives with such racy details as these; and who always hovered around the heroes of sensationalism, like blue-bottles around putridity?

But there was another reason why Mr. Faithful was not popular. His inferior brethren in the ministry, and their name was legion, were intensely jealous of his transcendent powers. Some of these brethren were the editors of little sectarian newspapers, under the management of cliques which were organized on the plan of a mutual admiration society. These men carefully excluded his utterances from print. Others of them started a whine about his orthodoxy. Amongst the number were some of those unctuous, sleek, pietistical scalawags, who are masters of the fiendish art of blasting a reputation by a whisper, a shoulder-shrug, or an innuendo contained in a public prayer. As the result of their combined efforts, it came to pass

was "not sound in the faith," and ought not to be listened to as a minister. But men of independent minds looked and laughed at "all that and all that," and saw with their honest eyes that Mr. Faithful was truly a great man. You might as well try to extinguish a constellation of stars with a fire-engine, as attempt by paltry detraction to suppress such thoughts as radiate from the soul of a man like that. Mr. Faithful shed a light upon every subject he touched. The entire absence from his public ministrations of all Cant and hearsay was owing to his purity and goodness. He realized the solemnity of life, and often felt overawed at the responsibility of the position which permitted him to expound to others the marvels of time and the mysteries of eternity. He had no sympathy with that priestly facetiousness which in order to attract a gaping crowd will play the part of Punch in the pulpit. He was a man of refinement and sensibility; and therefore the sensuality and morbid grossness of the popular theology which makes an inventory of the Saviour's groans and wounds, gloats over the fact of His personal agonies, and sings about His bruised body, battered brains and dropping blood, was to him unspeakably loathsome and profane. His nature was holy and reverent. Accordingly he felt a revulsion from that fashionable sanguinary fiction of the shambles which depicts a God of caprice as being in an ungovernable passion which could only be appeased by the unmerited murder of an absolutely innocent being—His only Son in whom He was well pleased. He was a man of warm sympathies, the friend of every child of sorrow. It grieved his heart to see a troubled world driven away from its only source of comfort by priests and mountebanks, who were every day misrepresenting as a Moloch or a Juggernaut the great loving Father of us all. He was a man of distinguished scholarship and erudition, and possessed great analytical power. He therefore declined to be imposed upon by mere traditional authority, by fashionable consents, or by popular votes. He saw the heart of things. Their wrappages were as nothing to him. Though poor, he was, too, a man of fearless independence. If all the Œcumenical Councils in the world had resolved to brand the truth as a heresy, he would have stood alone making his undaunted protest. This great man was of course unconscious of his own greatness. There was not an atom of self-complacency in his constitution. The reason why he did not move on the conventional plane of thought was simply because Nature had appointed him to move on a higher one. Created a spiritual star, he could not alter his component parts so as to coalesce with ephemeral elements, and join in fugitive pyrotechnical displays as a denominational rocket. He was no transient coruscation flashing over the sectarian horizon. He was as a burning and a shining light, and the beams of his great love shone tenderly on every created thing. Probably, not one of even the hundreds of men whom he had blessed with the affluence of his goodness ever comprehended the illimitable nature of that disinterested love.

Whilst Melville sat in his pew steadfastly looking at Mr. Caleb Faithful, and listening to the tones in which he spoke the grand thoughts of his sermon, he became conscious of that marvellous sense of nearness of relationship by which spiritual affinity asserts itself. He felt that he had met with a spiritual brother, who was on his own line of mental march. "Quit you like men" was the text from which Mr. Faithful discoursed. Not a sound of denominationalism, or of Falcon Small kind of talk, was heard from first to last. No miasmatic platitudes, no crude dogmatics, clouded the beauty of the truth. The sermon was like a grand clarion call to a manly and heroic life. Every hearer was quickened with mental vigour to see his duty, and braced with moral energy to perform it.

Melville, when he left the Chapel, felt himself stronger than ever to battle with the shams and villainies of the false and cowardly times in which we live. Tremlin saw him, and was soon by his side, eager to express the joy he felt at his presence. Hearty, and sincere, was the admiration which the two men expressed of the vitalising sermon to which they had listened. They walked together in happy conversation in the direction of Tremlin's house; for as Melville saw that he was able to cheer his humble friend, he was unwilling to hasten his departure.

As soon as they reached the residence, Mrs. Tremlin and the children came into view. The little ones ran to them with a shout of joy, which Mrs. Tremlin at once frowned down as anti-sabbatical. Immediately her jarring voice had discharged the duty of returning Melville's salutation, she said, "I much regret you did not go to my Chapel, Mr. Melville, instead of to my husband's. Dr. Jabez Blaze gave us a splendid sermon, most rousing and harrowing; many were crying in the congregation, and many sought him after the service. It is sad that Mr. Tremlin should prefer the preaching of such an 'unsound' and dreadful man as Mr. Faithful, and that he should also endeavour to lead others astray to hear him."

"For my own part," responded Melville, "I am personally indebted to Mr. Tremlin for mentioning Mr. Faithful's name to me. I am truly thankful I have had the privilege of being brought to-day into contact with the mind of that great man, and shall be eager to hear him whenever it is possible."

"Well," retorted Mrs. Tremlin, in a tone which was intended to be impertinent, "it is a fortunate thing that there are not many who appreciate that dangerous preacher. Whilst Jabez Blaze, Falcon Small, and other evangelical men have their Chapels crowded, he only preaches to empty pews."

"His Chapel was certainly not well attended," answered Melville. "But in estimating a congregation you must not only count numbers, you must weigh character, and sort quality. A ton of grass is not in value equal to an

potentialities of one acorn. Even the multiplication of mushrooms is not a matter of much importance. But to get twenty thousand oaks from one acorn is an achievement of absolute grandeur. If Mr. Faithful's scanty congregation be composed of men of the right sort of mental and moral calibre, they, though few, may be found in the long run to have more influence on the destinies of the world than any ordinary sectarian crowds."

"But surely," returned Mrs. Tremlin, "a large congregation is a proof of a good minister."

"I think not necessarily," responded Melville. "The opinion of one man is often more valuable than the opinion of a mob. Who would think of quoting the opinion of a crowd of nobodies in opposition to the opinion of Shakespeare or Milton? Depend on it if we want to estimate rightly a minister's influence, we must think less and less of the numbers who follow him, and observe more and more their mental and moral quality, and their capacity for virtuous performance."

After a little conversation on more general topics, Melville took a courteous farewell.

Mrs. Tremlin, however, was in a towering passion. She had been so accustomed to subdue and silence her poor husband, and other meek men, by the fierceness of her looks whenever her affectation of sanctity had failed for the moment to overawe them, that she chafed under the quiet judicial tones of the man who had this morning calmly opposed her views. As soon, therefore, as she was comfortably seated at home, she attacked Tremlin with waspish asperity.

"You have a great deal to answer for," said she, "in leading young men astray; and in endeavouring to make them as sceptical as yourself."

"I assure you, Mr. Faithful is really no sceptic," replied Tremlin; "but an earnest and conscientious preacher, who

"Yes, that is where it is," retorted his amiable partner, "head knowledge without heart knowledge. Not trusting to the Lord. Not leaving Him to make the dark mind light, but looking away from 'the blood' to poor human self. As Dr. Blaze said so beautifully in his sermon this morning, 'endeavouring to clean our own filthy rags, when Christ's robe of righteousness will cover us, and His blood wash us.'"

"My dear," said Tremlin timidly, "all those vagaries may suit you, but I cannot see any sense in them myself, I cannot even understand them."

"For shame, Maurice," cried Mrs. Tremlin, "to talk thus blasphemously to me who have passed through so much christian experience; who have been so specially tried of the Lord's afflicting hand, and thereby have gained so much christian perception. And you!—you who have never had a day's illness, who have never shed a tear for sin, to attempt to put me down. It is monstrous, disgraceful! and before the children too, whom I endeavour to bring up in the only right way. To hold me up to ridicule to them is, indeed, cruel;" and Mrs. Tremlin commenced gasping. She had resorted to the stratagem which she usually employed to secure her conjugal victories. Tremlin sighed as he rose from the table to get his wife's smelling salts. He knew that what she was pleased to designate "a fit of hysterics" was imminent, and the room for the next half-hour would be a scene of terrible confusion: so it was. Mrs. Tremlin's attack this time was "very bad," for she felt the absolute importance of showing her husband, in a way which could not be forgotten by him, the inconveniences, horrors, and dangers which would inevitably result from any renewed attempt on his part to question, in the presence of others, her religious knowledge or experience.

Poor Tremlin! "Quit you like men" is a wise command, but how seldom do men of your conformation attend to it in matters matrimonial!

CHAPTER X.

Cant on the Missionary Platform.—War and Christianity.—Sir Harry Grapeshot and Mr. Caleb Faithful.—Tom Decides to Enlist.

TOM'S fortunes had become exceedingly dark. Although he was always anxious for work, and grateful for any, even the most menial, occupation, starvation sometimes seemed to stare him in the face. One morning, when all hope was deserting him, he considered himself most fortunate when, in answer to his entreaties, an enterprising printer hired him for sixpence for the remainder of the day to carry out two large sandwich advertising boards, announcing a great missionary meeting under popular patronage. It was advertised that the chair would be taken by Sir Harry Grapeshot, K.G., and knight of the order of the elephant, etc., etc.; and that the Revs. Falcon Small, Jabez Blaze, Ezekiel Smallweed, etc., Dobbington Blooster, Esq., Dandy Filch, Esq., and other laymen would take part in the proceedings. It was also stated that an account would be given of the improvement which had been effected by missionaries in the condition of the heathen. Some curiosity to see his old master on the platform by the side of "the great Sir Harry"; and a very natural and pardonable eagerness to learn whether the persons who were helping the heathen thousands of miles away could do anything to alleviate the miseries of a wretched lad at home, impelled Tom to go to the meeting. He did not get there till late. The audience were in considerable agitation at the time he entered. They were witnessing an unprecedented spectacle:—the missionary report and the speech of Sir Harry

Grapeshot were being challenged by Mr. Caleb Faithful, who was speaking from the centre of the assembly. He said, " I consider that some of the noblest of the human race have been missionaries ; and the life of Williams, Livingstone, and Moffat are alone enough to prove that a true missionary is a real hero. But the language which we have heard from that platform to-night indicates that quite a wrong view is prevalent among you as to the aims and duty of the true missionary. You seem to think that it is the business of a missionary to promote sectarianism, and that he is successful only just in so far as he obtains new members for your denomination. Nothing can be more mistaken. Denominationalism is not Christianity. To make more Wesleyans, Baptists or Episcopalians is surely a task of very small importance. In my view no missionary is fit to attempt to introduce the gospel of Christ to any tribe unless he himself first understands enough of it to know, that it can never flourish in the pestilent atmosphere of the sects. Yet you will not subscribe money to send out the gospel of Christ. You want to send out the gospel of the 'cliques.' The fashionable missionary spirit is nothing but the rivalry of one denomination with another for the purpose of display in subscription lists. This is not the worst. In your report and in the chairman's speech you have applauded war, alleging that its conquests open up new regions for your missionary enterprises. In other words, you are so anxious to increase the number of your particular sect that you even welcome the assistance of wholesale murder and robbery. Both your object and your means are unchristly. Have you considered what war is? It means the aggregation, the totality of every villainy known to the human race. Its component parts are not only devilish, but you can mention no devilish thing which is not an essential part of it. It is Hell on earth. It is more. It means not only fiendish suffering for the human fiends who engage in it, but unutterable agony for the absolutely innocent and for the absolutely helpless; and that on an enormous scale. Nevertheless, you, sitting there on that missionary platform, actually approve this multitudinous enormity. Nor is this all, you approve it in its foulest form—the war of aggression for gain. You approve of England entering the territory of an Afghan barbarian under a false pretext and with an overwhelming army. You know that defenceless tribes are being massacred, and that your hordes intend not only to murder but pillage, and to permanently rob the natives of even their own land, and to annex it to the other possessions which you have wrested from your weaker foes. In South Africa, by way of a sequel to the brave labours of noble missionaries and explorers, you provoke quarrels with friendly tribes, and without a shadow of justification you wage war of aggression and extermination against poor and unclothed human beings, upon whom you discharge all the weapons which a highly armed military nation of vast wealth has accumulated during centuries of incessant practice in the most cunning arts of war. If the teaching of Christ does not condemn such proceedings, what does it condemn? If Christianity tolerates such infamies, tell me in what it is better than the heathenism which you wish to abolish! Tell me of any barbarian age in which more flagrant national crimes were committed than those wars which you are applauding! The extermination of your fellow-men in Africa and Asia is enough to make all heathendom recoil from you and your religion. I tell you this deluge of fire and blood is no fitting prelude to the gospel of the Prince of peace. Whoever else applauds such satanic infamy, you, at least, should not have added your missionary voices to those of the multiform and complex selfish interests in this country which, for greedy ends, perpetually clamour for any and every war. In opposition to all the bloodthirsty screams and brutal braggadocio which are now rife in England, it was to have been expected that you unhesitatingly would have raised a solemn protest in the name of Him who said, ' My kingdom is not of this world, else would My servants fight.' A missionary platform should proclaim the good tidings of great joy, 'Glory to God in the highest; peace on earth, and good-will to men;' and should recall the wandering and infuriated thoughts of vainglorious braggarts to the only true rule of life—to do unto others as they would have others do to them. Moreover, do you not, as citizens, shudder at the corrupting consequences on individual character of that Cant and hypocrisy which permit us unblushingly to say in Church every Sunday, 'Give peace in our time, O Lord,' at the same time that we are concocting, abetting, and extenuating the most monstrous wars in history? Depend upon it, my missionary friends, that the principles of Jesus Christ, faithfully proclaimed and honestly lived, will do more for the gospel in foreign lands than can ever be effected for it by battles' mightiest men, even though they overturn a thousand thrones!"

It would be as unnecessary as difficult to attempt a description of the annoyance and irritation which the meeting manifested during this speech. Of course Mr. Faithful was constantly called to order, and at the end of some of his sentences it frequently seemed very doubtful whether the lovers of order would allow him to commence another. The unthinking religionists in the assembly resented the shock to their habitual self-complacency. The geographical philanthropists were rudely shaken in those romantic morbid dreams which allure them to wander in search of duty in far-off lands, and to neglect their nearer moral obligations. The blustering sentiment, which counterfeits patriotism, was thrown into paroxysmal passion. On all occasions, appropriate or inappropriate, it always wants to bellow "Rule Britannia;" so now it naturally felt outraged that any one should dare to speak of England's

eulogium. Snobbery also felt itself grievously insulted. It could not tolerate any other attitude towards the conventionally great Sir Harry Grapeshot than that of servility. Pokey the chemist, and Fluffey the draper, who felt "'ighly honoured by seeing so great a man as Sir 'Arry on a missionhairy platform," could scarcely restrain themselves from turning Mr. Faithful out of the assembly. Besides Pokey and Fluffey, there were vigorous representatives of the other incarnate virtues at the meeting, so that between them all Mr. Caleb Faithful had, as Tom afterwards said, "a roughish time of it."

Successive speakers rapidly rose, and in noble indignation vindicated their gospel and their country from the aspersions of Mr. Faithful. They proved that the banners of all the regiments which went on foreign service were separately prayed over, and blessed and consecrated personally by those right reverend fathers in God the bishops, the successors of the apostles. They explained that consecrated chaplains accompanied the soldiers in their campaigns, and that all the murder was done on strictly christian principles, and under christian superintendence. Referring to the missionary aspect of our aggressive wars, it was shown beyond a doubt that every camp was well filled with Bibles, and that every English battalion was a kind of branch of the Society for the Propagation of the Gospel in Foreign Parts. The advantage of wars of extermination was also conclusively established, on the ground that tribes which could not be converted to the English faith ought not to be allowed to exist to perpetuate their ancient heathenism, and shock by their practices the tender sensibilities of the Anglo-Saxon race. It was also established beyond reasonable dispute that the aborigines, being much in the way of the territorial schemes of England, ought to expect to be pushed aside whenever the necessity arose, and merited condign punishment if they were so rebellious as to resist the invader who brought them the bayonet in one hand and the Bible in the other. When, at the end of the meeting, Sir Harry Grapeshot, that man of many war medals, presented himself to speak, there arose a perfect hurricane of applause. He vigorously denounced Mr. Faithful's "unpatriotic attack," proclaimed his own strong missionary zeal, defended wars by conventional christian reasoning, and explained how they opened up the way for missionary societies in foreign lands.

Whilst poor, wretched, hungry, homeless, unemployed Tom, listened to all this, his old idea of becoming a soldier came back to him with renewed attraction. His natural scruples at earning his livelihood by shedding innocent blood, began now rapidly to melt in the blaze of the rhetoric of the great religious soldier on the missionary platform. He walked away from the meeting half inclined to go and enlist. Circumstances occurred at a music-hall in the adjoining street that settled his decision. A great patriotic meeting to support the Government of the day had been held in the music-hall, under the presidency of an eminent civic pomposity who had just been created a knight. Magniloquent resolutions—asserting the infallible wisdom, and unwavering righteousness of England's foreign transactions having been spoken to by members of Parliament, clergymen, and others—had been carried amidst deafening applause. As Tom passed the doors of the hall, the well dressed assembly were surging forth in a mood of lofty patriotism. Inspired with the heroic sentiments generated in the meeting, they sang with tremendous force:

> " We don't want to fight, we don't want to fight ;
>   Yet by jingo if we do,
> We've got the ships, and we've got the men,
>   And we've got the money too.
> But we'll make the Indians do the work,
> And pay the money too, and pay the money too."

This was followed by other martial doggerel, which

exigencies of the hour. It was sung again and again, to the tramp and march of hundreds of boots and shoes, until the soldier-demon was roused in every street simpleton who believes in the gospel of numbers and noise. Tom felt himself in harmony with the prevailing sentiment. The voice of the missionary platform had sounded in one ear, the voice of the music-hall had sounded in the other. Both voices suggested the same thing to him. There was no difference between their declarations. He determined then and there that he would be a soldier.

CHAPTER XI.

Cant about Newspapers.—Hardcastle's Party.—Mr. Golding, M.P.

THE August sun shone brightly, and the blue of the sky was undimmed by a single cloud as Melville alighted from the train at the Broadcray station on a visit to the Hardcastles. A carriage was waiting for him, and after a drive of twenty minutes the gates leading to Leslie Grange were reached. The house stood in a park of eighteen or twenty acres, well situated about a quarter of a mile from the road, and on an elevation that overlooked a large portion of the surrounding country. It was a modern pretentious building of red brick, more bold than beautiful. The land for about a quarter of an acre round the house was completely bare of trees, and the terraces with a perfect blaze of flower beds were carefully exposed to view. An artificial lake, with swans and other water fowl, was at the foot of the terraces, and the glare of the sunlight, the sparkling of the water, and the many coloured flowers, were rather more dazzling than effective on a hot August day. Melville was ushered into a large drawing-room, the windows of which opened on to the terrace, and were screened from the sun by outside blinds. It was a perfect blaze of gilt, and yellow satin. Mrs. Hardcastle and Anastatia occupied the apartment; the former as loud in her welcome as a woman who wishes to be a man's mother-in-law could possibly be. "We are anticipating Lord Everton's company to-morrow, Mr. Melville," she said, "and Sir Nicol and Lady Giltspur have promised to come next week, so I trust we shall be able to make up some good picnic parties. Mr. Hardcastle is expecting one or two bachelor friends as well, I believe."

"This is a delightful neighbourhood for picnics, I should imagine," returned Melville. "I have not visited this part before, and I was charmed with the drive from the station here."

"Did you notice Mr. Golding's seat?" asked Anastatia. "You passed it soon after you left the station: it is considered the most picturesque in the county. He is member of Parliament for Broadcray, you know."

"I noticed a lovely place sheltered by a wood at the back, and very artistically built," replied Melville.

"That is Golding Hall," said Anastatia. "We must pay it a visit before you leave. Mr. Golding is such a nice man; is he not, mamma?"

"Yes, indeed he is," assented Mrs. Hardcastle. "Of course you know he was one of the owners of the wrecked *Rasselas*, in which you had such an adventure?"

"Yes," replied Melville; "the owners were Darnley, Golding & Co. Do you know Mr. Darnley?"

"Not well," responded Mrs. Hardcastle; "though I have seen him and also his wife, the celebrated daughter of the Count de Courtray. She was considered very lovely by some people; but she is not my style of beauty—too pronounced."

"I have heard Mr. Darnley spoken of as a man of munificent generosity," said Melville.

"Very likely," replied Mrs. Hardcastle. "But what he does he keeps quite to himself, and he renders no service to any evangelical cause. He is very peculiar, an infidel I believe. Mr. Golding and he have dissolved partnership quite lately, owing to his strangely irreligious views. Yes," continued Mrs. Hardcastle after a moment's pause; "you see Mr. Golding is such a true christian, Mr. Melville. He built the Baptist Chapel at Broadcray, and he takes a great interest in the cause. He is coming to dine this evening, so we shall be able to introduce him to you."

"We become Baptists," laughed Anastatia, "when we are down here. We always attend Mr. Golding's chapel. It is certainly the best dissenting place here."

"And who preaches," asked Melville, "Mr. Golding?"

"Oh dear no," replied Anastatia. "Mr. Ezekiel Smallweed is the minister."

"He is nothing like Falcon Small," declared Mrs. Hardcastle, "but he is thoroughly evangelical, and certainly a safe man to hear."

Mr. Hardcastle now appeared, and after welcoming Melville conducted him to the apartment he was to occupy, and there left him to dress for dinner.

When Melville re-entered the drawing-room, he found a party assembled, which included Mr. Chippendale Golding and his wife, the Rev. Ezekiel Smallweed, the Misses Hardcastle, and a young lady unknown to Melville. Mr. Hardcastle instantly introduced the M.P. and his wife to Melville, and the eldest Miss Hardcastle advanced to shake hands. The young lady, however, who was Miss Isabel Landor, was not introduced. Perhaps her uncle imagined Melville knew her. At all events she was completely overlooked. Melville seated himself by Anastatia.

"Who is your other friend?" he asked.

"Do you mean Isabel?" asked Anastatia with an air of surprise; then slightly blushing as she observed Isabel's eyes on her, she added, "I thought you knew one another. She is a cousin of ours, and having lost both parents lives with us. The tone and way in which Anastatia spoke had the effect she had intended, of conveying to Melville the idea that Isabel was some poor relation. But on looking at Isabel his opinion altered. Yet it was clear she was snubbed; and there appeared no reason for this, except that she was beautiful and refined. What a contrast she formed to all the company assembled! There was Mrs.

Chippendale Golding, in glaring attire of satin and velvet;—a noisy little woman chattering on in a squeaky voice about her house and her grounds and her servants. Everything of hers was so wonderful. Her conservatories had turned out so well. Her fruit was the finest in the neighbourhood, and her husband the most influential of men! There was Mrs. Hardcastle; talking vulgarly of "dear Victoria's" recent engagement, and of Lord Everton's expected visit. There was "dear Victoria" herself; joining in the conversation with an effrontery that spoke badly for his lordship's future happiness. Then there was the pompous yet mean-spirited Hardcastle; talking politics and trade to Chippendale Golding.

This much vaunted Golding was a self-idolater. The world had helped to make him so; for as he complied with all its maxims it had never rebuked his self-adoration. It had treated him kindly, loading him with all its riches, and dealing lightly with him for his early-day vices. In his youth he had been a fast young fellow; but at the age of thirty-five, having sipped the honey from every flower and exhausted all the sources of gratification in which vulgar minds delight, a certain *ennui* took possession of him, a sense of satiety that nothing relieved. Struck with the utter inability of his old pleasures to allure him, he began to count all as vanity, and from that hour dated his conversion, which he would describe in the blandest terms, and with all the technical phrases of Cant. No sooner was this new change effected in his heart than he redoubled his old efforts to attain notoriety. Of course the scene of action shifted. His ambition sought pre-eminence among sectarians. He saw that his success in that direction would be comparatively easy. Identifying himself with the congregation at Ezekiel Smallweed's, he soon assumed their leadership. Possessed of plenty of wealth, it was no difficult task for him to dazzle them with his pecuniary demonstrations. Sectarian sycophants, **who** value a co-religionist according to the number and amount of his subscriptions, soon placed him high up on a denominational pedestal, and surrounded him with a false glamour of glory. He was a far-seeing man, and knew how and when to make use of everything. When the applause of the various conventicles was at its height, he performed a few well timed local services for his neighbours, and during the general chorus of approbation announced himself successfully as a candidate for Parliament. By virtue of all these achievements he now sat in Hardcastle's assembly as its lion. He appeared to expect assent to all his opinions, so that when after dinner, in the course of a conversation about the newspaper press, he found himself opposed by Melville, he had the appearance of a man who is enduring a new sensation.

"I do not agree with you," said Melville, " in your belief that the newspapers represent national opinion. I believe they misrepresent and suppress it. People seem to imagine that newspaper proprietors are an association of philanthropic gentlemen, banded together simply for the purpose of enlightening the public mind impartially and disinterestedly."

"And surely they do enlighten the public mind," returned Golding.

"Certainly," replied Melville, "but not always. And not impartially or disinterestedly. A newspaper proprietor is simply a man who manufactures a literary article, which he, like any other vendor, seeks to sell at the highest profit. If his customers are Conservatives, he will manufacture his article to suit their taste. It is not to the taste of *Conservatives* to read impartial accounts of the progress of education, or the triumphs of liberty. Such customers as these want full details of old Tory politics, great speeches made by little lordlings, gossip respecting the court, and privileged personages; news about the State Church, army, out-door relief for the sons of the aristocracy. The Conservative newspaper manufacturer, therefore, takes care that his readers shall have what they like, and that the papers which he sells shall be free from all such intelligence as they would consider a blemish. But it is obvious that a newspaper compiled on such a plan as that, must necessarily close its columns to all that is best in the philanthropic, scientific, religious, and inventive life of the world. Whilst it may enlighten the public on some subjects, it intentionally keeps them in the dark on others."

"But," said Golding in amazement, "what of the Liberal papers?"

"Simply this," answered Melville: "they are conducted on a like trade principle; but as they cater for a class having a different taste, they supply a different article. Out of all the passing events, and current opinions of the great world, they select just that fraction which will be palatable to their party, and reject the rest. That plan suits party purposes, and pampers party pride and vanity; for thereby men who rely for their information on their party organ are made to feel that all the world is moving in the circle of their ideas, and that outside that circle there is merely chaos."

"I presume, however," said the Rev. Ezekiel Smallweed, "that you exempt our religious papers from your strictures."

"By no means," responded Melville. "They are more narrow-minded than the others, and differ from them also in that they are issued less frequently, but their mercenary spirit is just the same. In some respects they are worse than other papers, although and perhaps because, they pretend to be so much better. They are more occupied in puffing and advertising their favourites, and in writing up the big men of little cliques, than they are in representing the advanced religious thought of England. In point of fact they have always been the enemies of advanced thought. One paper, edited by Dr. Scampell, was written into a paying circulation by incessant and mendacious attacks on various members of Scampell's own denomination who happened to preach Religion without Cant."

"I hope so serious a charge may turn out to be an error," murmured the Rev. Ezekiel Smallweed.

"I wish it were error," replied Melville; "but it is not. It is within my knowledge that one of the best religious poets of our day—a Christian minister—was hounded down for fifteen years by this Scampell, because the fanatics for whom Scampell catered were glad to pay twopence a week to read ribald and brutal newspaper attacks on a scholar whom they would not understand. Scampell laughed in private at their folly, but as it was a question of making his religious paper pay, he was willing to scribble and print the piquant shamefaced falsehoods which pietists loved to believe. During the same period this maligner held a high conventional position as the pastor of one of the largest Chapels in London."

"Ah, yes, yes," said Golding, not wishing the matter to be further pursued, as he had once boasted of Scampell as an acquaintance, "no doubt—no doubt there must, in the case you speak of, have been faults on both sides—on both sides. But I was going to say, Mr. Melville, do not you admit that the newspapers publish much, very much, information which is not of a party character?"

"Certainly," assented Melville; "they publish freely such matters as both political parties, and all foolish parties in the state, agree to take a common interest in; for example, frivolous amusements, gambling, fashionable marriages, disgusting trials, gossip about the court and royalty, elopements, scandals, horseracing, pigeon-shooting, pageants, and trivialities generally."

"I must say," said Hardcastle, who, together with his family, exceedingly relished the things named in this category, "that I, for one, consider the newspaper press a grand and wonderful institution."

"So do I," returned Melville, "if I speak of it as a matter of mechanism. The arrangements by which reports are collected from all parts of the world, and the rapidity with which they are printed, is truly wonderful. Still I cannot agree that the press leads public opinion. It follows and panders to the conventional opinion of the hour."

"I feel that to be entirely true," said Isabel, who had listened attentively to the conversation. "I heard once of a grand enterprise to establish a paper which should discuss all questions not in the light of sect or party, or conventional opinion, but in the light of truth and justice, and which should proclaim fearlessly every day that righteousness which exalteth a nation. I wish we had such a paper. We should not then see the important utterances of our thinkers condensed into obscure paragraphs, whilst entire columns of letterpress are devoted to betting news, races, or court receptions."

"The enterprise to which you refer was indeed a grand one, Miss Landor," declared Melville; "and without a precedent in history. Its brave founder worked unceasingly until he enlisted the co-operation of ten thousand men; and the perfect realization of the project seemed at one time absolutely certain."

"By the way," inquired Golding, "why did the scheme collapse?"

"It was killed by the men of Cant, and their companions the men of avarice," answered Melville. "The honest-hearted founder of the association and his friends, just as they were successfully publishing their paper, allowed themselves to be allured into negotiations with some public men who cant about patriotism. The result of their misplaced confidence was that they were betrayed into the clutches of mercenaries who rushed on the scene, fought for the money, and ruined the whole enterprise."

"Those perfidious pirates, who, pretending to be pilots, thus leaped on the vessel and scuttled her just as she was launched, deserve the indignation of all honest souls!" exclaimed Isabel with great animation.

During this conversation Mrs. Hardcastle was in a constant fidget because Isabel was receiving attention which she wished to see directed to Anastatia only. Mrs. Hardcastle was aware that Anastatia could not sustain a part in the discussion, or even take an interest in such topics as those recently introduced. She was therefore anxious to divert the thoughts of the company to other channels; and accordingly suggested that some music would be agreeable.

Mr. Golding obligingly seconding her suggestion, and addressing Anastatia, said: "Do let us hear some of your delightful strains of music, Miss Anastatia."

"Oh, I am so fearfully out of practice, Mr. Golding," returned Anastatia, giving the usual excuses that young ladies who practise for four hours every day always consider proper.

"Mr. Melville," said Golding, "come and use your influence with this young lady; I want her to play."

"I really cannot," said Anastatia. "I have nothing that I can play perfectly."

Mrs. Hardcastle interposed. "Come, Anastatia, you can give us something, never mind what it is. Just to oblige, you know."

Miss Anastatia, thus persuaded, rose, and after a long search among a quantity of music produced a fantasia on some airs from "Robert le Diable." This piece, on which she had spent hours of toil, she executed in a thoroughly mechanical manner. Born with no musical ear, she had nevertheless laboured earnestly to become a player. Why she thus laboured was best known to herself. The ten minutes or so of patient listening which she extorted from

and growled in the bass, and squeaked in the treble, till you listened in vain for *Robert, toi que j'aime*, were wasted. Those who had heard the whole opera exquisitely performed elsewhere could derive no enjoyment from this rehearsal. Other persons only learnt from it that, under certain conditions, the piano is an instrument which possesses a powerful battery of annoyance.

CHAPTER XII.

Cant, Baptism, and Game-preserving.—Tom in Trouble.—
Rev. Ezekiel Smallweed, Baptist Minister.—Katie and
Annie.

CHIPPENDALE GOLDING sat in his luxuriously furnished library All that wealth need purchase for such a room surrounded him. Golding sat at a beautifully inlaid writing-table. He was well got up; and gems flashed from his shirt-front and his fingers. It was Sunday, and nearly Church time. Golding, who reigned supreme at Ezekiel Smallweed's Chapel, seldom failed to attend the services.

He will be there this morning, but has a little business to do first; a little business with yon wretched boy, who, pale and trembling, dirty and ragged, stands before him, a hideous contrast to the fresh rich beauty of the apartment. The gamekeeper, neat and smug, is by his side.

"Yes, Walters," speaks Golding in his most hard precise tones, "I shall certainly prosecute; most certainly. He shall be an example to others. He is young; but it will do him good. His career may thus be checked. A few months in a reformatory may alter his life."

At these words, Tom, for it is he, looks up. "Please, sir, don't put me in prison. I meant no harm; they gave it me 'cause I said I was 'ungry. Ain't tasted a bit since day before yesterday."

Golding smiled. "Ah, my lad, such stories are very fine, but don't go down with me. Take him off, Walters."

Tom burst into tears. "I walked all the way from London," he protested, "and hoped I'd find work in the country. And now mother's dead, I have no friend; and I'm a poor starving lad, on my soul, sir, and walked off with the hare because it was given me. I didn't know they were yours."

"My boy," returned Golding, "you do it very well; but we have had too much of it, have we not, Walters? And I gave my word that the next poacher I caught I should prosecute. Did I not, Walters?"

"You did, sir; and this young rascal is as bad as his mates, I'll be bound. He puts on very well, but I knew *you* would not be taken in by him."

"I think not, Walters."

In another minute the sobbing and begrimed Tom was pushed out of the room; and very soon an apartment that accorded more with his appearance was found for him. Now poor Tom to-day was really deserving of the pity of every humane person, for he had been in sore trouble. Acting on the decision at which he arrived on the evening of the missionary meeting, he enlisted in the army. The recruiting sergeant, who took him that same night to a public house and gave him the queen's shilling, spoke of the glories of the service in a strain of eulogy which corresponded with that adopted by Sir Harry Grapeshot. For forty-eight hours Tom positively thought he was on the road to honour and comfort. But, at the end of that time, he had to awake from his day-dream. For, when he presented himself for the ordinary medical examination, the regimental surgeon discovered and reported to the authorities that he was suffering from an incurable organic disease of the heart, which would render him absolutely ineligible for any position in the army. He was, therefore, not allowed to take up his residence in the barracks, but was turned adrift on the world once more in misery and despair. The account which he had given Golding of his subsequent movements was the literal truth, unalloyed by a syllable of exaggeration. But self-centred men of the

Golding type have not the spiritual eye to distinguish the true from the false. Destitute of any noble intuitions or keen sympathies, they imagine that a cultivated cunning will enable them to test the truth of facts. Golding, without intellectual or moral perception, never doubted for a moment that he was perfectly correct in regarding Tom's story as false, whereas it was quite true. He relied on what he complimentarily described as " his judgment." He was satisfied that by its infallible assistance in this poaching investigation he had reached the truth, the whole truth, and nothing but the truth. The matter needed no further attention from him, so he rose complacently from his writing table, walked to the mirror, arranged his cravat, threw open the window to freshen the apartment, and then strode downstairs to the dining-room, where he found Mrs. Golding ready for Chapel. At the same time that the Goldings entered their fine equipage to be driven to their place of worship, poor Tom was being cuffed and kicked by a policeman and the gamekeeper out of Golding Hall. The well-fed, well-clothed, saucy servants threw up their hands at "such a young vagrant, so old in wickedness;" and the scullery-maid, who was carrying a heap of broken victuals to the mastiff in his kennel, looked with disgust on poor Tom's eager glances at the dog's breakfast. Not one of those Pharisees—and Golding took none but religionists of his own type into his service—had a single kind word or pitying look for the starving lad.

The Hardcastle family were all in their pew this morning, and—grand triumph for "dear Victoria"—Lord Everton, the Tory and Churchman, sat beside her. Melville, too, was there, much to Anastatia's satisfaction.

The preacher to whom they had come to listen was the Rev. Ezekiel Smallweed, a "particular" Baptist. His conceptions of Divine truth were somewhat limited. His desire was to induce all his hearers to believe in the efficacy of a plunge into six feet of water for transforming them into the body of the "Elect." He preached a sermon this morning on the absolute DUTY of immersion, beseeching all persons to avail themselves of the tank with which their new chapel was supplied; and speaking words of special comfort to those who had done so. Golding, being one of this number, rocked himself in silent satisfaction as Mr. Smallweed discoursed on the paradise that awaited the "Elect" who had been satisfactorily soaked.

It was Golding's custom to walk home from chapel. He joined the Misses Hardcastle and Melville, who also walked.

"What do you think of Mr. Smallweed?" asked Golding of Melville.

"I think him a very erroneous preacher," returned Melville.

"He certainly laid a little too much stress on immersion this morning," said Miss Hardcastle. He does not always preach such discourses. I was sorry, because I wished Lord Everton to be favourably impressed."

"Must say—don't agree with him," spoke Lord Everton, "like our Church better than that."

"Ah! there is no other way to be saved," observed Golding, "it is a scriptural injunction, and that closes all argument. But we will not quarrel on theological matters; so to change the subject I may tell you that I caught one of my poachers this morning."

"Did you?" exclaimed the young ladies.

"Yes. He is only *one* of the gang, I am sorry to say, and but a youth of eighteen. Still, I mean to make him an example. He brings a pretty tale; says he got acquainted in the village with some men who told him they could give him a hare or two; and my gamekeeper caught him with a hare in his pocket, walking off from one of my preserves. He will not inform us as to the other men, that is the worst of it."

"That is rather a good trait in his character," remarked Melville

"One can hardly credit a lad like that with a good motive," said Golding. "His tale goes that he had walked from London seeking employment, and not being able to get any, he was starving; and these poachers would fain have filled him with my game, so he says."

"Poor fellow," observed Melville, "he has fallen into sore trouble."

"I am surprised at your pitying a thief, Mr. Melville," said Victoria.

"I do pity him for all that, Miss Hardcastle," returned Melville, "and I cannot help wondering, Mr. Golding, that out of all your abundance you could not spare the poor boy a solitary hare."

"Justice is justice, and stealing is stealing," remonstrated Golding. "I cannot encourage what the law of the country forbids."

"As to the law of the country," responded Melville, "the Game Acts being unjust in themselves and a disgrace to our statute book, the infringement of them cannot be a very serious crime. They are, in fact, maintained for the not very rational enjoyment of the rich at the expense of the poor; the preservation of game, especially ground game, involving a serious destruction of crops, and consequently reducing the food supply. To fine or imprison a starving man, which is often done, for breaking a law that is in itself an iniquitous institution, seems scarcely consistent with justice."

"*You* may condemn the game laws, Mr. Melville," returned Golding, "but your opinion will not receive much support while the landed aristocracy of England take pleasure in preserving their game."

"Really," exclaimed Melville, "it seems hardly credible that a large proportion of the landed aristocracy of our country should have no better mission to accomplish in this world than to devote themselves to the rearing of partridges, pheasants, and hares. And an intelligent

Red Indian would scarcely believe the fact that in this christian country the peasant who kills a hare or a rabbit renders himself liable to seven years' penal servitude."

"There would be a great many more poachers if the law were not severe," pronounced Golding. "The temptation is at hand to so many, and amongst a class of dishonest, needy poor it is hard to resist."

"Especially in the case of a hungry man," returned Melville, "who comes home to a poorly spread table at dinner time, with half famished children around it. It must be a hard struggle to him to resist taking the pheasants which are feeding just over his hedge; yet if he did so the law would commit him to prison as a poacher. Ten thousand of these wicked prosecutions were instituted last year."

"And who knows how many more there might have been if the game laws were not severe?" demanded Golding sternly. "I believe that punishment for small sins of theft is the right course. God will not hold us guiltless if we overlook the sin of a man who pleads poverty as an excuse to steal."

"As to the severity of the game laws producing a good result," answered Melville, "it is notorious that half the crimes of violence in the country are due to the operation of the game laws. And when you apply the word 'stealing' to poaching it is worth remembering that there can be no theft of property which Nature has made common to all."

"The law is framed by men wiser than ourselves, Mr. Melville," said Golding. "I stand up for the laws of my country to the very letter, and always shall."

"And what about Christianity, Mr. Golding?" asked Melville. "Are the words of the Great Teacher to be entirely ignored: 'I was naked, and ye clothed Me; I was thirsty, and ye gave Me drink; sick and in prison, and ye visited Me'? Excuse me, but does your Christianity include or exclude this?"

Golding coloured. "I believe my Christianity includes giving to the poor, as you may see by the numerous institutions supported by me. But I give only to genuine cases, not to poachers."

"Mr. Melville is right, I believe," said Lord Everton, "Mr. Golding—should give—boy—benefit of—doubt and believe his tale for once. Poor boy starving perhaps—very hard that."

"My mind is fully made up," returned Golding, complacently. "My wife agrees with me. I am not a man who requires pleading with."

Miss Hardcastle looked indignantly at Lord Everton, and he was instantly silent for the remainder of the walk. Nevertheless he found an opportunity to say to Melville when they were together on the lawn after they arrived home, "I think you quite right about that boy. I believe in being merciful. Pity some—have so much, and others so little."

That afternoon Melville walked over to the village of Redborough, which was about three miles from Broadcray. He went to see Mr. Tremlin's nieces, little Katie and Annie, whom, it will be remembered, he saved when the *Rasselas* went down. They had gone, at his expense, to live at Redborough, because Mrs. Tremlin was too selfish and too jealous to permit them to remain any longer in her house. The children were delighted with Melville's unexpected visit, and it rejoiced him to find that Mrs. Rose, in whose charge they had been placed, was a tender, motherly woman, well qualified for her task. She had already won their hearts by her unselfish, gentle ways. Melville's joy at the happiness of their present surroundings was complete, yet he was made anxious about the health of Katie, of whom Mrs. Rose spoke with some solicitude.

The little lily seemed fading.

CHAPTER XIII.

Cant, Conjugal Nagging, Bill Discounting, and Heresy Hunting.—Mr. Caleb Faithful's Perplexity.—Mr. Agnew Mumm.

LONDON was very hot and very dusty. The September sun all day baked the houses and parched the streets. Nor did the atmosphere grow much cooler toward the evening; and Tremlin, as he left the offices of Messrs. Mumm, Blooster & Co., contemplated with weariness the distance he had to walk. He was never allowed the luxury of a ride. He who clothed, housed, and fed the whole family, and worked early and late to do so, would have been considered by his wife extremely lazy and frightfully extravagant if he had indulged in a threepenny ride to or from town. "What could *he* want with riding, a strong man like him?" He had become so used to the walk that it scarcely even occurred to him now to think of a ride.

His pace was very slow this evening, partly on account of the intense heat, and partly on account of his thoughts. Caleb Faithful was in trouble. This was almost worse to Tremlin than if he had been in trouble himself. Mr. Faithful had become his hero, and drew from his soul love and esteem. He had never spoken to the Minister, for Tremlin shrank from attracting notice, and would do anything rather than obtrude himself. Mr. Faithful's trouble had been communicated to him by a friend the Sunday before, and Tremlin had not ceased to think of it. His one perplexity was how to get Mr. Faithful out of his trouble. It worried him by day and by night. He had not solved the difficulty yet. There was one way, however, that dawned on Tremlin soon after he left the office, and made him walk more slowly than before. Could it be possibly carried out? His wife, of course, was a terrible obstacle. Would she ever forgive him if he helped Mr. Faithful? For once in his life, Tremlin had determined that his wife should not stand in his way; and, this resolved, he deemed it prudent to strike off in a different road and walk in the direction of the Rev. Caleb Faithful's residence.

The pastor lived in a neat, unpretentious house near the Chapel. He was not married, and his sister resided with him. On the evening in question he was seated in his study, when the servant entered and announced that "a gentleman of the name of Tremlin" wished to see him.

"Tremlin, Tremlin," repeated Mr. Faithful, "I do not think I know the name. I will go downstairs and see the gentleman."

Mr. Faithful's visitor turned hastily round as the minister entered, and said nervously, "You do not know me, sir, I expect."

"By sight I do," returned Mr. Faithful; "I have seen you at Chapel often. Will you not be seated?"

Tremlin sat down, feeling he should never get through this business. He had not contemplated half the difficulties of his mission. Painfully struck, however, with the minister's altered appearance, strangely altered even from the preceding Sunday, he broke into his subject with abrupt determination. "Mr. Faithful, you are in trouble. I wanted to come and tell you how earnestly I sympathise with you, and also that I should like to be able to help you."

Beneath Tremlin's awkward nervousness Mr. Faithful could discover the true heart of a friend. He was almost overcome by Tremlin's words, but restraining his emotion he thanked him for his sympathy, adding, "I certainly am in great financial trouble."

"I do not want to know the circumstances of your

grief," said Tremlin, endeavouring to come to the point. "But—but, might I ask how much?"

"It is a large sum," said Mr. Faithful, "five hundred pounds. A very dear friend, for whom I became security, has met with unforeseen misfortunes. His brother and sister-in-law, Mr. and Mrs. Sinclaire, who were bringing home his foreign remittances, were wrecked in the *Rasselas*. I am responsible for the whole amount; and I cannot meet it all at the short notice which is allowed me, because there is not sufficient time to sell my trifling property."

Tremlin listened attentively.

"I may be able to help you, Mr. Faithful, now I know the amount."

"I am deeply appreciative of your goodness, Mr. Tremlin," replied Mr. Faithful, with emotion; "and I am sure you will not suppose me to be deficient in gratitude when I say, that, as I have no claim whatever upon you, I could not permit you to do anything of the kind."

"You have the most powerful of all claims on me, Mr. Faithful," protested Tremlin: "the claim of the teacher, —the man who has given to another priceless ideas."

"Your remarks," returned Mr. Faithful, "are intensely kind, and you must, please, consider that by your sympathy to-day you have more than repaid any good you may have received from my ministrations; and, that you must not attempt any other mode of acknowledgment."

There was real gratitude in Mr. Faithful's tones; but there was also a manly dignity and firmness which told Tremlin that a restraint was placed on any further allusion to pecuniary matters. Tremlin therefore conversed for a short time on a few other topics, to which, seeing his nervousness, Mr. Faithful gracefully led the way, and then retired to take his journey home.

"How late you are!" exclaimed Mrs. Tremlin the moment her husband entered the parlour. "We have finished tea long ago. I was far too poorly and faint to wait till now. This heat tries me fearfully."

Tremlin looked decidedly the worse of the two as he sank into a chair. The children gathered round him and whispered their delight at his arrival.

"I suppose you don't want any tea?" said Mrs. Tremlin."

"No; never mind. I will have supper a little earlier."

"You will not be able to do that," returned Mrs. Tremlin pettishly. "Martha has gone out for me to-night to get some reviving medicine that Mrs. Bertram recommended me to try, and she has some other errands to do also. I hardly thought you would care about supper this evening as it is so hot. How people *can* eat in the warm weather is a wonder to me. I can't." Here the invalid, commenced sighing with oppression owing to the hearty meal she had recently made.

"I had hardly anything for dinner to-day, my dear," said Tremlin. "Like you, I felt it was too hot to eat. But I begin to feel rather hungry now."

"Well! why did you not come in to tea? You know the time we have it. What were you doing?"

"I had a call to make," replied Tremlin, as he put the children from him and walked to the window for a breath of air.

"Pray do not open the window so widely," exclaimed Mrs. Tremlin. "I shall be in a thorough draught."

Where the draught was to come from on such a sultry evening was a mystery known only to the shrew herself.

"Where did you call?" she inquired sharply.

Knowing that sooner or later he would have to confess, Tremlin brought out the unpleasant truth at once: "On Mr. Faithful," he said.

"I am surprised at you, Maurice," remonstrated Mrs. Tremlin. "Knowing my views as you do about that man, you pay me great disrespect by seeking his acquaintance

But you are utterly careless of my opinions, and treat me shamefully."

Tremlin turned round. "Mr. Faithful is in trouble, my dear. I assure you I have never called there before. But when a man is in trouble that is an excuse, is it not?"

"Not in the least," pronounced Mrs. Tremlin. "I only rejoice to hear that the judgments of God have fallen on that man, and he is about to meet his deserts. 'The ungodly shall not always prosper.' Ah, how true that is!"

It goaded Tremlin fearfully to see his wife's gratification at poor Faithful's discomfiture. He felt more hurt with her than he had ever done. But being aware that any remark of his would prove useless, he held his tongue, and kept in the retort he could have made.

"What is the matter with him?" asked Mrs. Tremlin. "How has God visited him?"

"He stood surety for a friend," replied Tremlin, "and is liable for the money as the friend cannot pay it. Poor man! it is a sharp blow for him. He fears he must be a bankrupt."

"Then he will give up preaching, of course?" eagerly exclaimed the lady. "He will resign his pulpit. What a visitation from God! No longer will he be permitted to lead men astray, or lure them to destruction. I am rejoiced for your sake, Maurice, that he will not preach any more. At least, you will accompany me now to the pastures of a true shepherd."

"Mr. Faithful has not given up yet, my dear. I hope he may get out of this trouble," answered Tremlin.

"I trust you are not going to help him," said Mrs. Tremlin with a searching glance. "I am sure we cannot afford to give to others when we want so much ourselves."

Tremlin smiled. "I could not find anything like the money, my dear," he returned. "Mr. Faithful is liable for five hundred pounds."

"It is a blessing the sum is beyond you," said his wife, "or no one knows what you would do on the sly. But letting that alone, I should never forgive you, Tremlin, if you extended even your hand to help that unholy man. Mind what I say, I believe the Lord has marked him for destruction. God's long-suffering has indeed been great, but who shall dare to avert His hand when He strikes? Tremlin, the fall of that man will be brought home with good to your soul, I trust. Learn from it that the Lord will not always strive."

"He takes his affliction in a thoroughly christian spirit; not a murmur. Poor man! I do feel for him," declared Tremlin.

"What did you go to see him for?" asked Mrs. Tremlin, returning to the main point.

"I wanted to try and help him if I could," asserted her husband bravely.

"How could you?" ejaculated Mrs. Tremlin scornfully.

"I had a plan in my mind," said Tremlin.

"Then abandon it at once," insisted Mrs. Tremlin. "I have said it, Maurice, and I mean it. I will never forgive you if you help that man. As a Christian I protest against your interfering with God's judgments. Really, you are so headstrong and unfeeling you make me quite ill. Run, Fanny, and fetch the eau de cologne. Your papa always upsets me if he can. It is cruel in this warm weather. You might fan me, Maurice, instead of standing there when you see me so faint."

For the rest of the evening Tremlin was fully occupied in ministering to his wife, who did not permit him to be out of her sight. It was not till his dinner hour the following day that he found an opportunity of carrying out his resolution to help Mr. Faithful, from which even his fear of Mrs. Tremlin did not frighten him. When at last the hands of the office clock of Messrs. Mumm, Blooster & Co.

Tremlin could call his own, he sat down and wrote a capital letter to Mr. Melville, narrating the trouble in which Mr. Faithful was involved, and describing his interview with him. He felt sure that Mr. Melville, who was rich, and so much wiser than himself, would discover some way out of the difficulty, and of overcoming Mr. Faithful's scruples respecting pecuniary assistance.

The appearance of Blooster just as Tremlin was finishing this letter was not very welcome. Tremlin had embraced the quiet of the office dinner-hour to write his epistle, because he hoped to be free from interruption. Blooster nearly always announced his approach by a loud thick cough, and a wheezing breath, that foretold the appearance of a surfeited corporiety. He held in his hand a letter, and coming up to Tremlin said, "I want you to write a note about a bill of ours which falls due next week. We have been requested to renew it for another two months. We shall not do this; and I should like the endorser to be informed of our resolve. It is backed by Mr. Caleb Faithful, whose address I will give you, and you will be good enough to apprise him of what I have already told his friend."

Blooster cleared his throat loudly at this point, and then stared with surprise at Tremlin's look of utter stupidity. The fact was, Tremlin was so confounded by this intelligence that he hardly believed his senses. For the moment it seemed to him as if Blooster was aware of the subject of the letter he had been writing to Mr. Melville, and that his speech was a part of the same business.

"You understand," exclaimed Blooster with impatience. And on Tremlin's signifying that he did, Blooster returned to his private room, wondering if Tremlin were sober When Tremlin had recovered himself sufficiently to take a practical view of the matter, it occurred to him that he had lost an opportunity. If Messrs. Mumm, Blooster & Co. held the identical bill which was the cause of Mr. Faith-

and as a result Mr. Faithful and his friend would be able to make arrangements to meet it at maturity. Before posting his letter to Mr. Melville, he would see Blooster on the matter. Seizing the opportunity when he fancied him to be disengaged, he went to the great man's room; and on receiving permission to enter, he found Messrs. Mumm & Blooster in conversation. Blooster was quaffing champagne from a tumbler; Mumm, a rigid "abstainer," was drinking a cup of strong tea. Mumm was a wretched-looking man; the very opposite of his rubicund, bloated partner. He was thin, cadaverous, bald, and ignoble. His entire style and appearance seemed a protest against happiness. A poor talker with a croaking voice, he laboured under the hallucination that his forte was public speaking. Possessing a long purse, he managed to get himself invited to take the chair at anti-tobacco, teetotal, sectarian, and even political meetings, where the patience of the assemblies was sorely tried by the stammering platitudes which he articulated in remonstrative injured tones. Lately his vanity had whispered to him that Parliament was incomplete without his presence. When that idea attained the force of a conviction, he awoke to the great duty and privilege of giving money freely to the officials of such aggregations of social, political, and religious Cant as could appreciate his bounty, and would in return proclaim his parliamentary qualifications on the housetops. He professed to be strictly religious and "thoroughly sound" in his views; but he was by nature fearfully obstinate, and being of a disputatious, querulous turn, he was never happy unless at warfare with some one. At present he was actively engaged in quarrelling with the minister whose Church he attended; and as nothing could turn him from a preconceived opinion, it was hopeless to think of peace except by surrender. Seeing Mumm with Blooster, Tremlin was about to return to the office; but on Blooster's calling him in, he hastened to his subject.

"I wanted to have a word with you, sir, about that letter you asked me to write to Mr. Faithful." Tremlin's shyness almost overcame him here, and the colour mounted to his face as he added, "I know Mr. Faithful very well, sir."

"Ah, you do," said Blooster, as he tossed off the remains of his champagne.

"I fear he will not be able to meet the bill," continued Tremlin.

"I am very sorry to hear that," carelessly observed Blooster, as he thrust his hands in his pocket, and tilted himself in his chair.

"It would, I know, be a great convenience to him if you would renew the bill, Mr. Blooster," urged Tremlin.

"Eh, eh, what's that?" asked Mumm, becoming interested as he heard the word "bill," and looking from the *Times* over his spectacles at Tremlin. "What bill d'ye mean?"

"Why that Sinclaire affair," answered Blooster, "for five hundred pounds. We had the letter asking for another two months."

"Yes, yes," spoke Mumm. "I remember. The—the—the—endorser—" (Mumm had a peculiar way of repeating or stammering out some of his words in this manner, blinking his eyes at each repetition)—"we found to—to—to—be a substantial man, eh?"

"Yes. The answers to our inquiries were extremely satisfactory," replied Blooster.

"A minister. I forget what denomination," said Mumm. "But—but—but—ye said ye knew him, Mr. Blooster?"

"Yes; a Congregational Minister of latitudinarian principles. A Unitarian according to some," observed Blooster, as he winked his eye knowingly and refilled his glass.

"Thoroughly unorthodox, I believe," said Mumm.

"D'ye attend his Chapel, Mr. Tremlin? If so, I'm sorry for ye."

"I do attend there, sir," returned Tremlin. "Mr. Faithful is not a Unitarian though. And he is not rich, and to meet this bill without an extension of time would be very serious for him. And he has not had a penny of the money. He signed it to help a friend; and will be sure to see it all paid."

"We—we—we cannot renew it," remarked Mumm.

"I was with Mr. Faithful last night," said Tremlin with a last effort. He is in sad trouble, sir. He never expected to have to find the money, I assure you."

"We—we—we are sorry not to oblige him, but—but—but—"

"It is simply out of the question, Mr. Tremlin," asserted Blooster, as he waved his hand towards the door; "I believe we shall still look to Mr. Sinclaire or Mr. Faithful for the money in a week's time." And Blooster ended by affecting a tremendous cough that drowned all further remonstrance Tremlin might have offered.

"Then—then—then he attends Mr. Faithful's," whined Mumm in his thinnest tones, as Tremlin closed the door.

"Yes," said Blooster; "great pity."

"Eh, but—but—but we had better think if we ought to keep such a man in the office," croaked Mumm.

"Good fellow for work," replied Blooster. "Most reliable clerk in the office."

"But it ought to be considered, if—if—if a young man of such principles should—should—should be encouraged," muttered Mumm.

"Ah," said Blooster evasively. Then, having yawned, he took up a newspaper, intending that act to indicate his indisposition to pursue the collateral question of Tremlin's reliability, which he saw was warming Mumm's frigid heart. He meant to avoid it, because, though the religious opin-

were somewhat divergent. The difference between them was just this, that Blooster would have employed Satan if he could have made two per cent. profit by the business; and Mumm would have quarrelled with an archangel if he suspected him of heresy.

"It is all stuff about Faithful's not coming up to the scratch," remarked Blooster, returning to the main business, after a judicious pause. "A Minister is the very man who would be helped to do it, you know. Absurd idea to renew the bill, especially for a man who has offended all denominations. I never liked Sinclaire; so press it hard, I say. If Faithful *will* help such a man, they can take the consequences together."

Mumm's thoughts remained with Tremlin, however, and he scarcely replied. From that day Tremlin was a marked man for Mumm. The poor clerk little thought, as he sealed and directed his letter to Mr. Melville, that Agnew Mumm's persistent brain had commenced carefully to arrange his ruin

CHAPTER XIV.

CANT AND IGNORANCE.—MR. BEESWAX AND MR. TREACLES.—THE DEACON DESPOTISM.—REV. MR. RAINFORD, CONGREGATIONAL MINISTER.

IN one of the least important streets of the little town of Chenley there stood a small shop, with the name of "James Beeswax" in gilt letters over the door, and underneath, in letters of less pretension, "Boot and shoemaker. Repairs neatly done." The window contained three pairs of gentlemen's and two of lady's boots : a modest stock, which suggested that "repairs" were most in Mr. Beeswax's line. Inside, behind the counter, might be seen, early and late, James Beeswax in a leathern apron, tucked-up shirt sleeves, with wax and awl. He was a small, thin man, apparently about sixty years of age, and his face was only remarkable for its many puckers, and extreme thinness of the lips. His hair was still black as a raven's wing, and being very thick, did good service in adding to the size of his tiny head. All the six days of the week Beeswax worked at his trade; but on the seventh day he abandoned the leathern apron and tucked-up shirt sleeves, and appeared in a suit of the grimmest black broadcloth, which, though of coarse fabric, was free from the slightest speck of dust, and was brought out from Sunday to Sunday as regularly as the week passed round. In these clothes poor Beeswax always appeared ill at ease. He moved awkwardly, and sat with a hand on each knee, to avoid friction. But with these clothes he left off the shoemaker, and put on the theologian. Sunday was a high time for Beeswax,

in the week, he defiantly asserted that none knew better than he how to turn out a satisfactory patch on a customer's boot, so, on Sunday, with equal emphasis he claimed to be an authority on matters theological. The knowledge he possessed, however, was of the most meagre description. But Beeswax made short work of objections to his infallibility which were based on his want of education; he avowed that he had received "a large measure of the Spirit," and that, owing to its Divine teaching, he was fully competent to guide and spiritually educate the minds of those about him.

Down a narrow turning in the High Street, and between two shops, there stood the Independent Chapel of Chenley. It was an unpretentious building, adorned by no spire, and bare of all architectural beauties. The one iron gate that closed in the three narrow steps which led to the door, attracted but little notice from the passers-by. The Chapel had been there for some years, and the old-fashioned straight-backed pews, and the bare whitewashed walls, had known better times than the present. Unfortunately Independency was badly supported at Chenley. In James Beeswax we have introduced our readers to the chief deacon of Chenley Independent Chapel. Not that Beeswax was by any means the best man in the congregation. There were two or three others of certainly superior position to his own; but some years ago, when "the cause" was on the wane, he had been nominated a deacon, and no one seemed to care to supplant him in his office. In fact, the majority of the congregation looked upon him as a great authority in spiritual matters, and certainly a very good man. So frequently does the world rate us as we rate ourselves. There were three more deacons, but out of the quartette Beeswax, and a brother tradesman (a small grocer) were the two most active workers in the Chapel. As "active workers" they assumed it to be their foremost

pastor. They also thought it necessary to look out with a keen eye for his failings. Another portion of their "active work" was to attend the weekly prayer-meeting and take a conspicuous part in the service. Looking up absent members, and making impertinent inquiries into the cause of that absence, was another share of their self-imposed work; as was, also, seeing to the business affairs of the Chapel and keeping the books. And lastly, they paid the minister's salary—or made him wait for it if payment were inconvenient.

Beeswax was looked upon as a man of "very sound" opinions by the congregation, and Treacles the grocer, though of a more reticent nature, was also respected for his "orthodoxy." "No fear," said the people, "of a loose theology creeping in while they manage affairs." For Beeswax and Treacles scrupled not to impart their views of Scripture to their chosen Pastor. They were not backward in suggesting subjects for his sermons, and giving their recipes for "awakening sinners"; or for warning a church member who appeared in danger of "backsliding." In a word, the two deacons prosecuted their labours so untiringly that their Pastor was never free from their interference, unless the necessities of sugar, and shoes, called their presence away from him.

It might be deemed strange that Beeswax, who considered himself so capable of imparting instruction, should demand from his minister untiring attention to the spiritual requirements of his household. Yet so it was. He held four sittings in the Chapel, and paid for them thirty-five shillings. For this sum he expected two sermons every Sunday, and one on week evenings; addresses at prayer and any other meetings that might be held; a weekly ministerial call at his house; repeated visits, with prayer, to any of his family who were sick; special advice on any business or family changes; extra ministerial calls in bereavements and on occasions of rejoicing. When Miss

Beeswax lay sick of an infectious fever, the Minister, though he had young children of his own, was summoned to her bedside. Commercially viewed, what Beeswax received for his thirty-five shillings for spiritual requirements, was a far greater bargain for what he paid than he could drive on a week-day at either the shop of Brother Bullock the butcher, or Deacon Treacles the grocer.

Mr. Melville first saw Mr. Beeswax and his friends on the second Sunday of his visit to the Hardcastles. It came about thus. As he had been made anxious by the altered physical appearance of poor little Katie at his last visit, he resolved on this Sunday to walk over to Redborough and see her again. Now it happened that Chenley was on the road to Redborough ; and, as Mr. Melville justly entertained a higher opinion of the Independent denomination than of any other, he decided to worship at the Chenley Independent Chapel on his way. When he entered that edifice the kindly Beeswax was the gentleman who came forward to conduct him to a seat, and lent him books for the service.

Very soon the minister made his appearance. He was a young man of about thirty years of age. A profusion of fine wavy hair surmounted a noble forehead and an open countenance. His expression was exceedingly timid, and the lines of the face, movements of the lips, and expression of the eyes, indicated a character of great sensitiveness. He appeared in indifferent health, and not by any means the kind of person to grapple with the rough or harsh things of life. Melville judged him to be a man endowed with intellectual powers of a high order which had been sedulously cultivated. He had not proceeded very far in the service before Melville instinctively felt that the Minister was in trouble. The sermon was worthy of the man : logical, well arranged, expository, thoroughly thoughtful and deeply devout. The blasphemous allusions and **revolting details, empty platitudes, and inane assertions,** of sentimental orthodoxy were conspicuous by their utter absence. The preacher's manner was winning because of its natural grace and refinement ; and his delivery was fascinating by reason of the intense earnestness of his musical voice. Melville was sorry when the sermon came to an end ; and there lingered in his memory long afterwards the concluding words: "all love is sacrifice : the giving of life and self for others."

True to his impulses, Melville found his way to the vestry, after service, to thank the Minister for his sermon. He found him surrounded by his deacons ; and his weary face lighted up as Melville spoke his cordial thanks for the sermon he had heard. It was the smile of a new hope kindled by unexpected encouragement.

"Air you a visitor to this place, sir?" asked Beeswax.

"I am visiting near here," replied Melville, "and I wish I had known of the Independent Chapel before."

"We do not make much show, sir," spoke Beeswax, evidently gratified, and appropriating all Melville's kind words to himself, "but we are hee-van-gelical, and that, sir, is heverythink. As I hoften say to Mr. Rainford, we can but preach 'the one way,' and give hout 'the simple gospil.'"

Beeswax stood with his hands behind him, and emphasised his words in his usual way, which was done by raising himself slightly on his toes and letting himself drop on his heels with a jerk for the special word he wished to render impressive.

Melville took no heed of his remark. "Have you occupied this pulpit long?" he asked, turning to Mr. Rainford.

"Twelve months," spoke the Minister with a nervous look at his deacon Beeswax. He evidently was ashamed of that deacon.

"Hour congregation is small," resumed Beeswax, "but I grieve to say we air fallen haway greatly of late."

"But the opening of another Chapel in the next street

"Hall we can do," mouthed out Beeswax, with his eyes rolling, "his to put our faith hin the 'blessed gospil,' and preach it hin hall its simplicity."

Melville saw that Beeswax was not to be silenced, and that his broad hints about the "simple gospel" made the Minister uncomfortable. He therefore resolved to go; and shaking hands with Mr. Rainford said, "I shall hope to meet you again."

Mr. Beeswax and Mr. Treacles walked home arm-in-arm.

"What did *you* think of the sermon?" the former asked of the latter.

Treacles, who was a taller man than his companion, spoke with very little expression, and his sentences were as abbreviated as Beeswax's were long.

"More to 'ead than 'eart, brother," answered Treacles.

"That were gist what I were thinking, Brother Treacles. Hand, *gist* what I *hobject* to, and gist what we must guard agin with 'im. It is a sad thing, but we must hown it, that style of preaching his gaining ground in Hingland. Has I said to that gintleman, the 'simple gospil' is what we want. We want 'the blood' of a crucified Christ."

Treacles shook his head. "Honly one way," he observed. "We must speak to him."

"Young men," affirmed Beeswax, "require to be warned by those who are *more* experienced than theirselves. We 'ave seen the herrors of the 'ead, and 'ow they lead astray the sheep from the fold."

"Sich preaching don't dror," observed Treacles. "That gintleman seemed pleased, though," he added.

"A 'German philosophy,' I should *say*," said Beeswax grandly. This deacon had heard somewhere that "German philosophy" was associated with irreligion, but whether the term referred to persons or things, he never had quite comprehended.

Treacles was more ignorant, but too crafty to own it, and

observed, "Werry likely," though he had not the slightest notion of the meaning of Mr. Beeswax's remark.

"What a blessing, brother, that I and you know these dangers, and can warn others agin 'em."

"We have preserved that there Chapel more than once," remarked Treacles

"And honly the gospel will we 'ave," pronounced Beeswax. "Nothink helse shall come from that pulpit but the views that form our hanchor-'old—'the bleeding Lamb.'"

"Ah," said Treacles acquiescently. "We'll call on him, shall us?"

"Yes, and give 'im an 'int as to hour views," returned Beeswax.

And with this arrangement for their pastor's comfort and edification the deacons separated.

Meanwhile Melville was pursuing his walk to Redborough

CHAPTER XV.

CANT, PRIESTHOOD, AND ADVOWSONS.—THE REV. MR. GILMOUR, THE RECTOR.

ON the following day Melville decided to return without delay to town. He had received Mr. Tremlin's letter respecting Mr. Faithful, and was anxious to be where he could render some service in the matter. He had seen little Katie at Redborough, and her appearance gave such unmistakable signs of failing health as convinced him that poor Tremlin, her uncle, should be tenderly apprised of them. He was also desirous of performing some kindly offices for his friend Mr. Lorraine, who, shortly after his visit to Falcon Small's Chapel, to which we referred in the second chapter, had been in great personal trouble. Having suitably thanked the Hardcastles for their hospitality, Melville returned to London by the favourite mid-day train on Tuesday. A variety of considerations, arising out of the matters just referred to, necessarily occupied his mind; and when his thoughts took another direction it was towards Ezekiel Smallweed preaching at Broadcray, and Beeswax and Treacles ruling at Chenley. He was in wonderment as to what this thing, which such men as these, and such a woman as Mrs. Tremlin, called religion, really was. It was clear that it exerted a kind of freemasons' influence over a certain debased order of mind. But what was it? The people of that order described it as Christianity; but it had nothing, literally nothing, in common with the teachings of the great Founder of Christianity. It would be better entitled to any name than the one which, with characteristic effrontery, it had most unjustifiably and unrighteously assumed. It appeared to Melville an abuse of language to designate the Ezekiel Smallweeds and the Mistress Tremlins of society—Christlike. These reflections saddened him: he was indisposed for conversation. But soon his travelling companions changed. A new arrival was left with him in the railway carriage all alone.

The traveller was a jolly-looking man, possessed of strong social tendencies. He was not willing to endure a silent journey, and Melville's reflections were interrupted by a remark on the weather, evidently with a view to opening a conversation. Melville replied, and took a survey of the speaker. His first impression of him was that he had seen his face before. He was a noteworthy person with a conspicuously low forehead. The under part of his face was curiously large in proportion to the upper part. But a pair of sparkling black eyes and a well-defined nose redeemed him from positive ugliness. His florid cheeks and chin were cleanly shaved, but he had a thick moustache which was carefully trimmed. He possessed a tall, powerful frame, and a thick bull neck, which, together with his black and carefully arranged hair, and his fashionable attire, impressed you at once with the idea of a man who could and did take care of himself in the world, and who was more likely to bestow his attention on himself than on any one else. He wore a showy travelling suit, and an eyeglass dangled from his neck. The more Melville looked at him, the more he felt convinced that this was not their first meeting-place. That impression grew as the conversation between them proceeded, and Melville at last remarked—

"I feel sure we are not strangers to one another. Were you at Eton as a boy?"

The answer being in the affirmative, Melville discovered that they had been schoolfellows. The two men who had parted as youths thus unexpectedly met again after the

"I am surprised at your recognising me," exclaimed Melville's newly found friend, who was named Gilmour. "I doubt if I should have remembered you without a reminder."

"I can generally recollect faces I have once seen," returned Melville.

"And you could recollect Greek verses, too, in your youth," said Gilmour. "My word! what a fellow you were for study!"

Melville laughed. "And how has the world been treating you since we parted?" he asked. "By your appearance, I might suggest remarkably well."

"Well, lately very badly. I went abroad for a short holiday, and to have a little enjoyment with a few friends, and this wretched weather has beaten me. I have let them go on. I am bound for London now. It is true I have some business to transact which is rather important. But the weather really determined me; I would have let the business go."

"I wonder you allow the weather to vex you so much, for you were always so lighthearted about trifles," said Melville.

"You are right; from a boy I just determined to do the best I could for myself, and leave the rest."

"And how have you got on?" inquired Melville.

"I will give you a little idea," responded Gilmour. "I had two brothers, and my father assigned to us the three professions—the Church, the bar, and the army. My eldest brother, a rare fighter, and the bully of his school, took to the army as naturally as to his food, and has made a good thing of it. He is colonel now in the Forty-seventh, and doing well. My second brother was a plodding, studying fellow, generally to be seen with some book or other, and always ready to debate on every subject, till he would argue that your head was not your own. He chose the bar; and, of course, I was left to the Church; I had no choice. My uncle Parker told me it was just the thing for me, as I was such a fool I should never do anywhere else. 'You must do your own fighting and your own pleading,' said he, 'but you can get your sermons second-hand.' There was something in this, and I went into the Church. I have brains enough, however, to find it rather slow. But, on the whole, it has agreed with me remarkably well. There are plenty who are willing to do the work for small pay, and consequently I am left to take it easily, and to go on much in my own way, and follow any amusements I care for."

As a type of Church of England Clergymen, Melville looked at his old schoolfellow with more interest. Any one less like his notion of a Parson, in get-up, manner, talk, and style, he had never seen.

"Well, Gilmour, I should not have thought that preaching would have been in your line," observed Melville.

"Nor is it. To be serious, it does not suit me; and to be a Clergyman is a serious affair. But then, I leave the worst part to my Curate: there you find the advantage of the Church, and the truth of my uncle's remark. I only preach one sermon on Sunday, and that, to be candid, is not always my own."

"It is fortunate we are alone," said Melville smiling, "and that one of your parishioners is not sitting opposite; though I presume they would hardly know you in that costume."

"Oh, some of my parishioners behold me at times in unparsonly 'get-up'; in the hunting field, for instance, where I am often to be seen. They pretty well know that my Curate cures their souls. He is far more popular than I am. I take the fate assigned to me, and enjoy life in spite of it. The parish is a very small and insignificant one, and, to tell you the truth, I have been looking out for something better. No one seems to think me worthy a rise, however; and as to patronage, I have courted influential folks so little they hardly know I am in existence.

But they cannot do me out of everything, for all that; and I mean to *buy* what my talents and influence will not win. What do you think of that?" asked Gilmour, handing Melville a cutting from the *Times*.

Melville took it, and read the following advertisement:—

"For sale, the Advowson of a rectory in the best part of a favourite Cathedral city in the west of England. The Church is a handsome structure in the Italian style of architecture, and is endowed for repairs. The net income, principally derived from endowment, amounts to about £800 a year, and will eventually increase. The social and other advantages offered by this position are in their way unrivalled. Present Incumbent in his 80th year, and in bad health. Interest on purchase-money till a vacancy. Apply to Mr. Roy Woolfe, Southampton Street, Strand.'

"I should hardly care to give you my opinion of it," said Melville, as he returned the advertisement; "but it will answer your purpose, I have no doubt."

"That's what I think. But why reserve your full opinion on the matter?"

"Because it will not be flattering to you as a supporter of the sale of advowsons."

"Oh, never mind. I am not offended with any one for speaking plainly. Let us hear what you complain of: I am inquisitive."

"Well, if you will have it, I think the sale of Church livings as carried on at the present time a most disgraceful piece of business. Why should certain men have it in their power to sell a living to a Clergyman who may be very distasteful to the people of the parish? The congregation, it seems to me, ought to be thought of and consulted in the matter, and should have the power to choose a man who is suitable to their requirements. But where this shameful system prevails, the people are never thought of in the affair. The highest bidder, old or young, stupid or intelligent, is thrust upon them, to be endured whether they like or hate him. And I am of opinion that where the religious welfare of the people is supposed to be concerned, few things can be more repulsive to common sense than the sale in open market of the Office of Spiritual Instructor."

"I daresay there is something in your objection," answered Mr. Gilmour, "but I think it's an awfully convenient piece of business for men like me. And as to the responsibility of the thing, that never troubles me. A man must do the best he can for himself; that is my idea."

"Do you believe in a future state?" asked Melville.

"Of course I do; preach about it every Sunday," added Mr. Gilmour facetiously.

"Do you think our actions here will influence our future career in that state?"

"Yes. Well, I suppose if a man does not go to Church, or get baptized, or confirmed, and knows nothing of Christianity, it will be the worse for him in the next world. At least, this was what I was always taught, and we preach in that way. My father was most particular to make us go to Church every Sunday, and have us all confirmed."

"And if your parishioners go regularly to Church and are baptized and confirmed, you believe they do all that duty and virtue require of them?" asked Melville.

"Well, really you put it rather closely to one who does not pretend to go deeply into the matter. Of course we must live as straight as we can; and the straighter the better. You will get an *original* sermon out of me directly."

"But you profess to teach the doctrines of Christ, do you not?" said Melville.

"Oh, yes; Prayer-Book and Bible are our guides," answered Gilmour.

"Where do you learn from Christ's teachings as contained in the New Testament that it is a man's duty to be baptized and confirmed?" inquired Melville.

"Ah, there you have me; you have got too deep for me; you want my Curate here; he would prose for ever. You see I am simply the Rector of my parish, not the parson and teacher of the people."

"As you affirmed just now," observed Melville, "the Church is your profession, and simply confirms your *locus standi*."

"That is it exactly. My tastes really lead me away from arguing and reading. I love travelling, hunting, boating; and, to be honest, a little card-playing is within the range of my tastes. This rectory that I am now after is in a capital spot for hunting. I have corresponded already in the matter, and find the facilities for sport are first class."

"But you will be more observed and criticised in such a parish as, I presume, this is by the description in the advertisement, than in your own, which you say is out of the way and small."

"Right, my dear fellow; but I don't care a jot for their criticism. There I am fixed, you know; who can turn me out? I shall simply profit by the society the place affords, but not by their criticism."

"Do you belong to the High or Low Church party?" asked Melville.

"Oh, the Low, decidedly; the old-fashioned class of thing suits my taste best. I should be perfectly lost amongst all this ritual: vestments, and intoning; and turning, and bowing in the right place, must bother one considerably. My people would think I was going mad if I introduced such customs. They are a steady, sober lot in my parish, and live to a tremendous age; I have hardly any worry with burying them: some of them will live for ever, I believe," and Gilmour laughed heartily.

"And you think it perfectly fair," said Melville, when his friend's mirth had subsided, "to buy the right to teach people without at all intending to act on that right."

"I am afraid you will find me a poor arguer. I do not wish to vindicate my proceedings, I simply wish to do what others do. And, after all, the Church permits and advances these sales of livings; she is a better authority for what is right than I."

"You have no convictions about the responsibility of your post?" said Melville.

"Well, I shall put a good Curate in," returned Gilmour, "a working fellow, you know; he will do duty, and your humble servant will endeavour to make his life as happy as it is possible in a disappointing world. It is a bothering place, this earth, upon my word. Look at the weather, how disgustingly it has been against me; and before I left home a wretched groom managed to kill a favourite pointer of mine through leaving rats' poison about. That dog was worth twenty guineas; I wouldn't have sold him for that. And my mare fell lame just when I most wanted to use her; and, really, I was worried to death.

"You found it necessary to take a change of air, I presume, after such anxiety," remarked Melville smiling.

Gilmour laughed outright. "You are chaffing me. But, I can tell you I was thoroughly worried. There were other things too, for trouble always comes in company; I lost a good bit of money, and—ah, me, it isn't worth going back to it. Better times in the future, I trust."

"And *I* trust you may never have worse times, if that is the extent of trouble you have seen," declared Melville.

"Oh, dear me, no. I have had the same share as others in sorrow, I expect. I lost my father a year ago. Poor old man, he met with a bad accident, and being aged did not rally. He was a capital fellow, and I missed him a good deal at the time. I was his favourite too, and shared the best through his will. The old gentleman liked the Parson; he was always a church-going man; used to come and hear me regularly of a Sunday morning, and go to sleep just in the middle of the discourse. I think I see him now, nodding in front of me, and nodding as regularly as he came."

"You were unable to impress him by your eloquence, it seems," observed Melville.

"Oh, I never try eloquence ; it is out of my line. And what would be the use to such a lot as I address? Most of them have their Sunday's nap during the sermon. I don't care. It takes from the responsibility if they can't hear, you know."

The train stopped now to permit of the passengers taking refreshments, and Melville and Gilmour were separated for a time.

Gilmour's anomalous position as Clergyman of a parish struck Melville with intense wonder. The State Church appeared as a complete religious farce when it authorized such men as these to teach the people.

While in the refreshment-room, Melville could see his friend restlessly moving about, talking to one and another. The girls at the refreshment bar he chaffed for a time. A groom with a couple of dogs he conversed with for five minutes. He drank two glasses of neat brandy, and having lighted a cigar, walked up and down the platform with a newly formed acquaintance till the train was ready to start, when he vaulted into his place just as the whistle sounded.

"What a capital Parson you would have made! It is a pity you are not a Priest, Melville," was his first remark on observing the thoughtful look on Melville's face.

"I am devoutly thankful that I am not," was the reply. "In my present mood I have hardly sufficient respect for the Hierarchy. I make this remark without fearing to offend you : you are scarcely a Parson at heart."

"Oh, you will not offend me whatever you assert. But at the same time you will admit we are necessary evils,' remarked Gilmour smiling ; "though you may not respect our body, we perform some good services for mankind."

"A sort of superior police force," returned Melville, "that frightens the people into outside morality, and keeps them straight to a certain extent. In that way Priests may be serviceable to society. But a question arises as to the use of them as instructors of the race. Many are responsible for circulating the most flagrant errors."

"Well, I keep myself out of that responsibility by often reading to my people a better man's sermons," said Gilmour.

"It is questionable," remarked Melville, "if it be not better to give up all public discoursing on Christianity, rather than make it responsible for a set of doctrines which are in no way deducible from it. Your Prayer-Book, and your canons, perpetually assume that matters are of the essence of the Christian faith which have, in fact, nothing whatever to do with it. Your Priests, from time to time, for party or court purposes, have overlaid the teachings of Jesus Christ with a gloss which has so effectually obscured them, that numbers of Church people do not in the least know the difference between an attack on Christianity itself, and an attack on this mere gloss."

"Ah well, Melville," said Gilmour, " it has gone on too long now ; it will take a generation of men like you to reform us all. As long as Convocation and the Bishops sanction our Church theology, and as long as the Prayer-Book is the expounder of our Church's faith, I shan't quarrel with superior forces. I leave Bishops to be answerable for all that, and am very glad to escape the responsibility of deciding on such matters."

"Truth is independent of any number of Prelates, Gilmour," asserted Melville ; "the equitable truths of to-day which are termed heretical by the Hierarchy must live, and in time take the place of the shallow and false theories that are now dogmatically and untruly proclaimed to be the doctrines of Christianity."

"I trust it will not be in my day," observed Gilmour, "I am fairly up in the orthodox theology, but it would be a dreadful bore to unlearn the sayings of the present established faith, and to coach one's self up in a new creed."

"You are all right for life," returned Melville smiling; "the change I speak of is a thing of the far future. We shall, for a long time, continue to have as our Right reverend Fathers in God an order of men whose real concern is to preserve a State Church which serves them so well. They will take care that no new thoughts be introduced in the pulpit that shall in any way lead people to think for themselves; for they are alive to the fact that if men did use their brains, state arrangements and ecclesiastical offices might be imperilled. Vested interests may be trusted to do their utmost to hinder all progress and all advance of thought; and thus the march of truth must be very gradual. The spiritual rocking to sleep must be suspended before the nation can awake to think."

"I shouldn't mind possessing a bishopric for all you avow," said Gilmour knowingly.

"I must declare," responded Melville, "that when I look at the conduct of your Bishops, I do not think that the office is a very honourable one. In their legislative capacity, the Fathers in God will not support the right even when the opportunity to do so offers. Whatever political party is in power these lawn-sleeved Prelates always occupy the same seats in the House of Lords by the side of the Government of the hour, and give their votes, and often their voice, in favour of the maintenance of existing wrongs, and against the public good and the public liberties. They opposed both the Roman Catholic Relief Bill and the Reform Bill. They opposed the admission of the Dissenters into the Universities. They opposed the Irish Church Bill and the Burial Bill. They opposed the abolition of the Corn-laws, whilst hungry people wanted bread. Although they profess to be the ministers of the 'Prince of peace,' they will sometimes vote in favour of our wars of foreign aggression. Although they call themselves the Apostolical Successors of the fishermen of Galilee, these lords of Parliament forget, in their luxurious palaces, the cries of the poor and needy; and in the highest style of fashion, drive down to Westminster to show by their votes and voices that, as legislators, they have no popular sympathies."

"I do not trouble myself much with popular sympathies either," retorted Gilmour. "I find life quite vexing enough without them. We cannot make things go better if we would: let us bear them, and enjoy all we can. That is my theory."

For the rest of Melville's journey, Gilmour bore him company; and the lightheartedness of the Clergyman and his hilarious flow of spirits made him a pleasant fellow-traveller. Melville could not help a friendly feeling for his old schoolfellow, though he regretted his utter shallowness.

"You must come and see me at the rectory," were Gilmour's parting words. "No, I am not married. When you come to me you will find no female bugbear in reserve. Thank God, I am free as a bird. So you see before you both host and hostess, and you know how far you will be able to endure me as such. No, I am not married, Melville. I simply knew better how to take care of myself. A world of worry is a woman: she hampers you from moving, reduces your financial store, prevents you from being natural, sours your temper, breaks your spirit; in fine, takes every sweet from life, and impregnates it with the bitterness of her own discontent, selfish exactions, and morbid fancies. I have a little too much respect and love for Number One, and I may say too much sense of propriety, to see myself appear in the character of henpecked husband. Good-bye; come and see me."

CHAPTER XVI.

CANT AND BLACKGUARDISM STARTING A CHAPEL.—THE "WE" OF RELIGIOUS NEWSPAPERS.—THE REV. JABEZ BLAZE, D.D. —BOSS THE FIDDLER, AND JOYFUL GINGER.

MELVILLE took an early opportunity of conversing with Tremlin in respect to little Katie, and also on the subject of Mr. Faithful's financial difficulty.

Tremlin had not been inactive in Mr. Faithful's matter. He had seen Mr. Sinclaire, the friend in order to oblige whom Mr. Faithful had signed the bill, and had learnt from him that he could well defray the whole liability if only the time for payment could be extended to three months; though Mumm, Blooster & Co. did not believe this, and would not consent to any terms. In possession of this information Melville placed himself in communication with Mr. Faithful, and succeeded, contrary to Tremlin's expectations, in inducing him to accept the necessary financial assistance from himself; on the ground that it could be rendered without any personal inconvenience, whilst the acceptance of it would prevent unnecessary ruin. Perhaps no man in the city of London was more happy on the night when this negotiation was brought to a termination than was Mr. Tremlin, to whose prompt action the saving of a great man's home was due. Melville, too, felt sincere delight that he had been permitted to take a share of the good work: all the more so because it appeared as if there was a conspiracy afloat to ruin Mr. Faithful. Even the newspapers gave some evidence of it. When Melville took up the *Christian Comet*, he found two columns of scathing and malignant writing against Mr. Faithful for what was designated as "his diabolical speech" at the "great missionary meeting." In the pages of the *Christian's Cordial*, and in those also of the *Evangelical Corrective*, there were sanctimonious anonymous letters, and lofty leading articles, on the same subject, and in the like spirit. The assertions made by the editorial "WE," respecting the deserts of Mr. Faithful in time and eternity, made Religious Noodledom quake at the mention of his odious name. The editors of some of these papers were conventionally respectable men enough. But it is not always an editor who writes the articles.

The "We" of a newspaper is sometimes a very odd personage. For example, the "WE" of the first of the papers in question, was only a synonyme for the clever scribble of a little drunken, houseless profligate, whose friends would not trust him with a shilling, and whose social career had been one long disgrace. "WE" number two, merely stood for the present notions of a Mr. James Shuffle, who had been once a Roman Catholic, twice a Wesleyan, once a Mormon, twice a Baptist, once an infidel, and always a debtor, a liar, and a cheat. Behind the third awful "WE," there stood nothing at all but the besotted presence of poor vain Wamby Flamm, who for chronic inebriety and sad moral laxity had been ousted successively from two Chapels of which he was pastor; and who, to save himself from beggary, had now, in an empty garret, set to work between his intervals of delirium tremens to earn bread and brandy by the use of his religious pen. But, in the kingdom of simpletons, things are taken not for what they are worth, but for what they represent themselves to be. Therefore, the accordant "WE" of these religious newspapers was accounted in the kingdom of simpletons a mighty force of conviction. Accordingly when these newspapers demanded in the name of outraged Christianity, of which they were the especial guardians, that the ministry of Mr. Faithful ought to be superseded, and that an orthodox "cause" ought at once

heretic's Chapel stood, the people whom they addressed were forthwith satisfied as to the necessity of responding to the appeal. Thus it came about that, as a beginning of the "good work," these newspapers were now able to advertise "A Great Evangelistic Festival" at the public rooms near Mr. Faithful's chapel.

On seeing the advertisement Melville decided to be present. In order to ignore as much as possible the very existence of the work of Mr. Faithful in the neighbourhood, the meeting was fixed to be held on Wednesday, the very night of his ordinary week-day service. Immense placards had been pasted about everywhere, effacing even the notices on Mr. Faithful's Chapel board. Melville, therefore, had no difficulty in finding the place of meeting. When he entered, it was crammed in every part; and the eager assembly were quite ready to receive the "evangelical" gentlemen who were to address them. They soon appeared on the platform, followed by three very uncouth looking men, and by the great attraction of the evening, the newly converted "Boss the Fiddler."

One of the "evangelical" gentlemen immediately advanced to the front of the platform, and Melville stared on him with amazement. In dress, he was conspicuous for an elaborate fancy shirt, with three big sugar-loaf shaped gold studs; and a waistcoat most gaudily embroidered all over in fantastic flower-formed devices, across the front of which was flaunted a gold albert watch chain of the largest and most gaudy design. He was close shaven. Each whisker was cut into the shape of a mutton chop, and so there were displayed to the best advantage the audacious brazen face, and the play of the thin deceitful lips. The little grey eyes were sunken under a hard mischief-meaning brow. They resembled so strikingly those of a lynx that, when they glanced furtively around, Melville felt convinced that he had noticed their most peculiar ex-

was the Rev. Jabez Blaze, D.D., whom he last saw acting the coward's part with Dandy Filch on board the *Rasselas*. This reverend gentleman was one of the leaders in the orthodox movement against Mr. Faithful. He was therefore assigned a post of honour here. He prayed lustily for "a blessing on their work," gave out a hymn, made a speech full of sly hits at " the cause " over the way, insisted on the need of " a revival " in that part of the town, and then introduced to the meeting their " dear friend and brother, Boss the Fiddler."

No animal from a menagerie could have been viewed more inquisitively than the fiddler was by this sensation-loving audience. He was a little man, with a sharp quick eye, and a mass of black hair which was neatly laid on a low, narrow, felon's brow. He spoke in a cheerful voice, with a wonderful air of alacrity and self-assurance ; and the story of his numerous penal convictions was listened to with eager delight by his audience. He said the Lord had chastised him because He loved him : and as an account of his life would prove this he was there for the purpose of giving it. " On the completion of his first sentence" he related that he had "gone from gaol into the country thinking he would try some work, but it being unremunerative he returned to his old ways, and got convicted again. After that he stole some jewellery from a shop, and received a long sentence of imprisonment ; and since then he had been three times in Cold Bath Fields, six times in Holloway, and ten times in Wandsworth gaol. When a boy he had stolen the food from his helpless baby brother, robbed his parents several times, though they were poor labouring people, and as soon as he became a youth he planned a highway robbery with murder. But the Lord loved him with a jealous love, and therefore interfered on his behalf, and the devil had not been allowed to carry his designs on Boss quite so far as he wished. The very morning of

broke Boss's arm, and consequently the awful deed was never perpetrated. During his illness he made up his mind that if he got well again he would cut his wife's throat and murder his two children. Directly he was able he returned to stealing, and was again sentenced to twelve months' imprisonment. During this term of incarceration, however, he conducted himself so well that he was discharged with some good clothes and a pound in his pocket. Such success induced him to think of continuing the course of life that had brought this about, more especially as his youth had gone, and his strength and agility were failing. He determined therefore to try whether honesty was the best policy for him, and an old companion advising him to go to a service at the Mission Hall, he eventually acted on this advice, and there and then 'received his conversion,' which conversion had enabled him to appear before them as an honest, sober man. He could remember the time when for five years he was never sober, but now he could call upon them to enter the fold that had received him so graciously. Come to this fold," continued the little man, waving his two arms, "the devil is running, running like a mad wolf after you. Hold! hold! here is a safe pen where the shepherd guards and the dog watches, and the devil comes not here. There are false folds of many kinds: there is one at a Chapel near this hall. It's better in every way to be in my fold. Those who follow the devil only get stripes and bruises for their pains; but Jesus Christ has found work for Fiddler Boss, work that pays, my friends, in the long run. So it may be with you. Following the devil you will never prosper; follow 'the bleeding Lamb' and you are safe for ever. Thank the Lord, many a returned convict have I brought to this fold; and now, my friends, to-night I would call you in to join us. You are all of you as precious to the Shepherd as the Queen—God bless her!—herself. Come in, come in, and see if you don't like it

and destruction. Ah, Boss, if you had gone on with your little games you would have found a hot quarter in the next world. But now there is a paradise waiting for me, and for any of you, my friends, if you will listen to poor Boss to-night. I shall not have to play the fiddle any more, I shall listen to the golden harps. You may meet me there, my friends, if you take my word for it that if the Lord did not refuse Boss, He will most certainly accept you and welcome you to this fold."

Here the little man bumped into his seat; the breathless silence he had procured was broken, and the people coughed and moved once more. After a little whispering with Jabez Blaze, Boss again rose, and said, "I would now like you to hear a few words from my brother here. He was known among us thieves as 'Joyful Ginger,' and when I got converted I went straight to him, and told him he must go and do the same. He didn't the first time I talked, or the second, but last of all I conquered him, and here he is to-night, and will tell you himself what the Lord has done for him."

Ginger grinned and rose, and Boss grinned and sat down. And then there came another statement of a number of convictions for crimes committed, and the details of the history of a life of flagrant wickedness. Afterwards an appeal was made to sinners to accept the gospel, on the ground that it was "like a large leg of mutton," as to which you could "cut and come again."

Addresses from the Rev. Jabez Blaze, D.D., and two other reverend brethren followed; each one commenting in glowing terms on the speeches of Boss and Ginger, and each one full of gratitude for the "entry into the fold" of these sweet "lambs." Special appeal was made to the audience to rally round "the Evangelical committee." It was announced that they had arranged the

be consummated by the erection of a new Chapel in the street. A hymn closed the meeting.

As Melville passed out he heard on all sides exclamations of delight at the wonderful conversions of such men as Ginger and Boss. The crowd were evidently well satisfied with what they had seen and heard, and with some interest, mingled with astonishment, Melville surveyed them.

They were intellectual *protozoa*.

CHAPTER XVII.

CANT THE DESTROYER OF DOMESTIC PEACE.—MR. OSCAR CRAY-
FORD, PLYMOUTH BROTHER.—MRS. MILARD.—MR. AND MRS.
LORRAINE.

AN evening in Rome. An English traveller, as he crossed the bridge of St. Angelo, buttoned his coat tighter, and shivered as he faced the cold blast from the river. His memory took him back to the time when he had crossed that bridge before; when the sun shone brightly, and the sky was undotted by a single cloud. "Like my prospects," he murmured; "but the scene has changed, and general gloom has set in for me." So deep in thought was the traveller that the grand old dome of St. Peter's and the massive Vatican were hardly glanced at, as he passed quickly on his way, sorrowfully musing. He was well acquainted with the wonders of the great city. He had not come as a curious pleasure-seeker; his mission was more real, more earnest in its character: to the bedside of the dying he hastened.

A quarter of an hour's rapid walking brought him to the Piazza, which was his destination. At the Casa Maloné he rang the bell, and inquired for Mrs. Milard.

"I am expected, I believe," he remarked, handing his card to the servant who waited for his name. "I am Mr. Lorraine."

Pale, and agitated, he then paced the room till the lady he inquired for appeared. They bowed, but neither seemed inclined to speak. Lorraine broke the silence.

"I came, madam, at the earnest request of your daughter; and, because she wished it, I am ready and willing to see her. Understanding that her case was very serious, I have travelled night and day, trusting I may be in time to fulfil her wish."

"I am aware," replied the lady, "that my daughter has communicated with you. I can only say that I hope you will not attempt to shake her religious opinions. I grieve that she should be thrown on her death-bed into the society of unbelievers."

"Madam," said Lorraine, "I have never attempted to shake any one's religious convictions. Such parlance as this is unfitting for the occasion, and brings up again the past, which I would fain, in such an hour, obliterate from my mind."

"But," returned the lady in rather a supercilious tone, "I hold my daughter's religious opinions, at this moment, to be more precious to her than anything in life; and I cannot permit a visit from yourself to her unless I have your promise that the past shall not be touched on, and that you will not endeavour to extort any statement from her that she has been in error in her past actions."

"It is not my wish to extort confessions from her, madam; nor should I, in this the most critical moment of her life, think of asking her even to say how blinded she has been in the time gone by."

Mrs. Milard fired up. "There you are mistaken, sir. Were my daughter's time to be lived again, I would wish unaltered the last few years. And with her present wavering faith I think it most unconscionable that you should presume on a dying moment to shake a belief which will procure her salvation. My trouble is bitter enough in itself, I am sure, without the additional pain of beholding an unbeliever like yourself at the bed-side of my dying daughter. I acceded to her wish, and allowed you to be communicated with, but I have repented ever since."

"Madam," exclaimed Lorraine, "when I took this journey I did it in good faith that my forbearance in yielding to the proposal made by your daughter would be fully appreciated. Having thus far, by my actions, forgiven the wretched past, it is more than human nature can stand to be met and treated thus. I shall return to the Hotel d'Italia, and when you have decided to admit me to an interview, without annoyance, you can communicate with me there."

"I am sorry to find you have neither changed in temper nor opinions, Mr. Lorraine. The Lord sees fit to harden your heart, and, as Mr. Crayford was saying yesterday —"

"Hush!" remonstrated Lorraine, so loudly that the lady started. "Have I come here for that villain's name to be sounded again in my ears? Stand aside, madam; let me pass. I have lost my self-respect in submitting to be the dupe I am."

In another minute Lorraine was gone. But as soon as he had closed the street door a woman softly opened it, and running swiftly down the street overtook him.

"Sir! sir! stop!" she cried in broken English; and then continued in more fluent Italian: "The lady, my poor lady, would see you. Oh, she has longed for you to come; prayed for you; dreamt of you, oh! so many nights: do come to her!"

Lorraine stayed his steps at her voice.

"Who addresses me?" he inquired, his rage still kindling in his bosom; "any one from that insulting woman?"

"I come from the unhappy lady, sir; she is dying, dying fast. Her last, her only wish is to see you. Come back with me; I will take you straight to her."

"It is impossible. Are you the nurse?" inquired Lorraine.

"Yes, yes; nurse to the poor young lady. I beg you, come back and see her."

"Will you tell your patient that I have travelled from afar to see her; and, as usual, on entering the house where

long-suffering man; but there are things I do not feel called on to stand."

"You would not send such a cruel message to a dying creature, sir! If you have come a long distance at her request, you will never go back without seeing her! I promise you shall not meet Mrs. Milard. My poor lady will die in misery if she sees you not."

Lorraine hesitated; then, with a strong effort at self-control, and something between a gasp and a sigh, he said, " Lead the way; I follow."

On reaching the house once more, the nurse softly unlocked the door, and having let Lorraine in, she beckoned him to follow. Very astonished was she to behold him walk straight to the apartment where he had left Mrs. Milard. He entered. The lady was sitting in an easy chair, sipping some brandy and water which she had taken to revive her after the scene.

"Mrs. Milard," said Lorraine, "I propose seeing your daughter for a short time. This was my purpose when I arrived. With the spirit of forgiveness, of which you know and understand nothing, and as an ordinary matter of courtesy, I inquired for you when I came. This was my mistake. I find you are the same woman, and possess the same spirit as when we last parted. I am here to see your daughter; and without permission from you there are sufficient reasons for me to demand that interview at once. Nurse, you will lead me to your patient."

This the woman was only too glad to do; and without another look at the astonished Mrs. Milard, or a moment's delay to hear any remark she might make, Lorraine ascended the staircase. Arrived at the patient's door, he motioned the nurse to precede and announce him, whilst he endeavoured to calm himself sufficiently for the interview. A voice sounded on his ears: it was weak and faint, but Lorraine recognised it, and it awakened unspeakable emotions.

"Has he come? Oh, bring him here!"

Gently he entered the room and approached the bedside where the sick woman lay. She was quite young, and though wan from suffering, her face was extremely beautiful. As her eyes rested on Lorraine, they lit up with a radiant joy; and while the blood rushed into her pale cheeks, she exclaimed with astonishing fervour, "Stanley, you have come! I knew you would: you are so good!"

Lorraine did not speak. He took the hand she extended to him, but his voice would not come. He was gazing, maybe for the last time, on the woman whom he had married five years since, and whom for one year he had loved ardently as his wife.

"It is late to repent, Stanley; late to ask forgiveness. I can make no amends for the past, but I have lived to repent. O Stanley! can you forgive me?"

"I can and do, Evelyn."

"Ever since I was taken ill I have been thinking, Stanley. You said I should think some day. I see what a selfish wretch I have been, what a miserably narrow life I have led. How far from Christianity! O Stanley! I shudder when I look into my heart, and behold the real motives that influenced me. How you must have hated me!"

"No, Evelyn, I pitied you, for I knew you were misled. But I thank Heaven for this moment."

"My mother is in great trouble about me, Stanley. I have refused to see that man Crayford; and I have told her what I feel about the past. O Stanley, if I could live now and make you happy! But it is too late:" and Evelyn fell back exhausted with the effort she had made.

Lorraine, who was almost overcome himself, called the nurse to bring some nourishment for her patient; and after partaking of it Evelyn revived, and was able to speak again.

"I want to talk, Stanley," she murmured. "I have more

to say. Do not go yet. They will not let you return hither, I know."

Lorraine of course yielded to her request, and again seated himself beside her to listen to the history of the past years of separation, and to hear the confessions of his erring but penitent wife. She soon became exhausted, however, and Lorraine saw plainly that his presence was becoming too exciting for her.

"Tell me I am forgiven, Stanley," she whispered, ere he left.

"Fully and freely," he replied.

Downstairs he met with no interruption, and, passing into the street, he walked to his hotel. That night he slept not. The memory of the past, the strange bewildering present, and the agitation of his mind, caused all sleep to be banished.

In order to understand Mr. Lorraine's sufferings at this juncture, it is necessary to pause here for a few moments. We must tell the story of his previous life. Six years ago he had first seen Evelyn Milard. To see her was to love her. In three months after their introduction to each other Evelyn and Lorraine were married. And very fortunate Mr. and Mrs. Milard thought themselves to have secured as a son-in-law a man of high social position and great wealth, a liberal portion of which he settled on their daughter for her own absolute use. Lorraine, with his earnest, loving temperament, had anticipated a happy future. The period of his courtship had not revealed to him the true character of his future wife. Evelyn Milard in disposition was selfish, obstinate, narrow-minded, and fanatical. She was an only daughter, and indulged by parents who, simply because she was their daughter, deemed her a model of excellence. Accustomed to tyrannise over those who surrounded her, with whom her word was law, she neither understood nor would suffer the least opposition. Lorraine, soon after marriage, discovered traits of character in his wife that he could not respect, nor could he pass them by without remonstrance. He found, to his sorrow, that she brooked neither correction nor suggestion; but at first their points of moral divergence were too trivial to cause much disturbance.

The greatest annoyance to his married life he found in Mrs. Milard, who was never happy unless planning or manœuvring—sometimes with her daughter, but more often without her—the domestic and other daily affairs appertaining to his household. As Mr. and Mrs. Milard at that time lived near Lorraine, in Italy, she found plenty of opportunities for indulging her officious and mischief-loving tastes. She was a woman who grasped at power, and who never knew her proper place. Her haughty vindictiveness was a constant source of annoyance to Lorraine, who, bore it, however, as he bore many other things, for the sake of the woman he had married. There came a fortunate temporary deliverance to Lorraine from Mrs. Milard's attentions. She was obliged to give up her house in Italy, and go to England with her husband, who by reason of failing health, was ordered thither by his physicians. After her departure two months passed in Lorraine's home more happily than any he had experienced. But at the end of that time Evelyn was summoned to England to see her father, who was thought to be dying. It happened that Lorraine himself was just then very ill with a serious malady, and being confined to his room, was quite unable to accompany his wife to England. But, as he was always unselfish, he begged her to lose no time in joining her parents, if she desired to do so. Evelyn left him at once. In four months' time the father died. Lorraine received this intelligence in a letter from his wife, in which, among other things, she mentioned that she had "become acquainted with a friend" who had "quite reconciled her to her father's death," and

to mourn for the dead. She said she had obtained "true light" on religious matters; had learnt that "the believer ought to have nothing to do with the world"; understood that she and those who joined "the only true Church" were "specially illuminated by God"; and that their conclusions were necessarily right for that reason. She said nothing at all about returning to perform her duty to her husband; expressed no sympathy for him in his loneliness and suffering; made no reference to all his unselfish goodness to her, but filled page after page of letter paper with the technical terminology of dogmatic religiosity. By the time Lorraine had read the last few lines he was prepared for the tidings that she had renounced humanity. For by reason of a certain characteristic peculiarity in the hard icy Cant, he foresaw the news that she had joined the sect which terms itself " *The* Brethren." Mrs. Milard had associated herself with this sect many years before, when it possessed not a cosmopolitan but a local name—" The Plymouth Brethren." The saucy arrogance with which it usurped the grander title accorded with her consequential temper, as strikingly as the new designation itself disagreed with the narrow tenets of the sect. She had always meant that her daughter should ally herself with it, but Mrs. Milard, like others of her class—who select their particular religious communion on the ground that it seems to them to be the safest, if not the only solvent Heavenly Life Assurance Company—was well saturated with cunning and cupidity. Accordingly she was always mindful not to let her Plymouth Brethrenism prejudice her own or her daughter's secular advantages; but kept it well in the back-ground of her mundane stratagems, pending a suitable opportunity for its display. That opportunity had now arrived. Her husband was buried. She was fairly well off. Her daughter was well married, and possessed, through Lorraine's generosity, ample means independent of his control. Mrs. Milard had always known that Lorraine would not embrace her sect. With his heroic, liberal nature, no narrow dogmatism, or hollow pretence could possibly be blended. A man of warm and noble impulses, spotless life, and profound religious convictions, he loathed Cant and flippant, glib, pietistic, heaven-calculating talk; especially when it was divorced from all good actions. But he was now out of the way. With Evelyn in England, Mrs. Milard felt that she could make a successful fight for herself and her sect, and run no risk whatever. It was the moment to bring suitable influences to work for the subjugation of her daughter's soul to herself. To the ordinary pleasure which a proselytiser would take in the work she added the vindictiveness of a woman eager to be revenged on her superior, the son-in-law whom she had wronged but could not conquer. Her various artifices succeeded well with Evelyn. Lorraine, in consequence, was left in Italy to bear his illness as best he could. The teaching of the mother convinced the child-wife that the husband's illness was "a judgment from God on an unbeliever." Evelyn wrote to him to say quite coldly that she "should not return home at present"; and hoped in the meantime that "the affliction would be blessed by God to his conversion." Lorraine's heart revolted at the tone of this letter. He could not help seeing how selfishly his wife was acting in not returning to him in his long illness; and, above all things, he dreaded the prospect of Evelyn becoming a canting woman. His spirit sank within him as he read the letter, which seemed to whisper that his domestic hopes were dead. Several weeks elapsed before Evelyn wrote again, and then it was to say that she was "on her journey home"; and that she should bring with her Mrs. Milard, certain domestics, and the dear friend of her mother and herself, who had "done so much for her soul."

And verily she did arrive soon after, bringing with her a retinue of "Brethren." Of these, two were the respec-

housekeeper, and the fourth was Mr. Oscar Crayford, the "dear friend" who had helped Mrs. Milard in bringing Evelyn to "a saving knowledge of Plymouth light."

Mr. Oscar Crayford, though about fifty years of age, possessed all the charm of manner and vivacity of a man of twenty-five. His appearance was certainly not handsome: but it was more, it was fascinating. Under the basilisk influence of his eye, many a fair one had "become convinced of the error of her ways," and received his ministrations. The tones of his voice were practised in flattery and dissimulation, and had no ring of true manliness. They were the lute-like notes of an actor who wooes by flattery. He was tall and slight, with long tapering fingers which he displayed to the best advantage, and his tread was the stealthy creep of some wily animal that watches for his prey. He was a great man amongst *the* Brethren: one of their "lights" and preachers. Many converts had he made. And his influence was not confined to London only. During the excursion season he took frequent picturesque tours abroad, that he "might be useful," as he said, "to his Lord in many lands." His power over others was certainly remarkable, and under it Evelyn Lorraine had formed an attachment which held her captive.

By the arrival of this man and his companions, Lorraine was surrounded on all sides by people who were antipathetic to all his mental and moral proclivities. He was soon struck with Evelyn's change of manner; and not many days elapsed before he discovered that her affection had been diverted from himself during her residence in England. Before long it was visible to Lorraine that his wife's new religion caused her to depreciate all his unselfish actions.

Mrs. Milard, who had gained those secular advantages which she had sought from her daughter's marriage with

paraging him to Evelyn with the view of maintaining her own ascendency.

Mr. Crayford talked continually to Lorraine of the 'light" that his wife enjoyed, and begged him in the most unctuous terms to accept her faith and to be "converted." Mrs. Milard and Evelyn would look rapturously at one another as Mr. Crayford discoursed ; and Lorraine, unwilling to quarrel with Evelyn's friend, at first treated the matter lightly, and would listen as courteously as he could to Mr. Crayford's exhortations. But he soon found that the influences which were at work to separate his wife from himself were too strong for him. Mrs. Milard, who loved to domineer and to display, suggested to Evelyn that they should hold meetings of an evening for the servants and the rest of the household to hear Mr. Crayford speak. Lorraine strongly objected to this, nor would he yield. Mrs. Milard, who to all appearances had resolved to make her son-in-law's home her own, was in a terrible rage at Lorraine's firmness, and she so worked on Evelyn by dwelling on her "husband's tyranny" that Lorraine was drawn into his first quarrel with his wife. It was to him a bitter one, and ended in an estrangement which grew wider as the days passed on.

Sick at heart Lorraine was driven almost to despair. Wherever he turned in his house he was sure to encounter one of the "Brethren" domestics—who looked on him with a bold, pitying eye—or Crayford himself, whose expression was injured but resigned.

Lorraine still loved his wife earnestly, and for her sake forbore to come to an open quarrel, in the hope that Crayford would soon withdraw himself, and that Mrs. Milard would be too offended to remain. He fancied that, left with Evelyn, he could reason her back to her proper frame of mind. His efforts at self-control broke down one day when, on entering the house unexpectedly, he found that

holding forth to the whole establishment, and to some invited guests. It appeared that he was improving the occasion to depreciate Lorraine in the opinions of those present, for he spoke of him as "one who was very far from the fold, and whose proud spirit the Lord would, before long, most certainly bring low."

A stormy scene ensued. Crayford was told by Lorraine to leave the house; and Mrs. Milard was informed that after such a procedure, her daughter would be far better without the influence of such a mother. Evelyn, frantic with rage at what she considered Lorraine's "tyranny," declared that Mr. Crayford should not obey her husband's orders. Crayford, however, did eventually leave the house, and Mrs. Milard, who wept copiously, shut herself sulkily in her own apartment. That night Lorraine appealed to his wife, and urged her not to continue her strange infatuation. He begged her to dismiss from her friendship the man who had raised such a barrier between them, and appealed to her honour not to side with her mother against himself. It was useless. Blind in her infatuation for Crayford, who by this time possessed more influence over her than any one, and obstinate in her determination to side with her mother against "an unbeliever" like her husband, she refused to listen to Lorraine's words.

Mrs. Milard's indignation knew no bounds. "A godly man like Crayford turned from the house in the same way as a discovered thief or other criminal!" She advised Evelyn on the morrow to visit Crayford's hotel, and beg him to remain there till something was settled about her return to England. Evelyn, nothing loth, did so. She found Crayford perfectly calm and resigned. Magnanimous in his declaration of unabated friendship for herself, and "fervent in his sorrow for her passionate erring husband."

"We must expect this, dearest Mrs. Lorraine. Our Lord has told us we must have persecution in this world. The one

to the Lord. Ah, beloved one, if you had been brought to a knowledge of the Lord previous to your marriage, you would not, I am sure, ever have known the calamity of being unequally yoked with an unbeliever."

With such conversation, and with plenty of flattery, Crayford entertained Evelyn, and sent her away feeling what a wicked man her husband was, and how shamefully he had treated the angelic Crayford. Mrs. Milard improved on Crayford's conversation, and urged Evelyn to leave Lorraine.

"I dread his influence on your life," she exclaimed; "dread lest he should keep you out of Heaven."

She might not have dreaded this so much if Evelyn's fortune, which Lorraine settled on her at the marriage, had been less. As it was, a separation of Mrs. Lorraine from her husband would not involve the slightest pecuniary suffering.

Mrs. Milard's words produced their effect. The estrangement between the husband and wife grew. Lorraine was fearfully unhappy. When he tried to be kind to Evelyn, she treated him with the greatest coldness; and continually reproached him for his "unkindness to herself and mother." Things at last came to a crisis. Evelyn made a request that, before Crayford returned to England, Lorraine would see him and apologise for his conduct. This, Lorraine steadily refused to do. Meanwhile Mrs. Milard had laid her plans. She intended returning to England with Crayford, as she was anything but comfortable. Her great idea was to revenge herself on Lorraine, by causing Evelyn to abandon her husband, and accompany Crayford and herself. This was accomplished with little difficulty.

Fascinated, as Evelyn was, with the man whom she looked up to as her "spiritual adviser," and who took care to make his daily flattery necessary to her, she could hardly endure the idea of losing him, and being left with the husband from whom she had become estranged. Since Lorraine's refusal to see Crayford, she had hardly spoken to her husband, and though he still paid her every kind attention, and yearned with an aching heart to receive some acknowledgment of his own affection, she neither talked to him nor was with him more than she could possibly help. Crayford continually poured forth his "lamentations that she was yoked to an unbeliever," and pointed out to her the advantages that might have arisen had she made "a godly union."

As the time drew near for Crayford's departure, the wily Plymouth Brother, knowing that his views would find a ready seconder in Mrs. Milard, represented to Evelyn that it was *almost* her duty to leave such a man as Mr. Lorraine, and " to come away from one who was not a fit companion for a child of God."

The crisis of Evelyn's life now approached. She agreed to leave her husband. Without one parting word, she went off in the morning while he was absent, taking all her valuables, and leaving a letter for Lorraine, stating that she could never be happy with him after what had passed, or feel herself justified in living with one who had "treated her religious opinions so cruelly."

Mrs. Milard stipulated with Evelyn to depart in this manner. She feared that if husband and wife had an interview, Lorraine's entreaties might cause her daughter to flinch from the part she had to act. Evelyn's letter to Lorraine stated that any communication he had to make should be through her mother's solicitor, and no address of her future abode was given. Mrs. Milard had removed to an hotel some days previously, in furtherance of the plot, so there was very little stir with Evelyn's departure. The servants imagined she had gone for a drive, because her godly lady's maid, who was in the secret, left the house with her.

The shock that Lorraine received with Evelyn's letter was attended by a relapse of his illness. When he recovered he wrote a letter to his wife which principally related to business matters, and stated that as she had voluntarily left his protection and home, so he held himself irresponsible for her happiness or welfare in the future; and that all communication between them henceforth and for ever was at an end.

Lorraine's return to health was still further retarded by his father's death; and, left without a single relation he was almost heart-broken by his reflections. "If those Milards had wanted to make him a 'Plymouth Brother,' why could they not have said so at the outset of their acquaintance? If they could not agree with him, why did they so sedulously seek his society until he married Evelyn and settled a fortune upon her? But for them, he would still have remained happy in his pursuits of literature and the fine arts, surrounded by suitable companions, performing useful work, and enjoying golden hopes. He had dealt with them unsuspectingly, and with lavish generosity. They had acted towards him as only women can act when their humanity has been festered away by the poison of the most virulent Cant. They had made use of his house, his money, his protection, and his name. Then, they left him in loneliness and in despair, having played out a drama of perfidy which threw him into a dangerous melancholy."

It was at this conjuncture that Lorraine's old college friend, Melville, found him, and brought him out of the depths of his great darkness. Melville the brave, the faithful, the tender, and the true, was precisely the friend he needed. Under his vitalising influence, and following his wise advice, Lorraine gradually revived. The stimulating tonic of congenial companionship, combined with constant travelling, completed his restoration to mental and bodily health.

At the time when Mr. Lorraine was first mentioned in this book, as a casual listener to one of Falcon Small's sermons, he was unostentatiously devoting himself to scientific investigations, and philanthropic work, in London; and in the society of men of worth and culture he was once again realizing that life had still some joys. Again the Milard shadow came across his brightening path. Mrs. Milard, being aware that he had sold his property and given up his residence in Italy, considered she might gratify herself by sojourning in Rome with Evelyn and Crayford, without the fear of encountering him there. During her stay, Evelyn was seized with that last illness to which reference has already been made. Lorraine had to be sent for. In compliance with the summons, he made the journey to Rome, and had the interview with his wife which was described at the commencement of this chapter.

We have already recorded a part, but only a part, of the conversation which took place between the husband and wife on that occasion. The substance of that which we have not related will be surmised after a perusal of the proceedings recorded in the following chapter.

Twenty-four hours after her interview with her husband Mrs. Lorraine breathed her last.

CHAPTER XVIII.

CANT AND FRAUD.—THE PLYMOUTH BROTHER.—THE DISPUTE
BETWEEN MR. LORRAINE AND MR. OSCAR CRAYFORD.

LORRAINE sat in his apartment at the Hotel d' Italia. He was writing, and his face was cold and stern. A servant entered and announced that Signor Crayford was waiting to see him. Lorraine's cheek flushed at this intelligence. He hesitated, but after a moment's pause ordered that his visitor should be admitted. In another minute Crayford glided in. He commenced speaking directly he appeared, but his eyes avoided Lorraine's. "My business will not detain you long, Mr. Lorraine. It was necessary we should meet before you left Rome."

His tones were as silvery as of yore, and his manner as quiet and unperturbed as it was in those days long ago when he first came to break the harmony of Lorraine's domestic life. He took the nearest chair, and then brought from his pocket a paper.

Lorraine's soul recoiled from his visitor. He could hardly find words to speak, and he did not resume his seat, for he was unwilling that the interview should last long.

"You wrote me," continued Crayford, "that you intended to dispute the legality of your dear wife's will. I have brought you the document. It was entrusted to Mrs. Milard by her daughter at the commencement of her illness, which was some months back. I believe, after perusing that paper, you will change your mind."

Lorraine took the document and cast his eyes over it "Then," said he, "you assure me on your honour that my wife never wrote to you telling you that she had asked her mother to destroy this instrument, on the ground that she had altered her intentions with regard to the leaving of her property?"

"Ah, no," replied Crayford. "I had no letter seriously to that effect. Anything that Mrs. Lorraine may have said in her wanderings to her mother, and she did, indeed, wander most fearfully towards the last, of course were not taken as *bona fide* requests. I can assure you it was a fearful blow to both Mrs. Milard and myself that, at the last, our dear Evelyn should have appeared to have forsaken the religious conviction that had before ruled her life. I felt it acutely, acutely."

Crayford's eyes were raised towards an opposite picture, on which he now stared mutely, as if his whole soul were far away from the present scenes, endeavouring to solve the difficult problem of Evelyn's heresy. Tears at last exuded from his cold grey eyes, and a deeply bordered handkerchief was pressed to his face. The sight of that handkerchief irritated Lorraine. Crayford always had worn black, so the extra mourning he had assumed for Lorraine's wife was hardly noticeable till the broad black band on the white cambric called attention to the fact. It was true though strange: Evelyn's friend wept while her husband's eyes were dry. Intense irritation caused Lorraine to refrain from speaking for the moment. During the pause, Crayford's handkerchief was removed from his eyes, which resumed their keen yet bland expression, whilst he continued ;—

"Money, Mr. Lorraine, has little value for me, but the glorious work in which I am engaged will be benefited by my dear and lamented friend's munificence to 'the cause'; and under these circumstances I am ready and willing to appear in any court in favour of the existing will. I feel it my duty to do in the Lord's cause what, for myself, I should never even urge."

Lorraine's only wish now was to end the interview. He felt he should thrust Crayford from the room if he sat there much longer, with his smooth resigned face and folded arms So he applied himself to reading without further delay the document that Crayford had handed to him. When he had perused it, he laid it on the table, and turned his fine sincere eyes fully on Crayford.

"I cannot question the legality of that document, Mr. Crayford. You can keep it. You can get it proved. I have no power to interfere. At the same time, I believe with my deepest belief that if you act on it, you will be performing a deed unworthy of a man of the slightest honour. My mind at the time of my wife's illness was occupied with thoughts which had no relation to secular affairs. Our interview was a brief one. But she especially reverted to the satisfaction she felt that that document which you have produced had been destroyed. She mentioned it to me as a thing done. She told me that on her first being taken ill, which was in the summer of last year, Mrs. Milard had suggested to her the prudence of making a will, so that the money which on her marriage I had settled on her, might not revert to me, although it belonged to me. My wife was induced by Mrs. Milard to make part of it over to yourself; for you to use in the way you might think best for the promotion of 'Brethrenism.' The remainder she bequeathed to her mother. This will she consigned to the care of Mrs. Milard. A month before her death, though not confined to her bed, and in no more positive danger of the end than she had been for the last few weeks, and consequently quite able to make such an alteration, she told her mother of her determination not to abide by the will she had made. For, she felt it right that at least half of the money which I had settled on her on our marriage should revert to me, to whom it all belonged. Mrs. Milard was exasperated at the time, and my wife decided that in addition to telling her mother her wishes she would also convey them in writing to yourself. I believe she also gave legal effect to those wishes in a way which I admit that I cannot at this moment prove by strict evidence. These facts she related to me at our interview. I frankly state that there was no witness to our conversation, for the nurse each time was in an adjoining room. This money of mine, I can honestly affirm, I neither care for nor need. My vexation, sir, is that you, you of all men, should touch a penny of it; and that you, my greatest enemy, for such you have proved yourself, should profit by the unnatural and ungodly influence that you exercised over another man's wife."

Crayford's resigned smile was more provoking to Lorraine than a blow from his hand would have proved.

"Your words are hard ones, Mr. Lorraine, but I forgive you from my heart. In rescuing brands from the burning we do not mourn if we are stigmatised and upbraided by the world."

"Stop, sir!" cried Lorraine. "Cease your insults. Am *I* not the outraged party who have been long struggling to kill a sorrow that your baseness brought on me? You found me a happy man, and you never rested till you wrecked all my domestic felicity. Thank God that what you take from me now, my property, affects not my life or my hopes. Relentless in your persecution, you cannot touch me now. You took my all when you took my wife."

Lorraine could no longer master his indignation. Crayford at that moment appeared to him a monster of hypocrisy and deceit. Crayford, however, at whom his fury was directed, sat untouched. His grey eyes looked vaguely at the picture opposite, and his features were unmoved.

"Mr. Lorraine, you are in a rage," he said quietly, when Lorraine ceased speaking, and began pacing the room. "You are talking without previous thought. It is useless to argue with an angry man, or I might prove how false are your assertions. But those who suffer for conscience' sake suffer gladly and easily. The Lord has promised us persecutions, and to be spoken spitefully of, and to be falsely accused. Why should I expect to be exempt? In doing our Master's work we are exposed to all the storm of the battle's front. I am sorry you consider me your enemy, Mr. Lorraine. The time may come, and for that time I will earnestly hope and pray, when a knowledge of the same Lord will unite us in christian sympathy."

"Never, sir! never! Let this interview be ended," exclaimed Lorraine. "Take with you this unworthily possessed document, and with it the unutterable scorn that I feel towards a scoundrel and a hypocrite. And, as there is a God above, know you, that such blots on the human race as yourself will not go unpunished. My best wish for you is that you may be brought to an honest repentance, and thus evade your otherwise inevitable fate."

For a moment Crayford's calmness appeared forsaking him. He turned a shade whiter. But, ere he could reply, if, indeed, he had intended to do so, he found himself the only occupant of the apartment. Lorraine had retired from the room in deepest disgust.

Crayford soon recovered himself, and there was a momentary twinkling of satisfaction in his crafty eyes as he rolled up the document and buttoned it safely in his breast-pocket. He took a good look round the room, and seemed inclined to pry into the desk at which Lorraine had been writing, but a waiter's footstep on the threshold hindered him, and he left the hotel with the same self-complacent manner with which he had entered it.

CHAPTER XIX.

CANT "HEEVANGELICAL" RESPECTING THE "BLOOD."—A HEROINE—MRS. RAINFORD.—MORE ABOUT THE DEACON DESPOTISM.—VISIT OF BEESWAX AND TREACLES TO MR. RAINFORD.—MR. RAINFORD'S ILLNESS.

ABOUT half a mile from Chenley stood the house of the Rev. Mr. Rainford, the Independent Minister, with whom the reader became slightly acquainted in the 14th chapter, and of whom he will now learn more. The cottage was an old-fashioned pretty little place, standing in a small garden, which was well cared for. It was an insignificant abode, containing only six rooms. Rainford's means being very limited, he preferred the rustic cottage with its honeysuckle peeping in at the window, and the red roses climbing over the door, to one of the new villas which had recently been built in the town. Rainford loved nature; his garden was his paradise; he delighted in the country too. The pent-up streets of the town were his aversion, except when duty called him to them. How bright and fresh his pretty cottage and garden appeared when he returned from his pastoral calls. How charming the walk over the Chenley hills, with the town like a black spot lying in the valley, and the fresh breeze giving new life to his soul. On these spirit-reviving heights Rainford thought out many of his sermons, and his health, which was feeble, would have broken down altogether but for the fresh air of which he eagerly availed himself at every opportunity. His life was as simple as it was pure, and, had it been permitted to him, he would have passed his days without agitation or excitement

But this he could not do. He had opposing forces at work. Small as his congregation was, he found it a hard matter to please all its factions, and harder still to keep right with two of his deacons, Beeswax and Treacles. These men were constantly arming themselves to do battle with him on account of some of their pet prejudices, or as they chose to call them, "heevangelical views." In his home-life, fortunately, Rainford was wonderfully blest. How shall we describe Mabel Rainford! The world has been loud in its praises of heroic women. They have figured in battles, reigned as queens; been hailed as deliverers, and suffered as martyrs. As poets, as historians, as moralists, their names are immortalized. But the world does not recognise ALL its heroines or heroes. A life of heroism is often lived within the family circle whilst no admiring crowd confers the laurel wreath.

Mabel Rainford was a home heroine. Rising early, and working late, her hands were always active for the wants of her little family. No irritation was consequent on this. No harsh temper made the house a scene of discord. Quietly and calmly she laboured on. Domestic cares came to her plentifully. Her children, too, were delicate, and the one little maid-of-all-work was sulky. But Mabel seemed born to endure. She never gave way; she braved her trials. It was in scenes of tribulation that she had cherished the purity of her character. Poverty was the Rainfords' lot,— poverty which must preserve a respectable appearance; perhaps, the hardest poverty of all. To contrive, and manage to keep their heads above water, was Mabel's special duty; and to do this without worrying her husband or running into debt was her aim. With all her efforts and labours, she always found time to give her husband any writing assistance he might require. It was her delight to help him, if possible;—to read to him when his eyes ached; to act as amanuensis for him when he was

accomplish; and what was more, she knew how to bear with Rainford when the cares of his office, and the literary occupation by which he added to his income, over-taxed his nervous powers. She rejoiced to soothe him when ruffled, to cheer him when depressed; to distract his thoughts from things that vexed him, and to fight his battles in his absence. The poor folks of the chapel were well acquainted with Mabel. She used to flit in and out of their homes, and bring a kind word and a smile to many a suffering heart. She knew all their histories, was acquainted with all their troubles, and, out of her little, always had something to spare for them. How she found time for all her labours was the wonder. As minister's wife her duties outside her home were numerous, and not one was ever neglected. It was a difficult position too, that of the minister's wife of the Independent chapel. She could have no special friends selected from her own class in life. Directly there was a suspicion that she saw more of the educated families than of the official dullards, the Beeswax family and Mr., Mrs., and Miss Treacles were furious with vulgar jealousy, and ready to annihilate her. But, for her husband's sake, she held bravely to her post, and at all times she was ready to meet each duty as it arose. We think of her in connection with Solomon's "virtuous woman," whom the most original theological writer of the day has described as "erect in strength, with habits of diligence and honesty that gave a dignity to her bearing. Her neighbours would feel themselves, when they looked at her, in the presence of true nobility. Her conversation consisted not in simpering inanities, idle gossip, or unchaste narrations, nor was it ever tinged with unkindness. As there was no spleen in her nature, there was nothing sardonic in her speech. She was too rich in love for envies, too noble for jealousies, too confiding for suspicions, too truthful for falsehoods, too good for scandal."

and Treacles set forth one Monday morning on an evangelical errand. Beeswax had attired himself in his Sunday black. He felt more able to perform what he called his "official dooties," when attired in these clothes. On arriving at the cottage, the little servant ushered Messrs. Beeswax and Treacles into the parlour, and Mabel soon joined them.

"Mr. Rainford was very busy," she said; "could she convey any message to him?"

"We want particularly to see 'im," said Beeswax; and Mabel in despair went to her husband's study. He was sitting at the table writing, and looked up with a smile as she entered.

"Mabel! The very one I want. Are you ready to write a little, my dear?"

"I shall prove an unwelcome interruption, I fear," answered Mabel. "Mr. Beeswax and Mr. Treacles are downstairs; they want to see you. I tried to bring up their message, and mentioned that you were busy, but they *will* see you."

Rainford's face grew cloudy. He sighed heavily. "I wish they would leave me alone," he murmured. "I knew it was coming. Beeswax has given many broad hints lately. Bring the visitors up, Mabel; I must get through it."

Mabel stopped to kiss her husband's forehead, and to exclaim, "Never mind what they say, they cannot rob you of the consciousness that you try to do your duty."

"I daresay they mean well; let them come up," said Rainford, putting aside his papers.

The two deacons were received with proper courtesy by Mr. Rainford. Beeswax, as spokesman, occupied the chair nearest to him, and having assumed the position that his Sunday clothes demanded, he fumbled in his pocket and looked at the minister with a firm eye. In due time he laid a cheque on the table, which represented Mr. Rainford's quarter's salary—only two months after it was due—

and then commenced. " On the occasion of our presenting you with your salary, Mr. Rainford, we wished, that is to say, me and Brother Treacles, to give you a few words of hadvice and warning. It is the dooty of the helder to advise the younger, but *sometimes*, I do not say *always*, but *sometimes* the younger is not so hedified thereby as he might be."

Here Beeswax hemmed, and shifted a little more to the edge of his seat.

" I trust, Mr. Beeswax, I shall always take into impartial consideration advice which is honestly offered and is well meant," said Rainford politely.

" Of course, it is for your good," asserted Beeswax, " that we, in paying you your quarter's money, consider it hexpedient to make a few remarks about our views. How could we 'ave any other motive but for your good ? "

Here Beeswax rose. He generally felt most comfortable, when dressed in his Sunday black, in standing with his hands behind him. He then had more power over the argument, and could rise occasionally on tiptoe when the subject demanded emphasis.

As Beeswax paused after this last interrogatory Rainford observed, " You could have no other motive, Mr. Beeswax, I am sure."

Poor Rainford! He felt tired and irritable, and it was hard work to be patient with Beeswax.

" Well then, in paying the quarter's salary I would like to observe that we were not hedified with your discourse last Sunday morning, Mr. Rainford."

" I am sorry. What was the matter with it ? " asked Rainford.

" To be plain, there was *no* gospel at all hin it," said Beeswax decisively.

" Did I fail to convey the apostle's meaning ? " asked Rainford, " I endeavoured to give what I considered a correct exposition of the verse, ' We preach Christ crucified,' etc."

Beeswax was slightly puzzled for an answer, but Treacles came to the rescue, " What we mean is, it was not heevangelical : more to 'ead than 'eart."

Beeswax nodded repeatedly at this remark, and Treacles retired again for the present.

"It is my wish to preach to the heart, I assure you, Mr. Treacles," observed Rainford. "I was unconscious of naving missed this aim."

"I think no sermon heevangelical unless it introduces the BLOOD," emphasised Beeswax. "What are we without the *blood*, Mr. Rainford ? Where are we without the blood, Brother Treacles ? Sinners can only be brought 'ome through the blood, and the blood, sir," continued Beeswax, raising himself very much on his toes, " was NOT in your discourse."

At the word NOT the little man ended one of his tiptoe elevations and came down on his heels with a bump that shook the small study.

"But there are other and very important subjects to include in our teaching, Mr. Beeswax ; do you not think so ? " returned Rainford.

"Nothink without blood, sir ; nothink. When we read of those revivals, Mr. Treacles, 'ow are they done ? 'Ow do preachers bring so many into the fold as they do at these meetings ? The blood, sir, does it, I reply. The blood brings them hin when nothink else is of hany havail :—

> ' There is a fountain *filled* with *blood*,
> Drawn from Himmanuel's veins,
> And sinners plunged beneath that flood
> Lose HALL their guilty stains.' "

Rainford's pale face grew paler. He was evidently struggling to control himself. "Mr. Beeswax," said he, his voice slightly trembling with the emotion he was restraining ; "I think you must be under some misapprehension respecting the 'doctrine of the blood.' You appear to conceive that there was, and is, some theological merit and value in the sanguineous fluid itself, and that 'saving grace' was actually contained in Christ's blood corpuscles. Now, supposing that the mode of capital punishment in vogue amongst the Romans had not been crucifixion, and that, therefore, Christ had been drowned, poisoned, strangled, starved, slowly tortured, or put to death by some other means which did not involve the shedding of even one single drop of blood—do you really think that, in such an event, He would, as a consequence, have been valueless as a Saviour? Surely, the entire spiritual importance of Christ's mission to the world does not arise from the mere accident that there was selected, as the mode of killing Him, a plan which happened to involve the loss of blood! Will you tell me what you imply by 'the blood'? Your remarks hardly convey sufficient meaning to me."

Treacles gave a short "humph." He was certainly called upon to interpose and to speak at this juncture.

"The blood, Mr. Rainford? Why the blood that washes out the filthy sinners' rags, and makes them white agin. The blood that the Father plunged His fiery sword into."

"I can hardly suppose Mr. Rainford is in hearnest," spoke Beeswax, "when he puts that question. I 'ope he has *felt* the blood if he don't know its meaning."

Here Beeswax sniffed with dignity.

"It is your interpretation of Scripture I cannot comprehend," replied Rainford, struggling bravely to keep his temper. "The meaning of the Apostle, I think that I partly understand."

"Then, sir, I trust you will give hus a little more of the blood in your next, and hinvite others to its cleansing power."

"Ha," said Treacles, "Revivalism is very much needed 'ere."

"We must be plain, you know, Mr. Rainford," said Beeswax—unintentionally stating a dualistic truth, for they were both ugly men. "It is no use for me and Mr. Treacles to notice p'ints in your sermons, where we consider you fail, and not speak of 'em. Now is it?"

"Certainly not, Mr. Beeswax."

"Me and Mr. Treacles," continued Beeswax, "is as hinterested in the bringing hin of sinners as you, Mr. Rainford; and where we notice a p'int for himprovement we are bound to mention it. Another himprovement we wished to mention, me and Mr. Treacles, was that there should always for the future be a hinvitation at the hend, to sinners. We 'ave hurged this before."

Rainford bowed. "I am to bring that in whether it be in conformity with my subject or not?"

"Certinly, certinly. Sinners are more himportant than subjects," exclaimed Beeswax.

"Their 'ard 'earts want a deal of breaking," remarked Treacles. "One day in seven 'll 'ardly do it."

"A distinct and hearnest hinvitation, at the hend of heach sermon, does a deal of good," observed Beeswax; "and we should be glad, Mr. Rainford, to 'ear the same at sich times."

"Were these all the suggestions you wished to make?" asked Rainford.

Beeswax looked thoughtful. "These were the two principal p'ints," he returned. "But the 'ole thing last Sunday was 'ardly to our views."

"Not simple gospel," put in Treacles. "More to 'ead than 'eart."

"The friends was better pleased in the hevening," remarked Beeswax.

Rainford was standing now, and his fingers tapped the back of his chair impatiently. "I shall endeavour to remedy the defects you have mentioned," he observed. "I am sure you will excuse me when I inform you that I have some important writing to finish."

Beeswax looked annoyed, and Treacles seemed resolved

to sit. But Rainford had walked to the door, and with the most polite manner possible was extending his hand. They were therefore compelled to take their departure.

As the forms of the two deacons receded down the road, Mabel ran up to the study. Rainford had resumed his writing, but his face looked troubled, and his wife was struck by the utter weariness of his expression.

"Can I help you now?" she asked.

"I have a wretched headache coming on, Mabel; I think I shall go to bed. I am tired and ill," said Rainford, as he folded up the desk at which he had been laboriously working since the dawn.

"Those men have increased your sufferings," exclaimed Mabel, as the tears started to her eyes. "Let us get away from them!"

"Where to?" asked Rainford with a feeble smile. "I have no influence anywhere, or friends to provide me a new pastorate. Besides, I believe the men mean well. It is only their ignorance and arrogance that jars on me when nerve pains make me irritable. But I ought not to mind, I suppose. And yet I do. I cannot help it, Mabel. My patience forsook me. They pierce my very soul."

"What *do* they want now?" inquired Mabel.

"Only to tell me that last Sunday's sermon was unsatisfactory; and I prepared it so carefully."

"Never mind. Think of those you did please, my dear. Think of that Mr. Melville who came into the vestry to thank you for one of your sermons."

"Yes, yes. That is true. It is a pity they will be so bigoted. They are good men, I believe."

Mabel shook her head. "I do not see any of their goodness. And what is more, I believe no one else does either. It is the weakness of the Independent system of Church government that such men are able even to get into power. They seized office during a congregational squabble before we came here: and now, under totally different conditions, they insist on retaining it, although there are in the present enlarged congregation many educated and qualified men for the diaconate. It seems as if their only present work was to torment you."

"I feel that I am wrong to be so easily tormented and to get so irritable," said Rainford. "They meant nothing, perhaps, when they paid me that cheque, and made the paying of it so unpleasant that I could have tossed it back to them. Oh, if I could live without their cheques! Take it, Mabel. May it do us good;" and Rainford threw himself with a groan on the little sofa, and pressed his hand to his throbbing forehead.

Mabel deemed it more prudent not to prolong the conversation; and with a heavy heart she hurried downstairs to make arrangements for keeping the house perfectly quiet. She was soon by her husband's side again, bathing his head, and endeavouring to divert his thoughts from the unpleasant visit. He did not get better, however, but worse. And far into the night Mabel sat watching and tending the sufferer. No sleep visited that chamber. Racked with the pains of approaching brain fever, and tortured by utter despair at his ministerial failure, Rainford tossed from side to side, and longed in vain for sleep to bring oblivion to his physical and mental agony!

When the morning opened on Treacles and Beeswax— after a night of the most restoring and satisfactory slumber, broken only by their tremendous orthodox snores—those "heevangelical" worthies found themselves refreshed and ready to resume the profound duties of their calling. What mattered it to them that a painful day would dawn for the usually active pastor, and that the inmates of the sunny little cottage would be hushed to a sad and solemn stillness!

"The deacons had only performed their 'heevangelical **dooty.**'"

CHAPTER XX.

CANT AND PERSECUTION.—JOHN BLUNT, ON DOGMA DIVORCED FROM DUTY.—A CHURCH-MEETING WITHOUT BEESWAX.—THE TALE OF THE TEETH.

BEESWAX and Treacles returned home not very satisfied with their visit to Rainford. They had gone intending to extract a promise from him to preach more in accordance with their views for the future; but somehow they had come away without that promise.

"He was in sich a hurry," commented Treacles, as they talked over their visit.

"Yes. And not anxious to ear us, hevidently," suggested Beeswax.

The result was that the two deacons were even more prejudiced against their pastor than before.

The following Sunday Rainford was too unwell to preach. He had been ailing for some time, and the kind of irritation which men like Beeswax, and Treacles, can produce on the nature of a man of sensibility and refinement, was just the element to complete the breakdown of his nervous system. Beeswax and Treacles looked upon this illness as their opportunity, and as the doctor said Rainford must not preach for at least a month, a Church-meeting was called, to talk over what was to be done. Rainford had some firm supporters in the congregation, and two of the deacons were known to be on his side. Still, Beeswax, and Treacles were the working deacons, and, at this proposed meeting, Beeswax determined to make one of his stirring speeches.

"I and you," said Treacles, "would sooner he went, if

possible ; so you must just show up the gospil we are receiving, and ask them to stick to the hold religion, and then work on them to show what an expense it is—finding supplies when he gits ill, and whether, hunder all circumstances, we had not better sign a requisition to git him resign."

"I know, I know," returned Beeswax, rubbing his hard hands ; " I know just the speech that will touch 'em, and that speech they shall git. Mr. Treacles. I think me and you will have hour way yet."

Meanwhile, in the pastor's little cottage was trouble and anxiety. Poor Mabel, owing to the sorrow produced by her husband's illness, and to their poverty, had an anxious time of it. Their small income would hardly suffice in days of health ; and with the extra expenses of sickness it was quite in-adequate to cope.

"You must keep him up, Mrs. Rainford," were the doctor's words as he left the house. " Plenty of port wine, and soups, and everything nourishing he must have His recovery depends on this."

And, without troubling himself to inquire how such luxuries could be obtained in Rainford's modest circumstances, he left Mabel to follow out his instructions.

" His recovery depends on it," were the words that rang on Mabel's ears, and with an aching heart she sat down to consider how the prescribed viands were to be possessed. Procure them she must, but where should she find means to do so ? A thought had come into her mind when she first heard the doctor's orders, but she had quickly banished it. In her desperation it recurred to her. There was no other way open. The people did nothing. A few of them had sent to inquire after Rainford, but no one had interested himself to remember how hard was the time of sickness in a needy minister's household. There was nothing else. It must be done ; and when it grew dark

all pride, all past associations, and get wine and nourishing food by selling her jewellery for her husband. The resolution formed, her heart was lighter.

The twilight was fast settling into night, when Mabel clad herself in her poorest garments, and put a thick black veil over her face. She first went to a little drawer which was kept locked, and which contained all her own trinkets and jewels, and took from it a small box. She removed the lid to give one last look at the pretty treasures, and in another minute was wending her way to the town.

Passing on, she encountered Treacles, who was going to the Church-meeting. He did not recognise her, and she hurried onwards. They were going in opposite directions: the deacon to use his influence to promote what was "heevangelical," although the pastor's ruin would be the result; and the wife to sell the only fragments of a more prosperous past, to bring health to the victim of "heevangelical" bigotry. But the wine and the soup were procured for Rainford, and Mabel's happiness was great as her imagination pictured her husband once more in his study, with the glow of health again upon his face.

Alas, she had only to get over one trouble to encounter another! She learned that a Church-meeting was called for that very evening, for the purpose of preparing a requisition calling on her husband to resign.

"If such be the case," she sorrowfully mused, "he may never recover. Intelligence like that might kill him."

Leaving poor Mabel to deplore her bad fortune, and to nerve herself to the trial which appeared to await her, we will return to Beeswax. This "heevangelical" deacon, for the purpose of giving proper time and effect to his evening's speech, went down to the Literary Institute, of which he was a member, in order that he might, before the Church-meeting, arrange his thoughts. He knew the feelings of all the deacons in the matter, and just what would

retaining Rainford, and paying supplies to preach for him during his illness. But Beeswax could calculate on Treacles, and one other, to support him, and for the rest he trusted that his own speech would sway such of the general audience as were in the habit of looking to their deacons for direction on occasions when they were in Church-meeting assembled. Having noted down what he intended saying in a manner perfectly satisfactory to himself, he was met by a brother deacon, John Blunt by name, who was also going to the cabal that evening. Now John Blunt being a liberal-minded man, was generally opposed to Beeswax, and anticipated a tussle with him.

"You will be at the meeting, I suppose?" said Beeswax, after saluting Blunt.

"Yes. I have an appointment to keep first, so shall be a little late, I fear," answered Blunt.

"The best thing we can do," remarked Beeswax, "is to git the present pastor to resign. We can put it on the ground of his 'ealth. Now don't you think so?"

"To tell you the truth, I don't," returned Blunt.

"Well, well, you may like the man, but his *doctrine*, about the *blood*, is not the right sort; at least not for us; and we shall never have a better opportunity of putting a more heevangelical man in his place than now."

"To speak plainly, Brother Beeswax," returned Blunt, "I am sick of this talk about doctrine. Theories of right and wrong which merely float about in the brain, but never move the heart to noble deeds, do not seem to me worth half the time we spend in fighting about them. I think a pure and holy life, such as our pastor lives, does more to draw people of sense to Christianity, than public bickerings and hagglings over 'doctrine' can ever do."

"But a moral life, unless the *blood* has imparted saving grace, won't avail for 'eaven," drawled Beeswax solemnly.

"Oh, nonsense," quickly retorted Blunt. "If you ever

ventionally orthodox, but because your life was pure. I must also say this respecting to-night's meeting, though I know the majority is in your favour, that I shall not vote with you. If Christianity teaches me anything, it teaches me to be considerate, and kind, and gentle, and to do to others as I would be done by. It therefore forbids me to pain and wound our minister at such a time as this, when he is laid by, and cannot protect himself. Why, even common fair-play and decency should teach us better than to do that. And I do not see why we are to disregard fair-play and decency, which involve morality, in order to promote various notions of orthodoxy, which are merely speculations after all. You, Brother Beeswax, desire to have in our Chapel a Minister who will echo certain views which you have formed respecting God's plans—plans which are infinite, and therefore cannot be absolutely comprehended by finite beings, or be agreed upon by them. God has given us rules for our daily life, and placed Jesus Christ as an ideal before us. Why, then, wrangle about mere abstractions? Let us do that duty which is plain, and follow that ideal; this must be right. The work is quite enough for us to do in our short time. Let us not, therefore, waste in unchristian dogmatism and rancour respecting intellectual dreams, those hours which should be spent in exhibiting the actual practical virtues of a christian life."

During this speech Beeswax had looked aghast at Blunt, and at its conclusion he remarked in a most deprecating tone, "Ah, Brother Blunt, I have feared for a long while that your views were inclining to a course which is lattitoodinhary, and it is with much pain that I 'ear you make the remarks you have jist given hexpression to."

But Blunt hardly stopped to listen to this reply of Beeswax. He knew too well that the man was not to be reasoned with. He proceeded on his way through the club-lavatory to take a swimming bath. Beeswax followed him, at a distance, as far as the lavatory, shaking his head dismally as he hung up his coat preparatory to his own more limited ablutions. Certain that he would not be called on to speak again just at present, that he was in safe seclusion and quite unobserved, Beeswax then removed his false teeth, and, after a little mechanical manipulation, placed them in their customary morocco case, and the morocco case into a coat pocket, whilst he proceeded to make his toilet. But he was vexed by Blunt's remarks, annoyed at the prospect of Blunt's opposition at the Church-meeting, pre-occupied, mentally muddled, and altogether confused. So much was he bewildered that he did not notice that the pocket into which he placed his teeth was not his own.

Blunt was a rapid man in all his movements, and finished his plunge, and left the club, before Beeswax was even ready to readjust his mouthful of teeth. When at last Beeswax wanted to do so, he could not find them. He looked high; he looked low; he looked everywhere; and when at the end of two hours of anxious investigation it became evident that further search for the teeth was hopeless, his temper could scarcely be described as "heevangelical."

Meanwhile Blunt, having attended to the business appointment to which he had referred in his early conversation with Beeswax, walked down to the Chapel. It was then late, and he expected to find the "heevangelical" deacon in the midst of his oratorical flights, but Beeswax was not at the meeting, had not been there, and no one could explain his absence. Treacles was there; and Treacles, moreover, was in a state of dismay and disappointment. All the proceedings were in total opposition to the plans and wishes of himself and Beeswax; and because he was no speaker, he was obliged to content himself with listening to those who could talk. His exasperation was great when he found too that Rainford's friends were in the majority; and the mighty speech which might have secured a different result was still unspoken. The man who was to have carried all before him was absent. One result of Beeswax's non-appearance was the passing of an unopposed resolution, by which it was agreed to provide supplies for the pulpit, at the expense of the Church, during the pastor's illness. And, to crown the matter, many persons volunteered contributions then and there towards the object.

Why was not Beeswax at the Church-meeting, to lead, according to promise, the "heevangelical" opposition to all this? Because he could not audibly articulate without teeth, and every tooth he possessed was in the morocco case, and the morocco case was lost.

Why did he not send out the town-crier to announce his loss, since his own efforts to recover the property had been unavailing? Because, owing to his vanity, he would not for the world have had any one suspect, that the gleaming ivories usually seen in his mouth were not as much a part of his natural body as original sin.

Where were the teeth? At the time in question no one knew. But it was found out some time afterwards that, in the absence of their disappointed owner, they attended the meeting as his reticent proxy, and were comfortably accommodated all the time in Mr. John Blunt's pocket.

CHAPTER XXI.

CANT USURPING THE CHURCHYARD.—DEATH OF KATIE.—A SCENE BETWEEN THE REV. TANCRED LAWSON AND THE HIGH CHURCH VICAR.

ANY one who has passed through multiform and romantic experiences in life, and who possesses widespread and beloved social connections, is aware that the sound of the postman's knock, or the sight of the postman's budget, often excites a class of emotions which cannot be made intelligible to the uninitiated. If, when the postman's budget was placed before Melville on May-day morning, anxiety was in his mind, the opening of his letters served to increase it. His first communication was a long sad one from Lorraine, detailing those personal troubles which we have already described as having overtaken him in Rome. His second epistle was from Mrs. Rose, and stated that little Katie was sinking fast, and that she had repeatedly expressed, with even more than the eagerness of childhood, her longing to see him. It was very inconvenient to Mr. Melville to go to Redborough, but, as he was a man who never permitted personal convenience to stand in the way of a mission of kindness, he promptly decided that he would gratify the child. Accordingly, he reached Redborough on the evening of the following day, having first called on Tremlin in London and conversed with him respecting little Katie, the object of their common solicitude. It was well that he did not delay; for very soon after his visit to the sweet child, her beautiful spirit, having tenanted a human form only nine years, departed for ever. It became Melville's painful duty to communicate the sad fact of her death to Tremlin, and to make all the necessary arrangements for the interment, as the poor clerk, notwithstanding his feeble health, could not get leave of absence from his office, excepting for one day, to attend the funeral.

There are some flowers in the garden which compel the admiration of all tastes ; and there are some natures in the home which become the inevitable centres of everybody's affection. Little Katie was one of these. During her brief life she unknowingly had drawn to herself the admiration and love of many hearts. When she passed away, there was in her little circle a concurrence of feeling in favour of paying every tribute of respect to her beloved memory. But the Vicar of the parish, the Rev. Cavil Bartholomew, when application was made to him to bury her, indignantly declined to officiate, on the ground that there was no proof of her having been baptized by a Clergyman of his Church.

In this dilemma, Melville remembered Rainford, and decided to ask him to come over from Chenley and conduct the funeral service. To his sincere sorrow, however, he learned that Rainford could not attend, by reason of continued illness. But it was arranged that the Rev. Tancred Lawson, a ministerial friend who was doing duty for him at the Chapel, should attend on the mournful occasion in his place. When the melancholy day arrived, Tremlin, who came down to Mrs. Rose's house, and Melville, and a group of friends who sorrowed for the loss of little Katie, all met together to perform the last offices of love. As the High Church Vicar had declined to inter the little one, it was thought well to avoid the risk of wounding his ecclesiastical susceptibilities by even uttering a public prayer in the churchyard where she was to be laid for her long sleep. There was a common outside the churchyard, and it was decided that the short obsequies should be per-

could be taken on to the grave for silent interment. The *cortège* walked thither accordingly, and the numbers were gradually increased by the loving playmates and companions of little Katie, whose tiny hands were laden with the sweetest of spring flowers, which they had gathered to place beside her when she was laid in that narrow bed, which, to their tear-dimmed eyes, seemed so lonely and so dark. The common being reached, the mourners, and these little ones, gathered around the bier, and the Rev. Mr. Lawson proceeded with the devotional exercises. They were all suddenly startled, however, by the abrupt clamorous intrusion into their midst of two boisterous personages. The one was the burly High Church Vicar himself; the other was the corpulent, irascible, wealthy Mr. Bobson, brewer, and churchwarden.

The Vicar was the first to speak. Pressing forward through the throng to the coffin, he rapped on its lid with his ponderous walking stick, and shouted out to Mr. Lawson; "I require you at once to stop these proceedings."

"On what ground?" said Mr. Lawson.

"Because the child has not been baptized," was the reply, "and as such is not entitled to christian burial."

"That may be a matter of opinion," replied Mr. Lawson, "as to which we may not agree, and the discussion of which is not compatible with this moment."

"There can be no difference of opinion," vociferated the churchwarden. "The Church has declared what is the truth of the matter."

"Excuse me, gentlemen," said Mr. Lawson, "we are engaged, as we have a right to be, in a solemn service; in a very few minutes we shall have concluded it. Will you, therefore, be courteous enough either to be silent, or to withdraw from our midst?"

"Certainly not," protested the Vicar. "We shall not shrink from the duty we have to perform. I am here to say that no evidence has been given to me that this child, who was born in original sin, and in the wrath of God, was ever, by the laver of regeneration in baptism, received into the number of the children of God."

"But we are not using the Prayer-Book of your Church," said Mr. Lawson, "and you are not responsible for our dissimilar views."

"I say I am responsible," retorted the Vicar. "As spiritual head of this parish, I object to christian burial being given to those who are denied its privileges by the Prayer-Book—those who are excommunicated, who have committed suicide, or who die unbaptized as this child did; and in whom therefore the old Adam had not been crucified and buried."

"You are giving great and unnecessary pain," said Mr. Lawson, as he beheld the tears trickling down the face of Mr. Tremlin and others, who were harrowed by any harsh reference to little Katie. "May I beg you on grounds of humanity to desist?"

"I decline to talk about vague humanity and false sentimentality, and all that kind of thing," answered the Vicar. "My parishioners must be shown that christian burial can only be performed on christian terms. If a proceeding like this is permitted, I shall have them, and all those children who are gathered here, wandering into pernicious errors. They will begin to speculate that it may be possible for a soul to be made a member of Christ, a child of God, and an inheritor of the kingdom of Heaven, even without baptism by the Church."

"Surely, sir," said Mr. Lawson, "you do not consider this is a time or place for a debate about your Prayer-Book?"

"No," rapidly responded the Vicar, "I do not; indeed I decline to discuss. I have only to assert the truth as proclaimed by the Church, and to insist on its acceptance in my parish."

"Most certainly," roared the stentorian churchwarden.

"Well, gentlemen," replied Mr. Lawson with astonishment, but with admirable self-possession, "no doubt you think you are doing your duty, but it is obvious that there must be an end to this scene. In another five minutes our service will be ended. Kindly remain silent, or leave."

"We will not take either the one course or the other," asseverated the Vicar.

"Then let me tell you," said Mr. Lawson, "that your conduct is unseemly, and also that it is a piece of usurpation and tyranny. We are in a public place, and you have no jurisdiction whatever over the green fields of God, though we admit that you have it in the churchyard."

"Once for all let me give you warning," declared the Vicar, "that I am not going to waste my time any more."

"Your attendance here is quite unnecessary," remonstrated Mr. Lawson.

"I give you fair notice," continued the Vicar, "that if you do not instantly carry the corpse after me into the churchyard, I will lock the churchyard gates, and you can take the coffin home again."

By reason of the fact that the execution of this threat would have been quite within the Vicar's legal rights, no course was open to the mourners but compliance.

In humiliation and sorrow, to which was added the irritation of undeserved and unredressed insults, they therefore raised the bier, and followed the High Church Vicar and his churchwarden through the gates to the grave. The coffin was no sooner lowered, than the churchwarden gave orders to shovel in the mould, which the rough impatient sexton did with alacrity. Only a few of the panic-stricken children had sufficient rapidity of movement, or courage, to place a few of their lovely flowers near the tomb, and these were instantly and indiscriminately mixed up with the soil and clods, which, with childish horror, they saw hurled down rudely by the grave-digger upon the eternal bed of their beloved Katie.

The Vicar and churchwarden then marched to the gates, by way of signal that the time had come when they required all persons to leave the place. Pompous and triumphant there they stood, until all the sorrowful company had passed out into the public road.

Melville intentionally stayed behind alone. He was now free to speak to these men, and their attendants, without the former risk of exciting an insulted crowd to acts of indiscretion. Pointing with his right hand to the grave, and fixing on the Vicar a look before which even that bigot quailed, he said :

> "I tell thee, churlish priest,
> A ministering angel will my sister be,
> When thou liest howling !"

CHAPTER XXII.

CANT BARKING ACCORDING TO LAW.—MR. FERRET, SMUGGLE, ATTORNEY, THREATENS MR. MELVILLE.—THE TALE OF THE TEETH CONCLUDED.—MANŒUVRES AND SUCCESS OF "HEEVANGELICAL" INTOLERANCE.—MELVILLE ATTENDS THE CHENLEY TEA-MEETING.—DR. SOUND.

ON the following morning Melville determined to go over early to Chenley, with a view of ascertaining whether, whilst attending to some other matters of his own in that neighbourhood, he could in any way be of service to Mr. Rainford. He had scarcely finished his breakfast at the Old Lion Hotel, when the waiter brought him the card of Mr. Ferrett Smuggle, and announced that the gentleman wished an interview at once. Melville ordered that he should be admitted; and immediately an undersized, brazen-faced, vulgar coxcomb, with an impertinent-looking snub nose, jerked himself into the apartment.

"You will not be surprised, sir," said he, in the best style of a bully, and in a shrill, cantankerous, grating voice, "that my client, the Rev. Cavil Bartholomew, the Vicar, has consulted me with reference to your conduct yesterday. I came here to ascertain your name, which I have done; and I am to demand a written apology for your conduct, otherwise you must favour me with the name of your solicitor, who will accept service of the legal proceedings which, in default of your apology, as aforesaid, I am instructed to institute."

"What part of my behaviour yesterday is it that you consider yourselves aggrieved by?" inquired Melville, sarcastically.

"All of it, sir; all of it," vociferated Mr. Ferrett Smuggle. "But particularly the coarse, slanderous, defamatory language used by you at the gate, on leaving the churchyard. It is in respect of that defamation that the action at law will lie, and the innuendo implied in the words you at the same time used, will supply a head for special damages at common law."

Melville laughed outright, and repeated with annoying dramatic effect the reprehensible poetical quotation which was alluded to, and with which the last chapter ends.

"Bring your action, bring your action," said he, tossing to the pettyfogging solicitor his card. "There is my address."

"Do you defy us then?" demanded the man of law, in a voice which was intended to convey an awful threat of future consequences.

"Yes," was Melville's provoking answer. "I admit your desire to tyrannize, but I defy your power to move the legal machine. At your ignorance of law I laugh, and your attempt to intimidate is ridiculous."

"I presume, sir," snarled Mr. Ferrett Smuggle, strutting towards the door, "that you do not know to whom you speak. I am chairman of the County Conservative Association, chairman of the District Church Defence Association, chairman of the Board of Guardians, and one of the Churchwardens of this place."

"Had I been called on to guess the sort of people to whom your presence would have been endurable, I should have named just such bodies as those," retorted Melville. "But you called on me as a lawyer, and your legal knowledge is evidently not sufficient to tell you that you have no case which warrants your intrusion here."

"My legal knowledge, sir," blustered Mr. Ferrett Smuggle, returning passionately into the middle of the room, "my legal knowledge won the greatest ecclesiastical case of this century, and procured me the appointment of legal adviser to his grace the Bishop. I should think even you have heard of the great 'Tombstone Case!'"—continued Mr. Smuggle, oratorically waving his hand. "The wife of one Richard Baxter, an Independent Minister, near here, died, and was buried in our churchyard, and the family, sir, had the audacity to place over the grave a tombstone, stating that deceased was the wife of the Rev. Richard Baxter, Independent Minister. We served the parties with a notice that they were to erase the word 'Reverend' from the tombstone, or else take the stone away altogether. They asked reasons. We told them no one but a Clergyman of our own Church could be legally described as Reverend. They appealed to the Bishop: he was against them. They appealed to the Dean of Arches: he was against them. And so on, sir, the appeals went from court to court; and as solicitor for the 'Anti-Churchyard Desecration Society,' I, sir, won the case, and I had the stone removed."

"Be it so, sir," replied Melville. "It is only another case of priestly intolerance and ecclesiastical assumption; and as I did not invite you here to narrate to me the triumphs of rampant despotism, I beg you will excuse my saying that I am starting out on a journey, and have no further time to waste with you in listening to the recital of legalised enormities."

The solicitor felt chagrined and baffled. He had expected to intimidate some poor relation of little Katie's. He had met a wealthy man who was more than a match for his arts. He retired, with his vanity and self-love very much wounded; and Melville, whose carriage was waiting, drove off to Chenley.

Many things, sad and ludicrous, had happened in the Rainford world since that Sunday when, as our readers will recollect, Melville listened to the sermon in the Independent Chapel.

The most funny affair of the past week had been the

deacons' meeting to investigate a charge which Deacon Beeswax preferred against Deacon Blunt of abstracting, for a party purpose, the teeth about which so much has already been said. When Blunt, at his family dinner one day, suddenly realized that one of his pockets was uncomfortably hard to sit upon, and on looking for the cause, found the lost morocco case, Beeswax's secret was virtually at an end. For Blunt's wife and children were present; saw, with much merriment, the contents of the case, and afterwards assisted Blunt in making inquiries in all directions for the owner. When the matter came to the ears of Beeswax, he saw at once that if he were ever to recover his teeth he would have to abandon his vanity. He decided to humiliate himself, and thereupon he claimed his property. But his mortification, on every ground, was intense. And he determined to bring the conduct of Mr. Blunt before the deacons, and to ask them to find him guilty of "having purloined the morocco case for the purposes of a party trick," and to "censure his levity and fraud" by a solemn resolution. But the deacons, after an exhaustive inquiry, could come to no other conclusion than that the indicted deacon was not guilty, as aforesaid; and that the morocco case had been inadvertently placed in Blunt's pocket by Beeswax himself, on that particular evening when their coats hung in proximity in the lavatory of the Literary Institute.

After disposing of this business, they made their arrangements for the annual meeting of their Church; and as it was held on the evening of the day that Melville reached Chenley, he determined to be present. It was customary to celebrate this anniversary by a tea-meeting in the schoolroom, and a public meeting afterwards, when addresses were delivered. In the absence of Mr. Rainford, it had been arranged that the chairman should be the Rev. Dr. Sound, a very popular London Minister, a native of Chenley, who was staying for a few days in the place.

On this anniversary occasion the Beeswax people were very strong. Mrs. Beeswax poured out tea at one of the tables. Her daughters superintended at another. Beeswax, in the absence of the Minister, was quite a great man at the tea-meeting, and found himself taking cups of the invigorating beverage at nearly every table. He had resolved, with the help of the lost teeth, to deliver himself of an oration that evening which should bring in some of the best sentences of his great unspoken speech. He knew that most of the people were in a state of incertitude, ready to be led by authority, and that very few had manliness enough either to stand up for, or oppose, their Pastor. The meeting was well filled, many strangers being present, who were anxious to hear the famous Dr. Sound. The doctor was a thick-set man of about fifty years of age. His hair was brown and bushy, and brushed out so as to make the head look as large as possible. His eyes, like black beads, peered slily out from their sunken sockets. He was bull-necked. His lips were coarse and sensuous, and the whole expression of the face and form suggested that had this man been bred to poverty, he would very probably have turned to prize-fighting, rat-hunting, or burglary. He seemed formed for low delights, and entirely out of place in that religious world which he had selected as the arena for earning his livelihood, and gratifying his intense ambition. Nevertheless, he was a man of natural ability, and, with this to assist him, he made a great noise in the world. It was known to many that he was thoroughly artificial, and that he never spoke from his heart. But mankind are not repelled by a first-rate actor simply by the fact of his appearing in a dull conventicle. There were always numbers of people anxious to hear Dr. Sound go through his religious part whenever he acted. He spoke in a deep, sonorous voice, and every phrase was bombastic and inflated in style. His sentences were so arranged as to require at the end a long effective pause. He laboured at grotesqueness and individuality of style, and in this he succeeded. If his hearers did not recollect what was said, they remembered very vividly the tones and style of the man who had performed. At the annual meeting he gave one of his most grandiloquent speeches. The country folk of Chenley were prepared to be delighted with the great London Preacher, and so, of course, it elicited much applause. Some of his artifices made them stare with delighted wonder: the marvellous pauses after the sentences did so; so likewise did his fixity of posture. Sometimes, when even his voice was at its loudest, he moved not, till you might have fancied him a big roaring statue, dressed in the latest fashion, inflexible in all but the maxilla.

It might have been supposed that our friend Beeswax would have felt some timidity in speaking before so great a "light." But the self-complacence of men of his type knows no bounds, and he made a speech, as he said, "by the blessing of God," with as much confidence as if in his own room, with no listeners but wife and children. He expressed his hope that matters would soon become more settled with the Church, and deplored the results of their Pastor's enforced absence. He craftily insinuated that such absences were likely to recur; and threw out for the consideration of the meeting the suggestion that the time had come when it would be advantageous to the Church that the Pastor should be asked to consider if it would not be for the spiritual advancement of the "heevangelical" cause to appoint a man in energetic health to fill the pastorate. Mr. Wobbles, Mr. Ditch, and Mr. Grundy having all spoken in favour of the adoption of some such course; Beeswax rose again, and proposed a resolution, which commenced with politely thanking Almighty God for His general goodness, and concluded with an intimation that the time had come when His servant, Mr. Rainford, should retire from Chenley Chapel.

At that moment Melville rose, fired with a desire to say what was fair and just about an absent man. In a few brief sentences he called attention to the report which the secretary had read, proving that, during the twelvemonth that Mr. Rainford had been Minister, he had added a number of members to the Church, started a Working Man's Club and Institute, a Temperance Society, a Penny Savings Bank, a Dorcas Society, and a Cottage Hospital; and had laboured indefatigably for the good of the Church. " Would it not," asked Melville, " have been more like christian courtesy and gratitude to have agreed to a resolution recognising Mr. Rainford's services, and sympathising with him in the illness which had been developed by his overwork? Prayers had been freely offered on Mr. Rainford's behalf, and the Almighty had received minute details of information, and instruction, as to the requirements of the case. But the congregation appeared to decline all personal complicity with any plans which Providence might pursue for the restoration of their afflicted Minister. There were a few simple practical things to be done in the case, which would be of more service than thousands of plausible professions of goodwill. Let them first assure Mr. Rainford of their sympathy; secondly, continue to find ministerial supplies for his pulpit until his convalescence; thirdly, supplement his slender income by a grant, which would enable him to purchase those medicines and viands which, though absolutely necessary to his recovery, were beyond the grasp of his limited means. There were plenty of people, as a great wit had observed, who were always ready to play the good Samaritan, but without the ' oil ' and ' twopence.' Were they going to imitate—"

But Melville was allowed to say no more, for, at this moment Mr. Midge Long arose. This personified crotchet was a very important, officious man in all small societies. He was tall, lean, cadaverous, with a lack-lustre grey eye, cold as his heart. If he ever enjoyed anything, which was doubtful, it was the task of expounding some petty point respecting the technical procedure of meetings. His machine-like intelligence prevented his ever embracing the central aim of any assembly at which either beneficent or national sympathies were represented. But he surpassed every one else in his familiarity with all the smaller quibbles, stratagems, and objections, which technical procedure permits to a man who desires to interpose at any stage of business proceedings. He was master of the objection preliminary, the objection with a view to hindrance, and the objection with a view to quashing. He now rose to a "point of order," and to protest that Melville had no *locus standi*, because he was neither a member nor a seatholder; and he appealed to the chairman, Dr. Sound, to decide the validity of the issue. Dr. Sound took care not to point out that the same objection was fatal to his own right to speak to the meeting; but extending his hands over the heads of his hearers, as if pronouncing a benediction, and fixing his eyes heavenwards as if reading a message on high, he thus solemnly delivered his oracular judgment:—

"The cherubic legions who glitter upon the pearly battlements of the sempiternal profundities, and perambulate the sheening acclivities and declivities of the ambrosial immortalities, are homogenated in firmamental cohesion by one word. It glares through all the centuries, and gleams in perpetual coruscation throughout all our lower mundane sovereignties, from the myriad-chambered ant\ up to that gorgeous palace where bejewelled Victoria sits serenely on her emblazoned throne—the word 'ORDER.' Our brother is now doing violence to that God-engraven word, and is waging, against its laws, anarchic battle. He cannot be further heard."

Dr. Sound was succeeded by Beeswax, who, recognising in Melville the "German philosophy" of a former Sunday morning, was quick to give the reply he considered his speech demanded. He said—

"I think, Mr. Chairman, that you and this meeting are capable and ready to answer for our hacting as Christians, and for the merit and horthodoxy of our religion. We do not need to be reminded of our dooty: we do it as being accepted in The Beloved. And I am sure some of our worthy heevangelical friends 'ere assembled are as safe for 'eaven as any one can be. We know who is our sin hoffering.

> 'We at His footstool fall,
> Unite with all His blood-washed throng,
> And crown Him Lord of hall.'

We shall do our dooty 'ere to-night without being instructed by a stranger, and our dooty is to study the good of the Church militant. I therefore agin bring before your consideration the resolution which I proposed, and which has already been seconded by Mr. Wobbles."

Dr. Sound having put the resolution to the assembly, to the delight of Beeswax's heart, it was adopted and carried; and the meeting, having thus settled Rainford's fate, broke up, after they had lustily sung, "Praise God from whom all blessings flow."

CHAPTER XXIII.

Cant the Promoter of a Spurious Matrimony, the Destroyer of Modesty, and the Debaser of Woman.—Mrs. Hardcastle and Miss Isabel Landor.

MRS. HARDCASTLE believed that no christian mother performed her duty in life who failed in getting her daughters well married. Her interpretation of the words "well married," was a selfishly limited one. In her view, the comfort and well-being of a husband were matters as unimportant as his character. When she said daughters should be "well married," she merely meant that they should be married early in life, and that the most prosperous possible man should be secured by some means or other. She made extravagant professions of virtue, and if any heathen had hinted to her that a pure girl ought not to be legally tied for life to a bad man, simply because he possessed wealth, she would have raised her holy eyes to Heaven and declared, that it was because the man was so bad that he ought to be married to a good girl, that he might thereby be brought into "a saving knowledge of the truth." Her desire to bring the man into the "gospel fold" by means of matrimony was, however, always very much quickened when the man was found to be wealthy or distinguished. If he were good and poor, or bad and poor, no idea about getting him into the "companionship of the saints," by matrimony, or otherwise, ever stirred her cunning soul. In regard to her own daughters she practised exactly what she preached, and she indoctrinated them with her matrimonial creed before they had left off short frocks and pinafores. "Dear

Victoria" had made a good match. An equally good one was now needed for Anastatia. Every permissible and every possible effort had been made to entangle Mr. Melville into an alliance. But he was too sensible for flattery, and too shrewd for Cant and fraud. When the marriage conspiracy against him became confessedly a failure, Mrs. Hardcastle, like a wise strategist, led the spousal manœuvres, as she had often done, into another camp. The well-practised Anastatia peformed her evolutionary tactics with consummate skill. The new expedition was directed against Adolphus Bumpus, Esquire; and after desperate sapping, mining, and ambuscading, the citadel of that gentleman's heart was seized, and retained by Anastatia as proud conqueror.

Mrs. Hardcastle felt, after the victory, that her duty as a christian mother was done: but she was now fidgeting about her duty as christian aunt. The time had come when she could bestir herself in the hymeneal interests of Isabel without prejudice to her own daughters, and she considered she ought to take some decided action. Isabel had announced her decision not to make her permanent home at the Hardcastles'. She had arranged to live in a house of her own, so as to be surrounded by society which would be morally and intellectually congenial to her nature, and be free to engage in many philanthropic and social works which could not flourish in the vitiated atmosphere of Cant. Mrs. Hardcastle and family on all grounds, and especially on financial ones, strongly objected to losing the beautiful heiress. For a young lady to live alone seemed to Mrs. Hardcastle the height of impropriety; and to prevent such an anomaly she persisted with her nuptial schemes and advice. On the occasion when she had to communicate to Isabel the intelligence of Anastatia's betrothment, she determined to take an opportunity of thoroughly expounding her views on connubial politics.

"I wish, Isabel," she said—when she made her announcement to her niece of Anastatia's engagement to Mr. Bumpus—"I wish that you, too, had a prospect of a suitable marriage. It is really quite time that you should direct your thoughts to getting properly settled."

"You see, aunt, our views of settlement are different," was the reply. "I do not consider that marriage ought to be the great end and aim of a woman's existence."

"And pray, my dear," asked Mrs. Hardcastle, "why should you disagree with every one else? Society has certain rules, and it cannot be right for you to defy them."

"Society's rules are not binding on my conscience, aunt," replied Isabel. "They are merely the organized consent of men and women, more or less depraved, to do, or to abstain from doing, certain conventional things. They are transient fashions. They are ever changing like summer clouds."

"But my dear," remarked the aunt, "every girl should be married: it is really her duty; and with a little tact on her own part, and skill on the part of friends, most girls can get themselves married. Look at the Boodle girls, and the Slappertons, and the Gosjawks at Falcon Small's. There is no denying that some of them are even ugly, but they have all been got off, every one of them. And how was it done? Why they had been properly taught on these matters, and there was proper management amongst the relations and friends at Falcon Small's—proper management."

"It seems so hard to make you understand," said Isabel, her beautiful face suffused with the blushes of indignation "that conversation of this kind is revolting to my sense of delicacy."

"Well, Isabel," pursued the aunt, "as you have no mother, I feel I have a duty to perform in her place. By a proper diligence on their part and mine, both your cousins have been arranged for, and I believe it is only your own fault that keeps you from being equally successful."

"Cannot you see, aunt," returned Isabel, "that I am not aiming in that direction at all? I do not wish to pain any one, but I will frankly say that this idea of entrapping a husband, which is so shamelessly professed in your circle, is one which ought to be scouted by every virtuous maiden."

"Ah, my dear," said Mrs. Hardcastle in very patronizing tones, "your religious views are peculiar, very peculiar. It is not a question of entrapping. Holy matrimony is an estate specially blessed by God. Only read the Church of England marriage service, and you will see that your spiritualistic and mystical views are far beyond the Prayer-Book. We must take common sense and religious views of these matters."

"Permit me to say, aunt," answered Isabel, "that I interfere with no one's views; but in a matter concerning my own destiny I have a right to an opinion. My course in life is clear. I intend to travel, for artistic and scientific purposes, so as to continue my education. Then, when I settle down in my London home, I shall surround myself with the society of the accomplished, the true, and the good, and such persons as can enjoy the large library which I shall collect. I shall devote the chief of my income to assisting the poor and suffering; and a large portion of my time to active personal benevolence, in directions where I shall be untrammeled by sects or factions, committees or philanthropymongers. Socially, my great purpose in life will be to make all people better, and happier, who come within the circle of my influence: intellectually, it will be to understand more and more about this marvellous world and its pressing riddles. I may, or may not, be married, but marriage will be only an incident and not the great aim and end of existence."

"Well," remonstrated Mrs. Hardcastle, "all I can say, Isabel, is that you seem to me to propose to yourself a course which is not only unmaidenly and forward, but quite barefaced. I never heard of anybody at Falcon Small's who would entertain anything so outrageous."

"I can quite believe that," answered Isabel; "and also that you would think it more maidenly for me to angle for a husband, or to live entirely for the admiration of men."

"I do not put it in that way," explained Mrs. Hardcastle.

"No," said Isabel, "but that is what it comes to."

"At any rate, Isabel," returned her aunt, "I am quite shocked. Every girl but you seems to think marriage the object of life."

"And that to me," exclaimed Isabel, "appears the great fault of the present female generation. They make marriage the beginning and end of life, instead of mere incident which may or may not take place. On all sides one sees and hears this false notion of marriage urged and upheld. The popular novels do their best to create, and sustain, wretched matrimonial suggestions, which taint a woman's atmosphere soon after she has entered her teens. It is a disgrace to those who read, and disgusting to those who long for a healthier class of literature, that almost every successful novel should centre the interest of its plot on a girl's getting married. In most instances the marriage being accomplished the grand object is achieved, and the book ends. One hardly wonders at the class of girls which society abounds with, nor at their useless frivolous lives, when one sees how radically wrong is the instruction which they receive on this question of marriage."

"And pray," inquired Mrs. Hardcastle, "what is there which is so wrong in the way our girls are taught to prepare for the conjugal state?"

"This is wrong to begin with," replied Isabel: "you teach them—not to have some grand purpose in life, but to attach themselves to a husband who will keep them. Beyond that, they are not to look. As a rule, you do not even qualify a girl to be of any use in her husband's household. How many a lackadaisical worthless woman you may see dragging down to poverty, and a life of sorrow, the good-natured fellow who, as a mere boy, agreed to marry her. Did you teach her how to be useful in a married life or in any other sphere? No: you only taught her how to secure a person who should be legally required to maintain her."

"Is it possible, Isabel," exclaimed Mrs. Hardcastle, "you have so far forgotten what Scripture says—that for this purpose we are to leave father and mother?"

"Oh my dear aunt," responded Isabel, "what can be more unsatisfactory than misapplied scraps of Scripture! What horrible things have been made to appear good by a jargon of sacred words detached from their sense, and made to perform foreign service."

"It is not misquoting," retorted Mrs. Hardcastle, "to say that Scripture records much in favour of the holy marriage state, and nothing whatever commendatory of the state of an old maid. I should have thought, Isabel, that you would have wished to have been something better than an old maid all your days. However—"

"The term is not at all shocking to me, aunt, I assure you," replied Isabel. "Only children are frightened by tales of nursery bogies. Only frivolous persons should shrink at the horrors of that phantom which conventional opprobium calls up at the mention of old maids. The facts are simply these: unmarried women are divided into two classes, those who tried to marry and failed, and those who were superior to such a contemptible proceeding. Of course, the first class have reason to be sour and sullen, because their one aim in life has failed. But the other class, of whom alone I shall speak, includes the best specimen of brilliant, unselfish, noble womanhood. To whom does the aged parent turn for help in his declining days? Why, to the daughter who has not married. To whom do the married brothers go when in sickness they sorely want a friend? Why, to the sister who has not married. To whom does the married sister appeal for assistance when the cares of her little ones and household are a heavy burden to her? Why, to the sister who has not married. Who are the generous, vigilant, brave nurses, who, unfettered by home ties and domestic occupations, are always ready to leave anything at the call of duty and distress, and, defying disease and death, place themselves in hospitals and sick rooms to minister to all who need their aid? Why, for the most part, they are the unmarried women of the world."

"You may be as romantic as you like, my dear," returned Mrs. Hardcastle, "but I never myself knew anything good of old maids, and I say a woman cannot occupy her proper sphere unless she does marry—unless she does marry."

"And I," rejoined Isabel, "maintain, on the contrary, that marriage frequently prevents a woman from ever attaining her proper sphere. From the days of Hypatia to those of Joan of Arc, and from that period to the time of Florence Nightingale, there can be found innumerable instances of heroic women, who fulfilled their destiny only because they were free."

"Again, I must say," retorted Mrs. Hardcastle, "that I am shocked, truly shocked at such unchristian talk. Four times I have heard Falcon Small preach special sermons on different royal marriages, and they led naturally to much conversation about marriage throughout his congregation; but I certainly never heard any young lady in our circle indulge in anything so objectionable before."

"You must permit me, aunt, to remind you," replied Isabel, "that however objectionable this enforced explanation of my views may be to you, it cannot be more so than those sentimental sermons of Falcon Small's were to me; for I considered them, when analysed, coarse and indelicate. Besides, they were a mere pandering to the fashion of the hour. A court scheme, whereby two royal persons are married, and are to be maintained by legalized extortion from the taxes of unconsenting payers, is not an exploit over which a teacher of morals is called on to rejoice."

"I never discuss politics, Isabel," was the answer. "They are too deep for women. I can only regret that, by your unwomanly conduct, you seem quite determined to run in opposition to all proper opinions. I never expected to have to see a relation of mine left out in the cold as an old maid,—never."

"Pray do not agitate yourself, aunt, about that," said Isabel. "There are worse sights. The spectacle of two persons, between whom there is no moral or intellectual affinity, chained together for forty or fifty years as husband and wife, is far more terrible. So, also, are the sad and disappointed faces of those persons who have united themselves for life, in ignorance, or in violation of, the spiritual and temperamental laws on which alone permanent companionship can be based. You must not confine your gaze merely to the half-hour's wedding ceremony. Look beyond the faded orange-blossoms. Think of that great despairing multitude of haggard, wan, worn, weary men and women, who have to expiate, by a life of hidden sorrow, or open wretchedness, the transient error which they made when, as boys and girls, or through caprice, ignorance, or impulsiveness, they permitted some Priest like Falcon Small to tie them to incompatible associates."

"Why, Isabel," exclaimed Mrs. Hardcastle, "you surely know that if ever there is an unhappy marriage, people can go to the Divorce Court."

"Yes, I know there is a Divorce Court," replied Isabel. "But those who suffer most, the gentle, the tender, the sensitive, and the refined, endure a kind of agony which Acts of Parliament cannot recite, and which would be incomprehensible to the intellect of a court, which counts the number, and observes the colour of, wounds and bruises, and assumes as an axiom that all cruelty expresses itself in overt acts."

"Well, but if anything is very bad, you know," remonstrated Mrs. Hardcastle, "people can obtain a divorce. Not that I think it right. For the Scripture says that 'those whom God has joined no man should put asunder.'"

"I think," replied Isabel, "the case stands thus: man is always trying to join together those whom God has put asunder. Society is perpetually at work contriving irreconcilable life-unions. Men and women whom God has inexorably divided, by temperament, by family peculiarities, by inherited antipathies, by taste, by conformation, by intellectual and moral proclivities, by personal character, by moods, and by a hundred other things, and in a hundred other ways, society is constantly joining. This enterprise of society is disgraceful; and the Priests, and legislators, who give legal, and permanent effect, to the resulting arrangements, assume an authority which ethics and Nature alike deny."

"Well, Isabel," said Mrs. Hardcastle with considerable irritability, "I see it is no use my arguing with you. I have done my duty as a Christian in advising you for your good. I can do nothing more for you but pray that God may see fit to break down the atheistical stubbornness which seems to be depraving your heart."

CHAPTER XXIV.

CANT, FASHION, AND FRIVOLITY.—MR. ADOLPHUS BUMPUS.—
CURRENT REASONS FOR CHURCHMANSHIP.

IT was a bright and frosty Saturday afternoon, and two young men sauntered down Pall Mall. Their dress was of the latest style. Their hair was so closely clipped that their resemblance, about the head, to the little jail boy, who, hatless and shoeless, offered them a " box o' lights," was quite striking. They wore light kid gloves and dazzling coloured ties ; each brandished his cane, and puffed his cigar. The faces of both lacked intelligence, but their moustaches were properly cut and curled, and their clothes fitted exceedingly well. The set of persons by whom they were admired demanded nothing further in the way of personal excellence. They looked first of all at dress, then at style, and lastly at the size and quality of the moustache. Those who judge of men's characters through their faces, and appreciate breadth of brow and manliness of feature, might have passed by our adolescent friends with a look of contempt. But these young men were quite sharp enough to take care of themselves. They had sufficient sagacity to drive a bargain. They knew how to lay out their money so as to buy more macassar oil, and more lavender water, and more well-fitting clothes, and jewellery, and boots, and hats, and everything,—except the seeing eye to discern their own triviality and utter uselessness in the world, the poverty of their souls, and the ignorant folly of their lives.

" So, old fellow, I hear you are going to be married !' exclaimed the junior, and more insipid-looking, of these delightful youths.

"Ha, ha," laughed the other, with a swing of his dandy cane; "every one, I declare, is posted up on this subject. Wherever I go it is mentioned; till really, my dear fellow, the public seem to know more of my affairs than I do myself. For all that, you are rightly informed. I am caught."

The youngling who thus spoke was Adolphus Bumpus, Esq., to whom reference was made in the last chapter, wherein his future mother-in-law discoursed of matrimony to her niece Isabel.

"Who is the fortunate girl? Do I know her?"

"Haw, I don't know. She is a daughter of old Hardcastle. Rich fellow. Only two girls. Two sons abroad."

"What! old Hardcastle of Gutter Lane? Why, he's a rank Dissenter."

"Ye-es. But I don't marry him, you know. I shall soon make Anastatia leave off all that sort of thing. And, for the matter of that, the old folks need have nothing to do with us."

"But it's a pity, Adolphus. A girl is sure to keep up some of the old fandangle of her mother, you know."

"Trust Anastatia to do that. She likes the correct thing too well. I have bargained, of course, that the wedding is to take place at Church, and before a month has elapsed I will have her going with me to St. Saviour's."

"Or you with her?"

"Tush! Reginald. You will make me swear. It is years since I went within five yards of a Dissenting Conventicle. Oh no, I trust I know myself too well for that. Awfully low lot, those Dissenters."

Bumpus seemed to forget for the moment that he was going to marry one. But he quickly remembered himself.

"Anastatia is no Dissenter at heart, you know: she prefers Church. And, my dear fellow, her sister married Lord Everton, a great swell, and regular Tory. So, by Jove, I can marry Anastatia, I think. It will do well enough to introduce one's sister-in-law, Lady Victoria Everton, to one's friends; though, of course, I wish the family were Church people."

" Hardcastle has a seat at Broadcray, has he not ? "

"Yes, I shall get a nice lot of shooting down there."

" Hope you'll introduce me, old fellow."

"Oh, yes. Any time you like. By the way, you are ready to help at Pottledown election ? "

And the answer being in the affirmative, the two politicians decided that nothing but high Tory principles could save the country. They extolled the electoral league which exists between the parsons and the publicans; and exulted in the fact that when the beer barrel unites with the state-paid pulpits the parasites of the court are sure to succeed in their political adventures. They decided that a House of Commons had no business to control the crown: that its members ought merely to attend to the details of routine business; and always register the decrees of the sovereign, and levy taxes when required by the court to do so. They pronounced in favour of the Divine right of kings; that taxation without political representation was quite fair; that India and other lands, over which England wielded the sword, and whence she extorts money, ought to be "grateful for being governed by us at all," and ought never to be allowed to raise a voice of protest. They hoped to see the time when the plan pursued in India, of suppressing newspapers which complain of the tyranny of the government, or write disparagingly of high officials, would be adopted in England. It was tacitly understood between them, that the world was made for princes, dukes, earls, and aristocracy generally; and that the only duty of citizenship consisted in upholding the pretensions of such, and stamping out of society the men who preach the gospel of human rights. Having decided that, in furtherance of their principles, at the approaching election they would use all their efforts to get Sir Nicol Giltspur elected as member of Parliament for Pottledown where he was now a candidate, they began their farewell.

"Alas, the best of friends must part," said Reginald, as they came to a cross road. "I am off to the skating rink; and you, Adolphus, ah, well, Cupid has charms for you, I'll be bound."

"Well, yes, I shall give Anastatia a look up, and make her promise to accompany me to Church to-morrow. No more Conventicles for her. Ta, ta, till we meet again."

So saying, Adolphus hailed a hansom, and in about ten minutes was whirled to the abode of his lady-love. Anastatia was expecting him, and duly adorned for the occasion. He was to be presented to-day to Lord and Lady Everton; and her ladyship, who considered that the circumstance was a very important one in Bumpus's life, looked very stately and grand. Lord Everton was almost lost behind Lady Everton's tremendous and lengthy folds of silk, and with a consciousness of his own nothingness had to be brought out into proper importance by successive looks and gestures from his wife, who for the moment, and for the moment only, would wish him to remember his position. Lady Victoria's effect on Bumpus quite answered her highest expectations. To be in the company of people of title had always an elevating effect on the spirits of Adolphus. "A very fine woman," was his reflection, as, with glass in his eye, he surveyed the lady Victoria.

Lady Everton patronized Bumpus immensely. He was decidedly beneath HER, though very passable. Mr. Bumpus, in his turn, made a good imitation of a born aristocrat, and impressed ignorant Mr. Hardcastle by his "style."

"I have been persuading Anastatia to come to Church with me to-morrow, Mr. Hardcastle," said Mr. Bumpus. "You know we are all Church people in our family. My father is very High Church, oh, *very high* indeed. In fact we are all High Church, very high."

Bumpus emphasised "*very high*," as if the words referred

to some honourable personal distinction enjoyed by his relatives,—an impression which many who use those words seem anxious to convey.

"Have you ever heard Falcon Small?" was Mr. Hardcastle's answer. "He equals your Churchmen."

"Oh, no; I have never been in a Dissenting place, Mr. Hardcastle, and hardly expect I ever shall."

"Well, you come with us, and hear him to-morrow," said Mr. Hardcastle.

"Haw, no. I would rather not, thanks. Church is my taste: always will be, I think."

"What are your reasons for preferring the Church?" asked Victoria in her most chilling tones. As Lady Everton, amongst the Dissenters she was considered a very important personage, and all Falcon Small's attendants were willing to offer her any amount of flattery and homage. But, amongst the numerous titled people of West-end Churches, Lady Everton would play a very small part. Therefore, it was not likely that Victoria would become converted to the Church of England.

Mr. Bumpus, thus requested to substantiate his preference for the Church of England, returned: "Oh, it's the right thing, of course. True form of worship, and upheld by the state. Besides, when we consider that it has descended from the Apostles, we can hardly question its truth as a Church, and all that sort of thing, you know, haw."

"Then you believe in the apostolical succession of the Bishops, Adolphus," said Anastatia.

"Oh, certainly. That can be plainly traced back, you know. And, haw, we don't want much more than that, haw."

"Do you think the Apostles wore vestments as gorgeous as your High Church Clergymen, and waved incense, and burned so many candles?" asked the Lady Victoria.

"Well, that we cannot say," returned Bumpus. "But, haw, considering its antiquity, we are bound to respect the forms and ceremonies it enjoins, and all that sort of thing, you know. Besides, Lady Everton, it is hardly likely that so enlightened a community as the Archbishops and Bishops of the Church of England can be in the wrong, haw."

"You think their elevation to office by the state, is a guarantee for the truth of their doctrines and practice, do you, Mr. Bumpus?" inquired Lady Victoria.

"Well, yes, partly," returned Adolphus. "But they are all remarkable men, you know, and all that sort of thing, you know, haw."

"They are not superior to the Ministers of *our* Churches," said Mr. Hardcastle. "Look at Prodgers, Falcon Small, Sound, Gudgeon; and among the Americans there are Dalmage and Screecher."

"Haw, I haven't the pleasure," said Bumpus, as he stuck his glass in his eye, and stared at Hardcastle, who glowed with pride at the names he had enumerated. "I," continued Bumpus, "am so thoroughly imbued with the spirit of the Church, and all that sort of thing; and I think Lord Everton agrees with me, does he not, Lady Everton?"

His lordship had essayed to speak once or twice, but his wife had shot repressive glances at him, till his desire left him. He made bold, now his name was brought in, to remark, "Oh, yes, I'm—thorough Churchman,—been all—life, you know. But Lady Everton prefers—"

"Lord Everton believes sufficiently in my judgment to know I shall not mislead him in his religion," interrupted her ladyship. "And he considers it a privilege to listen to such a man as Mr. Small, I know."

Bumpus was hardly sure that his lordship acquiesced in this statement. But Lord Everton said nothing, and Bumpus murmured something about "the Established Church being the only thing in the shape of religion which was guaranteed as 'correct.'"

Anastatia thought it wise to end the conversation by opening the piano and rattling off a brilliant piece of music.

"A pity your father is such a Dissenter," said Bumpus aside to Anastatia, later in the evening. "Not at all the proper class of thing, you know. He and I shan't agree, I fear."

"Well, papa is rather old-fashioned in his views, I must allow, Adolphus; but I begin to see with you about the Church. Your arguments were very cleverly put, and quite past resistance."

"Yes, I put it well, didn't I? I believe my convictions are very sound. I speak from my judgment, and all that sort of thing, you know. Haw, all the best people go to Church."

"Yes," returned Anastatia reflectively, "I shall decidedly go with you to St. Saviour's to-morrow."

"Pity Lord Everton won't come too. His family are old Tories, you know, and all that sort of thing. He is a Churchman, is he not? Haw."

"Oh, yes; he went nowhere but to Church before he was married."

"Lady Everton's a fine woman. Shame for her to be a Dissenter and all that sort of thing, you know," remarked Bumpus.

Anastatia began to think so too, and heartily wished that his lordship had led his wife, instead of his wife having led him.

"Because, you know, Victoria," said Anastatia to her when Bumpus had gone, "it certainly is the proper sort of thing to go to Church."

"I am above that, my dear, as Lady Everton," returned Victoria loftily.

CHAPTER XXV.

CANT, CONFESSIONAL, AND RITUAL.—REV. DEMETRIUS MURIEL, THE HIGH CHURCH RECTOR.—THE ALMIGHTY "SHE."

ON the following Sunday, according to arrangement, Miss Anastatia Hardcastle accompanied Mr. Bumpus to St. Saviour's Church, Jasper Street. This large red brick edifice, with its schools, class-rooms, and all the appurtenances belonging to an important religious organization, occupied an imposing site. The interior of the Church consisted of a lofty nave, side aisles, and a large chancel. The altar was approached by an ascent of several steps, and was a gorgeous object, with a large brass crucifix, and decorated with splendid flowers. Six candles stood above, and six at the foot, of the cross, and on each side of the altar was a sculptured figure of a saint bearing a cross and crowned with wreaths of real flowers.

St. Saviour's was supported by what was considered an aristocratic congregation. Our old acquaintance Sir Nicol Giltspur, at this time the Lord Mayor, was an energetic friend of the cause. The Church was crowded. The female portion of the congregation was brilliantly attired, and Anastatia observed some good toilets to imitate. Most of the ladies wore large crucifixes, and kept up a moderate appearance of reverential attention. But a discerning eye could perceive that worship was acted, not felt. The anxiety was not about sin, but about the most effective and graceful postures and attitudes. This, of course, was more apparent in the ladies, but the men showed it to a great degree. The Rector himself, the Rev. Demetrius Muriel, was an admirable example for them, being a master of genuflexion and attitudinization. He was estimated highly by his congregation generally, but the ladies, to use their own expression, "really idolized him." They considered his face a perfect study. They said it was so pure, "so angelic in expression, so melancholy, and yet so earnest." They thought that, when he was kneeling before the altar, he would have served as a model from which an artist might have painted a saint. It must be admitted that Muriel really possessed very fine eyes, which he well knew how to use; but, in other respects, he could lay only a slender claim to be adjudged handsome. He had cultivated, for official purposes, an habitually sad expression, which well became him as the High Priest of St. Saviour's. His voice was mellifluous and clear. As a Performing Ecclesiastic he "made up well," and carried off his part to perfection. When he was not performing, and his face was in repose, an impartial observer could easily detect that he was just as shrewd, as sleek, and as sly, as ordinary Priests; and in his peculiar line, and by his own peculiar methods, he was quite as competent to assert, and enforce, his personal interests as any of the schemers in London city. The light of coloured Church windows, and the judicious tints of episcopal decoration, for which places like St. Saviour's are conspicuous, are very effective in showing off to advantage a man of this sort. For, such an one understands how to utilize them, and all other accessories, whether of tailoring, millinery, or bijoutry, so as to display himself to the best scenic advantage. Such a man, too, always knows how to produce great effects by public ceremonies.

Just before the service commenced, an acolyte, in scarlet cassock, came and lighted the candles on the altar, bowing low to the figure on the cross every time he passed it. The procession from the vestry to the choir was headed by a youth carrying incense, while on each side of him a boy in scarlet cassock and white surplice held a lighted candle. Mr. Muriel's two Curates, clad in eucharistic garments, came next, and lastly came Mr. Muriel himself, who wore a yoke on his chasuble, with the maniple and alb, and a magnificent stole. All the procession paused at the altar to bow before taking their places in the choir. The ritual was of the most advanced type throughout. At the communion table the Priests, the greater part of the time, turned their backs to the people. The Gospel for the day was read from a book which was held before the Priest with much formality by an acolyte, having a boy with a lighted candle on each side of him, while the whole group was enveloped in clouds of incense. At the time of consecrating the elements a hand-bell was rung; and, throughout, the most profound adoration was paid to the elements.

The Rector having ascended the pulpit crossed himself in the name of the Father, and the Son, and the Holy Ghost, and then commenced his sermon. From the Epistle to the Romans he selected for his text the words, " Every one of us shall give an account of himself to God." Specifying the things as to which God would require an account, he said it would be with regard to man's conduct respecting— first, Baptism ; second, Confirmation ; third, the Eucharist ; fourth, Confession ; fifth, Absolution by the Church. He extolled perpetually the infallible teaching of the Church ; by which, of course, he meant that section of it which is established by Act of Parliament. This section, too, he always described as " *She.*" " She " says this, and " She " says that ; " She " covenants for this, and " She " covenants for that, were descriptive assertions constantly on his lips. He said no more about the holy and distinctive teachings of *Him*, whose minister he professed to be, than he did about his reasons for considering the gender of his Church to be feminine. His discourse was simply a series of assertions respecting the dogmas and requirements of this wondrous " She." But he grew positively rapturous when he had to speak of what " She " had to say on the subject of the Confessional. He of Nazareth, was ignored on this point, because "She," by Act of Parliament established, had uttered her dictum. "Oh," exclaimed the Rector in his most tender tones, "what a delightful duty is it which 'She' imposes on you when 'She' tells you that you are to confess to her Priests. What a privilege, too, is the opportunity which 'She' affords you of systematically unveiling your hearts and their everyday secrets to '*Her*' priests, who are willing to lead you. When, through 'Her' sacraments, we enter paradise;—when we look with dazzled gaze on our God and His holy Mother;—when, through the mortifications of the flesh, through opposition, persecution, and much sorrow, we have reached that heavenly land, bright with the presence of saints and martyrs;—when, I say, you throw your crowns at the feet of the blessed Jesus and His holy Mother, then you will look back with delight on the efforts which you made on earth to comply with the requirements of the Church, and on the bravery with which you mastered your confidence and personal pride, and went regularly to 'Her' priests, confessing fully the most minute and secret affairs of your daily lives." At the conclusion of the sermon a hymn to the Virgin was sung, and after the benediction,—pronounced by the Rector, who previously made the sign of the cross in the air,—the congregation dispersed.

On leaving the Church, Anastatia was accosted by Sir Nicol Giltspur. She was much gratified to find that he was accompanied by Mr. Melville, because an opportunity was thus unexpectedly given her of proving to that gentleman, by the presence of Mr. Adolphus Bumpus, that all men had not been so indifferent to her charms as he had been. Sir Nicol offered the party seats in his carriage, which Anastatia, in particular, was willing to accept—first, because it was a most gaudy equipage; and secondly, because a storm of rain had set in.

"Well," said Sir Nicol, as they drove off, "and what do you think of our Rector, Miss Anastatia?"

"Oh, he is charming," was the reply; "so handsome, so winning. And the service, how beautiful! And what a lovely Church! Adolphus told me of the fascinations of St. Saviour's, but I was not prepared for anything half so divine."

"Ah," rejoined the much-pleased Bumpus, "I never overstate a thing. I knew that a person of taste must admire St. Saviour's. And the ritual is apostolic, and all that sort of thing, you know. Hope you liked it," said he, turning to Melville.

"I hesitate to express an opinion which will give unnecessary offence to you all," was Melville's reply.

"Oh, we do not mind," exclaimed Sir Nicol. "We of St. Saviour's are quite proof against criticism. What is your indictment?"

"The sermon," answered Melville, "seemed to me 'much ado about nothing.' The Preacher did not grasp the essentials of morality."

"Why," said Bumpus, adjusting his eye-glass, with a severe look, "I myself heard him mention Baptism, Confirmation, the Holy Eucharist, Confession, Absolution, and all that sort of thing, you know."

"Yes,' replied Melville, "he mentioned them all, and quite seriously, as actually being the momentous matters about which the great God of worlds requires His creatures to busy themselves."

"Pray, what are they then?" inquired Sir Nicol.

"In the sense in which he referred to them, they are mostly details of Church machinery, to which, for exhibition purposes, Priests have often given fictitious importance. They are technical terms understood in different senses by conflicting sects, and used for ever-varying objects by ever-changing ecclesiastical factions."

"Their meaning," protested Bumpus, "is decided by law, and all that sort of thing, you know."

"Yes, I am aware," returned Melville, "that now and

then an appeal is made to some aged lawyers, and other unspiritual, or spiritual, old gentlemen in the House of Lords, or Privy Council, respecting the sense in which these phrases are to be understood in state-paid Churches; and they settle the application in this way, or that way, according to the strength of political, or other parties. And the various factions in the Church, either accept the ruling, or rebel against it, according to the exigencies of the hour, or their particular locality."

"But do you attach no importance to these dogmas of the Church, Mr. Melville?" asked Anastatia on behalf of indignant Adolphus.

"I do not say," replied Melville, "that they are absolutely insignificant and trivial. That would be nearly as inaccurate as saying that they are often true. I admit that within certain little limits, and for certain very exceptional sectarian purposes, some of the dogmas we heard to-day may possibly be of temporary service, where religiosity is feeble and needs a crutch; but to affirm them as the whole truth of God seems to me very blasphemous."

"I never heard Clergymen and Bishops charged with blasphemy before," exclaimed Bumpus. "Successors of the Apostles too."

"Do you not think that the gullibility of congregations explains the fact that you have not?" inquired Melville. "People accept priestly assertions on trust. Hence crude nonsense, and revolting barbarity, pass unchallenged amongst us for religious truth. I often hear the Priests of all sects ascribing to God, as His most holy attributes, cruelty so abominable, and meanness so despicable, as would, if they were proved against any gentleman of my acquaintance, disgust me with, and sever me from, him for ever. And, what sort of a God was He of whom your Rector spoke to-day? A God of trifles. A great Master of small ceremonies. A punctilious Despot, spending eternity in watching that His liliputians get themselves baptized, confirmed, and christened, with regularity and circumspection."

"But saving ordinances surely are to be attended to," expostulated Sir Nicol, "and the Almighty will require an account as to our performance of them."

"Depend upon it," replied Melville, "you lay too much stress on all these inventions of your Priesthood. Which of the Apostles would consider St. Saviour's to be a Church consecrated to the simple faith which was taught by his Master? What has your ritual in common with the worship of The Twelve humble men of whom your enthroned and wealthy Bishops affect to be the successors?"

"But do you not think, Mr. Melville," interposed Anastatia, "that in our times it is most important that the Church services should be conducted with striking effect?"

"I cannot think it really important to the cause of truth," answered Melville. "It seems to me that we fail to appreciate the solemnities of life, when our Church systems arrange for Clergymen what vestments they shall wear; what position or attitude they shall assume at this or that stage of the service; whether the cope or the chasuble should be worn in the administration of the sacrament; to what height they may elevate the paten; when and where genuflexion may take place; whether, and with what fervency, or frequency, the Prayer-Book may be kissed, and matters of that kind. The conscience of humanity must ever stand aloof from it all."

"Pray," inquired Bumpus, who, having now recovered himself, was determined to pose Melville outright: "pray, since you think our Rector wrong, let us know what you suppose God *will* require an account of."

"Willingly," responded Melville. "I pass at once away from such details as your Rector insisted on, and from such matters as lawn sleeves, hats, aprons, or ecclesiastical tailoring and millinery, bishops' mitres, crucifixes, baptismal

less to be weighed in the scales of even common morality. The paramount duty of man is contained in these words, 'Do justice, love mercy, and walk humbly before God.' If preachers would proclaim, and congregations would recognise that duty, it is true we should not hear so much about 'our Church,' and what '*She*' ordains, but we should soon see an improvement in public and private morals. We should have fewer commercial swindles, and no unprovoked aggressive wars, like those fiendish ones which fashionable society now applauds. It is time that we heard less of what '*She*' has to say, and more of the teachings of Him whose right alone it is to rule."

CHAPTER XXVI

Cant and Inquisitorial Effrontery.—The Soppet and Larby Grand Revivalistic Exhibition Explained.—The Story of Dandy Filch.

ONE good point in Sir Nicol Giltspur's character was his unwillingness to take offence. Within less than a month of the discussion in the last chapter, Melville received a letter from him bespeaking assistance on behalf of a person deserving his charity. Melville's liberality, and active benevolence, were unbounded, and he at once replied, fixing a day and hour when he would receive Sir Nicol's *protégé* at his town residence in Park Lane. He intimated the appointment to his footman, and gave instructions that the gentleman introduced by Sir Nicol, when he arrived, was to take precedence of all other visitors, and be ushered into the library without delay.

At the appointed time the door opened, and the servant introduced a melodramatic young man, with a pale dissipated, pimply complexion, and a self-satisfied face. He was dressed extravagantly and whimsically, and his perfumed hair was thrown back from a low brow. His manner was affected, and objectionably obtrusive. He was followed by a servile-looking small-headed youngster, who was dignified by a black cloth costume, and carried a bundle of books and tracts under his arm. Melville was rather taken aback at the saucy appearance of these visitors, for it seemed incompatible with the character of charity applicants. He was just conjecturing which of the persons could be the one of whom Sir Nicol had written, when a few sen-

had obtained an entrance by sheer tact and adroitness in leading his servant to suppose that they were expected on urgent business.

"Ah, good morning," said the young man with the pimply complexion, pulling his handkerchief from his breast-pocket, and stylishly waving it from one hand to the other. "If it were not," he continued with a condescending smile, "for the importance of our mission, we—er—er might apologise for our call; but we consider the work sufficient—er—excuse for our intrusion." He spoke in the most affected tones, with his head thrown back.

Melville was puzzled. "You came, I believe, according to an arrangement I made with Sir Nicol, did you not?" he asked.

"We came because—er, well—er, we are going everywhere, all over London. We are giving our time—er to—er—evangelizing London, and we take each house that comes in our district, large or small. We—er—trust to—er—complete this work in time. There are—er—several others assisting us. It is, indeed, a most—er—important work, and—er—we feel anxious that—er—it may pass off with —er—the surrender of—er—er—many souls."

This speech was delivered with much hauteur, and with a constant bending and swaying of the figure, which appeared strangely ludicrous to the onlooker.

"I hardly comprehend you," spoke Melville. "I imagined you were keeping an appointment I had made for this hour. I find I am mistaken. Therefore, will you explain your business, as time presses?"

The melodramatic visitor then took a book from the young man in black. "If you will allow me, I will—er read with you a Scripture portion."

"Certainly not," returned Melville. "I have asked your reason for calling. I should be glad to know it."

"Well—er—er—we are going to every house to introduce—er—to all the glorious salvation for—er—their souls."

"I have really no wish," observed Melville, "to discuss this subject with you, consequently, I will not take up your time, which may very likely be better bestowed elsewhere."

"I fear, sir," said the melodramatist's companion, "you are not a believer."

"Pardon me, but I really cannot see on what ground you are justified in putting inquisitorial questions to me," replied Melville.

"We do not expect to be—er—hailed with delight wherever we go," observed the melodramatist audaciously, "but we put up with this—er—in order to—er—drop a word in season. We are quite sure that—er—the whole of London will—er—quake one day, at—er—the Judgment Day, and you must—er—flee for safety now, if—er—you will find it then."

"Is this all you have to say?" asked Melville, "because, if so, I deem it a most unwarrantable intrusion on your part to have gained an interview with me."

"Is—er—your soul of no importance?" was the next question.

"My soul is no excuse for *your* presence in my library," returned Melville, "especially when I have business of importance to transact."

"Very different to—er—the generality of our visits," was the retort. "The nobility of our—er—devotion to the cause, in—er—giving so much of our time to—er—such a large undertaking, has impressed almost every one, and—er—we have been the means of inducing numbers to think."

"Of what?" interrogated Melville.

"Of saving their souls," put in the younger Evangelist.

"I should have deemed it impossible," declared Melville, "that two presumptuous young fellows like yourselves, going about with, it seems, no real excuse for your visit, could have produced any impression except annoyance."

"The Lord has certainly called us to this work," observed the younger Evangelist, "and it is His power that helps

"Your impudence in assuming this," said Melville, "exceeds your profanity. Is it ignorance, or madness, you are suffering from?"

" We—er—expect persecution," was the rejoinder, "but—er—we also, I am thankful to say, meet with much success. The apostle Paul was once accounted mad, and—er—we think it no degradation to suffer with him."

"There is no fear of your doing that," pronounced Melville, "and there could be no excuse for making such a comparison. But do you mean to tell me that over this business you waste the whole day?"

" The entire day. We—er—do not think it too much for the Lord. We have read and prayed in seven houses already this morning. We allow—er—a quarter of an hour to each house. Here is our map. You perceive we —er—have certain streets marked out, and—er—we do so much each day."

" And your object," Melville said, " is to—"

The melodramatist interrupted : " To make London stop and *think* about the Bleeding Lamb."

" You consider," remarked Melville, " that you, and this youth who accompanies you, have the power and the right to do this. On what grounds is this assumption based? I should conclude that four-fifths of the people you visit have more right to stop you, and set you thinking ; even if they have not the right to stop you and carry you off to Bedlam."

"Your heart—er—appears to be hardened towards the Lord," said the visitor, assuming an injured air, "but we are not to be deterred from the Lord's work by—er—such a discouraging visit as this. We—er—however, shall not look upon you as a failure ; we—er—trust that the seed now dropped in this unhallowed house will appear at a future time. Much of our work is—er—success. The meetings I have held have—er—all been triumphant. I have the

meetings. I will read them, and—er—then you will, perhaps, understand my character."

Here some canting periodicals were produced, but Melville remarked,—" Your credentials are unnecessary: I have no respect for the good opinion of any one about your work, nor am I ambitious to understand your character. I think our interview may be at an end."

"If—er—you will not hear, I am not responsible, and the sin must be on your own soul," returned the melodramatist, replacing the papers; "but I will leave a few—er—tracts on your table, and some little works by Mr. Gudgeon and Mr. Falcon Small, trusting—er—that your conscience will one day prick you—er—about the treatment we have received."

"I can allow no rubbish on my library table," affirmed Melville.

"But, I have too much pity for—er—your ignorance," was the answer, "to—er—leave you without some instruction," and the Evangelist laid on the table a small paper-covered book, pointing at the same time to the words, "*Fly for your life*," printed in large black letters on its red cover.

Melville glanced at the title, and observed,—"I should recommend you to do the same. You have tried my patience quite long enough. For, let me tell you, that since you have been in this room I have recognised you as a person whom I have seen before. You were on board the *Rasselas* with one Jabez Blaze, and like cowards, you and he deserted the two orphan children who were under your care. I rescued them from the shipwreck, and I can feel nothing but contempt for the base and heartless way in which you left them, as you thought, to die. It is not men of your type who are needed to speak about God's ways. Were London converted to your principles we should have a city of sneaks, fops, and tyrants."

Dandy Filch and his companion, Mr. Tonkin Sappey,

before he made his exit, "You—er—will not hear any explanation; but I believe—er—that *still* this visit will not be without its good effects on you. I trust it will bear fruit, and—er—be the means of your conversion. I—er—have a conviction that this will be so."

In another minute the door closed on the retreating Evangelists. Melville was quite correct. The man whom he had just addressed was, indeed, Dandy Filch. We last mentioned him when the *Rasselas* was wrecked. Our history must now go back to tell that he, and Jabez Blaze, suffered not the smallest inconvenience, beyond their fears, on that melancholy occasion; and that, on safely reaching shore, they invented a story of their bravery, and deliverance from death, which was of perpetual popular service to them in their respective circles. Dandy was now exhibiting himself in a new character. He was one of those creatures who crave to be always "on show." All his life he had gratified his passion for notoriety in some form or other. In his early days he had distinguished himself by the most absurd eccentricities in dress, habits, and recreation. Possessing no qualities whatever that could have commended him to the public in any legitimate manner, he nevertheless hungered to obtain notice, even the notice due to a fool. Not that he for a moment deemed himself one, or fancied that others estimated him as such. A "genius" was the name his family applied to him, and a genius he regarded himself. With that wonderful conceit and self-assertion which distinguished him, and with a good capital, he was placed a partner in the wealthy business of an aged relative who retired in his favour. During five years the wildest stories were circulated by himself and his admiring family respecting his financial successes, and his commercial marvels. But his schemes were like himself, hollow and superficial, and at the end of that time his business collapsed in bankruptcy, with a deficit of upwards of ten thousand pounds, amidst the moanings of certain trustees who had entrusted their money upon its security, and the indignation of the creditors, whose eyes had been completely blinded by the false *glamour* which this melodramatic debtor contrived to shed over all his exploits. Nor was the wrath of his creditors, who received about twopence in the pound for their losses, mitigated when they discovered that the bankrupt, whom they were asked to forgive on the ground of his youth, inexperience, and incapacity, had been shrewd enough, out of their money, to secure a handsome pecuniary provision for himself and family. He had made an ante-nuptial settlement on his wife which was indefeasible in law. Upon the proceeds of that settlement he was able to live in luxury. And, as he sallied forth from his comfortable home to meet, at the Bankruptcy Court, from time to time, the creditors who protested that he had cheated them, his equilibrium of spirits was so happily maintained, that, with unblushing generosity, he told them that they had his full forgiveness. In fact, this bankruptcy crash did not disconcert Dandy Filch. A supreme audacity made him impervious. He certainly perceived that he could no longer display himself in his former social and commercial circles; but as his bankruptcy only pauperized other people, and did not deprive him of his luxuries for even a day, the only problem which he proposed to himself was, with regard to the shortest, and easiest, method whereby to bring himself into notoriety in some other sphere.

Now, it so happened, that just at this time England was being startled by a sensational revivalistic novelty, conducted on a gigantic scale and advertised with unexampled skill. Messrs. Soppet & Larby, who invented and arranged it, possessed consummate tact, and had become inordinately popular. It was said that their work had the direct personal assistance of God. But their popularity could easily be accounted for without invoking a supernatural explanation. In the first place, they propitiated all the newspaper proprietors, and advertising contractors, by a lavish and unprecedented financial expenditure. In the next place, they abstained from attacking any of the institutional iniquities of the land. Those stupendous and multiform organizations and interests which are bound up with the maintenance of war, and of intemperance, were spared exposure and castigation. The reckless race for riches, was practically unrebuked ; as also were caste, the worship of sham heroes, and snobbery generally. By statesmanlike management they avoided giving offence to any class prejudices or sectarian interests, and abstained from irritating national and individual vanity. Their mission was to show people how, by a mere volition of the mind, they could infallibly secure for themselves very comfortable quarters in a future state. The natural selfishness of the world induced it to go to hear what was so obviously advantageous and cheap. Especially, as the entertainment included the finest collections of sensuous hymns, and music, ever performed in England. It was, therefore, not surprising that the Soppet and Larby movement grew to great proportions.

Just at the time when Dandy Filch was seeking a new arena for his vanity, there was an opening in the Soppet and Larby ranks for a coadjutor. Dandy offered himself, and was welcomed. His melodramatic antics passed for deep emotion, and his vagaries were accounted spiritual phenomena in that fetid atmosphere in which popular Cant loves to dwell. Here, as he could sing a little, and chatter a great deal, he was able to disport himself without the help of brains or character. In the occasional absence of Soppet, at the less important demonstrations, he conducted the musical performances ; so that, whilst his creditors were launching unavailing epithets at his dishonest head, he was serenely singing to rest those nomadic, morbid souls, who followed in Soppet and Larby's wake. Of such is the kingdom of fools !

CHAPTER XXVII.

CANT AND CALLOUSNESS.—MR. TREMLIN IS MADE ILL.—THE CANTING WIFE AS NURSE.—MR. MELVILLE APPEALS TO MR. AGNEW MUMM.—THE GOD OF ONE MAN MAY BE ANOTHER MAN'S DEVIL.

MRS. ROSE, of Redborough, of whose excellence mention has been made already, was enabled by Mr. Melville's generosity to establish herself as the principal of a girls' school in the West End of London. One day, after having paid her a visit in order to see little Annie, who was still in her care, Mr. Melville decided to make a call on Mr. Tremlin, to report to him Annie's satisfactory condition, and ascertain if there was anything further in which he could promote her happiness, or relieve her uncle of anxiety. When he reached Mr. Tremlin's house, he heard with much sorrow from the servant that her master was confined to his bed by illness, and could not see any visitor. He, therefore, saw Mrs. Tremlin. In answer to his inquiries, she started off into a vigorous dissertation on her own health, and her husband's imprudence.

"Yes, it is true that owing to his nervousness he is in bed to-day," said she, "but I am so thankful I did warn him, and can clear *myself* of all blame. But he would persist in his own way, and the judgments of God, of which I forewarned him, have fallen upon him."

The nature of Tremlin's attack could not be gathered from this statement, and Melville rather impatiently exclaimed, "But is he seriously ill?"

"Oh no," returned the lady in the calmest of tones. "But, of course, he fancies himself at death's door. Men are bad ones to endure. Ah, if he had suffered what I have! If he had had one tenth of my agony!" Here Mrs. Tremlin lifted her eyes most piously to Heaven. "But God's will be done. He hath seen fit to afflict me, and I bow in submission to His will. As I observed to my husband a short time ago, we *must* submit: we must *not* rebel against God's judgments. And, oh, if this illness is the means of leading him to the fold, who for a moment would regret it? He is a sad wanderer, Mr. Melville. He has acted most cruelly to his wife and little ones since *you* last saw him."

Here Mrs. Tremlin raised her pocket-handkerchief to her eyes and whimpered.

"What has he done?" asked Melville bluntly, for Mrs. Tremlin's behaviour impressed him unfavourably.

Mrs. Tremlin put down her handkerchief rather suddenly, roused by the tone of Melville's voice.

"He sacrificed us all for that freethinker, Caleb Faithful," she answered indignantly. "I begged him not to do it. Told him God would surely visit him if he did. I warned him not to meddle with the hand of the Almighty. But he turned a deaf ear to my entreaties, and went his own way. And where has that way led him to? I tell him repentance is too late—too late; though I fear he is not sorry. He sees not the error of his ways. But MY words have come true."

"That is a satisfaction, madam," said Melville drily, for he could find very little sympathy for a canting woman.

"Scarcely a satisfaction," retorted the lady, "to lose his situation through his assistance of that Caleb Faithful, and for all *I* know we may become penniless in a short time."

"Dear me!" exclaimed Melville with interest. "How did that happen, Mrs. Tremlin?"

"Oh, *I* hardly know. He tells me so little. He is so close at all times, but especially on subjects where he

firm to which he is clerk are very godly men, and one of them, Mr. Agnew Mumm, feels towards Mr. Faithful as I do. He discovered that Maurice had assisted Mr. Faithful, and in consequence of this gave him notice to leave. My husband has been too proud to confess this to me, and told me that he had his dismissal without a reason being assigned; but he has wandered occasionally during his illness, and from what he has then said I have gathered the true state of affairs. He has, indeed, acted most basely. He was afraid even to tell me he had been able to assist that Minister. He evidently felt guilty."

"To what lengths will not bigotry carry us," said Melville, "when it deprives a man of a situation because he renders assistance to a fellow creature. It hardly seems possible. But may I see your husband, Mrs. Tremlin?"

"I think it is as well for you not to," returned the lady. "He is better when left quiet."

"Is he so very bad then?" inquired Melville.

"Oh no. There is nothing really wrong. It is only his extreme nervousness. I, who have suffered *so* much, can endure illness like a Christian, and perhaps that causes me the displeasure which I experience when I see others less resigned."

"Has he a medical man attending him?" asked Melville.

"Oh no. It is not necessary. In fact, in such a position as ours now is, it would be extremely wrong to indulge in such a needless expense. Of course, I put this to him very plainly, as *I* always desire to be very straightforward, and not incur expenses we cannot, through his obstinacy, meet. I will tell him you have called, Mr. Melville, and he shall visit you when he is better."

"I should very much like to see him, Mrs. Tremlin. Just for a minute or two," urged Melville.

"I really do not think he *would* see you," observed Mrs. Tremlin, hardly knowing what excuse to offer.

hand on the bell, which he rang, while Mrs. Tremlin searched her brains for an excuse. She frowned slightly as the servant entered the room, and tried to hide her vexation in her smelling salts.

"Did you ring, ma'am?" said the girl.

"This gentleman wishes to see your master. Ask him if he feels well enough to see any one, and say I think he had better not," directed Mrs. Tremlin in a very injured tone.

"Take him my card," said Melville.

During the servant's absence Mrs. Tremlin was too annoyed to speak, and Melville did not commence a conversation.

"Master would like to see the gentleman, mum," said the girl after a minute's absence ; and Melville without a word to Mrs. Tremlin followed the servant upstairs. He had expected to find Tremlin ill, but not so completely changed as he was. His eyes were terribly glassy, his face ghastly pale, and his lips parched with the fever that was fast consuming his frame.

"My poor fellow," said Melville, as he held the hand that was feebly extended to him, "I am indeed sorry to find you thus."

A weak voice returned, "Oh, Mr. Melville, I am so glad to see you. I have laid here, and longed for you to come."

The tears were in Tremlin's eyes as he spoke. The excitement was almost too much for him.

"Do not talk," said Melville. "Let me talk to you. And first : do not want for anything. You may draw upon me for all your needs ; and I have come to tell you that your niece Annie is in perfect health and happiness, and wants nothing. Let your mind be quite at rest about pecuniary matters. What do you take in the way of nourishment ?"

"I have no appetite, Mr. Melville. A little beef tea occasionally is all I want."

"How I wish you had communicated to me that you were ill," observed Melville; "I had no idea of it."

"I should have done so, Mr. Melville," replied Tremlin, "but that I am too weak to write, and my head is fearfully bad sometimes. I try not to give way. But I fancy I am very ill."

"My dear fellow, we will soon get you better," said Melville very tenderly. "I will have my own physician to see you, and we will have you strong and well once more."

Tremlin smiled gratefully, and murmured his thanks. "I did want to see you, to thank you for your goodness to Mr. Faithful. It was so kind."

"Not a word, Tremlin. Not a word. You were the hero in that affair. I did nothing."

"I have been unfortunate since we met, Mr. Melville. I have lost my situation. I hardly know for what reason; but I fear Mr. Mumm is very prejudiced against Mr. Faithful. He told me he could not keep a man with such principles as mine in his office, and that I must leave in a month's time. This has worried me terribly." Tremlin paused for breath, and closed his eyes. Even this explanation was too long for his strength. "Oh, Mr. Melville, I want to tell you so much," he whispered, "and my breath has gone."

"I know quite enough, my dear sir," answered Melville, "and can guess the rest. But let me comfort you by the hope that all will come right. I will see Mr. Mumm, and, perhaps, get him to revoke his decision. He very likely will when I explain matters to him. And if not, I will soon get you another post. Just try and get better now, and fill your mind with pleasant thoughts. A little ice would relieve your head. Have you tried it?"

Tremlin smiled mournfully, as he replied in the negative.

"I will send you some directly I leave here. I will also

at once provide you with a competent woman to nurse you."

"Oh no, Mr. Melville. Pray do not do that. My wife is too much of an invalid to wait on me, but she sends the children up with things, so that I get what I want. I could hardly expect her to attend on me, could I?"

"I think you will be better for having a nurse," replied Melville. "I will speak to your wife about the matter. But I have talked sufficiently, I see; I will call in to-morrow. And believe me, you may command me in anything. My warmest sympathy is yours."

Tremlin tried faintly to return Melville's grasp, and looked up earnestly as if he would have said something more. Melville waited.

"If you could,"—commenced the sick man, and paused.

"If I could what? Do not be afraid to ask," said Melville.

"If you could see Mr. Mumm."

"I will see him to-morrow," answered Melville, at once writing down the address.

Mrs. Tremlin, who had not been too much fatigued to remain in a most uncomfortable attitude listening, outside the door, during Melville's talk with her husband, here entered the room, and pitching her tones in an unusually high key commenced, "Well, Mr. Melville, he is not very bad, is he?"

"I will give you my opinion of your husband downstairs, madam," said Melville, so sternly that Mrs. Tremlin was completely overcome for the moment.

She rallied, however, and continued: "You would be far better up, you know, Maurice. I wish Mr. Melville could persuade you to get up for a little time now you are so much better. There would be some chance then of your returning to work again. But so long as you lie there moping you simply get weaker and weaker. I might have remained in bed all my life, if *I* had given way."

"I will try to-morrow, my dear," murmured Tremlin, as he moved restlessly on his pillow, and wearily closed his eyes, as if wishing to shut out Mrs. Tremlin's voice and face simultaneously.

Melville, thereupon, invited Mrs. Tremlin to follow him, and in such a manner that she felt compelled to obey. He then ushered the lady into her own sitting-room, and closing the door, commenced, "How long, Mrs. Tremlin, has your husband been in this condition?"

"About ten days he has been ill," returned Mrs. Tremlin, slightly discomposed by Melville's manner.

"And you have had no medical attendance for him during that time?"

"Dear me, no. It was merely a chill Mr. Tremlin caught through being out in the rain one night. He got up a few days back, and was much better. But he really wants rousing, and I do trust you may be able to do this for him."

"If your husband dies, Mrs. Tremlin, I shall consider that your neglect has sacrificed his life."

"Dies, Mr. Melville!" cried Mrs. Tremlin. "Ah, you are frightened by the way he talks. With *my* experience of illness I know there is very little the matter with him. If he had suffered like *I* have. If he had lain for hours as I have of a night racked with pain, he might talk of dying. But, really, Mr. Melville, you are not in earnest."

"Madam, I am intensely in earnest when I say that your husband is in a most precarious state. Now listen, I shall send my physician to him at once. I shall also send a nurse whom I can trust to carry out the physician's directions. I shall—"

But at the word "nurse," Mrs. Tremlin screamed, and threw herself into the nearest chair.

"Nurse! I will have no nurse here. My house to be upset in that manner! I am surprised, Mr. Melville. Oh dear, my poor heart! this excitement is too much. I shall faint. Call Fanny to bring me the eau de cologne. I should have thought you would have had more pity for me, Mr. Melville," continued the lady as she sobbed hysterically. "Harrowing up my nerves in this manner, and upsetting me when I am in such a weak state, and surrounded with trouble. It is very, very, cruel."

Melville saw that neither reason, nor tenderness, could touch this woman. He also perceived that by making her an enemy he would be less able to assist her husband.

"Pray calm yourself, Mrs. Tremlin," he remarked. "Of course, if you object to the nurse we must consider how to meet your objections. And for the rest, I was about to add, that I should, with your permission, send Mr. Tremlin a few little strengthening delicacies and necessaries."

But Mrs. Tremlin lay back with her eyes shut, and her breath coming and going in gasps, and Melville bit his lips with vexation as suddenly the air was rent with the lady's screams. The servant came running up, and the elder children were despatched in all directions for eau de cologne and brandy. Amidst the general confusion, Melville would have been glad to leave, for the attack was only a fit of the shams; but he waited till she could keep it up no longer. Yet he waited in vain: for she then was seized with a fit of the sulks, and declined to talk to any one until he had departed in his brougham.

The next morning, true to his word, Melville found his way to the offices of Messrs. Mumm, Blooster & Co., and having sent in his card, was ushered into the private room of Agnew Mumm.

"You will pardon my intrusion," spoke Melville, as Mumm, having declared himself unacquainted with his visitor, gazed at him over his spectacles, "but I wished to see you about a young man you are dismissing from your office, very suddenly. Mr. Tremlin, I mean."

"Eh, eh," returned Mumm. "He—he—he is ill, I believe, and is unable to come now."

"He is very ill, Mr. Mumm. And I am sure you will be grieved to hear, that it is the worry of losing his situation which is acting on his brain and keeping up the severe symptoms of his malady. You found him a good servant, did you not?"

"Ye - es. He did his work well enough, but—but—but, he was a young man of no—no—no principle. And I—I —I learnt a thing or two of him that—that—that I did not like."

"I am sorry to hear that. He was morally right, was he not?"

"I—I—I daresay he was. But I believe him to be a freethinker, and—and—and being a religious man myself, I—I—I cannot stand such men about me. They ought not to—to—to be encouraged. It is keeping good men out of a good place."

"Is this your only reason for dismissing him?" asked Melville.

"Well, yes; I—I—I believe so."

"And you have nothing to say against his character?"

"Only that—that—that he was a freethinker, I believe, and—and—and that to me is—is—is as bad as a thief."

"Which comes to this: he differed from you in his faith," spoke Melville.

"Yes, of course he did."

"But you surely would not quarrel with him for that if he suited you."

"Well, I—I—I would. For if a man's wrong in—in—in his religion, he—he—he is wrong everywhere. In fact, I would not keep any one who sits on Sundays under that Mr. Faithful. And—and—and this man not only sits under him, but—but—but he tried to get money for him."

"A very noble thing to do, Mr. Mumm, under the circumstances. We cannot all think alike. But we can all help one another. And as to religious differences, we ought not to persecute one another for their sake. The term

'Christian' embraces people who hold very widely divergent opinions. You and I may call ourselves Christians, but, at the same time, your God may be my Devil. The Deity is not changed by our conceptions of Him. To almost all men He appears in a different character. Therefore I think we ought to be very charitable in our judgments on another man's religious convictions, especially when we know his private life to be blameless."

"I—I—I do not go with ye at all, sir. I—I—I am shocked at such a doctrine. There is only one faith—substituted righteousness—that will save us, and—and—and I think ye are far short of it."

"Well, be that as it may," returned Melville, smiling at Mumm's consternation, "your feeling as a fellow-creature, as a human being, will draw you towards a suffering man, who, in a measure, is dependent on your leniency for his recovery. And you will permit me to give him hopes of his restoration to your favour, will you not?"

"I—I—I will do no such thing, sir," said Mumm, rising from his seat. "I—I—I think myself well rid of such a fellow. 'My God your Devil,' indeed. I—I—I beg you to understand my God is—is—is the God, the only God; is—is—is—"

Here Mumm paused, hardly knowing how to express himself.

"A most respectable idol, I have no doubt, sir," put in Melville. "Your God, probably, is a fiction of your own intolerance. You assume that He places you at the head of a small band which He has reserved for His paradise, whilst He consigns the rest of the vast creation to eternal damnation. I wish you good morning, sir; and my best hope for you is, that your God may be more merciful to you, than you are to others."

On his way home Melville called, by appointment, on the physician whom he had sent many hours before to Tremlin.

The physician's opinion of the patient was very unsatisfactory. "He has had brain fever," said the doctor, "and his life now depends on nourishment and good nursing. And, even at the best, I can give but small hope. What a strange thing he did not have advice sooner. I gather, from his wife, that he has been wandering in the head several times, and she ascribed the syn ptoms to the effects of a violent chill, and so dosed him with nitre and weak gruel."

In deep dejection at this intelligence, Melville, later on, wended his way to Tremlin's house. Mrs. Tremlin received him with much coolness; but, considering that she was just sitting down to some turtle soup, and that her table was adorned with the hot-house grapes and other delicate fruits which Melville had sent for her husband, she did not feel quite free to use towards her visitor that insolence which she found hard to repress. When asked about her husband's health, she responded, of course, that he was "very much better." "But," she added, "I cannot get him to touch the soup you sent, so I thought it was a pity to let it get bad, and we are having some of it for dinner."

"Does he fancy the wine?" asked Melville.

"He drank a little of it this morning. But I have not pressed him to take more, as I think it very heating for him."

"You saw the physician, and heard his opinion, I presume," said Melville.

"Yes."

"Did he tell you Mr. Tremlin was to take plenty of nourishment?"

"Oh yes. But it will not do to overload the system. With my experience of illness, Mr. Melville, I know how bad that is. The heaps of nourishment that I am always ordered, but from which I refrain, knowing its injurious effect!"

"I have no doubt of it, Mrs. Tremlin. But as that soup

is nice and hot, I will, if you will allow me, take some to your husband, and see if I can tempt him," said Melville.

Mrs. Tremlin could hardly refuse such a disinterested offer, and with a very bad grace, ladled out the soup, observing, " I trust it *will* do him good, and, not harm."

Melville found Tremlin sleeping; but it was that sort of sleep which foretells that eternal rest is near. Melville waited until the slumber ended ; then, with infinite gentleness, leaned over the invalid and spoke to him.

Tremlin's eyes opened at the words, and a smile of pleasure illumined his features. " How kind to come again," he murmured.

" I have brought you something you must please me by taking," said Melville, helping him to the refreshment.

It was painfully clear that the sufferer was far worse to-day. Conversation was scarcely endurable. Lethargy was extending over all the faculties. Melville remained with him as long as he could be serviceable, and then descended with a heavy heart.

Mrs. Tremlin met him on his return. "As you seem to think the wine *will* do Maurice good, tired as I am, I was endeavouring to carry him up a glass."

" Nourishment may save him, Mrs. Tremlin ; but I fear he will not be long in this world."

There was an expression in Melville's face that struck even the hard, selfish woman before him.

" Not long for this world ! " she exclaimed. " Why, there is nothing *dangerous* the matter with him, is there ? "

" I have," replied Melville, " tried to impress on you, madam, apparently without effect, that your husband is very ill. I have had the physician's opinion, and he is not at all sanguine of his recovery. Nourishment is his only hope, and you do not approve of nourishment. So, it seems to me, your husband must die."

" ' Approve of nourishment ! ' Why, I am sure, Mr.

to keep up his strength. In my critical state of health I often marvel how I have been supported under this terrible affliction. I have indeed been blessed with sustaining grace."

"Pray, madam," said Melville as he departed, "be good enough to let me know if your husband should ask for me; or if there is anything more which I can do for him"

CHAPTER XXVIII.

CANT STRAINING AT A GNAT AND SWALLOWING A CAMEL.—WARRIORS AT AN ANTI-VIVISECTION MEETING.—THE ASSASSINATORS OF MEN PROCLAIMING THE INVIOLABILITY OF THE BLACK-BEETLE.

DO what we will to escape the nuisance, we are certain to have our eyes offended by the perpetual reappearance, during our journey through life, of the more loathsomely corrupt personages of The World of Cant. The stream of time fails to carry them into oblivion. Their very rottenness raises them to its surface; and by reason of the alarming moral putrescence of their qualities, they exact from our unwilling gaze the very notice and attention which, in the result, produce our nausea.

Melville hoped, after his interview with Agnew Mumm, that he might be spared the pain of ever being brought into contact with such a man again. Nevertheless, a very few days afterwards, when he was attending an Anti-Vivisection meeting, Melville, to his surprise, again beheld him, heard him speak, and saw him treated with every mark of honour by a whole platformful of professional philanthropists at Courtray Assembly Rooms.

But, without dwelling upon him, or his speech, we may refer to the meeting. It was very interesting, and an instructive illustration of the sincerity and vehemence with which people may proclaim inconsistent opinions. Lord Everton occupied the chair. Resolutions were unanimously passed very properly denouncing the practice of vivisection, on the two grounds, that man is bound to defend weaker creatures from suffering, and that he has no right to destroy life, excepting under the compulsion of paramount necessity. Surgeons and anatomists who, for the purposes of scientific investigation, destroyed the life of a mouse, a cockroach, or a frog, were held up in scathing language to the opprobrium of mankind. Strange to say, the qualifications of the speakers for the task of censuring the cruelty of others was somewhat slender. For example, the first of them was the Rev. Malcolm Steel. Three days before the meeting he, as the Rector of his Parish, and as a Minister of the Prince of Peace, publicly read and presented an address of thanks to Captain Bullgore for his war services.

Now Captain Bullgore had just returned from mutilating the bodies of thousands of men in South Africa. All the demonstrations in all the vivisecting rooms in the civilized world, would not, in the course of half a century, produce a tithe of the physical agony which Bullgore was in the habit of causing in a few hours to defenceless savages; yet because Bullgore, under the falsehood of patriotism, blew away from his guns in detached fragments, not vermin or insects, but human beings, and was reckless both of human torment and physiological discoveries, this Mr. Malcolm Steel had called upon a christian congregation to applaud him as a hero, and now came here to denounce the dissectors of a cockroach as inhuman brutes.

The gentleman who moved the second resolution was a worthy cousin of Sir Nicol Giltspur, Lieutenant Spearpointz. Lieutenant Spearpointz had been engaged in all the legalized burglaries and massacres incidental to the British invasion of Afghanistan. He wore many medals because he had committed many murders. It was recorded among his illustrious deeds that, in a recent campaign, he had entrapped a half-clothed native regiment in a mountain pass, and hewn them to pieces. He covered the ground with maimed men, and fragments of shattered limbs. Deprived of all help, his mangled victims lay upon the barren rocks bleeding, thirsty, and utterly deserted; scorched by a burning sun all day and shivering with cold all night. Several days and nights elapsed before merciful death released the last of them from their unutterable tortures. But the object of this, and the similar exploits in which Lieutenant Spearpointz had been engaged, was martial glory and not physiological discovery. His innumerable dissections of men were performed in order to extend the "scientific boundary" of his country. He was, therefore, conventionally regarded not only as a respectable person, but as a patriot, and, as such, entitled to attend this meeting, and utter his indignant protest against the cruelty of those anatomists who, for the purposes of science, are guilty of practising vivisection on frogs and fishes.

Another speaker, who was very effective, was the Rev. Dr. Grillman. He considered that professors who resorted to vivisection, whether for the purposes of discovery or tuition, were a disgrace to a christian country. He believed that God abhorred all such cruelty. Yet the doctor propounded from his pulpit every Sunday that this same merciful God, who would not sanction the wounding of a caterpillar for scientific purposes, had deliberately created the bulk of the human family for the purpose of burning them in Hell fire for ever and ever. The doctor was, also, one of the prominent exponents of the blasphemy that God derived lawful satisfaction, and moral gratification, from the physical agonies endured by Christ upon the cross; and that it was only because He was so "well pleased" with the tragedy of the crucifixion, that He consented, by way of recompense, to save even a fraction of the human race from unending miseries in the burning lake which He had prepared for their eternal home. The doctor asserted, and very properly, that the practice of vivisection, in so far as it was brutalizing, was injurious to morality. At the same time he maintained, against all comers, that a daily contemplation of the wantonly cruel proceedings of the God whom he preached, would awaken the world to righteousness; although by reason of their malign and excessive baseness those proceedings would necessarily shock the moral sensibilities of even prize fighters of ordinary depravity.

"Don't you think, sir," said Melville to a gentleman who sat next to him at this anti-vivisection meeting, taking elaborate notes, "don't you think, that the anti-vivisectionist speakers, to-night, are like those of whom we hear as being able to swallow a camel though they strain at a gnat?"

"I do not see any resemblance," replied the ready writer.

"It is in this," said Melville, "that whilst these persons accept and applaud all the unnecessary horrors and brutalities of war, they are shocked at the sufferings which science, in prosecuting her discoveries for the amelioration of the physical condition of the race, incidentally and unwillingly inflicts upon a few mice and insects. They do not object to the destruction of even the highest forms of life by slow, lingering torture, provided that war, and not science, gives the command. But they shudder at sacrificing a black-beetle in the interests of biological research."

"I do not agree at all with you," replied the note-taker testily. "What would become of our glorious constitution without war? But vivisection is wicked, and against the law of God."

"I respect profoundly all ordinary anti-vivisectionists," said Melville; "but a sportsman's, or a soldier's claim, to be considered an anti-vivisectionist, seems an abhorrent absurdity."

"I do not agree with you at all," repeated the little man.

Melville said no more; and his neighbour continued his writing.

He was a homœopath of the old narrow school, and was incubating a leading article which he intended as a vigorous attack upon orthodox surgery; proving by the speeches delivered that evening, that the cruelties practised by the tutors, students, and professors, of the art, were so horrid as to shock even the veteran warriors who had witnessed, and caused, mutilation, and carnage, on innumerable battle-fields.

The little man wished to convert the world to his own opinion, that all the diseases of mankind could be successfully treated by means of the globule.

CHAPTER XXIX.

CANT GLOATING OVER MORAL PUTRESCENCE.—PENDANGO AND THE CHRISTIAN PRIZE CHAMPION.—A REVIVALISTIC FESTIVAL.—MR. TREMLIN DIES.

THE physician's opinion of Tremlin proved to be quite correct. It is true the sufferer rallied a little, by reason of the nourishment which was given him, and would wake up and talk, and take some interest in surrounding objects, but there was no permanent improvement. Mrs. Tremlin's fright, on being compelled by Melville to realize her own responsibility in the matter, produced satisfactory results. For a few days she remembered to give her husband either food or medicine at the right hour; and when she was unable, from what she termed her weakness, to go to him herself, which was very often, she sent the servant. So poor Tremlin was better cared for than he had ever been in his married life.

Melville called regularly, and was satisfied and delighted to notice that there seemed to be occasionally some improvement in the patient. Mrs. Tremlin at once protested that her husband was "almost recovered" now, and, but for her fear of Melville, she would have made him get up. When poor Mr. Tremlin, one afternoon, asked for his children, and tried to talk to them, Mrs. Tremlin was of opinion that her husband's health was again quite equal to her own, and that she could relax her duties and enjoy herself. She accordingly set forth to a tea-drinking at the house of a "dear christian friend," preparatory to attending a great religious festival in the "Ezekiel Gospel Hall"

This "festival" had been well advertised for many weeks. The local evangelical revivalists, both Churchmen and Dissenters, had combined together to make it a grand success. They announced, in all the newspapers, that they had secured the services of a splendid choir under the leadership of Mr. Dandy Filch. Also, that the speakers at the meeting would include Messrs. Gudgeon, Jabez Blaze; an African Bishop who had been a slave, and who was advertised as being "blacker than any ordinary negro"; and, as the great attraction of the evening, Brother Pendango, the great christian prize-champion. Blessed by such a play-bill as this, properly displayed on mammoth posters by skilful printers, and aggressively placarded everywhere by enterprising advertising contractors, it was no wonder that the originators of the "festival" had their hall crowded to suffocation.

Mrs. Tremlin's "fainting" did not trouble her, even in a close atmosphere, when the place was sanctified. She was able to get a good seat, and to enjoy herself vastly, for the proceedings were deeply interesting. The usual formalities of singing and praying having been got over, and speeches having been made by various gentlemen, the ebony Bishop was put up to say a few words ; and the people gaped and stared their delight at this ecclesiastical curiosity which religious good taste provided for their delectation.

But the desire of their heart was Brother Pendango, and their eagerness to hear him was intensified when the Rev. Palfrey Dasset, the chairman, spoke of him. He said that "Brother Pendango was the great reformed prize-fighter. He had been thirty-four times before various criminal courts in nearly all the counties in England. He had been charged with every variety of offence, including bigamy and murderous assaults, and had been convicted no less than thirty times. His various imprisonments had caused him to be incarcerated in as many as eighteen different jails. He had also been one of the most daring and cruel of our prize-fighters. He had horribly maimed six men and two youths; and no less than four eyes had been knocked out of the heads of four different women by Pendango in his drunken brawls. But as years came on he was less and less inclined and able to fight, and in a happy moment he resolved that in his closing years he would 'fight for Jesus.' And what a cause of rejoicing it ought to be to all the followers of Christianity that Pendango had turned his efforts now to gain the heavenly championship."

Here the meeting broke into rapturous cheers. The reverend chairman then announced that they would "glorify God" by singing a hymn. We can supply the first verse, but can give no information as to how God gets "glorified" by such people or by such hymns.

> "I plunged into the fountain,
>   And it washed my sins away;
>   'Twas filled with blood from Jesus,
>   And floweth night and day."

Brother Pendango then came forward. He was a disgusting specimen of a coarse, brutal prize-fighter, with a broken nose. His style, as might be expected, was low in the extreme. He described how, in fighting for the devil, he had always been a complete conqueror; "but," said he, "when Jesus Christ came into the ring, He licked me the first round. Jesus wanted me to be a champion for Him, and here I am ready to meet all the infidels who are unhung. You, come up out of the slums of sin, and join me in fighting for our Jesus. His is the only blood to wash in. He is the One to fight for. I'm not ashamed of Him. When we have smashed all His enemies here we shall reign with Him for ever and ever as kings and conquerors."

A good deal more in the same strain followed, and it was very keenly relished by the evangelical audience. At the end of the address a meek little Clergyman rose and prayed, thanking God for the conversion of Pendango, and for His mercy in giving the Church militant such a champion. Then a wealthy layman, Mr. Pigley, gave out an altered doxology, which the meeting sang with grand effect, led by Dandy Filch's choir :—

> "Praise God from whom all blessings flow,
> Praise Him for Brother Pendango."

After this, a gentleman stood up and said that he "would like, before they separated, to ask a little explanation. It had been reported that Pendango, since his conversion, had been one of the principals in a great betting transaction, with reference to a match between champion terriers and four hundred rats; also that Pendango had been present at the match, and had on the same day been one of the seconds in a prize fight between Brawny Billy and Crushing Tom. It was alleged that several witnesses could corroborate these facts."

Pendango replied. The truth of this report he did not dare deny; but he wished it to be understood that it was "the last successful attempt the Devil would make to lure him back to the paths of wickedness." Pendango then sat down amidst vociferous applause. Then he rose again, shaking his head cunningly, and asked the meeting to join him in singing,—

> "The Devil had me once,
> And he wants me now:
> He wants me again,
> But I don't mean to go.
> Singing glory hallelujah."

This jumble was sung with great spirit by the entire audience. When it was ended, the rapturous "festival" terminated, without one single Christly truth having been uttered; and Mrs. Tremlin, much edified, returned to the home of her "dear christian friend" to supper.

Meanwhile, the little flame of life, which medicine and nourishment had replenished in the feeble frame of Tremlin, was again flickering into exhaustion for want of sustenance. Throughout all the weary hours of his wife's absence, the suffering man was absolutely alone.

With the advancing night he realized that he was dying, and he longed to say a last farewell to his children whom he loved so tenderly. But in his solitude, and utter prostration he was powerless even to make his wishes known. Alone, in his dark, desolate room he awaited, in reliance on the goodness of God, his impending change.

When Mrs. Tremlin returned home that night, her husband had ascended where the "wicked cease from troubling, and the weary are at rest."

CHAPTER XXX.

CANT THE DEBASER OF CHILDHOOD.—THE MISSES HAUHARD'S SCHOOL, THE NURSERY OF CANT.—MRS. ROSE'S SCHOOL, THE HOME OF TRUTH.

WITH characteristic kindness Melville undertook to attend to all arrangements in connection with the obsequies of Mr. Tremlin. Mrs. Tremlin protested that she was "far too upset to see to anything." The shock which her nerves had received when she returned from "glorifying God" at the revivalistic "Festival" on the evening of her husband's death would, she asserted, "leave its effects on her to her dying day." This she affirmed to every friend who came to sympathise in her bereavement. She kept her room, and would on no account venture downstairs. She pronounced herself "perfectly unable to survive the tremendous blow her nervous system had received;" and her own doctor was summoned to prescribe for her. She said she was "far too ill to think of funerals, or tombstones." So Melville settled those details in his own way. Over the grave of Maurice Tremlin he placed a beautiful marble slab engraved with the words, "The pure in heart shall see God."

When all was over, and it was necessary to look into business matters, Melville fixed an interview with Mrs. Tremlin, in order that he might make arrangements with her respecting the future; for he was anxious about the welfare of the little children. The invalid received him with an affectation of deep emotion. She was well dressed in the most fashionable mourning. Melville could not find it in his heart to offer her sympathy, and might have found it difficult to commence a conversation, had not the lady burst into a long harangue about her own sufferings consequent on her recent shock. She ended with remarking, "Of course, this bereavement comes not to me in the same way as it would to a worldling. I receive it with a sanctified spirit, and as coming for some good purpose: some wise discipline especially arranged for my good. And I am sure that the Lord is chastening me out of His love, and not from His wrath; and whatever He does must be done to show how He loves me."

No words from Melville could have penetrated this woman's vanity, or could have revealed her to herself in her true colours, so he proceeded to business.

"It is a very sad thing," groaned the lady, "that, considering the age of my husband, and the time we had been married, he was unable to make any provision for his family, except to insure his life. What we shall all do I cannot tell. But Maurice was always so thoughtless. Always so extravagant in matters concerning—"

"Mrs. Tremlin," interrupted Melville, "the memory of your husband, to me, is sacred. I can say what I have to say without the mention of his name, and this I would prefer."

The suggestions that Melville generously offered were, that as Mrs. Tremlin was determined to send all the children away from home, she should avail herself of the proceeds of the insurance policy for her own personal use; and that he should send the children to school, and pay the cost. To this Mrs. Tremlin agreed, provided she selected the school. Nor would she yield on this point for her own children, though she consented that Annie should remain at Mrs. Rose's academy. This plan being settled, the interview ended. Mrs. Tremlin, when she made the arrangement, had secretly decided upon the school to which she would send her own children. In her

trained at an establishment kept by the Misses Haghard, at Stepney, and Melville's munificence would now make it practicable for her to do so.

The prospectus of the Misses Haghard's school stated that the "proprietors paid particular attention to instilling the principles of a sound orthodox evangelical creed into the minds of their youthful pupils." The seminary, moreover, was advertised in *The Christian Weekly Baptistry* and had a recommendation from the preacher whose ministry Mrs. Tremlin attended. Consequently she considered the eligibility of the place guaranteed beyond question. The little girls, Fanny, Mary, and Clara, the eldest eleven, and the youngest six years of age, were consequently placed with all speed in the care of these Misses Haghard. Mrs. Tremlin was particular to inform Miss Haghard, when she left the children finally to her care, that "the late Mr. Tremlin held very peculiar views, and *she* was not responsible for any erroneous religious notions" the erring father might have planted in the young minds of his daughters. Also, that she would be very thankful if such opinions could be rooted out.

The regulations of the Misses Haghard were as follow. On arriving in the schoolroom at an early hour in the morning before breakfast, the young ladies were called to prayers. Miss Haghard's plan of reading the Bible at this ceremony was opposed to any selection of topics. She commenced at the first chapter of Genesis, and read on each day until she had finished the book of the Revelation. Then she began again. After the chapter of the day, came an extempore prayer of at least ten minutes, and then the girls were permitted to partake of breakfast. The first lesson after this meal was a Bible one, when a chapter was selected, and a verse read by each pupil. At the end, Miss Haghard expounded the chapter read, and put her own doctrinal interpretation, which was highly

During the morning, each girl was expected to repeat by memory a portion of the Old or New Testament; and if any of them misbehaved themselves, they were punished by being required to commit to memory a long psalm. At the close of school in the afternoon, another chapter was read; and immediately after tea, evening prayers were conducted in the same manner as the morning.

In fact, with the exception of reading, writing, arithmetic, and meals, it was nothing but Bible. Bible before, and Bible after breakfast; Bible morning, noon, and evening; Bible for reading-lessons, Bible for memory exercises, Bible as punishment sentence; Bible misinterpreted, Bible misdirected, Bible made wearisome; everlastingly the letter of the Bible, in contempt of its spirit. The holy book was made repulsive by the purposes to which it was desecrated, and its beautiful teachings were trampled out of sight by the fanatical harshness of the women who pretended to explain them.

Sunday was a dreadful day at the Misses Haghard's. Both in the morning, and in the evening, all the little children were taken to hear doctrinal sermons. One part of the afternoon was devoted to reading the discourses of Gudgeon, Dalmage, or Falcon Small; and the other part to the singing of dismal hymns.

Poor little Mary Tremlin, a child of eight, with more spirit than her sisters, behaved herself so badly during the weary reading of a sermon one Sunday afternoon, that she was informed by Miss Haghard that God would be very angry with her for not listening, and would never take her to Heaven.

"I would rather He did not," returned the child, "for I hate Sunday, and you say that it is always Sunday in Heaven."

The Misses Haghard looked at one another, and turned up their eyes. "The father is certainly coming out in *that* child." remarked the one to the other.

he told me that every one would at last go home to God and be happy, and I believe him."

"No one will go to Heaven who is wicked," declared Miss Haghard. "Those who behave like you, Mary, will go down, down, down into a dark pit, and burn, and burn, and burn for ever and ever."

"Why, they couldn't burn for ever," said Mary scornfully. "They would all be burnt up in less than a day."

At this, Miss Haghard glared with indignation, and requested one of the under-teachers to remove the impertinent child and set her a Bible lesson for a punishment. She then asked one of the girls to recite, as a warning to other children, an awful description of the agonies of the wicked, and the "joys of the elect," which she had been compelled to commit to memory from the sermon of a great revivalist.

The principle of punishment employed in this school was such that it weakened the child's self-respect, and produced an inanimate, spiritless air, unnatural to the buoyancy of youth. If one of the girls were discovered telling an untruth, she had to wear, for the remainder of the day, a big card on her back with "liar" printed in large letters on it. Whoever visited the schoolroom, beheld the poor offender. Many were the children's manœuvres to hide the card when a visitor came. The same form of punishment was made use of with other different offences, namely impudence, ill-temper, obstinacy, and such faults; for all of which the white card with the black letters was hung on the back of the offender; the length of the punishment being proportioned to the offence. Twice a week an evening prayer-meeting, which lasted for an hour and a half, was held in the schoolroom, the Misses Haghard officiating, and the under-teacher being allowed to take part. Even the smallest child was doomed to be present at these gatherings; and if one of them was discovered sleeping, she was awakened with the startling intelligence that God was frowning at her, was noting down her wicked inattention, and would assuredly punish her for it at the awful Judgment Day.

The children were daily instructed in the gross theology that is termed "orthodox." They were told, that they could only propitiate the Deity by "bathing in the blood of His Son;" and as such doctrine is totally incomprehensible to the most intelligent mind, the girls were oppressed by the consciousness of their utter inability to procure salvation, or safety, from the awful Hell that was yawning under them. God was constantly represented to them as an angry and malignant ruler, watching each action, and ready at any moment to cast the offending soul into boundless torment. Hell was described in all its horrors, and the millions who were doomed to that awful place had their agonies depicted in the most terrible manner. No Juggernaut could have been painted in blacker colours, than the God who was held up for worship in "the Misses Haghard's christian establishment."

Nor was this all. The mind of a child, which, like a growing tree, naturally puts forth its powers in all directions, was treated by these people as if it were some dangerous plant, which required to be perpetually stunted, and dwarfed, to save it from growing into dangerous proportions. It never occurred to the Misses Haghard that Heaven intended it to grow freely and grandly, and without trammels; and, that their only duty towards it, consisted in removing all existing obstructions to spiritual light, and intellectual liberty.

Caleb Faithful once pointed out to these ladies their mistake. He said that "those who would train a child should make its faculties and potentialities a matter of profound study. They should place, before its mind, the subjects that will tend to develop the dormant talents, and should also give a right turn and a noble aim to all the strongly marked idiosyncrasies of its character." For example, when destructiveness was a trait, they should direct its possessor to the work of pulling down shams, and destroying old abuses. In the case of strongly marked individuality, they should encourage the pupil to dare, and to do, those noble things which weaker natures cannot attempt. Where acquisitiveness was strongly marked in a child's character, her ambition should be aroused to buy the truth and to sell it not for any of the trivial possessions of earth.

But the advice annoyed the Misses Haghard, and they, therefore, proceeded on totally different principles. Their school was a hotbed for rearing fanaticism and dogmatism; and its atmosphere was rank and reeking with Cant. Girls were taught hymns the sentiments of which their hearts completely disavowed. They sang, "I want to be an angel," well knowing that this was not the case. They were taught to express exaggerated love and admiration for the Misses Haghard's God; and the child who spoke in the warmest terms of affection for this execrable dragon was rewarded by the commendation of the teacher.

Now it was utterly impossible for any human creature to feel affection for that repulsive being; consequently a spirit of hypocrisy was instilled into the pupil's character. Indeed, dissimulation pervaded the whole training. The children were never natural: to have been so would have been considered rude and reprehensible. To succeed in making them assume, what they were not, was counted the purpose and end of all education. They were taught to seem, not taught to be.

But they were not only made hypocritical, but miserably nervous, and pestilently selfish. This was a consequence of the Hell-doctrine. The poor little creatures realized so vividly the horrors of the awful place to which, unless they were very circumspect, they were assured that they would be "inevitably doomed," that they were constantly brooding over every means of escape. The disinterestedness which is the essence of Christianity, and characteristic of childhood, was educated out of them; and in its place was planted a cowardly, slavish, anxiety respecting personal safety, here, and yonder.

In this unlovely home, the little Tremlins soon forgot the lessons that their father had, at sundry times, endeavoured to teach them. Slowly, and surely, they imbibed the spirit of Cant that surrounded them.

After the lapse of six months they went home for their first holidays, and they had grown sufficiently artificial, wily, and fanatical, to give satisfaction even to their mother.

Very differently situated was little Annie, who, as we have already stated, was with Mrs. Rose in her new school. The fundamental rule of Mrs. Rose's academy was, that learning was to be made a delight. To stimulate the inquiring faculty, which is inherent in the child, and to feed it with such food, and in such quantities, as to increase the craving for knowledge, was her constant aim. No petty prejudices of any kind were fostered, for the teacher knew that they debased the moral nature, closed the heart to the reception of pure impressions, and blinded the intellect to the reception of new truth.

The God who was worshipped in this school, had no attributes in common with the Misses Haghard's God. The pupils were encouraged to regard The Great First Cause in the light of Fatherhood. Taught to revere, and adore, the character of their God, they eagerly applied themselves to all such studies as enabled them to comprehend, in any measure, the spiritual, and physical laws whereby His Almighty will works out its stupendous results. The natural sciences, instead of being considered as dry uninteresting drudgery, became superlatively interesting to minds whose curiosity was awakened, by a loving sympathy, to understand the works and ways of a Beneficent Father.

With the life of Jesus Christ placed charmingly before them, the students constantly strove to imitate the example of Him who did no sin, and in whose mouth no guile was found. Consequently, the vices of the Misses Haghard's establishment were never heard of in Mrs. Rose's school.

The children were taught to loathe Cant, hypocrisy, and unreality, both of thought and expression. Sincerity, frankness, and nobility, were as characteristic of that bright circle as were the happy intelligent smiles on all the radiant faces.

One reason why these girls excelled all others in educational proficiency was, because their every-day life was a joy, and knowledge was made a delight.

Their physical education, too, was properly attended to. It was refreshing to watch them as they bounded about in the playground after school. Thorough joyousness was depicted in their courageous, beaming countenances; and the light-heartedness of childhood resounded in their jubilant mirth.

As a rule, these brave happy girls developed into brave, happy women, and were, therefore, blessings to the world.

CHAPTER XXXI.

CANT AND WILINESS.—REV. HAMILTON CARNEY.—REV. MR. RAINFORD REMOVES TO LONDON.—A MISSIONARY WORKING PARTY.—A PRAYER-MEETING.—AN ENTIRE DAY WITH REV. FALCON SMALL.—AN ACCOUNT OF THE INVALUABLE AND UNOSTENTATIOUS WORK DONE THEREIN BY THIS POPULAR PREACHER "TO EXTEND HIS MASTER'S KINGDOM."

WHEN Mr. Rainford received official intimation of the resolutions passed at the meeting presided over by Dr. Sound, the shock to his nervous system was so severe as to protract his illness. After many months he became convalescent; and then he at once began to look about for another sphere in which he might resume his pastoral work. Towards this end he wrote to a gentleman, who stood high in the ranks of Congregational officialism, whom he had always regarded as a friend, asking if he could introduce him to a pastorate. The Rev. Hamilton Carney, in a reply full of profuse good wishes, regretted that, as Mr. Rainford "was living so far away from the metropolis," the opportunities for helping him would not be many. As Rainford's money resources were well nigh exhausted, and there was no reason why he should remain in Chenley, he forthwith proceeded with his wife and family to London, and took furnished apartments.

He at once called on his correspondent, who, on finding that the excuses about non-residence near London were no longer available, began to invent others, at the same time promising to "bear in mind" his friend's application. The fact was, that the Rev. Hamilton Carney did not much like espousing the cause of any brother against whom there had been any whisper of heresy, even though the whisper had emanated from an idiot. In this matter he was determined to be very cautious. Accordingly, when Rainford left him, he wrote to Mr. Beeswax, "as the senior deacon" at Chenley Chapel, to inquire the reason of their late Pastor's withdrawal from the Church; and Beeswax, as he put it to Treacles, "felt it his dooty to acquaint the Rev. Hamilton Carney with Rainford's heterodoxy."

On receiving Beeswax's reply, the Rev. Hamilton Carney wrote to Rainford, "regretting that he was not likely to be able to introduce him to a new sphere of labour," but suggesting to him that it might be well to call on the Rev. Falcon Small, "one of the most popular Ministers in London," who might be able to help him.

To the house of the Rev. Falcon Small Rainford accordingly went. Mr. Small, as usual, was absent from his home, but Rainford was informed that he could be seen, and conversed with, in the vestry of his Church after the prayer-meeting the same evening. Rainford determined to seek him there.

Meantime, we may see for ourselves that the Rev. Falcon Small was devoting his day to the work of uplifting humanity. In the morning, he made an ostentatious attendance at the fashionable funeral of a nobleman, all the proceedings in relation to which were certain to be reported in the newspapers. At noon, he was outside a committee room of the House of Commons, extorting a promise from a fat civic M.P., to patronise a public meeting in connection with his Church. He gained his point, because he knew how to manipulate the alderman's vanity by means of tactics which he justified by the too liberal construction which he always placed upon the scriptural permission to be "all things to all men." An hour later, he was seated in a conspicuous place in the Queen's Bench, impatiently listening to an important trial. This he was soon obliged to leave, to put in an appearance on the right hand side of the chairman at a meeting in Willis's Rooms. As soon as the reporters had transcribed his little speech, he dashed away to the private room of the editor of a daily paper, to place in his hands a puff paragraph concerning an organization in connection with his Church. Having propitiated this editor, he rushed to the Ministers' Club, saluted those of the fraternity whose social position was unquestionable, and gobbled up a hearty dinner with a speed unattainable by any other man. Proceeding thence to the reading room, he allowed himself ten minutes in which to master, for purposes of superficial conversation, the contents of all the newspapers of the day, and the latest magazines and reviews, preparatory to his appearing at the "Ladies' Missionary Party," in connection with his Chapel.

We must leave him at his reading, because we have to turn aside to draw the curtain, and obtain a view of this missionary party scene, in which he will presently appear as the lion. First of all, then, it is easily observable, that this missionary institution was conducted as those of its kind usually are in the World of Cant. The meetings were held in rotation, once a month, at the houses of the various members of the society,—the number of persons attending being, generally, contingent upon the reputed wealth of the entertainer. Gossip and slander were freely indulged in, for the enjoyment of the party in general; and needlework was done, for the benefit of the natives of Flatskumski in particular.

To-night, the meeting is to be held at the residence of Mr. Small's notable official, Mr. Blooster—who, having just performed some very lucrative tricks in wrecking and plundering a public company, seizes the present occasion for an ostentatious display of hospitality, which he intends shall amaze every beholder. When Mr. Small arrives, he finds himself surrounded by a glare of gaudy grandeur of all sorts, which begins in the entrance hall, and culminates in a blaze of colours in every part of the drawing-room.

Directly Mr. Small enters, all the ladies instantly leave off work. He glides with the greatest celerity to Mrs. Blooster, and shakes hands with an appearance of almost convulsive affection, saying, " How d'ye do, Mrs. Blooster? So pleased to see such a fine gathering. I returned from North Wales only yesterday, and have been immensely busy all day; but thought I should like to close the meeting."

Then saluting the other ladies in their turn, he made an unctuous remark to each. This business ended, he said to all, in fervent, emotional tones, " My dear friends, it is such a pleasure to see you all so indefatigable in your labour of love. I am sure you must be charmed at the numbers present. Shall we sing now? Are you ready to close? I have a meeting I must attend when I leave here. It is some little distance hence. After that I shall go to our special prayer-meeting. Say a few words first? With pleasure." As Falcon Small rose, the ladies dropped their work, and arranged themselves in a respectfully listening attitude.

" My dear friends," he commenced, " it gives me great pleasure to see the Missionary Working Association so well represented this evening. Your labour of love will be hailed with gratitude by the poor natives for whom you are spending your time. In our annual reports this year we learn that at Flatskumski the number of converts had increased to six hundred. Four hundred of these have agreed to adopt the civilized dress of the European, so that I may safely predicate that, at the present time, in Flatskumski the becoming, and sensible, costume that we see in these very streets of London is gradually being adopted. The women ask eagerly that their babes may be clothed like the English children. Flatskumski and England, hand in hand, in civilized robes, and civilized ways! The chiefs have discontinued the gorgeousness of their attire, and often now appear dressed like the English Christian on the Sabbath-day! In dividing their food they begin to abandon the use of skewers, and may be found separating it into portions, with the English knife and fork, like our own families in this christian land! Our civilizing influence has induced them to organize a small standing army in place of their warlike hordes. And eventually, no doubt, instead of the mission-room where services are now held on that island, we may assist them to erect a magnificent edifice with stained windows, lofty tower, and conspicuous in all those features which characterize the most attractive of our own religious temples. It is a pleasure, also, to me to state, that in the pockets of the clothes which are exported from this country to Flatskumski, are always enclosed a copy of my little works, 'What You Want,' and ' Nothing but the Blood.' Twelve thousand of these have thus found their way into the hands of the Flatskumski natives! And, as there have been six hundred converts during the past year, from each score of copies we have obtained one convert! Bibles, too, are distributed, and though, with the benighted darkness of heathen tribes, the people, on reading them, have exclaimed, with a Flatskumski native's incredulity, 'These Englishmen do not act up to the principles of their faith,' yet, on a closer investigation, they have left their idols, ejaculating, ' The white man's religion is the religion for us. There is nothing to DO! We have simply to believe.' Such a religion, you may imagine, must, in the long run, commend itself to those whose barbarian faith extorts from them the greatest self-denial to please their gods, and the offering of sacrifices to procure their salvation. Dear friends, let us go on! Let us be true to our faith! Let us, —leaving the Romanist to torture himself with penances, and work out his salvation by fancied righteousness,— content *ourselves* with the merits of Him who is our Representative, and who requires us *only* to believe. And may every tribe and kindred, every land and nation, be speedily brought to the only true faith, which is our own. **We will now sing a hymn.**"

A few words of prayer from Mr. Falcon Small closed the meeting. Almost before the last words of the benediction had died from his lips, the reverend gentleman sprang like a jack-in-the-box to Mrs. Blooster's side, and was holding out his hand to say good-night. Fervently uttering the words, "So pleased to see you all," he rushed off.

Having spoken at the meeting to which he had referred, he leaped into a hansom cab, and rattled over the streets to his Chapel, to attend the special prayer-meeting.

Mr. Rainford was there long before him, eagerly waiting.

The prayer-meeting was held in a room adjoining the Church. It was well filled when Rainford entered. On the platform were assembled the deacons and Assistant Minister. The latter, perceiving by Rainford's dress that he was a Divine, invited him, with official pomposity, to sit on the seats of honour beside them.

"I want to speak to Mr. Small," said Rainford, as he took the place which was offered. "Is he here?"

"Not yet," returned Mr. Twaddle, the Assistant Minister, "but he will be present shortly."

The proceedings commenced with a hymn; then followed a prayer from one of the deacons; and Rainford found himself once more in the region of Cant. The theology of Beeswax was displayed in full force here. It was arranged by Mr. Small that the prayers should be limited in duration, in the same way as the speaking of a debating class is limited; and as only five minutes were allowed each supplicant, it was noticeable how each man's pet hobby stalked through his whole prayer. One man solicited the return of the Lord's "peculiar people" to Jerusalem; another, devoted his five minutes to the various members of the royal family, including an infant princess thirty-six hours old; another, entreated for the heathen that their darkness might be enlightened; another, prayed for the British army

struction of Roman Catholicism; and a sixth, requested that the weather might be altered. But, for personal wisdom, purity of heart, honesty of purpose, humility, or charitableness, not so much as a single aspiration escaped their lips. It never seemed to occur to them to pray for that spirit, and disposition, which would enable them to acquiesce in the ways of God. They impiously assumed it to be their duty, to make impertinent suggestions to the Creator as to how He should amend His plans to their views ; and, with marvellous audacity, they coaxed Him to stay the laws of Nature, and work innumerable small miracles in consequence of their request, and for their personal convenience.

Weakened by illness, and full of despair at his position, Rainford, when he had heard the second prayer, almost forgot where he was ; and, with his hands to his face, he was unconscious of its finish, and would have remained in the same position during the singing which followed, had not Mr. Twaddle touched him on the arm and whispered, " Mr. Small is now coming in."

When Rainford looked up, Mr. Falcon Small had bounded on to the platform. Having wedged himself, between two or three deacons to get to Mr. Twaddle's side he whispered, and vociferated to the Assistant Minister for a second or two, and then taking the hymn-book which was humbly offered, walked to the edge of the platform, and with a loud voice commenced—

" Dear friends, only this morning I followed to the grave an evangelical nobleman. Surrounded by all the luxuries that wealth could give, and with the Queen's physician in attendance, nothing could keep away the angel of death. At the costly and magnificent family vault of that noble lord we sang a hymn, which we will now all join in singing once again, and rejoice that his soul, through faith in the Atoning Blood, has passed to those realms where the earthly coronet will be surmounted by the crown of right-

This was extremely touching, and the people seemed to think it so. They were perfectly quiet while Mr. Small spoke, appeared overawed by their Pastor's intimacy with aristocracy, and overwhelmed by his announcement. The dolorous hymn was sung with solemn fervour, and Rainford was the only person who endeavoured, and endeavoured vainly, to discover what connection the nobleman's funeral had with the prayer-meeting. After the hymn, and while a member of the congregation was praying, Mr. Twaddle lent forward and acquainted Mr. Small—whose eyes, though apparently covered by his fingers, were wandering all around—with Rainford's presence. This statement, accompanied with Rainford's card, brought Small, after the prayer, to Rainford's side. He shook hands, saying, "These are very nice meetings, my dear friend. *We* enjoy them very much."

When all was over, Small took the visitor to his vestry.

"I shall be able to give you five minutes, my dear friend," he said, "and then I have to be at a meeting presided over by Lord Toffee. Let me see, you would be glad to get a charge? You resigned the Independent Chapel at Chenley, did you not?"

The colour stole into Rainford's pale cheek.

"I was called on to resign, because two of my deacons persistently represented that I was "unsound" with regard to what they designated the doctrine of the Blood. It is sometimes fearful work in these country places: the minds of the people are opaque, and will not admit light."

Rainford rejoiced in the impression that he might speak openly to a man like Falcon Small. He ignorantly imagined that such a popular preacher would be thoroughly liberal in his opinions, and would have sufficient intelligence to be anxious to teach his congregation as well as talk to them.

"Then you had a little disagreement?" interrogated

"We had two or three disagreements," blurted out Rainford honestly, "and, for these disagreements, I am cast on the world with my wife and children, having nothing but my ministerial work to depend on for subsistence. They acted very cruelly to me, Mr. Small."

Falcon Small seemed quite to understand the case now.

"Your opinions were not considered sound, I presume, Mr. Rainford?"

"I believe not," said Rainford firmly. "But I respect truth more than popularity, Mr. Small. And my convictions are dearer to my heart than success or power."

"Ye-es, ye-es," returned Small, stroking his chin. "I will see what I can do for you, my dear friend," he added, with a dart of his eye at the clock on the mantelpiece.

"There was a man at my Church named Beeswax," pursued Rainford, "a coarse, uneducated fellow. He was constantly wishing me to introduce the 'blood,' as he termed it, into my discourses. I could not conscientiously respond to his request. This doomed me. Such bosh, is it not, Mr. Small?"

The cold sardonic smile again returned to Small's face.

"People will have that sort of thing, Mr. Rainford; and we must give them the truth as they can bear it, you know. We must conform a little to the tendencies of the public mind, my dear friend."

Rainford looked astonished.

"I would *teach* and *educate* the mind, Mr. Small."

"Ye-es, ye-es. I am sorry our interview must end. My important engagement. I must keep it. My dear friend, I will bear you in mind. You shall hear from me. So pleased to have had- -"

Rainford was bowed out by this time, and, the vestry door closing, he was prevented from hearing the remainder of the sentence. To do Falcon Small justice, he did not

recollection of Rainford for ever after. It simply was this: Falcon Small could never deem anything important enough to be remembered which was outside the circle of his own personal interests.

Having disposed of Rainford, Falcon Small dashed off to the meeting at which Lord Toffee presided. He there distinguished himself by the delivery of an exaggerated panegyric on the character of the noble lord. He observed the reporters taking notes of what he said. He assumed that some of his speech would be printed in the news papers. His heart rejoiced.

When he reached home, at twelve o'clock that night, he felt that he was indeed a workman to whom Humanity might say, "Well done, good and faithful servant : such a day's work as this, is unquestionably well worthy of a popular preacher!"

CHAPTER XXXII.

CANT AS A REMUNERATIVE PROFESSION.—THE BLASPHEMY O_i POPULAR THEOLOGY.—REV. JEHOSOPHAT DANKS.

AMONGST the numerous inhabitants that peopled one of the blackest alleys of London some years since, there was a family which consisted of a man, his wife, and two children—a boy and girl. The father had fits of intemperance which bordered on insanity. The mother was more industrious than the neighbours that surrounded her, and kept her one room cleaner, and bestowed more care and affection on her children than is usual with the drunken women of these places. She managed to send the boy to a Sunday-school, where he picked up a smattering of reading, and early developed a pietistic tendency by singing hymns in the street, to obtain a few pence when the father was tipsy and there was no money at home. The boy's voice was eminently suitable for psalmody; and his face, which was strangely old for his years, he cunningly trained into the religious expression which he had observed in the features of his superiors at the Sunday-school. Thin, pale, and cadaverous, with an expression of mock humility on his countenance, he sang his morbid, mawkish melodies, and attracted the attention of the passers-by, till they formed a small group at his side. Then the wily boy would choose his most pathetic hymns, and shake his crafty head with each drivelling sentiment, till, from the gaping crowd, he gathered numerous coppers. After the receipt of these he would shuffle home with the old cunning shining out of his eyes.

This state of things went on for some time; the boy, with increasing years, developing excessive shrewdness for earning money, and doing so more with his tongue than his hands. He had always ready a clever tale about his own and his mother's miseries, and this tale, which was well saturated with Cant, drew many a sixpence from the listener. Thus he lived till his fifteenth or sixteenth year, when his Sunday-school teacher—impressed by the ready flow of glib, trite, pietistic talk which the lad could always indulge in at a minute's notice, and considering this a manifestation of early religionism highly creditable to his Sunday-school which had produced it—took up his case. The result was an introduction to a college where young men of the coarsest class were, if considered eligible, received and trained for the ministry.

A few years glide by, and the sickly, starving, canting boy, has changed into the well-fed, well-clothed, complacent student. He wears a ministerial wide-awake, and has donned a grand official-looking black coat, also a white neckcloth. His hair is long, and parted down the middle; and the cunning, that was born in his eyes, has been exchanged for an expression of priestly religiosity. The tale of "me and my poor mother" is now obsolete; he tells another, respecting "me and the Master," and he does it equally well. He is no longer called "Jossy." He is now designated in the denominational directories, and year books, as "The Rev. Jehosophat Danks."

Whilst Mr. Rainford was in London seeking a pulpit, this gentleman became his successor at Chenley, in response to what was termed "an earnest and prayerful call." The history of his promotion, and the causes which led up to it, are not without interest. After Rainford's connection with the Chenley Church was severed by the resolution of the meeting over which Dr. Sound presided, the deacons deputed Messrs. Beeswax and Treacles, to select "supplies" for the pulpit, from amongst the most eligible of the large number of reverend gentlemen who had already offered

the diaconate, and the Church members generally, feel themselves for a long time afterwards. They were a grand tribunal. Before them all the eager candidates for the pastorate—doctors of divinity, members of Universities, writers, and elegant preachers—had to appear, and receive sentence.

This tribunal, having summarily disposed of the claims of scores of applicants, and having swept aside as unworthy of notice some of the holiest of men, and best scholars of the day, began, at last, to grow weary of its unpaid functions. Nevertheless, it had not yet discovered a candidate in whose favour its august judgment could be pronounced.

At this crisis Beeswax came again "to the rescue," as he said, of the "Hark of the Lord." As his picturesque description does not exactly supply the necessary details of his exploit, it may be better to forsake the metaphor and to pursue the history. What he did follows.

He wrote "to a valued Christian friend" in London (a little tailor by trade, and a deacon of a Chapel), and requested him to be on the look-out for a "*thorough, blood-bought, evangelical sin-convincer.*" The tailor thought that the Rev. Jehosophat Danks answered precisely to the description given by Beeswax of his spiritual wants. So it came to pass that Danks, once the miserable street-singer, found himself, on a certain Sunday morning, in the very pulpit from which the accomplished Rainford had been ejected by those who, in scriptural phrase, may be called the "beasts and the elders."

To the more thoughtful portion of the people, Danks was a sad contrast to the man who had formerly occupied that pulpit. His appearance was essentially vulgar and gross, and the combined efforts of the hair-dresser, and the tailor, were impotent to give him the slightest appearance of gentility.

The most prominent feature of his face was his mouth.

naturally strained them, as if his great physical aim in life was to alter, what once was a mouth, into a vast chasm of utterance. Though his complexion never lost the unhealthy hue produced by the cellar, which for sixteen years had been his home, he never seemed to permit that, or any other circumstance, to keep him humble, or to make him serious. His sudden good fortune had only added to his self-confidence ; and so steeped in conceit was the vapouring youth, that nervousness, or the slightest consciousness of responsibility at the solemn position he was filling, never occurred to him. From the first moment of his appearance before the Chenley congregation, he was a great success. Beeswax and Treacles well prepared the way for him ; and as he boldly stated that he "came on a mission from Heaven," the people soon rallied round him.

The first Sunday of his settled ministry was signalized as a grand day. The morning service was long after spoken of as having been "an especially blessed opportunity, and a season of refreshing." The Rev. Jehosophat Danks chose the most sensuous hymns, and summoning all the strength of his street-practised voice, sang them as loudly as in the olden days when he sang in the London thoroughfares for his supper. Beeswax, who had much approved the conversation he had had with him before the service, arranged himself in his usual Sunday position, but gave out the hymns with a more satisfied and less critical look upon his face than in the Rainford times. He felt, as he afterwards expressed himself to Treacles, that the young man was about to expound the "heevangelical" way of salvation, and give them the old-fashioned gospel. Whatever this might be, Danks seemed determined to make an impression. He roared and bellowed like a bull. He paused to take breath only when it became absolutely necessary. He never faltered for an idea, because he never wanted one. He was a popular Preacher : and therefore he was able to rush into subjects and through scenes where even angels fear to tread. He knew the secrets of eternity, and had construed the covenants of God.

His entire sermon would occupy too much space here so we must be contented with a summary of his glowing, soul-uplifting, argument. It was this: the Eternal Father having got into a muddle, by permitting the beings whom He had created to fall into sin, was at a loss to know how to let them live, and yet show His hatred of wickedness. Justice, which was a principle outside Himself, to which even He was amenable, required that they should die. His own wrath, roused by their criminality, also required that they should die. But Mercy, which was another principle partly independent of Him, and by which He was bound, stepped forward, and requested that they should be permitted to live. In the midst of this perplexity and hocus-pocus, the Son presented Himself, and offered to die in the place of those who had sinned against their Creator. And, the Father, having quenched His burning sword in the blood of His own Son, was able once more to look with equanimity on all the creatures whom He had hated before. The Son, having thus been slaughtered for us, we had only to believe this fact, and we were safe for all eternity. Nothing but belief was required of us.

Such a picture of the dying agonies of Christ did the Rev. Jehosophat Danks draw, and so graphically did he paint all the ghastly details of death, that a female hearer, who had lately lost her dearest relation, was affected to tears. No sooner did Danks's quick eye observe this, than he took care to "improve the occasion;" and fixing his attention on the supposed convert, he wrought her up by his declamatory fervour, till her hysterical sobs were audible all over the Chapel, and she was assisted out by Treacles—whose face suggested that such results as these were of a highly important character, and the sort of thing they had long desired to see. Anything poorer, more blasphemous, tautological, or more absurdly ignorant, than Danks's wretched twaddle, could hardly be offered to human ears. But, so great is the love of some religionists for gross sensuousness, mawkish sentimentality, and putrescent Cant, that the chief portion of the congregation was delighted with the sermon, and talked with rapture about the grand effects which had already been accomplished in the hearer whose "heart had been overcome" by the eloquent "servant of the Lord." Beeswax was very much elated, and even excited; so much so, indeed, that when, at the end of the sermon, he rose and shouted,

"'Ail to the Lord's Anointed,"

it might have been thought, from his exceptionally jovial tones, that he was at a convivial supper, calling out for a libation, had not the words "Number one hundred and seventy," and the waving of his book, demonstrated that he was announcing a hymn for the congregation to sing.

When the Rev. Jehosophat Danks was fairly installed in regular work, Treacles and Beeswax enjoyed a rest from the anxiety caused by preserving the orthodoxy of the Church. They even felt that, occasionally, they were justified in a nap when the sermon was very long. They knew that, on awaking, they should find Danks at exactly the same place as they left him, in the same train of thought, with the same sentiments, altered slightly in the construction of the phrase, and interspersed with the correct number of "ohs" and "ahs." There was no fear of a stray word of heterodoxy creeping in while they slept. Though Danks selected a text, they well knew he would take nothing out of it; he would simply gyrate round it in a well-beaten track. Whatever the text, the track traversed would be just the same. It was very comforting to wake up and know that they might at once nod their heads approvingly, and lift their eyes to Heaven with a sigh, thereby rendering

Danks soon rose to an extensive popularity in Chenley, and all the district round about. He had the satisfaction of knowing that all the young ladies were endeavouring to fascinate him, and all the old ones were smiling in commendation of him.

Hardly a thought of their former Pastor ever troubled the Chenley congregation. Having driven him from them, they were careless of his future, or his welfare ; careless as to whether, in attaining their own mean object, they had blighted for ever his success in life.

Thus it always is with the fanatical mob. The true teacher they crucify. They call aloud for Barabbas.

CHAPTER XXXIII.

CANT AND COLLEGES.—OVERCROWDED STATE OF THE DENOMINATIONAL HARVEST-FIELDS.—MR. DARNLEY'S PROTEST.—MR. MELVILLE AND MR. RAINFORD MEET.

THE Canary Congregational College Committee decided that their anniversary proceedings should arouse the attention of all the religious public. They arranged a morning service, at which no fewer than six great denominational lights were brought forward to shine around the star of the day, the Rev. Dr. Sound, who coruscated in the College pulpit. Of course collections were made in aid of the funds. In anticipation of them, the hymns were selected, the prayers were framed, the passages of Scripture were chosen, and the sermon was preached, with the express intention of producing on the minds of the audience the impression that there were "not enough labourers to gather in the Lord's spiritual harvest," and that it was a religious duty to subscribe money to enable the College to procure, prepare, and despatch, the number necessary for the purpose.

It was reiterated that the spiritual fields of the world were white with a harvest which was wasting for the want of reapers. At the grand evening meeting all the speakers repeated that same assertion, in every variety of form and phrase. The tutors of the College, on the platform assembled, acted to perfection the part of brave, resolute men, who were able, and determined, to qualify for the required harvesting any number of students who would come forward and help the Lord in the present pressing emergency.

ingly self-satisfied. They felt that they had a mission, and a most important one. Some of them, indeed, seemed even to smirk with vanity and conceit. Among this number was young Pupsley, the son of old Pupsley, the eccentric soda-water maker. This youth was found worthless in business from the moment when he fancied he had a "call" to the ministry. There were no external evidences that Nature moulded his organization with a view to his being a teacher or a leader of men. She had given him dull eyes, a very narrow retreating forehead, a snub nose, a crooked spine, a refractory liver, and, as he often boasted, "a very weak constitution." He possessed scarcely any logical faculty, no poetry, and no imagination; he was a very poor hand at composing a sermon, and a wretched speaker. But, in answer to the urgent College appeals "for men to gather in the spiritual harvest," a still small voice whispered within him that he was "set apart" for the "glorious work." His friends were satisfied that he was "called by the Holy Spirit." And he, and they, were proud, as well they might be, of the selection thus made. From the day on which he was admitted into Canary College, Pupsley's feelings of self-consequence had been ostentatiously writing their lines upon his priggish countenance. Among Pupsley's companions were several students whose capacity for "gathering in" any spiritual harvest were not even equal to his. Out of the entire number of students there were only about six on whose behalf any reasonable excuse could be put forward for the position which they were assuming.

The youths themselves were not to blame for the anomalous position which they occupied. The College authorities had assured them, and their vanity had made them anxious to believe, that their services were urgently wanted in the "gospel field"; and the Church, as if mindful of their feebleness, had sung for their encouragement that

"Satan trembles when he sees

The senior student was, according to custom, put forward at the evening meeting to make a specimen speech, which was intended to show the College subscribers the kind of harvest-reaping talent which *Alma Mater* was rearing. The honorary secretary, Dr. Scoreby, delivered a telling address; in which elaborate arithmetical calculations as to the pecuniary cost to the subscribers of each of the students, were relieved by grand and glowing pictures of the moral future of the world when its spiritual harvests should have been garnered by their hands. All went on very well indeed until a most gentlemanly, intelligent-looking man, arose in the body of the assembly and demanded to be heard.

"Who is he?" inquired the pompous Rev. Mr. Podgers, impatiently nudging his ministerial neighbour on the platform.

"He is Mr. Darnley, lately the head of the great firm, Darnley, Golding & Co.," replied the Rev. Hamilton Carney. "Unfortunately we shall be obliged to allow him to speak as he has been a munificent donor."

But Mr. Darnley was not in need of any concession from official magnates. He was one of those men who, by their very presence, compel even the involuntary attention of crowds. After a few graceful, but manly, introductory sentences, he went on to say, "I address you because it is my right, because it is my duty, and because this will be my last opportunity. Some years since I conveyed to this College committee, as trustees, a valuable piece of land, on part of which was erected a beautiful Chapel. I am here to complain that, in spite of my intentions, and in defiance of the protestations of the congregation, you have obscured that Chapel from view by the erection of a brewery, which in itself is a nuisance; but on this land, and in this association, is profanation. You allege that when I conveyed the site to you it became yours to do with as you please, and you say that a brewery pays money, which enables you to maintain more students at the College. But I remind you that the liquor traffic is the greatest obstacle to the spread of Christian truth. Moreover, the congregation assembling at the Chapel will always have to endure a nuisance created by you, the men whom I had constituted their legal protectors. My next remark has reference to your cry for more men to enter the ministry. I say it is an unjustifiable cry. I give you statistics. There is a vacant pulpit at Pantin; salary one hundred pounds per annum: there are fifty candidates for the pastorate. For the vacant pulpit at Tynt, salary two hundred pounds per annum, there are seventy candidates. For the vacant pulpit of Yesborough, salary three hundred pounds, there are ninety candidates. I could multiply instances almost indefinitely with the like results. Of course, in order to justify the continued existence of your College, you must keep on getting students. But does it ever occur to you that your responsibility is very serious? How can you reconcile your proceedings with the notorious facts against you? What reparation can you offer to those young men who find, too late, that you have allured them into a mistaken career? You have besought them to prepare themselves for the pulpit, yet you well know that the pulpit is so crowded that there is not room left for them to squeeze into it. I am aware how terrible is the offence I am giving; but as I am responsible for having assisted this College, I was anxious, before I leave England, to place plainly before you the altered views which I now take as to this and similar institutions. The storm of vituperation which may follow is very unimportant. I have seen sufficient of religious Cant and intolerance to separate me from them for ever; and if I make this announcement here it is simply because I wish it to be known, for the benefit of others, that I withdraw my name and assistance from this, and the allied institutions, with which I have been identified."

Naturally enough there was some little disturbance made

by the audience during these observations; and something like consternation was apparent in the faces of some of the platform men.

Mr. Melville, who was in the meeting, and who was slightly acquainted with Mr. Darnley, felt a peculiar interest in this unexpected speech. This was not only because it in part shadowed forth some of his own views, but because he knew that Mr. Darnley spoke under the influence of intense conviction; and that his conclusions had been reached by painful processes. People in the meeting who endeavoured to interrupt Mr. Darnley found themselves well called to order by Melville. But, it was obvious, that the great majority regarded the utterances as insults which ought not to have been uttered.

Of course, the speech was indignantly replied to by various vehement College apologists; and resolutions in favour of the College were carried amidst applause. The fact was that most of the audience were in various dissimilar ways personally interested in discrediting the new critic.

As Melville looked around he noticed, however, one attentive, earnest, quiet face, which did not seem to share the sentiments of the majority, and he was delighted to find that it was that of Mr. Rainford. At the end of the proceedings he went across to him, and it cheered Rainford's heart to be welcomed with a greeting more cordial than he had yet received in London.

Leaving the building together, Mr. Melville and Mr. Rainford walked homeward conversing; and soon Melville was in possession of those facts which we have already related concerning Rainford's Chenley and metropolitan experiences. It required very little insight to enable him to understand that, though too brave to confess it, Rainford was in actual pecuniary distress. Indeed, Mr. Rainford had attended the meeting in the desperate, forlorn, and now disappointed, hope of finding some old fellow-

to get employment. By reason of his being in his present terrible plight, notwithstanding that he had passed through that very College with high honour, it had been most exasperating to him to listen to speeches urging men to come forward to do that pulpit work which he himself could not anywhere find, and which the denomination could not find for him.

Many years ago, in answer to appeals similar to those which had just been ringing in his ears, he unreservedly devoted himself to the ministry; and having consecrated his life to the office for which he was well qualified, he now found himself not only unable to obtain a pulpit, but without direction as to the means of procuring one even at the hands of those same College notabilities who were dinning into the ears of the public the palpable untruth that there were not sufficient Preachers to meet the requirements of the time.

Melville sympathised greatly with Rainford's position. It came out inadvertently, during the conversation, that to such straits was Rainford's little family reduced for the bare necessaries of life, that the brave Mabel had been compelled to obtain needlework in order to add to their scanty funds.

Melville found that Rainford was greatly distressed at the failure of his visit to Falcon Small, from which great things had been expected. He therefore offered to call on Mr. Small with a view to obtaining a better result; because he was sanguine that his friend Mr. Hardcastle might use favourable influence in the matter.

Rainford went home with a lighter heart.

The following morning he experienced the greatest surprise of his life. On opening a letter, directed in an unknown handwriting, he found himself the possessor of fifty pounds' worth of bank notes, enclosed in a sheet of paper, inscribed with the words, " A present."

CHAPTER XXXIV.

CANT AND SHUFFLING.—MR. MELVILLE'S VISIT TO THE REV. FALCON SMALL.—THE VALUE OF A POPULAR PREACHER AS A HELP IN TROUBLE.

TRUE to his promise, Melville, the following Sunday went to see Falcon Small at his Church. With no desire to listen again to that gentleman's preaching, Melville entered the Church at the close of the service, and inquired his way to the great man's vestry. He, however, first found out, to his great regret, that he could not be introduced by Mr. Hardcastle, because that worthy deacon was out of town. Impatient to execute his mission, Melville went straight to the vestry door—which the awe-stricken group of Small's admiring bystanders seemed to regard as that of the holy of holies—and, after knocking, entered the presence of the Rev. Falcon Small, being invited thereto by a sonorous "Come in." The popular preacher was sitting in an armchair by the fire, and three of his deacons stood obsequiously around him. Falcon Small was performing his hollow laugh, a laugh peculiar to himself, all noise but no merriment. The deacons were softly and reverently echoing the mirth. Small's eye instantly fixed on Melville, and seemed to interrogate his business.

"I must apologise for introducing myself, Mr. Small," spoke Melville. "I had hoped to have been presented to you by Mr. Hardcastle, but as he is from home, I must introduce myself."

"I am pleased to see any friend of Mr. Hardcastle's," replied Small, bowing affectedly, and placing a chair for Melville.

"Thanks, Mr. Small. I came to ask the favour of your influence for a friend of mine who is seeking a charge. He has already paid you a visit, but I am anxious to tell you more of him than he could say of himself. I know you have the power of recommending many Ministers, and I can honestly affirm that my friend is worthy your commendation. He is an excellent preacher, and a genuinely good man. But, in order to have a fair start, it is necessary that his case should be taken up by some one like yourself."

Falcon Small smiled his cold smile.

"What denomination does he belong to?" he asked.

"The Independents. Mr. Hardcastle would know him by reputation, I believe, for my friend comes from Chenley. He was Minister at the Congregational Church there."

"Ah, yes," said Small, "now I remember. I have had the advantage of meeting Mr. Rainford, and we went into his case very thoroughly—very thoroughly indeed."

Here one of the deacons spoke up.

"I have heard Mr. Hardcastle mention Mr. Rainford. There was a strong feeling against him in his Church, was there not? He was surely ejected for not being orthodox."

"He was treated abominably," protested Melville, his eye kindling, "and by a wretched little clique of the most ignorant of men. The congregation as a body liked him. The opposition to him emanated from only two or three of the deacons."

"Did you say he was ejected from his Church, Mr. Knowall?" asked Small of the deacon who had just spoken.

"He was asked to resign," explained Melville.

"Mr. Hardcastle was my informer," returned Knowall, "and he told me they turned him away for being unsound in the faith."

"Rather an awkward affair," mused Small. "I should think Mr. Hardcastle would know."

"Oh I am sure this was the case," continued Knowall, "and I heard from Mr. Hardcastle that Mr. Rainford was considered a most heterodox preacher. He was not sound on many points."

"Can you tell me what those points were?" inquired Melville.

"The doctrine of the 'blood' was one," said Knowall; "and 'original sin,' I fancy, was another."

Melville cast a glance at Small, who had drawn his chair to the table, and was resting his arms on it; but his face was unmoved.

"I am sure Mr. Small will agree with me. It was only the men's frightful ignorance that caused them to squabble over such nonsense," said Melville.

"Sir!" exclaimed Mr. Knowall, "the doctrine of the 'blood' is of all importance, I consider; and Mr. Small, I am proud to say, preaches it faithfully."

"Heresy is a very easy charge to make," replied Melville; "and as to the doctrines to which you refer, it is certain that even the ablest thinkers differ in opinion respecting the sense in which they are to be understood, and their practical bearing on morality seems quite debatable."

Small said nothing, but played a tattoo with his fingers on the table. He seemed anxious to convey the impression that his time was of immense importance, and that he should have to depart in a moment.

"Is it possible?" asked Melville, "that men of thought and learning still proclaim such barbarous dogmas as essential to salvation? I smiled at the ignorance of the little country shoemaker, and grocer, with whom my friend had to contend. I little thought that in a Church like this, and amongst a civilized London congregation, dogmas about the blood, and original sin, would acquire any importance."

"The old tried religion, sir," said Knowall, "is good

many a long year, and we never want any new-fangled doctrines. Mr. Small preaches salvation by blood only."

Falcon Small raised his eyes, but it was only to glance at the clock. Melville was vexed at his stubborn silence.

"I will leave my friend's case in your hands, Mr. Small," he said. "I hope your opinion of him will be favourable. May I arrange another interview at which you and he can discuss all necessary matters, with a view to forming your independent judgment respecting his fitness for the ministry?"

Falcon Small looked up quickly.

"There would be some difficulty in bringing him forward," he observed blandly, "after what I hear from Mr. Knowall."

"Is it necessary then, in order to secure his introduction to a Church, that he should preach the doctrines of the blood, and original sin?" inquired Melville.

Small rose from his chair, and his voice was louder and his manner more decisive and oratorical as he proclaimed, "There is one faith, as my dear friend here observes, and the doctrines of that faith are plain and simple. To these doctrines, of course, we, as a body, must remain true."

Melville was listening eagerly, anxious to see how Small, who affected to play the part of an educated progressive man, could support his deacon's views. But he was not prepared for the second part of Small's speech, or for the extended hand, and suave smile, that the Minister gave him as he concluded: "I am sorry not to be able to help your friend. Another time when you have a request, I trust I shall be more fortunate. So pleased to have seen you."

By this time Small had opened the door, and Melville found himself bowed out, before he could collect his thoughts. Stung by Small's civil impudence, Melville paused outside the vestry door, hardly aware he was so doing. The people pushed past him, some one way, some the other, buzzing, chattering, and on the watch for a glimpse of the great popular preacher. In a few minutes he came out, accompanied by Knowall, who was talking very earnestly. Small was not listening. His cold eye was wandering far away from the Church and its people. He stared at Melville, but without any recollection of him, and in another minute he strode rapidly away to dine with a wealthy vulgarian, at whose Chapel he was to deliver, in the afternoon, his grand sermon from the text, " He went about doing good."

CHAPTER XXXV.

Cant and Crime.—Golding's Gamekeeper Dies in a Scuffle with Tom.—Newspaper Marvels.

WE must return to Tom. We described the circumstances under which he was removed from Golding Hall. It remains to be related that he was sentenced, by a game-preserving magistracy, to six months' imprisonment for the poaching transaction, which, as we know, had excited the implacable severity of Mr. Chippendale Golding.

By a singular coincidence he was liberated from his penal duties at the time when the prorogation of Parliament, and the termination of the London season, permitted Golding to return to his country house. The worthy member, in view of an approaching general election, commenced a series of ostentatious hospitalities. But the very first of them was destined to have a tragic ending.

The story which Tom told on the Sunday morning when we last saw him, was strictly true, and he had been convicted unjustly. This had preyed on his mind during all the period of his incarceration. Society had always been cruel to him, and this culminating atrocity made him thirst for revenge.

He determined to inflict a terrible beating on Walters, Golding's fierce gamekeeper, who had been the cause of his being sent to prison. He reached Golding Hall for that purpose on the evening when Golding gave the first of his series of dinner-parties. The gamekeeper was close to the hall, whither he had gone to obtain his share of such remnants of the feast as found their way to the kitchen. Tom challenged him. The gamekeeper struck out brutally, and fell on him with an open knife, calling all the time lustily for help.

Golding and his friends, who were sitting over their repast, heard the screams just under the dining-room window, which was at once thrown open. Tom saw that he would soon be overpowered by the assistance which was coming to his adversary, who by this time was sprawling over him, brandishing the knife close to his throat. He made one desperate lunge for the knife, and partially extricated himself from his position. But Walters, who was now lying at full length, seized him violently by his leg, and Tom fell heavily forward upon the hand in which the gamekeeper still held the open knife. The effect of the fall was to drive the weapon into the gamekeeper's heart.

By the time Golding, and others, reached the scene of the affray, Walters was in his death spasm. Tom was, of course, captured, taken to prison, and charged with wilful murder.

After the usual preliminary inquiry before the magistrate, he was committed for trial at the assizes.

In the meantime the tragedy was one of the leading topics of conversation throughout the county. It was also of great service to newspaper editors during the "dull season," when their columns required something to supply the vacant place usually occupied by the platitudes, swagger, and twaddle of the official, and parliament men, who had, for a few weeks, left off speaking in order to consecrate their powers to grouse-killing.

Several of these admirable editors wrote splendid moral articles on the subject of "the increased use of the knife for pugilistic purposes in England." It was marvellous how these literati, although often residing hundreds of miles away from the scene of the struggle, were able to supply the public with even its most minute details! Four illustrated papers gave four different, and contradictory, pictures of the combatants, apparently sketched by their artists on the spot, at the very moment of the occurrence.

The most sensational and enterprising of the London papers, *The Daily Bluefire*, supplied its readers, in the course of three weeks, with fifty-four columns and a half of printed particulars relating to the affray. So indefatigable, painstaking, and enterprising was the "special commissioner" of *The Daily Bluefire*, that within a few days of the occurrence he was able to supply facts about Tom's parentage, and history, never before known, because never existing. He was able to tell the outraged British public, on the authority, as he said, of "persons of the highest credibility," that Tom was "not an Englishman at all, but the vagrant son of a proscribed Russian citizen." It was explained that Tom had long resided abroad among political conspirators, one of whom had presented him with the un-English weapon with which, since the day of its coming into his possession, Tom had stabbed no less than seven men! It was also hinted that he had long been in the pay of the Leader of the great Liberal Party in England.

CHAPTER XXXVI.

CANT AND ELECTORAL TACTICS.—A DRAWING-ROOM PRAYER-MEETING.—COLONEL SAMMEY'S "GREAT WORK AT THE BARRACKS."—MISS IRENE GRAHAM BETROTHED TO MR. OSCAR CRAYFORD.

GOLDING was too good a strategist to allow the tragedy, or its consequences, to interfere in any way, with his electoral tactics. He busied himself in all directions in consolidating party interests, conciliating waverers, and planning schemes for securing new political adherents. Some of his supporters, in conjunction with local magnates whom he was most anxious to convert into supporters, were just now fanatically active in connection with the latest fashion in religion—" drawing-room prayer-meetings." They invited Mr. Golding's co-operation, and, in his present popularity-hunting mood, had no difficulty in obtaining it. The gentleman who had been mainly instrumental in introducing the drawing-room prayer-meetings into the county was Mr. Oscar Crayford, who, shortly after his interview with Lorraine, at the hotel in Rome, returned to visit some of his connections in this locality. As a compliment to some of his constituents, and as an evidence of his own religious zeal, Mr. Golding invited Mr. Crayford to stay a short time at Golding Hall. Here Mr. Crayford enjoyed himself very much, for he met the most beautiful girl he had ever seen, and under auspices which favoured his design of making her his wife.

Irene Graham was an orphan. Her mother had died during her infancy; and her father, Golding's uncle, when she was twelve years of age. This uncle had been Golding's guardian and benefactor. When he died, greatly impoverished, partly by Golding's conduct, he begged the wealthy and childless Golding to take care of Irene, and a small sum of money which she possessed. The money was only just enough to give Irene a thorough education, and on her leaving school Golding arranged to take her to his home; his idea being that she would not trouble him long, as her face gave great promise of beauty, and, with his assistance, he believed she would soon find a husband. For five and a half years Irene remained at one school. It was fortunately an excellent academy, and she obtained a capital education. She only saw her cousin twice a year. Once, and only once, she spent her Christmas holidays at Golding Hall. But, whenever Mr. Golding met her, he always represented how grateful she ought to be for all his care of her, till Irene fully believed that the money for her education came out of his pocket, and she was consequently under a sense of the deepest obligation to him. As a fact, she had never cost Golding a penny, but when her schooldays were ended he found himself with sufficient money in hand to furnish Irene with a handsome wardrobe, by which means she was able to maintain an appearance at Golding Hall that did not disgrace him.

"Now, my dear," exclaimed the generous Golding to his wife when Irene finally came home from school, "she must marry at once, or we shall be considerably out of pocket. At present I have managed so well that she has cost us nothing, and has received an excellent start in life. If only now we can marry her to a man of unquestionable piety, I shall be more than repaid for all my trouble."

"Ah, yes," replied Mrs. Golding, "Irene has had no religious training. I do trust she may marry an evangelical man."

"Of course I shall see to that," returned Golding. "I

shall certainly forbid any attentions from a worldly man. So rest satisfied on that point."

Meanwhile, Irene, ignorant of all this, was quite overcome by the apparent generosity of her grand relations; and never did a day elapse but Mrs. Golding made the remark, " What you would have done Irene, without your cousin, I dare not think. How good you ought to be to him."

Irene felt that this was painfully true. She had been very happy while at school, and often now wished she might return there; but Golding impressed her with the fact that she was a woman, and her actions must be regulated accordingly.

Soon after Crayford's arrival at Golding Hall, Irene was informed by her cousin of the visitor's desire to make her his wife. She was also told by Golding that she would be most fortunate in obtaining such a husband, and Irene, who was well nigh crushed by her sense of indebtedness to her relations, did not feel justified in raising any opposition till her cousin mentioned his solicitude that the marriage should take place shortly.

" I believe that this union will be for your spiritual good," said Golding, " and I am also anxious that the marriage should be hastened, in accordance with my dear friend's wishes."

" But, cousin, I do not want to be married yet," pleaded Irene, her eyes filling with tears.

Golding was irritated at her speech, and her grief.

" What do you intend doing in life ? " he asked. " Whom do you expect to keep you ? Here is a christian gentleman of affluent means, and with a character for piety and excellence, willing to take you, and do all he can for your spiritual and temporal comfort ; and you, forsooth, the favoured party, object. You put me out of all patience After all my goodness to you ! After all my care for your education ! After taking you to my home, and treating you like a father! I say such ingratitude can only come of an unregenerate heart, and is base in the extreme."

"Oh, cousin, I do not mean to be ungrateful," exclaimed Irene earnestly. "Do believe that I am conscious of your goodness to me. But, my life has been so changeless hitherto, that such a sudden alteration quite bewilders me."

"All I ask of you is to do what I bid you," returned Golding. "I must know best. I do not expect you to be a judge. See the expense your wedding will be to me. Of course it must take place from my house. What interest can I have in hastening such an event?"

Irene sighed. The helpless poverty of her condition had never appeared so forcibly before her. She left her cousin's presence with a heavy heart, and sought her own room.

Golding, and Crayford, afterwards had a further conversation respecting the pecuniary questions incidental to the marriage, at which each tried to outwit the other in selfishness. "Anything more which Irene may have will be at my death," Golding had said, when he had mentioned the trifling balance of Irene's money which was owing to her, and which he represented as being his own gift. He was rather taken aback at certain worldly manifestations on the part of his "dear christian brother;" and he felt it impossible to broach the point of the wedding breakfast. His intention had been to make Oscar Crayford, if possible, pay for the *déjeûner*, and the other wedding expenses. But that now appeared impossible. Crayford, on the other hand, was rather disappointed about the marriage settlement, but he was too much in love with the person of the beautiful Irene to break off his engagement on this account; and, besides, he had some enjoyment from feeling that, if she were poor, Irene would be, perhaps, more plastic under his autocratic will.

"Irene," said Golding, a few days after this conversation, "I wish you particularly to attend our drawing-room prayer-meeting this afternoon. If you have any lingering uncertainty as to whether you have done right in fulfilling my wishes, and accepting Mr. Crayford's hand, it will, I trust, be removed when you again see the remarkable powers and piety he possesses, and how highly everybody esteems him."

"I will, of course, attend, cousin," Irene said meekly; and she did so.

The company assembled at four o'clock in Golding's drawing-room. They were all fashionably dressed. It was noticeable that many of the plain girls had conspicuously fanciful attire, as if to make up by that for their lack of personal charms. Amongst the gentlemen were some officers from the Broadcray Barracks, who, with their well-trimmed moustaches and military airs, formed a prominent attraction to all the young ladies.

Crayford stood near the door, waiting to grasp the hand of each comer. Who could resist the fascination of his gaze, which seemed to speak the earnest interest of the man for each fair female soul? When Irene arrived he led her a little aside, and said: "Irene, I shall pray for *you* to-day. You are a jewel I must place in my Redeemer's crown."

Irene felt the blood tingling through her frame. His words were flattering to her ear, but oh, how hard it was to become what he wished. She seemed to herself the chief of sinners at that moment; and the tears rose to her eyes as Mr. Crayford glided to the harmonium, and beautifully played one of Boobey and Crankey's hymns, of which Golding had read the words.

At the conclusion of the singing, Mr. Sarney Ribble engaged in prayer, and made a pert appeal to the Almighty for blessings on the company assembled. He spoke to God as if to a younger brother to whom he was giving orders, and whose actions he felt it his duty to direct.

Another hymn, another prayer, and then Colonel Sammey, renowned as the christian officer who had done a

periences." Colonel Sammey was a diminutive, over-ripe, man of fashion, who possessed less than the average intelligence. His hair and whiskers were faultlessly dressed, and his tiny boots and gloves fitted without a wrinkle. He, at first, seemed nervous at the sound of his own voice, but his overweening conceit soon came to his rescue, and he related what he termed his "successes" since he last met the Drawing-room Prayer-meeting Association. He spoke slightly through his nose, in a weak, thin voice, and told of "the numbers he had sent weeping away" from the meetings he had held at the barracks. Two or three men had come to him late at night at his rooms, and, knocking loudly at his door, had demanded the way to the "golden city." It was discovered, afterwards, that they were the worse for drink, but the colonel had used the opportunity to reveal to them the way to Heaven, and he felt sure that his words would return to them when sober, and the results might be marvellous! This was spoken of subsequently in religious circles as the "startling work which was going on among the soldiers of Broadcray Barracks."

But the great event of the afternoon was when Mr. Crayford rose to speak. The ladies' eyes were riveted on him, and the men readjusted their eye-glasses. Little Colonel Sammey was resolved this time to see (as he expressed it) "how that Crayford did it," and put himself in a listening attitude.

The voice that now sounded was singularly sweet and clear. In low but distinct tones Mr. Oscar Crayford commenced:

"Before me this afternoon I behold a picture: it is a scene of fairy loveliness. There are fields waving with yellow corn; there are woods with leafy trees, the homes of birds of every plumage. They bask in an everlasting sunlight, glinting and sparkling in the golden beams. The flowers are growing in rich profusion, and the flowing river

this radiant spot, and their laughter and mirth fall on the perfumed air. Merrily they play, and dance, and sing, and intoxicated with the mundane loveliness, they walk on and on, hardly heeding or caring where;—till, suddenly, the scene changes! On the summit of a grassy hill a precipice appears, and the unthinking, giddy crowd, who have gaily climbed the hill-side, are startled by the frightful chasm that arrests their steps. They turn to retrace their way, but night overtakes their wanderings, and, in the awful darkness that succeeds the sunlight, they are dashed to pieces in the terrific gulf. My friends, I have pictured to you the doom of the sinner. How terrible it is to me to realize that this afternoon there are those in this room who are hastening to the precipice's brink! Must we clasp hands in the closest friendship here, and must your unwillingness to believe in The Blood, eternally part us! Who can tell how near is the night of death which will land you in the eternal abyss!"

The speaker's acting was perfect. His words flowed with ease, and his white hands gracefully gesticulated, whilst the tremulous pathos of his voice, as he asked his friends to join him in the road to Zion, must have tempted the ladies to do so without delay. After detailing, in most forcible language, the horrible doom of the unconverted, he proceeded with great solemnity to ask, "Who will come on the Lord's side this afternoon?" pointing at the same time to a row of chairs which had been specially kept vacant to receive the bodies of any who might answer to his appeal.

After this question the speaker paused, and his eyes rested on Irene.

She was sitting spellbound by his words; they awakened a strange feeling within her, but she could not tell if it meant conversion or not. Her heart was touched, but by what? She was trying to analyse her emotions, when a stir in the room attracted her. A young lady moved towards the vacant chairs, and in an agitated voice made the response,

"I will come." The look of tenderness that she received from Mr. Crayford when he took her hand in welcome, was sufficient reward for her boldness. Her example was imitated by two other young ladies, but Irene remained where she was. The ladies looked so very awkward in their new position that she felt disinclined to make a similar exhibition.

After a few moments of silence, Crayford observed, "Let us pray for those who remain unconverted." A torrent of energetic pleadings for the "unawakened souls" followed. In simulating pathos, this accomplished actor exerted himself with so much violence that his very frame shook, and his pale face glowed. To use his own expression, he "agonized" for the sinners before him. He begged deliverance, as from some tyrant's grasp, for the souls of the "unconverted" that day. At last, as if literally exhausted with his efforts, his voice sank into a murmur as he requested the company to engage in five minutes' silent prayer. When the last word died on his lips his head sank upon the desk, and his hands were clasped above his forehead.

During the first part of the five minutes complete silence reigned, but after that coughs were heard; the gentlemen peeped at the ladies through their fingers, and one or two yawned. Irene was rather frightened. The "appeal" was over, and she was not standing where her future husband expected her to be. It was too late now, and she tried to resign herself to the fate that she was conscious awaited her.

Precisely at the end of the five minutes Crayford's white hands unclasped, and he raised his head. He spoke not, but fell into his chair. Another hymn was sung, the benediction was pronounced, and then the meeting closed.

"What a delightful meeting!" was the general remark. "What a success!" "What a powerful speaker he is!" "How thrilling his appeal!" The company separated in high spirits, for most of the females had a gentleman to

Before Irene could retire to her room Crayford sought her. His vanity, which was considerable, was hurt that she had not made "a surrender of her soul" that afternoon. He had certainly counted on it, and was disappointed.

"Irene," he said in his quietest tones, "I want to talk to you."

He took her arm and led her into an unoccupied room. Irene had dreaded this interview, but it was unavoidable.

"Irene," he began, standing in front of the seat he had led her to, "those dear young people I have just been talking with, have entered the kingdom. Why have you not?"

Irene could find no words for an answer.

"I would rather my Irene had come than any one in the room," he added, taking her hand.

This was true, for he might then have felt that his control over his future wife was sure. He was really irritated, but not a shadow of that irritability appeared.

"Irene," he demanded, "why do you not speak?"

She looked up at him for an instant with a steady eye.

"Because," replied she softly and slowly, "I cannot be a hypocrite, and say I believe in a religion which I do not even understand."

He did not flinch in the least, but he dropped her hand, and rested his elbow on the mantelpiece, and his head on his hand. In this attitude he surveyed the rebel, and Irene felt him looking down on her. There was silence for a minute, then he said, "Irene, shall we never walk together in the same path? Oh, my dear Irene," he exclaimed earnestly, "think how soon death might seize you, and what would my feelings be if I knew you were unprepared, and that the unpropitiated wrath of God would consign you to the endless flames. Why will you not decide now while there is time to do so?"

Irene moved restlessly in her chair. She would have given anything to have got up and run away.

"Irene," he continued, "the great God is watching your rebellion now. How awful is your state! Cannot you understand your danger? or will you torment me with ceaseless pain at your unrelenting heart? Did you feel no contrition this afternoon?"

"I think I did," she replied. "But I hardly know what I felt."

"Irene, do not anger a just God any longer. He can send you to perdition at any moment."

His voice was so solemn and hollow, that Irene exclaimed, "What is it I am to do? You frighten me."

"I will teach you if you are willing to learn," returned Mr. Crayford. "Do you feel your ignorance?"

"I believe I feel that I am very wicked," she answered, in a melancholy voice.

"Then I will pray for you, that comfort may come to your heart."

And with such sentences as these, Crayford made her feel in some mysterious way that he was necessary for her eternal peace, and that, under his guidance, she was safe for this world, and the next. He mused thus:—if only she remained undisturbed in this frame of mind, his influence over this lovely woman was for ever secure. He cared little then whether she loved him or not. She would have to marry him, not only to please her cousin, but of her own choice and will. He would be necessary to her, and this would satisfy his vanity.

When Irene retired that night—full of anxiety for her future fate, and with her distorted imagination crowded with forebodings respecting the many horrors that were reserved for lost souls,—she hid her face on her pillow and sobbed hysterically.

What was that influence whose horrors were surrounding her, and preparing to darken her destiny? It was Cant.

Let us pause for a moment to meditate on this equivocal and hideous word.

What is Cant? It is a verb; it is a noun. It is a trade, a profession, a show, a vitiated appetite, a conspiracy, a charm, a mischief-maker, a talisman, a saleable article, yet an unreality; a school, a faith, an institution, a pet, an imposture, a miasma, a hydra, a conundrum. It is gross and tangible; yet it is subtle, impalpable, and all-pervading. It would require volumes to describe it; but as its forms are protean, and its origin and its goal are invisible and inscrutable, no definition could be complete.

Nevertheless, the fact is obvious that in modern England, it is the Heaven in which sentimentalists, traditionists, pharisees, dunces, adventurers, and impostors love to dwell, and the Hell which all honest men shun with hatred implacable, unappeasable, unextinguishable.

CHAPTER XXXVII.

Cant, Persecution, and Sly Slander.—Mr. Melville Visits Tom in Prison.

AMONGST the many philanthropic societies which Melville had initiated and sustained, was "The Deserving Prisoners Defence Society."

At one of its meetings the secretary laid before the council, of which Melville was a member, the case of Tom, who was then awaiting his trial. The secretary felt that although nothing could be urged in extenuation of the revengeful feelings which had induced the unhappy lad to thrash Walters, there was, nevertheless, not sufficient evidence to make it certain that Tom had intended murder.

Tom was in prison without a friend in the wide world, protesting, in the ears of incredulous officialism, that Walters had caused his own fatal stab by dragging him forwards, and then falling himself upon the open knife. The council considered that the case deserved a thorough investigation. Melville, for the reason that he was about visiting a place not far distant from where the prisoner was confined, and because, also, he was able to recall the circumstances connected with Tom's antecedent alleged poaching offence, was urged to undertake the task. Always the willing defender of the defenceless, he cheerfully complied with the request.

Two days afterwards he visited Tom in prison. He listened to his heart-rending tale. He heard how he had tried, for his mother's sake, to keep honest, and he witnessed his distress as he murmured, "I'm not afraid of dying: my life's been too hard for that; but what would my mother have said if she had known I should go to the gallows!"

In his heart, Melville believed the lad innocent of wilful murder; and he determined to have him ably defended at the Assizes. He thought it right to mention this to Golding, so he walked up to his house one morning. The great man received him rather coldly.

"I was sorry to hear of the death of your gamekeeper," said Melville, plunging into the heart of the business on which he had come.

"A more cold-blooded murder I never heard of," said Golding warmly.

"I am inclined to think the fellow is innocent of the intent to murder," observed Melville. "And as I am going to have him defended, I thought it only polite to tell you so. I also wanted to ask if you could assist me with any evidence which would make in his favour at the trial."

"Have you heard the facts?" asked Golding.

"Yes, and from the lad's own lips," replied Melville.

"He is an awful character," said Golding, vehemently. "It was so much wasted time on your part to go and see him. You know, I suppose, he was only just out of prison for poaching?"

"Yes," answered Melville, "I remember conversing with you respecting him at the time of his capture. But there was a great excuse for the poor fellow; he was starving when he was found in possession of the game which he said was given to him."

"I have no sympathy with poachers and murderers!" exclaimed Golding.

"And my position," replied Melville "is this. I have no sympathy with poaching, or with murder, but I have human sympathies for every man, simply because he is a man. I think it no degradation to seek and to save the

"Justice is what I believe in," said Golding coldly; "and these creatures are thoroughly aware, when they poach and commit murder, that the law of the country is being broken by them."

"This lad declares he is innocent," spoke Melville. "He tells me he only intended to thrash the gamekeeper, but the man rushed on him, and drew his knife, and in the scuffle which ensued pulled him down so that the gamekeeper fell on the knife."

"A likely tale, but it will not go down with a jury, Mr. Melville," said Golding scornfully.

"It goes down with me," declared Melville, "because I always wish to give a fellow-creature the benefit of any doubt which makes in his favour in an equivocal transaction."

"Well, time will prove. But, mark my words, Mr. Melville, that fellow is certain to be convicted. I thank God my interests, and my opinions, are respected in this county."

"If so, you will surely use your influence to save a human being from a judicial murder, Mr. Golding. You should have heard him tell his tale of misery, and of his hard life when he first came to Broadcray. He begged his way the whole distance to escape starvation, and—"

"Young thief," interrupted Golding. "I suppose he thought if he murdered the man who looked out for the poachers, he would be able to continue his old games unmolested."

"Well, I must beg to differ from you," asserted Melville. "He assures me he never saw the inside of a prison till he was punished for poaching, and he is more overwhelmed at the humiliation of dying like a felon than he is terrified at the prospect of death itself. He spoke of his dead mother with a pathos that moved me. Her last injunction to him was to keep honest."

"Mere craftiness, used as a final resort to get up an in-

listen to such talk, but have the bare facts of the case placed before an intelligent jury. I shall be content with their decision."

"That may be so, Mr. Golding," said Melville. "Yet, with no wish to offend you, I may state that I shall engage the services of the most eminent counsel of the circuit to defend this lad, and I shall do my utmost to prove him innocent of the capital charge. I thought you could have had no personal interest in his being hung, and would not hesitate to suggest how I might obtain details on your premises which might elucidate the transaction."

Golding was in a rage, but to all appearances he only grew colder in voice and manner. "You may engage whom you please, and do what you please, and I will engage to beat you," he said slowly and emphatically. "My poor gamekeeper is the only wronged party in this case, and *justice* is what I desire, and what I always will contend for. I believe in a God of justice."

"And I, in a God who combines justice with mercy," returned Melville, as he rose to go.

"I trust you will reconsider your determination to defend that worthless vagabond," exclaimed Golding.

"I do not think that is likely," said Melville. "My mind is made up on that point."

"And who are you, sir," cried Golding, his rage getting the better of him, "who would dictate in a matter which concerns no one but myself?"

"I am the friend of the friendless, and the antagonist of the despot wherever found," replied Melville—in tones which continued to ring in Golding's ears long after his visitor had departed from the hall.

As Melville walked out of the grounds he met Crayford entering them. He knew this man slightly, and also that he had been the cause of Mr. Lorraine's unhappy domestic

night, Crayford made this remark, "I saw a man in your grounds to-day, Mr. Golding, whom I have not seen for some time. His name is Melville."

"Ah, do you know him?" inquired Golding, cautiously refraining from saying more till he heard what Crayford had to relate of him.

"I used to know him," answered Mr. Crayford. "He disagreed with me because I tried to bring him, and a friend of his, to a knowledge of the truth. He was "—and Crayford raised his large eyes from his plate, and resignedly helped himself to an orange—" a great persecutor of mine."

"Ah," said Golding, "a conceited opinionated fellow. I dislike him extremely."

Crayford inwardly rejoiced, but his face affected a look of pain, as if at the recollection of Melville's ungodliness. "He has not forgiven me for taking an interest in the soul of a lady whom we both knew. I was the means of her conversion, and in consequence of her husband's unkind treatment and atheistical conduct, she separated from him. Her husband was Mr. Melville's dearest friend, and though I endeavoured to convince both of them, at different times, of their ungodly lives, I only made myself their enemy, and exposed myself to the most unkind treatment. But that is the way of the world."

"He is a nice fellow to go about defending murderers and thieves," ejaculated Golding : "a man who could uphold a friend in the ill-treatment of his wife. But it is just what I expected of him. I read that man through and through."

"And what has become of his friend, and the poor lady?" asked Mrs. Golding.

"Oh, I have heard nothing of the friend for some time, but the wife died recently. Poor thing! hers was a cruel fate. She died of a broken heart."

could not compete with men of her husband's type, or Mr. Melville's. Certainly Mr. Melville was the more to blame in this case, for he influenced his friend to such an extent that he could make him do anything ; and I believe his conduct to have been extremely harsh and persecuting towards his friend's wife in this matter. He assailed her religious convictions most cruelly."

"And comes here," exclaimed Golding, "talking about God's mercy, and pleading for a murderer ! A cool piece of presumption."

"*Great* impudence," asserted Mrs. Golding.

"Mr. Melville is very strange in what he shamelessly calls his philanthropic notions," murmured Crayford. "I have known him to assist the most abandoned-looking tramps, perfectly aware that the money would go in drink, and he has observed, on being remonstrated with, that he believed in cheering the lives of even the drunkard, and the thief."

"An infidel!" remarked Golding scornfully; "cares neither for the laws of God nor man. I thank God, however, that I very soon understand these fellows. I read him pretty quickly."

"I fear he is an infidel," sighed Crayford, "but we can pray for him, though he turn at present unheedingly from our voice."

The prayer, however, did not seem to be deemed an immediate duty, for, at Mr. Golding's solicitation, Crayford helped himself to a fifth glass of old port ; and the worthies soon forgot the horrors of infidelity in their epicurean delights.

CHAPTER XXXVIII.

Cant neglects the Waif and protects the Felon.—Tom in Prison.—The Jail-Chaplain's Theology.

TOM was better cared for as a felon in prison, than he had ever been as an honest lad outside of it. He had never had a clean and comfortable bed to lie upon, nor had he before had regular meals, and enough of them. If, when he was struggling for a livelihood, half the brain power had been available for his advancement which the State now employed to keep him safely in his cell and to prepare him for death, he would have become quite a respectable citizen. Not only were his hair-cutting, bathing, feeding, sleeping, clothing, and other requirements, admirably provided for, but even his theological belief was now a matter of the most careful solicitude.

The Chaplain devoted to him an immense amount of valuable time, for he considered the claims of so notorious a criminal justly entitled him to the most assiduous attention. But that reverend official was not satisfied with the results of his labours. As a Low Churchman and also a sentimentalist, he talked to Tom much about "the blood" and the physical sufferings of Christ. He spoke exultingly of the crucifixion, and of God's goodness in arranging all the tragedy of Gethsemane ; and explained to Tom how grateful sinners should be to Christ for agreeing to bear, and to God for condescending to accept, so much unjust torture for the purpose of saving believers.

Yet Tom did not see it at all. He only protested that if he had been present at Calvary, and had seen the Roman

harm to anybody, he would have tried to smash them, even though there had been a gallows at hand on which they could have hung him at once for the attempt."

Pressed by the worthy Chaplain to acknowledge, at least, that God was worthy of eternal thanks for having permitted His only Son to die such an awful death, Tom refused acquiescence; alleging that as the Deity could easily have saved sinners by other methods, and indeed need not have created men at all, such cruelty on His part was unnecessary. Then the reverend gentleman would try to show the lad how horrible was murder in the sight of Heaven. So far as the observation applied to his own case, the poor youth simply remarked that he had not committed murder, because he had never intended to kill Walters. With regard to the general proposition, he perplexed his spiritual instructor with questions.

He asked why, if murder were contrary to God's commandments, a judge sitting calmly in court, unmoved by personal passion, was justified in judicially ordering it to be committed. He related how he had once enlisted as a soldier, and asked whether, if he had been ordered to the wars and killed a hundred men, he would have been called a murderer a hundredfold, or a hero? He asked why it was that if a person killed one man, who had injured him, he was called a murderer; but when another, caused thousands to be killed whom he had never seen, and who had never injured him, he was called a patriot, and created an earl? He said that if the Chaplain was right in declaring that God had commanded them not to take human life, then society was wrong in applauding those individuals who slew mankind on a grand scale, whilst it punished those who killed a single enemy.

Much more of the like kind of thought did he give expression to, in his own peculiar vernacular. It was sadly evident that his mind had never been moulded and com-

to receive the arguments which satisfy a great christian country. He was so stupid that he was not familiar with the topics now treated of by the Chaplain, and all his talk was merely the crude articulations of unsophisticated human nature, "unregenerated by grace."

Indeed, so often did Tom bring the pertinacious Chaplain's incessant arguments to the test of what he called "common sense," that the indefatigable official soon despaired of inspiring any awe by his pompous allusions to either the sacraments or the authority of the Church. But, as the felon was the fashion of the hour, the spiritual instructor, always anxious to do his duty, continued his exemplary ministrations. Not that poor Tom enjoyed them much. He had neither talent nor taste for theology.

"Poor mother! she told me God loved everybody, and it was our duty to be honest, and that all things would be put to rights in the next world." That was his simple creed.

He was glad when Melville called to see him, very glad, for he felt that this man knew and understood him, knew all the good, and all the bad, that was in him, and yet warmed with sympathy towards him. During the greater portion of his time, however, he was silent and melancholy—not morose, not nervous: he was simply stricken with an overwhelming sense of failure. His brooding memory dwelt again, and ever, upon the fact that during all his unhappy life he had tried to do what was right according to his ability. He had tried for his mother's sake to be honest, and now they told him he was a murderer. He fancied that society had been against him all through the piece. He had been willing to work, but society said "No." He had striven to be honest, and society had starved him. He had acted in ignorance, and taken what was offered him to allay his hunger, and society had pounced on him, and imprisoned him for stealing. He had

character for honesty, and the revenge that he had intended should end in a thrashing had, accidentally, become a murder.

All this was too much for Tom ; it bewildered him. He was, however, in no dread of the future. The failure of his life had so stunned his faculties and crushed his hopes, that the prospect of death could hardly add to his wretchedness.

The foppish governor of the prison, who was an equivocal relation of a member of the aristocracy, pronounced him a fool ; for when he held a general conversation with Tom, the lad maintained that rat-hunting in Whitechapel was no worse than pigeon-shooting at Hurlingham. He refused to believe that God took special care of queens, kings, and princes; or that they deserved to be the objects of the special prayers of the poverty-stricken multitudes.

Moreover, he protested that a poacher who took a rabbit from a wood, where it was not wanted, and gave it as food to a starving fellow-creature, was a more honest person than the statesman who, by force and bloodshed, stole territories, whether Afghan or Zulu, from their legitimate owners, and gave them to a sovereign, who stood in no need them and had no excuse for their acceptance.

CHAPTER XXXIX.

CANT THE CONSECRATOR OF MONSTROUS MARRIAGES.—MR. AND MRS. OSCAR CRAYFORD.—THE PLYMOUTH BROTHER IN HIS HOME.—HANNAH.

IN the Golding circle there was no one sufficiently blasphemous to talk about the laws of Nature in connection with such a topic as "holy matrimony." Crayford's engagement to the beautiful child Irene proceeded, therefore, not only without opposition, but altogether in harmony with Golding's selfish wishes. It ripened into marriage three months after the great drawing-room prayer-meeting, and religious society was not at all shocked to see Oscar Crayford, aged fifty-nine, married to Irene Graham, aged seventeen.

There was, in fact, no particular reason why society should be shocked; for marriage and incongruity are ideas which have long been associated with each other in the public mind. Even English marriage laws are a collection of anomalies. A marriage may be perfectly valid in one part of the British possessions, which is null and void in another. Courts judicially decide one thing in one place, and a different thing in another place, respecting the same subject-matter. The Church considers marriage as a "religious ordinance;" but the test in any given case, as to whether the ordinance has been properly or improperly performed, has to be sought in the geography, and the statute book.

In England itself we are very particular in some of our matrimonial matters. For instance, we especially forbid a man to marry either his grandmother, or his mother-in-law. Nor do we allow him to marry his deceased wife's sister, though she may be of suitable age, and peculiarly qualified to take care of his children.

Men like Crayford take very high ground in any debate on this last question of marriage with a deceased wife's sister. They protest that any relaxation of this prohibitory law would be subversive of morality and the Bible. They are of opinion that matrimony, as now managed, is a peculiarly "holy institution." When a Plymouth Brother, or a Clergyman, officially marries a man of eighty to a girl of fifteen, all parties consider that the union " is sanctified by God." Mr. Crayford, for example, claimed for his own marriage that it was entirely in accordance with Heaven's intention, and well symbolized the "relation which Christ sustains to His Church."

But the real reasons which induced Crayford to marry, though he deceived himself as to them, were worldly enough. He wished to be the legal proprietor of the woman whom he considered the most lovely of her sex. Besides this, he could not disguise from himself that advancing years might make it desirable for him to have in his house a wife who could minister to his domestic wants, in case of his failing health. He loved admiration, and felt a keen zest for female society; but he well knew that as old age approached he might lose some of his powers to fascinate and charm the weaker sex. So he considered that, as a matter of prudence, it would be well to secure Irene whilst the opportunity offered; and he deemed it providential that Golding's indifference to her welfare made this acquisition so easy. Of course he intended to rule her. He had been so long accustomed to dominate others, that any serious apprehension as to encountering difficulties with her scarcely occurred to him.

But before his brief honeymoon was over, he began to have uncomfortable misgivings as to whether, after all, he had not overrated his powers, as self-confident men are apt to do when they employ them in ways to which they are not accustomed. He could not complain that Irene was a scold; neither was she sulky nor unreasonable. His apprehensions of prospective difficulties with her, arose when he began clearly to perceive that she was no coward, and could not be frightened; no hypocrite, and would not cant. But, as she was only a girl, and possessed a very high sense of marital duty, he did not despair of being able ultimately to educate her into the kind of wife he wanted.

He commenced the good work at the end of the wedding tour. It is true that he returned home with some forebodings, yet still he was strong in the hope of being able eventually to complete her subjugation.

The house at Knightsbridge, to which he took his young bride, was the same as he had occupied before marriage. It was small, but situated in a fashionable part. Crayford loved luxury, but he loved money better. By nature he was mean and grasping, and he conducted his establishment with rigid penuriousness. This economy he justified on religious grounds. "The disciple is not above the Master," he observed to Irene, "and I could not, as a consistent christian, live in extravagance and show. The sum I am able to devote to my Master would be very small if I spent more on myself; therefore I know, Irene, you will agree with me in the plainness of my home."

But Irene was not prepared for the barely furnished rooms, and the utter absence of the comforts she had been accustomed to. The drawing-room was the only well furnished apartment; it was here she concluded the "prayer-meetings" would be held. She was not prepared, either, for the greeting that awaited them on arriving at home from their short tour. The person who opened the door to them was warmly accosted by Crayford—each saluted the other in terms of conventional Cant.

"This is Hannah," remarked Crayford, by way of introduction to Irene; "my housekeeper, my worldly adviser my conscientious worker, and my humble christian friend,"

Hannah smirked at this eulogium, and held out her hand to Irene, with a familiarity that surprised her. She was a strong, bony-looking woman of about thirty. All Irene saw of her, at that moment, was that her face was contorted into a fictitious smile, and that her dress was dark and ugly, and unrelieved by apron or cap.

Crayford entered the dining-room and seized eagerly the letters which were awaiting him, and Hannah led Irene to her room. When she descended Hannah and Crayford were so deep in conversation that they hardly noticed her presence. Irene took a chair by the window, and at this moment Crayford saw her. He instantly ceased speaking, and folding up the papers that lay before him, he dismissed Hannah to see about tea.

"You are so young and so inexperienced, Irene," observed Crayford that evening, "I shall not require you to perform any housekeeping duties. Hannah can do it very much better. And I confide in her, for we both worship the same Lord. Hannah is a sincere believer amongst the Brethren, and a most useful christian worker. You may safely trust her."

Irene concealed her astonishment at this arrangement, but she felt that Hannah would not help to make the place home-like. She saw little of this trusty Abigail till the next morning, when, Crayford being out, Hannah entered the dining-room most unceremoniously, and with a bundle of tracts in her hand.

"I should like you to read this," she observed, holding out one to Irene. "It is so convincing. I was grieved to hear from Mr. Crayford that you were not one of the Lord's followers. It must, indeed, be a trial to him to have known you so long, and to have failed to touch your heart. I shall be pleased to do anything that I can to remove your doubts, or difficulties. I should like to read to you every morning at this time. I would willingly spare you an hour."

Irene looked up from her fancy work with amazement at her intruder. She was a tall, thin woman, with a low forehead, high cheek bones, and coarse, sensuous lips. She spoke with the peculiar self-assurance of her sect. Her dress affected quaker simplicity, and her hair was drawn from her face and arranged in a plain knot at the back of her head. Her cold grey eye told of relentless determination. That she was one of the uneducated class was indicated by her speech.

"I do not understand you," answered Irene, when she had recovered from her first surprise. "I have no doubts to remove, that I know of; and I scarcely think it becoming on your part to offer to teach me."

Hannah, unbidden, took a seat in front of Irene.

"That is because your heart is hard," she affirmed. "You must become lowly and humble, my dear young lady, before you can enter the kingdom. I see you are too proud to come, too self-satisfied to be taught better. But I will not give you up. I will read to you; and I shall come each morning at this time; and I trust it will be blest to your soul."

"When I require you to read to me I will tell you," said Irene, her wrath rising at Hannah's presumptuous words.

"Mr. Crayford wishes me to read to you," exclaimed Hannah rather fiercely.

"Then I will tell him I do not wish it," returned Irene emphatically.

Hannah rose from her seat.

"You speak very rashly to one who has come as the Lord's messenger," she observed; "but," and her cold eye looked its determination, "if you are in this house, you will have to hear me some time."

Irene felt the effects of this visit the same evening.

"Irene," said Crayford, "that fancy work is not agreeable to my feelings as a Christian. I cannot permit it."

"Why?" asked Irene. "What harm is there in it?"

"It savours of the world, Irene; and, though I cannot call you a Christian, still, in the house of a man who professes what I do, it appears incongruous. You must discontinue it."

Irene was annoyed.

"If I see no harm in it I shall certainly continue it," she exclaimed, with the first show of spirit she had evinced to Crayford.

"You will not," returned her husband calmly, "for I shall not supply funds for the purpose; and much as it may pain me to revert to the subject, unless I find the funds you cannot continue to disobey me. For, Irene you are aware, and it would be better for you to realize this at once, you are utterly dependent on me for everything you possess."

It was impossible to dispute this cruel speech, and Irene was silent, but her heart ached terribly; and the misery, and loneliness, of her position, so overcame her that she rose to leave the room.

"Wait, Irene," said Crayford. "You must understand that I wish a portion of your time to be spent in studying books that will benefit your soul; and I have asked Hannah, as my time is so occupied, to read to you instead of me. She thinks, and I agree with her, that your hours are too frivolously spent. She is a most valuable coadjutor of mine, and I trust you will meet her with proper respect."

Having said this, Crayford resumed the letter he was writing to a young and anxious female inquirer, and Irene was allowed to go.

Hannah entering the room a few minutes afterwards, Crayford laid down his pen, and with a sigh remarked, "Ah, Hannah, I apprehend you are right. I *have* made a mistake in choosing an unbeliever for a wife, and in fondly fancying that I could bring her to a knowledge of the true light. This, I fear, will never be, and we shall ever be unequally yoked."

He was correct in declaring he had made a mistake; but the mistake lay in *marrying* the lovely creature he had become enamoured of, instead of remembering that he would tire of her, as he had of scores of others in his wicked life.

Upstairs, Irene came across the one servant that the establishment boasted besides the immaculate Hannah. She was crying, and Irene, whose sympathy was easily kindled, at once asked her the cause of her grief.

"Miss Hannah has given me notice," said the girl; "and she says she shall not give me a character."

"For what reason?" questioned Irene.

"Because I will not go and hear Mr. Crayford at The Room on Sundays, and I won't, for I don't believe in his humbug, or hers. I know all about them. There is no religion in beating down the tradespeople as *she* does; and grinding down the poor folks as makes things for her and Mr. Crayford. She tried to cheat me out of part of my wages the first quarter, and said I agreed for less; and Mr. Crayford and her are always trying to cheat people, and then she wants me to go and hear him preach. But I little knew she would refuse me a character; all I stayed for was because I didn't want a short character."

"I am sorry," said Irene. "I will speak to Mr. Crayford for you."

"Thank you, ma'am," said the girl; "but it won't be of any use. *She* does what she likes in this house."

And the disconsolate maid turned away and left Irene to her own reflections.

The religious business that was conducted in Crayford's house was astonishing. Mr. Crayford was evidently a great light amongst the Brethren, and was looked up to almost the same as a Minister of a Church. Ladies were constantly calling for religious advice, and the evenings were generally spent in meetings at home, and abroad. Irene was thankful that her presence was not required at these assemblies. Crayford never asked her to attend them now. He had given up the hope of converting her.

There was a considerable commotion and preparation one morning, and Hannah even omitted the usual reading with which she persecuted Irene every day. There was to be a baptism in the evening, and Crayford was to officiate. One of the rooms had been recently converted into a baptistery, and fitted with a tank of sufficient depth to admit of a grown person's immersion. Crayford kept the key of this room, so Irene had not been in it before. That morning, on looking in, she saw Hannah busily arranging carpets and seats.

"Ah," she remarked on observing Irene, "if the Lord had only blessed the measures taken, you might have gone down into the water with the six others whom Mr. Crayford has converted."

"If I were converted I would not be immersed," returned Irene, whilst Hannah sorted some large towels which had been obtained for this special occasion. "It seems to me simply disgusting."

And, with this remark, she left the room, unwilling to hear any more of Hannah's talk. On trying the drawing-room door, where she fancied she might obtain quiet, Irene found it locked from within. It was strange, but of little consequence. Very likely that room, too, was being prepared for the evening's proceedings. Entering the dining-room, she observed, from the window, an elegant brougham with two well appointed servants on the box. A carriage was no novelty at Mr. Crayford's door, but Irene, with natural curiosity, felt desirous of seeing the visitor who was evidently in the drawing-room with her husband. Some time elapsed, then footsteps were heard in the hall, the street door opened, and a young lady beautifully dressed passed to the carriage. As she raised the brougham window, Irene perceived that the visitor was very lovely. Turning quickly away, Irene confronted Hannah, who had come into the dining-room unobserved, and who now exclaimed—

"That is a remarkable case of conversion. A most worldly young woman, and brought to the Lord's side entirely through Mr. Crayford. She will be here to-night, and will be baptized into the fold. Mr. Crayford's influence over her is marvellous. She believes—"

But Irene did not stop to hear any more. She hurried off to her room, where she quickly attired herself for walking, and then hastened away into the fresh morning air, where she could again breathe freely. Away, away, from that home of Cant; away to the busy crowd, which, if it did include paupers, thieves, and vagabonds, would, at least, be free from the suffocating atmosphere of the World of Cant.

CHAPTER XL.

CANT AND INDECOROUS CEREMONIES.—A BAPTISM AT MR. CRAYFORD'S HOUSE.—MRS. CHRISTABEL DARNLEY.—MR. OSCAR CRAYFORD UNMASKED BY MR. LORRAINE.—MRS. CRAYFORD'S INTERCESSION.

THE baptism of which Hannah had spoken was anticipated by many as a great event in their lives.

By seven o'clock in the evening the preparations for the solemn service at Mr. Crayford's house were all completed. Seats were arranged round the baptistery, the gas chandelier was lighted, soft carpets had been laid down, and Hannah had kindled a fire in the adjoining dressing-room, and prepared blankets and towels for the use of the converts. Six ladies were to be immersed, but, as seemed generally the case at Crayford's house, it was a baptism for females alone. Three or four gentlemen from what the Brethren call "The Room" were present to address the meeting, and about fifteen or twenty spectators who had already received baptism.

As Crayford was rather late in appearing, one of the gentlemen gave out a hymn, and proposed that they should sing it, as he expected that Brother Crayford was engaged in religious conversation. This was true: the lady who had called in the morning required much encouragement to perform the "christian duty" that was required of her, and Crayford was busy settling her doubts.

At the conclusion of the hymn he arrived, looking sanctified and resigned. It was a way he had whenever he appeared before the public, and was intended

front of the baptistery, and every eye was at once fixed on him. Knowing this, he looked solemnly down for probably two minutes, and during that time the six converts made their appearance, and took the seats allotted to them.

They wore white dresses and capes, and small white caps. Their appearance was altogether so ludicrous that in any assembly of ordinary creatures, the risible faculty would have been excited.

The self-complacency, however, of this sect of "Brethren" is impervious to the ludicrous. Ever ready to ascribe to themselves extreme individual holiness, they assume in the most brazen manner, that their absurd antics, and their stubborn inanities and formalities, are being accepted by the world as evidences of it.

On looking up Crayford's eyes rested in all their brilliancy on the convert he had just been talking with. Then he said in his most bell-like tones, " Let us pray." In the prayer he was much moved. His tones trembled as he thanked the Lord for His goodness in making him the humble instrument of bringing so many souls to the kingdom. His heart "swelled with gratitude for these new jewels that would sparkle, he hoped, in his heavenly crown in all their exquisite loveliness." Certainly one of the "jewels" was very lovely, and if any one had observed her at that moment they might have noticed the blush that rose to her cheek. She evidently took the compliment to herself. Crayford then spoke of other converts he had baptized into the faith, and gave thanks for them. Might " all these dear ones in their turn follow his humble example, and bring home the lost ones to the fold."

Follow his example! What would the young wife upstairs in the solitude of her chamber say to this? Unnoticed, and in recent days almost uncared for, her gentle spirit chafes at the thought of the solemn farce that is going on under that very roof. The light by which

scared away all the poetry and romance of her life. If ever a prayer could cross her lips, it would be a cry that others might be preserved from his dangerous influence. She, however, is far from praying. Such men as Crayford wither up, in the heart of any honest girl, all faith in such prayer. Not that it would have pained Crayford had he been conscious of the fact. So he prayed on, and said "Amen" to his own requests. Then he gave an address to his christian sisters who were about to show by their actions that they "had found the Lord."

Afterwards came the baptism. Crayford never moved inelegantly, or he might have made the scene more ridiculous than even it was of necessity. He performed his part well, but some of the ladies appeared very comical. The first one, on rising out of the water, became hysterical, and was led off in blankets to the vigilant Hannah, who, surrounded by towels, stood in the adjoining room, with the servant, ready to dry the dripping corporeity of the saturated saints. The second convert was rather frightened, and struggled with Crayford to keep her head above water. On coming up he observed, "My dear sister, you are not baptized yet," and she had to go down once more. The second time was ineffectual, and Crayford repeated his words. At the third attempt she yielded, and with a scream went right under the water; but the poor creature looked terribly scared as she was hurried away, and it was some time before she got over the shock attendant on her three immersions. Last of all came Christabel Darnley, the wife of that Mr. Darnley who addressed the Canary College meeting. She was the lady of whom Hannah had spoken to Irene as "the remarkable case of conversion." In Crayford's eyes she was the heroine of the evening.

Crayford's sect, more than any other, enjoys the task of dividing families, and breaking up households. Its religiosity freezes the natural home affections of those whom it touches. As an excess of ice in a conduit, will cause a disruption of the ordinary water-courses, so this frozen sentimentality of Plymouth Brethrenism, breaks up all the ordinary channels of domestic intercourse.

In the case of Christabel, Crayford had the proud joy of knowing that he was tearing her from her husband; and that, in opposition to her husband's wishes, he was now successful in making her perform a ceremony which Mr. Darnley loathed with all the hatred usually entertained towards it by decent persons. To baptize Christabel was, therefore, a keen pleasure. He took her hands very tenderly, and looked into her eyes with the most enthusiastic fervour. Christabel's beauty defied the disfigurement of even her baptismal dress, and her rare loveliness this evening was only heightened by the exciting occasion. Whether Crayford's dazzling glance, as he held her, was too much for her, or whether the water was too chilling, it is impossible to say, but she fainted immediately after the immersion; and, to prevent her from falling, Crayford was obliged to hold her in his arms till Hannah came with a blanket, and assisted him to carry the unconscious belle to the dressing-room.

The immersing business being over, Crayford appeared rather exhausted, and sat down while a hymn was sung. Prayer was afterwards offered by one of the "Brethren," who thanked the Lord "for the addition of these converts to fight under His banner," and begged that more might soon follow their example. With this, the meeting concluded; and the room quickly emptying, Crayford sought the drawing-room, where he had requested the recently baptized ones to meet him before they left the house, as he had a few words to say especially to them. They were all there, including Christabel, who had quite recovered from her fainting attack.

Crayford had just seated himself and commenced to speak, when Hannah entered—bearing a card. Crayford was surprised at this interruption: for he gave no admittance to the outside world on these occasions.

"The gentleman insisted on my bringing you his card, and would not leave," she explained in an undertone.

Crayford took it and, on reading the name, for once in his life, changed colour.

"You have told him I am engaged?"

"He will wait till you are at liberty to see him," returned Hannah, as she hastened to make her exit. It was greatly against her principles to disturb her master at such a time.

But the religious joys of the evening were ended for Crayford. He continued to play his part, but his heart was not in it. Yet he did not omit to see Christabel to her carriage, or forget to press the lovely hand that rested on his arm, or to arrange an early meeting for the young convert to relate her experiences, and to receive further christian advice and encouragement.

Then he went to the dining-room; and he encountered once more—Mr. Lorraine. He had neither seen nor heard of him since they parted at Rome.

Mr. Crayford bowed and expressed his regrets for having kept his visitor waiting.

"We have been holding a religious meeting this evening, and it was not quite finished when you arrived. I trust you will excuse the delay in my appearing."

He placed Mr. Lorraine a chair, then sat down himself, and waited calmly, with an unruffled face, to hear his visitor's business.

Mr. Lorraine did not take the chair which Mr. Crayford had placed. He stood looking at Crayford. He mused to himself thus: "Not one whit changed is this man Crayford. Inflexible, incorrigible, unshameable."

Then after a moment's silence he said—

"Mr. Crayford, does this religion of yours suggest to you the expediency of destroying other people's wills, in order that you may reap the benefit of their money?"

"No one but you would ask such a question, Mr. Lorraine," replied Crayford. "Wherever I go I am trusted and confided in. You, I believe, are the only one who would attribute to me actions, and motives, unworthy a christian gentleman."

"Mr. Crayford," observed Mr. Lorraine, "I have learnt by bitter experience that your words are mere subterfuges. The last time we met I believed this, but I could not prove it. Now I can prove what I have all along been convinced of."

At this point Lorraine produced from his pocket a letter which he opened and read aloud. It was as follows:—

"Copy of letter to Mr. Crayford.

"DEAR SIR,—On thinking over the matter of my will, it seems to me more just that my property at my death should revert to my husband, to whom most of it really belongs. I am determined, therefore, to make a fresh will, and write to acquaint you with this alteration which I am about to effect. I grieve to say that, with the prospect of death before me, the actions of the past that were committed under your and my mother's influence, do not appear to me in the light in which they did; nor would I desire at this moment to leave any of my money for the benefit of that sect which has blighted the best years of my life. The present is very dark, but the past is a never-ending regret to me. I do not blame you. It may be that you acted according to your convictions, but I blame myself for deserting, without a cause, the husband whom I had promised to love and honour. I confess that there appears no godliness, but deliberate wickedness in such an act.

"I remain,
"Yours in deep affliction,
"EVELYN LORRAINE.

"To Oscar Crayford, Esq."

"Did you ever receive that letter?" demanded Lorraine.

holding the writing before the eyes of the unmoved Crayford.

"I had," answered Crayford, "so many hysterical and other letters from Mrs. Lorraine on numerous subjects, religious and otherwise, that it really would be impossible for me to remember the details of all."

"This is mere evasion," thundered Lorraine. "A matter of this sort would certainly impress itself on your mind, seeing that it would make a great difference to you at Mrs. Lorraine's death."

"Not so much to me, as to The Cause," returned Crayford blandly. "If Mrs. Lorraine had changed her mind, Brethrenism would have suffered. As for me, in doing my Master's work, I find little time for luxuries, or leisure to procure them; and however poor I may be, I am rich if I have on high one Friend."

Crayford's eyes were raised to the ceiling, in the old manner; and Lorraine was chafing with an irritation that no one but Crayford ever excited in him. Controlling his indignation, however, he remarked, "All this is away from the point. You have evaded my first question; I therefore draw my own conclusion, and proceed to my second interrogatory: "Did you destroy the fresh will, which I find, by a memorandum on this very letter, was made a week afterwards by my wife?"

"If I did not believe," said Mr. Crayford, "in the spirit of christian forbearance, Mr. Lorraine, I might exclaim, How dare you ask me such a question? But I will never resent this continued persecution of yours, which arises from the ignorance of unbelief, and a total alienation from the Lord's people. If this is all you have to ask of me, I would beg you to excuse my presence, as I have still some work for my Master ere the day closes."

"It is *not* all I have to say," retorted Lorraine, "or, depend upon it, I would never have come into the presence of so wily a man as yourself. It is true, indeed, that you would never confess your wickedness, nor would I have wasted more time in endeavouring to compel you to. I have proofs to lay before you now, and proofs that would satisfy any court of justice. The solicitors who made the will to which Mrs. Lorraine's memorandum refers, and which you have destroyed, kept a copy of that will; therefore I am at liberty to say that not another shilling of my wife's money shall go into your pocket. And I shall require you to make restitution."

Mr. Crayford listened attentively, but his face remained unmoved. Mr. Lorraine waited for him to speak. There was a pause, then Mr. Crayford remarked,—

"Have you reflected, Mr. Lorraine, that you are not taking the money from me, but from the Lord's cause? One of your wife's last wishes was that her money should be devoted, at my discretion, to the precious work of saving souls."

"It is impossible for you to think this after that letter," declared Lorraine. "And I may add, that the observations which it contains would have caused the greatest remorse in any heart but your own."

"It is your intention then, Mr. Lorraine, to take from me all my property."

"It is my intention to take back what you have swindled me out of too long," retorted Mr. Lorraine. "Whether that includes the whole of your property depends on your own income. Just now you informed me that it was The Cause alone which would suffer, and I can only reply that The Cause, as represented by such men as yourself, deserves to suffer.'

"I will be frank with you, Mr. Lorraine," returned Mr. Crayford. "I have little pride in my nature, for God's people are enjoined to be humble, therefore I may state without shame, that at present I am entirely dependent on the money your wife left me. A short time after I made the acquaintance of Mrs. Lorraine, I lost the whole of my income by serving a christian friend. Mrs. Lorraine heard of my suffering. She knew I had acted as one Christian should toward another. She behaved well to me during her lifetime, and assured me that at her death, if it should please God to take her first, she would not forget me. When she was ill, she sent for me and handed to me that will which you say was revoked by a subsequent will. Therefore, I am now entirely at your mercy. But why should I say this when I remember that the Lord will not forget His own. I have had so many proofs of this during my lifetime, that it may surprise you to learn that I feel sure He will provide now, and I shall not be left penniless."

"Then," answered Lorraine, "I shall leave you to your God's mercy. I have too much of the spirit of justice in my nature to pension a man who ought to be in jail."

"You may become the instrument, in God's hands, of ministering to a soul in sore distress, Mr. Lorraine," said Crayford. "I appeal to you now, not for myself, but for another. My wife must suffer with me: my wife whom I love more than my life; who looks to me for protection and for sustenance; and who, hitherto, I have shielded from every trouble. Unhappily situated in the house of an elder cousin, who was too eager to get the orphan girl off his hands, I married her from pity: a christian pity which led to a love that now influences my whole life. Could I for one moment have foreseen the misery I was bringing that young and guileless creature into, no machinations of her cousin, and no pity for her wretched fate, should have moved me to marriage. How shall I tell my wife, Mr. Lorraine, that I am a ruined man, and that she is once more at the mercy of the cold world? I am unable to break to her this intelligence. I make one request of you: that you will communicate to her the misfortune you have decreed for her."

Before Mr. Lorraine could answer, Crayford had glided from the room.

In another minute the husband stood before his wife. His old cunning had suggested a rescue.

"Irene," he implored, "I am pursued, and hunted down, by one who delights to persecute the Lord's people. The man you will see downstairs has plotted to ruin me. Go to him and alter this determination, or your ruin and mine are certain. If necessary, throw yourself at his feet and implore him to show mercy."

Irene was almost bewildered at her husband's words, and frightened by his manner and appearance. His tones were so imperative, that without asking a single question, she ran downstairs with the feeling uppermost that she was about to defend her own and her husband's life.

Mr. Lorraine was tying up some papers, previous to his departure, for he had not intended waiting for Mr. Crayford's wife. He was rather perplexed at the sudden entrance of Irene; and her exquisite beauty, and imploring yet timid eyes, could not pass unheeded.

"My husband says you can ruin us," began the breathless Irene, her fright overcoming the shyness which had been considerably augmented by the appearance of the gentlemanly visitor instead of the ruffian she had pictured. "But you look too kind for that," she concluded, as Mr. Lorraine's eyes met hers.

There was a pause, during which time Irene collected her senses, and began to feel that her readiness to obey Crayford's commands had landed her in some confusion.

"You *will* help him," she commenced again, finding that the stranger did not reply.

Mr. Lorraine hardly knew what to say, but he observed with some gentleness, "I do not think you know all, or you would not ask me that."

Instinctively Irene felt, that Mr. Lorraine was right, and she returned, "I know nothing except what my husband has just told me, that you could do us some great harm; and I am sure if that is so you will be merciful, and—and—forgive."

The colour rose to Irene's cheeks; for she had lately learned to feel ashamed of her husband's actions, and with a woman's intuitive perception she guessed that he needed the forgiveness for which she craved.

Mr. Lorraine placed his papers in his pocket as he exclaimed, "Forgiveness would be ill bestowed in his case."

"But forgiveness is better than revenge," suggested Irene timidly. "And great natures can forgive great wrongs."

"Ah, madam, your husband wants more than forgiveness from me to save him from ruin," remarked Mr. Lorraine; "he wants my assistance, and for the love of justice I must withhold that."

"Is he your enemy, then?" asked Irene. "Has he wronged you?"

"He has been my most inveterate enemy," returned Mr. Lorraine, his compassion for the wife's ignorance forbidding him to reveal the whole truth.

"And you can punish him now?" inquired Irene.

"I can," said Lorraine, "and justly he deserves it."

"Then forgive him," returned Irene, her courage rising as she pleaded, "and restrain the vengeance you might take. My husband's religion would never be mine; and I do not profess to be, in his sense, a pious person; but, does not the Bible say, 'Love your enemies, do good to them that hate you and despitefully use you.' We see little of this in practice; but it is so beautiful in theory, I often think if I had some bitter enemy I would try to carry out that injunction. It is noble, and would make one feel noble. You will act as those beautiful words dictate. I feel sure you will."

"Madam," cried Lorraine, "you have touched the right chord in my heart. *I believe* in the words you have quoted; they are the essence of Christianity, though disregarded in the World of Cant. I will think over this matter. You shall hear from me in a day or so. And, be assured that, whatever is the decision I may come to, I will not make the innocent suffer with the guilty."

CHAPTER XLI.

CANT, PECULATION, AND INHUMANITY.—THE SANCTIFIED RASCALITY WHICH ELUDES THE LAW.—BLOOSTER DEFRAUDS CARTER THE CRIPPLE: DRIVES HIM MAD, AND PRAYS FOR HIM.

CRAYFORD was not the only man in The World of Cant who, at this time, was taking liberties with other people's money. A humble plumber and glazier who attended Mr. Falcon Small's Chapel, being possessed of a thousand pounds, settled that sum, just before his death, upon an only son, James Carter, a widower with eight children, a paralysed cripple who had seen better days, but who was unable to work, and in the greatest distress. Of this settlement, Mr. Knowall and Mr. Blooster were, by reason of their reputation at Mr. Small's Chapel, appointed trustees. Knowall, who was an old man, died a few weeks after the Sunday service at which Mr. Melville met him; leaving Blooster sole trustee. Up to this period, the trustees paid the cripple fifty pounds per annum, being interest at the rate of five per cent. But when Knowall died, Blooster at once withdrew the money from the satisfactory security on which it had long been placed, in order to use it for his own speculative purposes. He gambled with it very profitably to himself for several months, without even consulting Carter, but, at last, a speculation attended with enormous risk made it prudent that he should get the cripple to sign a document of indemnity.

Accordingly, he set out after one week-night service to Carter's poverty-stricken rooms. The cripple had never

his own helplessness, and utter inability to provide for his children, not one of whom was old enough to work, he was appalled at being unexpectedly called upon by Blooster to sign his name to a document relating to the only money which he possessed, without comprehending completely its scope and importance. He, therefore, respectfully begged Blooster to grant him time for reading that document, and thinking over the matter. Blooster was baffled and annoyed, but hid his disappointment under plausible arguments, all of which, however, were unavailing.

The cripple asked that the matter should stand over for consideration until the following day, and wished to keep the document. Blooster upbraided him with ingratitude, and declined to leave it; but to the unexpected application which Carter made for permission to copy parts of it, Blooster was puzzled how to reply. He was most anxious that no copy should be made, yet he feared that if his refusal became notorious it would rouse suspicion in people's minds. Moreover, he reflected, that by the aid of his arts of jugglery, and obfuscation, it would be easy for him to prove that his meaning had been misunderstood. He, therefore, managed to control his passionate vexation while the cripple wrote out the extracts which he wished to make.

On the following day Carter took into his confidence his oldest friend, a lawyer's clerk. By his help there was no difficulty in clearly understanding the nature of the document which Blooster was trying to get signed. The legal effect of it, though disguised by all kinds of technical terminology, was to give Blooster authority to risk Carter's money in any speculative adventure whatever. And it released him from all liability, and responsibility, in the event of the whole being lost. In return, Carter was still only to receive five per cent., and Blooster was to pocket the rest.

indemnity. He also requested that Blooster would kindly allow the money to remain upon its original safe security. Blooster at once went to Carter in a great rage, did his utmost to induce the cripple to alter his decision, inquired whether he dared throw any aspersion upon his honour— the honour of Falcon Small's valued friend; and tried all his tricks, first of flattery and afterwards of bullying, to get back the transcript of the discarded document. He was unsuccessful.

As he walked back moodily to the city, all the malignity of his heart asserted itself. Not only had his selfishness received a blow, but his vanity was stung. The very trick in which he had now failed, he had, quite lately, performed triumphantly in the cases of three persons, whose trust money he had got hold of by virtue of his official connection with Falcon Small's Chapel. The consciousness that he, the crafty Blooster, had been foiled by a paralysed cripple was unendurable to his tyrannical soul. Meditating a tremendous act of retaliation on poor Carter, he, with his bloated face now purple with passionate spite, hurried himself, wheezing and snorting, up a long flight of stairs to the office of Mr. Scorpion, "the highly respectable solicitor" whom he always employed to give a legal, and decorous shape, and appearance, to such of his proceedings as were specially disreputable.

The result of the conference between Blooster and his lawyer was seen a week afterwards in a letter to Carter. Instead of sending the usual cheque for £25 for the half year's dividend, Blooster wrote inclosing only five shillings in postage stamps, and his lawyer's receipted bill for twenty-four pounds fifteen shillings. The items in the bill consisted of a number of charges for alleged advice given, and services rendered to Blooster as a trustee, extending over a long period. The account was a fraud: as there never had been any litigation, nor had any questions arisen

Blooster to be correct, and the trust deed enabled him to pay it.

Remonstrance on Carter's part was, therefore, utterly vain. He wrote to Blooster expressing regret that the various items of the bill had not been paid as, and when, they became due; because that method would only have involved a moderate deduction from time to time from his income, whereas the course adopted robbed him, and his children, of the means of sustenance, and left him with only five shillings in postage stamps, instead of the usual twenty-five pounds, to provide for all the requirements of the coming half-year.

He begged Blooster to reconsider the matter. In reply he received a frigid letter from Blooster's solicitor. The man of law regretted "that as his estimable client, Mr. Blooster, after all his sacrifices for Mr. Carter, had been treated with an ingratitude which was highly unbecoming, it was impossible that disputed matters could be re-opened. At the same time, he had no objection to add, without prejudice, that if Mr. Carter agreed within two days to sign that most reasonable paper, on which Mr. Blooster had most kindly agreed to continue the onerous duties relating to the trusteeship, the question of lending him a small sum of money might be entertained."

To this Carter replied, adhering to his refusal to sign the paper, and inquiring whether Mr. Blooster, since he found the trusteeship was onerous, would object to resign it to some other person.

The result of this suggestion was a long and pompous communication from the solicitor. In the first place, the letter recommended that "for the purpose of saving the trust estate further expense, the correspondence had better close." In the second place, it stated that the additional costs recently incurred in advising the trustee, and otherwise incidental to the matter in hand, amounting to ten

deducted from the capital sum of one thousand pounds, the balance had been this day invested in government three per cent. annuities."

The cripple was plunged into the depths of distress, for this letter made it apparent that he would get no dividend at all for another six months, and then only about fifteen pounds instead of his usual twenty-five pounds. He renewed his efforts to awaken Blooster's mercy. They were in vain. The great man would neither give up the trusteeship, nor alter the investment.

Carter then appealed to the relations of the deceased Knowall, and to Falcon Small more particularly, to use their efforts to induce Blooster to resign the trusteeship. This attempt, besides being utterly useless, was the means of bringing the cripple three severe letters. The respective epistles of Falcon Small, and the representatives of the late Mr. Knowall, were almost identical in their expressions of sorrow that "their dear christian friend, Mr. Blooster, should have had to suffer so much through his generous care of Mr. Carter's temporal interest." The writers deprecated and declined any interference with Mr. Blooster, "whose high christian character, and extensive commercial experience, made him, of all men, the best judge as to the right course to pursue in this complicated business." They concluded by reminding Mr. Carter that "any pecuniary inconvenience which he might have to endure would only be the punishment which he had quite unnecessarily and recklessly brought on himself by his ungrateful and unkind treatment of his christian benefactor." The third letter was from Blooster's solicitor, Mr. Scorpion, threatening him with legal proceedings, on the ground that his "attempts to get a new trustee, and the statements put forth in justification thereof, amounted to defamation of Mr. Blooster's character."

Wretchedness more appalling than that which shrouded

cult to find. He was an incurable cripple, unable to walk beyond his room, and possessing only just sufficient power in his right hand to write a letter, or, on his best days, to do a little wood-engraving, by which he was able, now and then, to earn a trifle. He was, moreover, very intelligent, and very sensitive. Before a railway accident had shattered his physical strength, he had followed a lucrative business, and lived in comfort. During the lifetime of his wife he had, always at hand, a loving gentle help who mitigated his sorrows. Death, however, had lately taken her suddenly from him, and he was now overwhelmed by mental prostration and despair. Eight little children were around his desolate hearth, starving, like himself, for want of sufficient bread.

In this agonizing extremity of his distress a neighbour recommended him to send two of his little girls, one eight, and the other six years of age, to Miss Scampion's "Home for Children," and most kindly offered to supply such funds as might be needed. To this generous suggestion the grateful cripple gave his ready assent. Painful as it was to his morbidly tender heart to part from these little ones, it was far more harrowing to him to witness their daily hunger, and to gaze on their emaciated little forms. To Miss Scampion's Home, therefore, the girls were sent without delay. Six children, however, and his own necessities remained to be provided for.

As a desperate resource he, very unwillingly, made his case known to the "Society for the Help of the Helpless," of which Mr. Melville was the chairman. It was his last sane act. His reason broke down under his accumulated misfortunes. When his children next saw him he did not know them. In terror they implored the assistance of the other lodgers in the house. These persons communicated with the parish doctor, and the local authorities. Steps were forthwith taken to confine him. He never

evermore that Blooster was God, and God was Blooster: and that each child must be offered to Blooster separately as a burnt-offering, "because he was great, his ways were past finding out, and his tender mercy endured for ever!"

When Blooster heard of the cripple's condition, he at once behaved as became him. He sold out all the trust stock from the Bank of England, and placed it in his own bank. He instructed his solicitor to take proceedings in Chancery to "obtain the direction of the court respecting the proper mode of administering the trust estate under the present circumstances."

By this proceeding he opened two new sources of income for himself. In the first place, he shared profits with his solicitor, Mr. Scorpion, for the three subsequent years, during which the fictitious legal proceedings were, by all sorts of dilatory and expensive manœuvres, kept before the court. In the second place, he speculated with the trust moneys to his heart's content, none daring to make him afraid. He managed at the same time, to get great credit for "his goodness" to Carter and the children. He headed a subscription list with ten shillings, to pay some debts of Carter's, amounting in all to four pounds, which were due to a member of Falcon Small's Church.

He also introduced a new topic into his public "prayer" at Falcon Small's prayer-meeting on the night when Carter's fate became known. He thanked God for giving to His saints the light of reason, and earnestly begged Him, "for mercy's sake, to restore it to one who was unfortunately outside their communion, upon whom, in His wrath, His heavy judgments had fallen."

CHAPTER XLII.

CANT COMMITTING LARCENIES ON THE CHARITABLE.—THE BEGGING CIRCULAR IMPOSTURE.—MISS SCAMPION'S "HOME" INVESTIGATED IN COURT.—MR. MELVILLE RESCUES CARTER'S CHILDREN.

"THE Society for the Help of the Helpless" went to work immediately they received the cripple's application. But before even their kind reply reached Carter, his madness had too far advanced for him to comprehend its import; and their efforts to get at the history of his case were attended with many difficulties. Mr. Melville's first concern was that Carter's six children should be provided for. And this was admirably managed.

Groping their way to the salient facts respecting the trust funds, the society eventually obtained sufficient information to justify them in instructing their secretary to write to Blooster. They received a reply from his solicitor, Mr. Scorpion, intimating that he was "awaiting the directions of the High Court of Chancery, and that any interference with the trust estate would, of course, be highly irregular and improper."

This part of the letter was couched in terms of propriety, admonition, and reprimand, so admirable, that one member of the council, on hearing it was, for an instant, appalled by a misgiving that the secretary must, in a weak moment, have been making some wicked overtures to one of the guardians of public virtue. The rest of the letter was filled with expressions of "pleasure" that the society had taken up "this truly deserving case;" and with information respect-

gentleman, had already made on behalf of Mr. Carter," in proof of which assertion a reference was given to the Rev. Falcon Small.

Unable to do anything with Blooster, the committee decided that their next duty was to make inquiries respecting the two children that had been sent to Miss Scampion's Home. To save time, the matter was placed in the hands of Mr. Melville, with plenary powers.

On returning to his residence in Park Lane, after attending the meeting of the committee at which his services had been thus invoked, Mr. Melville made it his first duty to read all the letters, and other documents, which the secretary of the society had given him respecting the institution in question. His distrust was soon awakened by the canting tone of these effusions. The circular letter soliciting subscriptions was a sample. It read as follows:—

"Dear Friend in our most blessed Lord,

"Will you give a trifle to assist a fold maintained for Christ's sweet lambs? We cherish here the babes and sucklings, giving them home comforts, and the sincere milk of the word, which alone, through the merits of our precious Saviour's blood, will qualify them for saintship on earth, and the crown of righteousness which fadeth not away. Do spare something for our homeless lambs. Pray for me that I may be supported in these great works. Your sister in Jesus Christ,

"Susan Scampion."

"The Report of the year's work" contained some incidents which seemed to Mr. Melville, to say the least, somewhat improbable.

It recorded, amongst other phenomena, that "little Polly Fletcher, aged seven, had discovered her need of being plunged into the scarlet fountain opened for the cleansing of sinners. Asked, after a day of fasting, to take her supper, she begged to be excused, alleging that if she

to be awake all night, talking to Jesus, feeling that His arms were around her, and her head was on His gentle breast."

It also recorded that "Mary Ann Denny, aged ten, implored permission to remain away from the children's annual holiday, because she wished to prepare herself for being an angel, by a day of prayer; and that she remained on her knees all day; resumed, and continued prayers, all night; and rose in the morning, 'having received the seal of the Holy Ghost to the perfected work of the Spirit.'"

Mr. Melville carefully perused the rest of the Scampion literature. All of it was filled with exaggeration, false sentiment, morbidity, and the other vices usually incident to the achievements of Cant. At the conclusion of the unsavoury task, he formed a strong opinion that he ought, at once, to go and see how it fared with the two little children whom a cruel fate had drifted into the unwholesome place whence these literary productions emanated. He recollected, moreover, that this Susan Scampion was the cousin of Mrs. Tremlin, and this fact increased his forebodings of evil.

Accordingly he set out, early the following day, for the Home, Zion Mount, Little Clarkley Street. On arriving there he found the house almost deserted. A miserable child opened the door, and said that Miss Scampion had gone out with all the other girls. An old woman who resided at the adjoining house, and who happened to be standing near, volunteered the information that Miss Scampion had been summoned before the police magistrate; that her case had been adjourned several times, and was now to be fully investigated.

To the police court, therefore, Melville proceeded. In answer to a few judicious inquiries there, he obtained information enabling him to comprehend the nature of the case which was then proceeding. A father, whose child had died at Miss Scampion's Home, as was alleged, through her ill treatment, had instructed a lawyer to pro-

detail the incidents of the trial, or to distinguish the evidence which was given in examination, from that which was elicited in cross-examination. It is enough that we give a summary of the facts which were brought to light.

Mr. Sharpe, an accountant, proved that Miss Scampion had received for three years upwards of five hundred pounds a year in contributions from the public, exclusive of sums collected by the children, and the payments which some relatives made for the board of some of the inmates of the Home. Miss Scampion had destroyed her account books, but extrinsic evidence remained which proved this statement to be approximately correct.

Jerusha Hogg, another witness, said, "she had often worked as charwoman at Zion Mount, and, with the exception of the little girls, the oldest of whom was twelve, no one else was ever employed to do any housework or cooking. The house contained altogether only eight rooms, and of these, two belonged to a married sister of Miss Scampion, and two were filled with the warehoused furniture of a person who was travelling. Of the other four rooms, one was Miss Scampion's bedroom and parlour, another was an underground kitchen. The remaining two rooms, of which one was an attic and the other an underground structure leading out of the kitchen, were the dormitories of the thirty girls. The passages, and the kitchen itself, were frequently used for sleeping purposes. The children had two meals a day, at no fixed time," and Jerusha Hogg believed that "meat was never provided. There was no bath in the house, and the children were filthy, and badly clad. Miss Scampion often beat them when in a passion, and was in the habit of throwing at them the first object which came in her way. Miss Scampion drank freely, and often had merry parties in her own room. The children were taught nothing systematically,

seemed like prolonged scolding, for half an hour, every now and then, when disposed."

Mary Blackwell, another witness, an emaciated little girl aged eleven, deposed that she "had been in the Home twelve months. Her father was at sea. He paid four shillings a week for her support. He paid Miss Scampion for six months in advance before he last went away. She never had enough to eat. She slept with two other girls on a straw mattress on the floor in a room behind the kitchen. They had one blanket, and their own clothes, to cover them, nothing else. The girls did the work of the house, and had to go out collecting every day for the Home. If they did not take back some money they were generally beaten. They were not taught anything. There was no fire in the kitchen, or in either of the rooms used by the girls. Miss Scampion took her meals upstairs."

Emma Tiley, another witness, a wan-looking girl about twelve years of age, said, "she had had the care of Fanny Stevens, the child who had died. Four other little girls had died during the last six months. She had not the care of them, but only of Fanny. Fanny was ill nearly three months. She grew thinner and thinner; her bones seemed coming through her skin. For a long time she was too weak to walk. She used to sob for food, and wanted them to send some one to find her father. Miss Scampion often whipped Fanny, chiefly because she cried with the cold during the winter nights, and wanted a fire, and something to eat."

Annie Leigh, another witness, a half-starved child about eight years of age, said she "recollected calling for a subscription on a lady, who gave her ten shillings, and sent a great lot of books and toys. Miss Scampion kept the ten shillings, and sold all the books and toys. The other girls never saw them. She looked at them at the lady's house. The girls had to wait on Miss Scampion, and Miss Scampion's sister. Some of them had to sit up to let Miss

Scampion in of a night. It was often very late. Sometimes the sun was rising. If they kept her at the door a minute she would beat them violently, especially if she was very tipsy, which the girls thought she often was."

Judith Headland, the last witness, a diminutive girl about twelve years old, whose face was badly scarred and bruised, and who had lost the sight of one eye, in consequence, as she alleged, of a blow from a jug which Miss Scampion had thrown at her, gave corroborative evidence. She added, however, that she "often had collected ten shillings a day for the Home. She had once bought a loaf out of the money and taken it to the girls, for they were starving. As a punishment she was locked in the coal-cellar for a day without food, where there was neither light, nor air. Any girl who was called for by a friend, was put into clothes specially kept, and taken to Miss Scampion's room. Miss Scampion was always present. They never saw their friends alone. They dared not complain. Edith Tiley, who was now dead, once told a visitor that she wanted more to eat, and she was beaten so awfully, and kept in the coal-cellar so long without food, that the girls had ever since been too frightened to tell the truth."

When all this sort of evidence had been heard, Mr. Flicker, Q.C., the brilliant criminal advocate, to whom a magnificent retaining fee had been paid by Miss Scampion out of the funds she had collected, rose to address the court. With masterly skill he exposed the discrepancies, absurdities, improbabilities, and contradictions apparent on the face of the evidence, which had been given. In his cross-examination he had intimidated, and confused, the half-starved children, until the truth appeared like prevarication. And now, he was at liberty to comment on all the facts of the case, and characterize the statements made against Miss Scampion as being, in the first place, irrelevant to the specific charge before the court; and in the second place, a tissue of children's falsehoods. Standing erect, and personifying indignant virtue, as only a great actor like himself could do, he called on the bench to hear the testimony which he was able to adduce to the eminently christian character of the estimable lady, who had been so foully slandered.

Hereupon Mr. Golding, M.P., stepped forward, and paid a warm tribute to the high moral worth of Miss Scampion. The Rev. Falcon Small, Mr. Oscar Crayford, the Rev. Jabez Blaze, and last, but by no means least in his own estimation, Mr. Blooster,—as one of the patrons of the Home,—stepped forward and gave similar testimony.

Upon the judicial mind of the worthy magistrate, the opinion of these gentlemen, and the eloquence of Mr. Flicker, produced a profound impression. He decided, without a minute's delay, to dismiss the summons which had been obtained against Miss Scampion; and begged that it might be understood by the public at large, that she "left the court without a stain upon her character."

At this announcement Miss Scampion and her friends arose, and having bowed to his worship, left the court.

"Ah," said Miss Scampion to Mr. Crayford, as she passed out, speaking in tones which were intended for all hearers, "it is, indeed, a blessed thing to be sustained by my risen Lord in a world of cruel slander. I *knew* He would not forsake me in this trying moment."

"Madam," returned Crayford, "you will receive the reward of your work in another world."

"But," screamed the shrill voice of an elderly woman, "it would have pleased me to see her get it in this world also. My poor child was starved to death in her Home, and she knows it. Say what you will, I believe that other child was killed there too."

Mr. Melville had not been all day merely a passive spectator in court. He had found out poor Carter's two little children, and heard from their own lips their wretched tale, which was corroborated by their death-like appearance. Finding that they could talk without any fear of Miss Scampion pouncing down upon them, they opened their hearts to him freely. Their child-instinct told them that they could trust this benevolent man. They implored him to take them away with him: anywhere, so long as it was to some place where Miss Scampion could not come. They cried bitterly when, from his silence, they feared he would not grant them their prayer. Then, in the intervals between their sobs, they redoubled their piteous entreaties. It had been far from Mr. Melville's design to take them under his charge, and there were not a few difficulties in the way of his doing so. But if he had closed his eyes to their infant misery, or turned a deaf ear to their infant supplication, he would have been recreant to his manhood.

He therefore bade the little ones to sorrow no more. Then, taking them with him, he led them away from their home of horrors and bondage.

When Miss Scampion was leaving the police-court, he made himself known to her, and explained that it was his inflexible purpose to remove Mr. Carter's children.

Holding their trembling hands, he told her that they were neglected and starved, and even she did not dare deny a fact which their appearance so clearly proved.

CHAPTER XLIII.

CANT AND SELF-DECEPTION.—RELIGIOUS CODDLING, QUACKERY, AND SILLINESS.—REV. MR. MAWKSLEY, ARMINIAN METHODIST.—REV. MR. HOWLING, CALVINIST.—MRS. TREMLIN BECOMES MRS. CHARLESWORTHY.

MRS. TREMLIN contemplated the affairs of her cousin, Miss Scampion, and of the scandalous "Home" with serene equanimity. She knew that Miss Scampion had ingratiated herself amongst a clique of professional Samaritans who were well versed in all the legalised tricks of a prostituted philanthropy, and that Cant, and Rant, would, therefore, strain their utmost powers to snatch her from the hands of justice. Mrs. Tremlin understood, too, the strength and value of Cant and Rant in such cases. Her cousin's deliverance from the hands of the police magistrate was, therefore, only a fulfilment of her shrewd expectations. But, in her confused category of the several, and dissimilar, forces which move the personages, and arrange and readjust the scenery, on earth's little theatre, Mrs. Tremlin habitually used wrong names, and Cant had so muddled her mind that she invariably ascribed results to wrong causes. So, when she wrote to congratulate Miss Scampion on her acquittal, she asserted that the result was a direct answer to her own prayers. Her self-complacency made her quite happy in the fancy ; and as she never had an honest thought, it was never revealed to her that her notion that she had been instrumental in inducing Heaven to save Miss Scampion, was nothing more than a monstrous illusion which was the offspring of her own vanity, falseness, and fanaticism. She never consulted her memory very much, or she would have ascertained, that even her statement about her prayers was altogether a fiction and an after-thought. Mrs. Tremlin was, however, very happy just about this time. Several things conspired to make her so. She found that she was secularly better off than she had ever expected to be. She had discovered a nice little house in a new neighbourhood, and had settled herself in it most comfortably. Her delicate health, too, was greatly improving, "now that she had no longer the incessant work and anxious care which for years had always been entailed on her by her dear Maurice." She was able to go out alone very much more frequently. In fact, she was completely re-juvenized, and the miserable, complaining invalid had changed into the sprightly, voluble widow. She had severed her connection with the Baptist Chapel because it was some distance away from her present residence; and since Maurice could no longer oppose her going thither, she had lost her zest for the place. A new Church and a new circle of "dear religious friends" now interested her.

She had found out the Wesleyan Methodists. There were two of their Chapels within an easy walk of her new home. She tasted alternately the joys of each. At the Paragon Chapel, the Rev. Mr. Mawksley preached. He drew around him a considerable flock. His doctrines were those well-known ones which are very enjoyable to a certain order of minds. His conception of the human soul was, that of a battle-ground on which God and the devil were perpetually waging a relentless war. According to his view, it was often difficult for man to satisfy himself as to which of these two warriors had obtained the upper hand. He taught, that a man's best impulses might really be only the tricks of the evil one, and that promptings which were ascribed to the Devil were often the whisperings of the Spirit of God. In this terrible state

man, according to Mr. Mawksley's teaching, was incessant self-inspection, with the object of catching Satan at a disadvantage, and turning the odds of battle against him, in favour of God. The disciples of this reverend gentleman were mental hypochondriacs and religious valetudinarians. They spent their time in analysing morbid conditions and in feeling their Wesleyan pulses. They were always afraid of "falling away from grace," and were perpetually watching for every appearance of the indicative symptoms, in themselves, and in others. For example, if a man, owing even to physical conditions, failed to enjoy his Sunday services as usual, he began to perplex his understanding as to whether his "call" to salvation had really been effective. Was not Satan, after all, playing him a trick? Had the Devil's temporary disappearance from the soul been just a crafty device for its subsequent subjugation? Was the heart hot? Was the heart cold? Was the heart indifferent? Was the heart lukewarm? Had the ears waxed deaf? If so, was it through personal neglect? If not, was it because the voice of grace never had intended to deliver a saving message? After exasperating his whole nature with these, and similar questions, the man would take himself to the "class," or consulting room, which the Wesleyans keep open for the diagnosis, and treatment, of such cases. Here he would relate all his emotional and mental experiences. Then the question would arise whether, and when, he had really dropped "the legal yoke;" and to ascertain this a minute examination of all the symptoms which occurred in his religious history and constitution many years ago would be entered on. Then would follow an elaborate inquiry as to what he did when "the plague spots of sin" were first made visible to him. Did he defy Satan at once? Did he go and tremble before "Admission Gate"? How long did he stop there? How often, and how loudly, did he

"voice of thunder," or the "still small voice"? Did he really pass into the "covenant of grace"? Was he happy for a short or a long period? What was the origin of the present lack of spiritual warmth? Had he encouraged Satan to "retake possession" of him? At the end of these questions, and the subsequent clinical observations, and pathological arguments, the man's egotism and vanity would probably have been placed in good tone; and, for a time, he would "go on his way rejoicing." But he would often relapse; and, as often as he did so, it would be his pleasing duty to present his case to the renewed consideration of the "class room."

In this religious society, what were called the "experience meetings" derived the chief part of their interest from cases like this. Men, and women, were all expected to present to their class a history of their moans, and groans, their attempts, and failures. Very often, the conventional language employed was so exaggerated that speakers unintentionally conveyed utterly erroneous impressions as to matters of simple fact. In that tropical heat in which these worthy people kept their religiosity, all hopes and fears assumed abnormal proportions, and grew into the most artificial, and fantastic forms. A perpetual fuss and excitement was constantly kept up among them, and as their frequent assemblies afforded the additional attraction of plenty of opportunity for spicy personal gossip, it was no wonder that vulgarity and fanaticism crowded the ranks and filled the Chapel.

Notwithstanding all these alluring influences, Mrs. Tremlin decided that she would not join the worthy people who were under the pastoral care of Mr. Mawksley; but would enter into religious fellowship with their brethren of the same denomination at the Rattling Street Chapel, near her own house. One of the reasons why she preferred this branch of the Methodist body, was because the teaching of its ministers was Calvinistic. She certainly enjoyed the excitement which resulted from the acceptance of Mr. Mawksley's Methodism; and the task of microscopically investigating her own symptoms, to see whether "grace was working properly" in her heart, was very delightful to a mawkish woman, who selfishly loved the incessant contemplation of her own mental, moral, and physical operations, to the exclusion of all the grand and vast things of creation. Yet, still, she could not accept any doctrine which in any way admitted that man had "free will." Mr. Mawksley's exposition of Methodism seemed to imply that man could help in the work of his own salvation. She preferred to believe that, "God had settled from before the foundation of the world what men should be saved," and what men should "be damned;" and that all the wriggling, and all the struggling, of penitent sinners, was utterly useless in cases where the names of the parties had been "omitted from the Book of Life." She knew that Mr. Howling was "sound on the great doctrine of the elect," almost as sound as Mr. Jabez Blaze, and as all the advantages of Methodist organization could be enjoyed at his Chapel, Mrs. Tremlin decided that to his Chapel, and to no other, would she go.

Mr. Howling was one of those many popular men, to be found in all pulpits, who, like Falcon Small, claimed to be especially "inspired" by God. Whether he took a pleasure jaunt on the river, or caught a cold in his head, whether he lost an umbrella, or found a purse, he always contrived that the incident, whatever it was, should be so dexterously manipulated, and so skilfully represented to the public, as to compel them to believe that the whole transaction had been carefully planned by God, for the express purpose of proving to mankind that He had been careful so to arrange the affairs of the great universe as to make everything come right for Mr. Howling. A fluent speaker was this Mr. Howling, but he would not have been content with that estimate of his oratorical powers. He claimed that his words "proceeded from the Holy Ghost," who had deliberately made choice of his wide mouth for purposes of sublunary articulation. It was this assurance that enabled him to meet, with an unblushing face, any persons who charged him with ignorance. "What is book learning? What is philosophy? what are ancient languages? what is ancient geography to us who are set free by the Spirit?" This was the defiant question with which he confounded Biblical critics, and restored the faith of his flock in himself as a great teacher, on the occasions when his transparent historical, arithmetical, geological, and other blunders, staggered the boys from the board schools. His friends met all interrogatories by the statement that Mr. Howling was not only "one set free by the Spirit," but also "a man mighty in the Scriptures." By this last phrase they meant that he quoted the Scriptures prodigiously. So he did, but it was in the oddest fashion. He never seemed to see when, or where, any given text was disjointed. Scrap by scrap he wrenched poetry, history, law, genealogy, out of their accustomed and proper places in the Holy Book, and threw particles of them pell-mell into any discourse, on any subject; and by tremendous muscular energy, and vast rhetorical heat, made the whole mass cohere as solid gospel before the startled eyes of delighted crowds. If those same people who applauded Mr. Howling's manner of treating the Scripture, had been taken to a dwelling-house to see wheelbarrows thrown on to pianos, mouse-traps nailed to oil paintings, kitchen fat thrown upon books, feather beds hung upon picture rods, and the whole furniture, and utensils, of a modern villa eccentrically jammed together with these in one monstrous amalgamation, they would have been disgusted at the stupid, and incongruous, spectacle. Yet, the kind of Biblical treat which they so highly appreciated, was, in truth, a far more absurd, and certainly a far more wicked entertainment. In the case of the furniture and utensil jumble, it would be possible for even an ignorant observer to distinguish dissimilar articles; but in

Mr. Howling's sermonic medley, such an one would have struggled in vain to detect the true from the false, the blasphemous from the holy, what was really Christian from what was merely Wesleyan. For Mr. Howling perfectly dazed his hearers.

> " Louder and louder grew his awful tones ;
> Sobbing and sighs were heard, and rueful groans ;
> Soft women fainted, prouder man expressed
> Wonder and woe, and butchers smote the breast ;
> Eyes wept, ears tingled ; stiffening on each head,
> The hair drew back, and Satan howled and fled.
> With outstretched arms, strong voice, and piercing call,
> He won the field and made the Dagons fall ;
> And thus in triumph took his glorious way
> Through scenes of horror, terror, and dismay."

Under his "arousing ministry" Mrs. Tremlin was very happy, and when Mr. Howling paid her a pastoral call she became happier still. She found him to be such a "dear" man ; he was so thoroughly orthodox, particularly on the question of the "call." He agreed with her that "grace" was not a gradual growth, but an instantaneous act. He was always so very comforting when he spoke of the "call," for he showed that those who received it, like Mrs. Tremlin, had no further cause for anxiety in this world or the other. When such persons received the "call," they became possessed, he said, " of a certificate which discharged them from the penalties of original sin, and of all their debts to God." At the same time it was to be remarked, that Mr. Howling's opinion that God had predestinated men from before the foundations of the world to their respective fates, did not at all lessen his zeal for the spread of Wesleyanism. He cared nothing about the logical consequences of the dogma that men were good or bad irrespective of their own works—which would appear to render all preaching unnecessary ; what he did care about was, that in any event the world should be Wesleyanized. The zealous intentions of himself, and his friends, were thus expressed by one of their local preachers in the kind of poetry in which the more ignorant of the fraternity delight:—

> " By the powers of Noah's dove,
> This gospel through the world we'll shove."

A few weeks after her introduction to Mr. Howling, Mrs. Tremlin received her Wesleyan Methodist Society ticket, " Admitted on trial." Then she had her " Lord's Supper " ticket, and finally her ticket of admission to the " Love Feast." She attended the "class meetings," and soon attained an enviable celebrity for the volubility with which she descanted on her "christian experiences." Greatly did she enjoy the " Class-room," though, perhaps, her felicity reached its height at the " Love Feasts," where, sitting around well-made cakes, and listening to well warmed Cant, her gastric and sentimental needs were respectively satiated.

> "'Tis a point I long to know,
> Oft it causes anxious thought,
> Do I love the Lord or no?
> Am I His, or am I not?"

This was a favourite song on these occasions, and it indicates the intellectual capacity, and moral tone of the *habitués*. It is, of course, simply impossible to conceive of a man or a woman of vigorous understanding articulating such maudling jargon, but it expressed perfectly well the religiosity of these people, and of their equals in other Churches. They do not know their own mind. Spending a lifetime in religious ordinances, and devoting an infinitude of pains to the task of investigating every symptom of their nature, they can come to no conclusion as to whether, or not, their spiritual compass points in the true direction!

Mrs. Tremlin was determined that Wesleyanism should not only forward her heavenly schemes, but should also contribute to the advancement of one of the most important of her earthly plans. Mr. Tremlin having been dead six months, she resolved to select, and, without unnecessary delay to wed, a "prosperous believer." The gentleman upon whom her hymeneal choice had fallen frequented occasionally the meetings which she attended regularly.

Mr. Charlesworthy was a speculative builder, and some years her junior. She felt sure that, under proper control, he would become a docile husband. Now, as Mr. Charlesworthy did not himself appear to be a candidate for that position, she deemed it necessary to catch him by flattery, and a variety of other snares.

"What are you going to call this house, Mr. Charlesworthy?" said she to him one morning, as he stood surveying some architecture which he had just completed.

"I thought of calling it 'Violet Villa,' ma'am, or else 'Victoria Lodge,' as a little compliment to our queen."

"Dear Mr. Charlesworthy," she exclaimed, "you are not only a great builder, but full of poetry and loyalty. The first name would show how you love even the humblest flower, and the other, that you respect our glorious sovereign. But, why not call it 'Charlesworthy House,' after your own name? The 'chosen people' in Scripture are commanded to call their lands after their own name, before the places that know them now shall know them no more for ever."

"Well, ma'am," replied the gratified builder, "there's a good deal in what you say, but I don't think my name is a pretty name."

"Oh, indeed you are wrong," protested the aggressive widow. "It is a charming name. What house, or what woman, would not be proud to bear it? Call it 'Charlesworthy House.' That would do beautifully. Oh, call it that for my sake."

He hesitated. She knew, at once, she had gained her advantage. She pursued the matter; and she induced him to give his name that same day to the house, and, some few weeks afterwards, to herself also.

The married life of Mr. and Mrs. Charlesworthy was not a happy one. Charlesworthy understood building houses, but not managing widows. Mrs. Charlesworthy understood how to crush a man of the Tremlin order, but had no receipt for subduing the passionate master-builder when he lost faith in her. When Charlesworthy realized the base hypocrisy of the woman who was esteemed a saint at her Chapel, he "fell away from grace" at a rapid rate.

"I am sick of all your noise," said he to the class-leader who called on him. "It is true that since I was fool enough to get married to one of your people, my worldly matters have got into a muddle, but I do believe that your religious affairs are in even a greater muddle. You say God has put aside some fellows to save, and has given over some to the Devil to damn, and matters cannot be altered. Then, you tell me the Devil is trying to get away from God some of those whom God never intends him to have. As God is almighty, of course, there is no fear of the Devil's success. Then, you tell me, that the Wesleyans are trying to snatch souls from the Devil. Of course, if God intends the Devil to have them, you cannot hope to upset God's plan. So you, and the Devil, are both wasting your time and labour, for God has already settled matters independently of both of you."

With feelings of despair the class-leader left the degenerate builder to his fate. He reported on the "case" to the "class meeting," that the man had "fallen from grace and had become a dangerous backslider and freethinker."

Charlesworthy did not remain in England long after the date of the class-leader's visit to him. He left his wife enough property to live on, and sailed to America, determined never again to see her face, for it had become absolutely hateful to him.

When far away from his home and country, with his faith in wife and Church shattered, he, in his sadness, might have plunged into recklessness or despair, but for some words of Caleb Faithful's which he had heard long before, and which repeatedly rose to his memory.

"Never lose faith in God. Sectarianism is only a fog. Do not let its foul darkness dismay you, or prevent your mind from pursuing its heavenward road. Heed not the hideous voices which shout in the darkness, and threaten you with damnation when you cry for a better light. Be brave and struggle on your way, seeking ever for fresh gleams of truth. Very soon you will leave the sectarian fog behind; and walking erect, and happily, in the vast expanse of fearless thought, your eyes, undimmed by the exhalations of denominationalism, will behold Him who dwelleth in the light, and whose inspiration will guide you to Himself at last."

CHAPTER XLIV.

CANT AND INTRIGUE.—MR. LORRAINE'S MAGNANIMITY.—MR. CRAYFORD IS CONFRONTED BY MR. DARNLEY.

WE must not linger over the petty affairs of Mrs. Tremlin Charlesworthy. Nor must we stay to tell the history of her husband, who, when freed from all emasculating influences, eventually groped his way out of sectarian Cant, and grew into a brave and good man.

What we have to do now is, to follow the fortunes of Mr. Crayford. A fortnight elapsed after his last interview with Mr. Lorraine without his receiving any communication from that gentleman. It is only due to Mr. Crayford to say that, during the period, he had felt some anxiety with regard to his future fate. He well knew that, though Mr. Lorraine had not communicated with him, he was still in Mr. Lorraine's power. The consciousness of this, however, did not suppress his religious ostentation. He still held meetings at his house, and conversed with "anxious inquirers." But, in preparation for a collapse, if such collapse should come, he wore a look of the utmost resignation, and his eyes were constantly welling with a grief which he seemed unable totally to overcome. Of course his female friends and admirers noticed all this, as it was intended that they should, and their consternation was great. " Mr. Crayford was certainly in trouble; what could it be? The world was undoubtedly ill-using him, persecuting him for his spotless life maybe, as it has many a holy man before.'

After Mr. Crayford had endured a fortnight of suspense, by reason of the silence of Mr. Lorraine, his anxiety and fear prompted him to bestir himself to invent contingent arrangements. Irene must move once more on the scenes: she must play mediator again and call to see Lorraine. Crayford had been far more attentive, nay, even affectionate to Irene since Mr. Lorraine's visit; and he had exhibited such deep dejection in her presence that Irene's impressionable soul was touched with pity for him. She knew nothing of the nature of her husband's trouble, but she was sure it was a terrible one. She readily assented, therefore, to call on Mr. Lorraine, when requested by Crayford to do so.

"The Lord's chastening hand is very heavily upon me," he had observed. "I am suffering acute mental pain. This anxiety you can relieve, Irene. You must see Mr. Lorraine for me."

This speech, prefaced as it had been by Crayford's refusal to eat his breakfast, caused Irene to make all possible speed to Mr. Lorraine's house.

During Irene's absence, Christabel Darnley's elegant carriage drove up, and the fair lady was ushered into Crayford's presence. We may remark, in passing, that this was not an arranged visit, and Crayford's look of surprise as Hannah announced his visitor was genuine. He led the way to a seat, with as glad a smile as his intense grief permitted; and Christabel evidently caught his depression, for her lovely face was sad.

"My husband returns to-morrow," she explained; "so I came to-day. Oh, I cannot welcome him as I once did! I feel I am separated from him now."

"There is no barrier like the barrier that separates a godly, from an ungodly, heart, my dear Christabel," said Crayford. "I grieve to say I am situated like yourself, and in my trouble I can only turn to my God."

"Yes, I knew you were in trouble," exclaimed Christabel, "and that was why I wanted to see you. Do tell me, can I help you?"

Mr. Crayford shook his head. "Your Christian sympathy helps me," he said, smiling mournfully; "and a knowledge that the wicked shall not always thrive."

But Christabel was not to be put aside like this, and very soon she gathered from Crayford's craftily arranged tale, that his trouble was a pecuniary one. With this information her sympathy at once took a most practical turn; and the comfort which her visit afforded to the heavily tried Crayford induced him, at parting, to press the ministering angel to his heart, and reward her faithfulness to one of "the Lord's people" with "a holy kiss."

If any one had entered the dining-room shortly after he would have been surprised to behold the change in Crayford's face. Instead of the sullen gloom which had settled there before Christabel's visit, his features were lighted with an odious smirk, in which crafty self-complacency struggled for predominance. What was it that had wrought so great a change in his expression? It was this: Christabel had placed her wealth at his disposal; and though Crayford would have preferred his present position to an elopement, yet, rather than face poverty, he had determined that he would accept the good which was offered him. Should Irene's visit to Lorraine prove a failure, the future could not assume that hopeless, poverty-stricken aspect which he had contemplated with something akin to horror. He had taken care, however, not to commit himself too definitely to a plan of action with Christabel, because he wished to leave himself free to act according to the sudden exigencies which any hour might require.

Meanwhile, Irene had reached Mr. Lorraine's house, and was waiting in the drawing-room for Mr. Lorraine's appearance. Mr. Lorraine was ill, and had been so during some days. Mr. Melville, who came every morning to visit his friend, was with him when the servant brought up Mrs. Crayford's card.

"You will see her for me," suggested Lorraine. "You know all about the matter, and can tell her my decision."

Melville readily complied with this wish. Poor Irene! Her heart beat violently as the drawing-room door opened, and she tried, in vain, to recall the little speech which she had concocted on her journey. It was almost a relief to find that it was not Mr. Lorraine who entered.

"My friend is too unwell to see you this morning, Mrs. Crayford," explained Melville, "and he asked me to speak with you in his stead."

"We were anxiously waiting to hear from Mr. Lorraine," said Irene, "and I thought, as he did not write, I would take the liberty of calling. Perhaps I had better explain a little."

"I know all, Mrs. Crayford," rejoined Melville; "I have Mr. Lorraine's confidence. He is my dearest friend."

"Oh, can you tell me if he is going to help my husband?" asked Irene anxiously.

"For your sake, Mrs. Crayford, he will."

Irene took a long breath. "It is kind of him," she observed, "and I shall never forget it. I dreaded so to go home with bad news. What message may I take to my husband?"

"Mr. Lorraine is writing to him now, Mrs. Crayford. Mr. Crayford will have to settle all the money he has in his possession, on yourself."

"Will Mr. Lorraine compel him to do this?" questioned Irene timidly.

"He will," responded Melville. "He can think of no other way of preserving you from future suffering."

"It will be very unpleasant for Mr. Crayford," said Irene.

"He deserves a far heavier punishment, Mrs. Crayford, and may think himself very fortunate in being let off so easily. But, surely such an arrangement will add to your comfort."

"I would not wish to profit from my husband's troubles," returned Irene. "If it lies in my power to help him, I trust I have the courage to do so without considering my own interests. He is depressed, and in sorrow now, and I would assist him in every way that I could. May he not keep the money? I do not want it."

"But you surely are speaking without reflection, Mrs. Crayford," observed Melville.

"I am not acting under a momentary impulse," said Irene. "I am only doing as I would be done by. If Mr. Lorraine would let my husband keep the money, I would much rather."

"Mr. Lorraine's mind is made up, Mrs. Crayford," said Melville. "I cannot bring the subject before him again. It has already given him much anxiety, and brought back to him scenes which he would willingly have banished for ever. You do not know all, or you would wonder at my friend's generous forbearance in this matter. You must be satisfied with his final decision."

Irene's sense of propriety forbade her urging her request any further, and Melville having given her Lorraine's letter, she left the house with a lighter heart than she had on entering it. She walked very quickly, for she was anxious that her husband's burdened mind should be speedily eased.

How little she knew that another ministering angel had already relieved it, and that the footsteps of the charming Christabel had hardly died away as her own crossed the threshold!

One unexpected consequence resulting from Irene's visit to Lorraine was, Christabel's salvation from a fate over which Crayford would have had absolute control.

When Mrs. Darnley appeared at Crayford's house three days afterwards, in pursuance of an arrangement which she had made with Crayford, she found him bearing his sorrow more resignedly than she had anticipated. Christabel's "conversion" had acted very unfortunately on her character. From a comparatively cheerful, amiable creature she had become discontented, fretful, and ill-tempered. To use her own words, she pined for the "congenial society of those who believed with her;" and her husband, who would never tolerate Cant, appeared to her now as her natural enemy, and the opposer of her wishes. Crayford's influence had done its work. He had fascinated her, and she pined for *his* society. There was nothing interesting in life for her apart from him. She realized this on the morning of the visit in question, and she was prepared to give substantial proof of her sympathy in his affliction.

But Crayford's future had brightened, and his way seemed easy again. He had completely conquered Christabel, and he had no inclination to risk any more on her soul. He felt that matters had gone quite far enough for his reputation with the public; consequently, when Christabel declared her intention of leaving her husband, it answered his purpose to counterfeit the part of christian counsellor, and remonstrate with her about such a determination.

"My dearest friend," he remarked, "how can I, as a Christian, permit you to take such a step without showing you that it would be wrong! We must *bear* the fate that God has assigned to us, not run from it, and in the Lord's good day you may be the means of your husband's conversion to Brethrenism. Then how joyful will your heart be, what a triumph for your soul!"

Christabel's brow clouded, and she returned, "But you did not talk like that when I saw you last. You said then, that it was miserable to have to attend meetings on the sly, and not to be able to come here as often as I liked. I cannot bear my fate; and you have frequently told me that there is great danger of falling away from grace when one has such a worldly husband."

"I could never for a moment urge you to leave him," observed Crayford. "Oh, Christabel, my child! it is, indeed, a dark way for you; but the Lord sees fit that for the present your path shall be dark, and you must bear it.

yes, bear it, remembering how precious you are to the Lord; how He singles you out to endure heavy afflictions for Him, and be glad that He so honours you, Christabel. Run not from His chastening hand, but bow in holy submission."

"I cannot stop with him!" exclaimed Christabel, who by no means enjoyed the lesson Crayford read her. It contrasted so strangely with the persistent, and successful efforts, he had hitherto made to induce her to think badly of the husband whose character she had never doubted until she knew Crayford. "I cannot remain with him," she repeated; "he has forbidden me to attend any meetings, and though I have talked and tried to convert him, it seems all useless; and I shan't stop with him, when he makes me so miserable."

"Have patience, my dear friend; nothing is too hard for the Lord," murmured Crayford.

"But you told me his worldly views made him a dangerous companion for me," remonstrated Christabel, "and that the happiness of your life depended on your having my constant companionship."

"You must, indeed, be very watchful," observed Crayford evasively. "But think of the delight of leading him to renounce The Old Adam. Oh, my friend, it is worth struggling for; and if, after enduring all sorts of discouragements, you succeed at last, this is grand compensation."

Christabel was surprised and disappointed. She had anticipated a very different reception; for Crayford, on very many occasions, and notably at their last meeting, had acted as an admiring lover. She burst into a flood of tears.

Crayford was consoling her in the tenderest fashion, when the door burst open.

Before Crayford could turn his head, he felt himself seized by the collar, and flung to the other end of the room.

Christabel's tears vanished at the sight of her husband, who stood confronting herself and her companion.

Mr. Darnley placed his card on the table, exclaiming in excited tones,—"There is my address, Mr. Crayford! Seek satisfaction in any way you choose, I am ready to meet you; and before I leave, let me have the pleasure of telling you, to your face, you are a villain!"

Crayford's passivity had by this time returned to him. "I do not know what you mean by this unprovoked assault," he complained. "Mrs. Darnley came to me for christian advice, and I have endeavoured to direct her in the ways of the Lord. Is it for this I am to suffer violence?"

"Most certainly," returned Mr. Darnley; "if the 'ways of the Lord' mean alluring other men's wives."

"As a Christian, I must expect to be misinterpreted in my work for the Lord," said Crayford meekly.

"So the Lord is to answer for all your goings on," cried Mr. Darnley. "What roguery will religion not have to be responsible for soon! But, talk as much as you like to me, sir, you have met with one, at last, who is not taken in by your hypocrisy: who knows your language, and can interpret it; who detects the rogue by such phraseology as you have used, and who will not hesitate to expose you to all the world!"

"Then," sneered Crayford, "you will expose your own wife; for, had you been here five minutes ago, you would have heard me expostulating with her on the unnatural course she had determined to pursue. The only influence I have exercised over the lady has been such as a brother in the Lord should exercise. I grieve very much that there should be family quarrels, and family differences. Religious feuds between those who ought to be *of one mind* are much to be lamented."

"Reserve your grief for your own sins," shouted Mr.

believe. Of your canting duplicity I am absolutely certain; and as I said before, I will expose you."

"Your wife must admit that what I have alleged is correct," protested Crayford, who did not at all relish the exposure Mr. Darnley threatened—for by reason of Lorraine's arrangement about the money, he felt that Irene's good opinion of him was of the greatest consequence. "I was advising her," continued Crayford, "as a christian friend, and expostulating with her about the unwifely course she had determined on."

Christabel, who had buried her face in the sofa-cushion, did not look up during Crayford's speech, and Mr. Darnley impatiently thundered: "Silence! scoundrel! Such words shall not be spoken of my wife."

"They are true, for all that," coolly retorted Crayford, "and Mrs. Darnley cannot say to the contrary, or I have no doubt she would."

But Christabel spoke not. The beautiful daughter of the Count de Courtray was overcome with emotion, and only her sobs were audible. At that moment the contrast which her noble, and long-suffering husband, presented to the ignominious, and cowardly Crayford, was appallingly clear to her.

"Listen!" exclaimed Mr. Darnley. "I will have no tales about my wife. I can settle matters well enough with her, and did settle them, and got on smoothly and happily till *you* came between us. Since then, my home has been totally different. I have lived long enough to know the power of Cant; and you have exercised an influence over this lady which I intend you shall suffer for. My only feeling towards those who come under your influence—is intense pity. A knowledge of your true character would make them loathe you as I do." Thus speaking, Darnley raised Christabel from the sofa, and led her from the room, pausing at the door to remark, "I could say more to you, sir,

"I am unsullied by your taunts," replied Crayford, "and your incredulity of my good intentions cannot harm me."

Christabel, who was overpowered by her husband's sudden appearance, hardly raised her eyes as she left the room. The double shocks, of Darnley's unexpected visit and Crayford's treachery, were more than she could sustain.

Immediately after the departure of the Darnleys, Irene entered. "What has been the matter?" she asked. "I heard such loud voices, I was quite frightened."

Crayford's face was the picture of dejection. "Ah, Irene!" he began; "I have indeed to suffer wrongfully for the Lord's sake. A lady, whose soul I had brought to a knowledge of saving grace, has been here this morning seeking christian counsel. Her husband entered during our conversation and insulted me—yes, insulted me, with remarks that wounded my very soul. I had to endure all this, and yet answer him as becometh one of the Lord's servants."

"What did he come for?" inquired Irene. "On purpose to quarrel with you?"

"I will tell you one thing, my dear Irene," said Crayford, with a slight smile. "The most beautiful woman in the world, I should say, offered to-day to leave her husband to be with me. She, also, would have shared with me her magnificent fortune; but, though I refused on christian grounds, my unchanging affection for my wife would have caused me to spurn such an offer, even if I could have entertained it consistently. Irene, you are my life, and my hope!"

Such remarks as these were not uncommon now, from Crayford to his wife, and Irene's domestic lot was far brighter since the money had been placed in her hands.

"Did her husband know she had spoken thus to you?" interrogated Irene.

"I told him she had. I would never deceive a fellow creature; and I made him acquainted with all. I felt then I had done my duty. I, also, told him that I was convinced that his wife was only led away for the moment; and that her christian faith would return to her, for I believed she had entered the fold."

As we shall not have occasion to refer again to Mr. and Mrs. Darnley, it may be well at once to record the fact, that Crayford never succeeded in bringing Christabel again under his influence. Mr. Darnley was a strong-minded man, and his steadfastness of character enabled him to control properly the transient religious hysteria of his beautiful wife. He removed her beyond the enervating malaria of Cant; and, in the atmosphere of strong common sense, and healthy occupation, in which he compelled her to live, her intelligence developed, until at last she matured into an exemplary character. In subsequent years she was wont to look back with disgust upon her temporary association with the "Brethren;" and, unlike many women, she had the honesty, and the gratitude, to thank her husband for the energy, and firmness, with which he had insisted on saving her from spending a life of Cant in their company.

CHAPTER XLV

CANT A LADDER BY WHICH THE UNSCRUPULOUS ASCEND TO POWER. — THE REV. DANDY FILCH IS EXALTED. — MR BLOOSTER IS TRUSTED.

AMONG the many evangelical vultures who pounced upon Tom, when he was in jail awaiting his trial, and regarded the lessons of his life as so much spiritual food which ought to be distributed amongst their faithful followers, was Dandy Filch.

The time which intervened between Dandy's bankruptcy, and Tom's committal, marked Dandy's transition from the condition of a questionable bankrupt, to his development into a popular Low Church Divine.

It happened thus. Dandy had heard that the Established Church, though well satisfied with the scholastic attainments of its Ministers, was not altogether contented with their capacity for popular declamation. He obtained private information that a man with an aptitude for religious panic-making, and evangelistic pyrotechny, would stand the chance of getting a licence to preach, even though he were somewhat deficient in educational attainments.

Dandy, therefore, frequented popular seaside places, and, in season and out of season, managed to keep his name before the religious public in their periodicals, as a man who was "doing a great work for the Lord." Shouting to the mob from the top of a bathing machine, a sugar-barrel, or any other grotesque position, he managed, by his extraordinary antics, to raise such unexpected obstructions in the thoroughfares of astonished visitors as attracted general attention. Then, he collected a choir of young

moonlight nights, and prevailed on them to join him in serenading the Lord and His angels at the pier-head.

As soon as the papers began to speak of him as "an evangelist who had a mission," "an enthusiast who was burning with zeal for the Master," he became still bolder in his aggressiveness. He would rush into the middle of a well-dressed group, generally of pretty girls, sometimes of men and women, and in distracted tones beseech information as to their spiritual health. Immediately afterwards he would distribute a few sensational leaflets, similar to those which, it will be remembered, he obtruded on the attention of Mr. Melville, when he made his revivalistic visit at the house in Park Lane. Occasionally, he would induce persons just emerging from their lodgings to retrace their steps, that he might "pray with them."

In due time all this evangelistic seed-sowing bore him the fruits he desired—the fruits of notoriety. He announced, in the proper quarter, that the "marvellous manner in which the Lord had blessed his work, convinced him that it was his duty to consecrate his life to the saving of souls." He said that he "preferred, if possible, to work in the ranks of Episcopacy; but, if he were not welcomed there, the Lord would make an opening for His servant *elsewhere*."

The authorities to whom this crafty intimation was given, thought it undesirable that the Lord should be called upon to make any schismatical "opening" for this evangelist. Accordingly, they invited him to work for ever in their own episcopal fold, securely protected by their Thirty-nine Articles from all Dissenters and heretics.

At the time when Dandy preached his grand sermon on the career of Tom, the reverend gentleman was the chief ecclesiastical light in a leading London suburb, not more than four miles distant from the very school which he had left as a confirmed dunce, and the social circle in the midst of which he had passed his life as a conspicuous

One of his old trade-creditors expressed amazement at Dandy's audacity; but Dandy replied that "the Lord, and no one else, had lifted him up for a special work, and caused his face to shine with the oil of gladness above his fellows."

With his holy face thus shining with that holy oil, we must now take a long farewell of the Rev. Dandy Filch.

Another man who preached, what his admirers called, a "ighly gospel sermon" on the career of Tom, was the Rev. Falcon Small.

Useful as this topic was to this hollow sentimentalist, it was, however, of infinitely greater advantage to Blooster. This pompous deacon delivered a special address to the Sunday-school on the subject, explaining to his spellbound audience his own personal knowledge of the celebrated murderer; how he had "warned the criminal to shun worldly ways," and how he had predicted a murderer's end for him. Blooster's fictitious account of his connection with the felon, enhanced his own reputation for religious zeal, personal sagacity, and benevolence of heart. Not a few of the garrulous old women who were communicants at Falcon Small's Chapel delighted to boast to their neighbours that they "were well acquainted with the good Mr. Blooster, who knew the murderer through going out to seek and save the lost."

Altogether fortune smiled on Blooster at this period; for that reason Mr. Hardcastle thought it would be a proof of good sound sense, on which he especially prided himself, if he smiled too. He therefore yielded to Blooster's repeated suggestion, and Falcon Small's importunity, and constituted Blooster one of the executors of his will.

As Mr. Hardcastle died shortly after this climax of folly, Blooster became possessed of ample trust funds. Some clauses in the will being somewhat ambiguous, he was able, with the cunning assistance of his old accomplice, Mr. Scorpion, the solicitor, to speculate with the money

CHAPTER XLVI

CANT AND PERFIDIOUSNESS.—MR. HARDCASTLE'S UNJUST WILL.
—LORD EVERTON AND MR. BUMPUS HARASSED BY BLOOSTER
AFTER MR. HARDCASTLE'S DECEASE.—BLOOSTER DIES.

THE evil which men of Cant do, lives after them. Lord Everton, Bumpus, and Mrs. Hardcastle, discovered this truth very soon after Mr. Hardcastle's decease.

Lord Everton's case was especially deserving of commiseration. It will be remembered that it was only owing to the exertions of "dear Victoria," and the intrigues of her mother and family, that Lord Everton was inveigled into marriage. The Hardcastles were most proud of the connection, had made it a conspicuous boast; yet old Hardcastle in his heart felt uncomfortable in the presence of his son-in-law. He was oppressed by that sense of inferiority which not unfrequently vexes a coarse-minded, vulgar man, when circumstances bring him into intercourse with a gentleman.

By way of making the little lord acknowledge his power, Hardcastle's first act was to shirk the performance of the financial engagements into which he had entered preparatory to the marriage, and on which Lord Everton as he was not very rich, had in part depended to enable him to support the flaunting style in which "dear Victoria," when created Lady Everton, insisted upon living. His lordship's next trouble was that Lady Everton, even when she found that her faithless father had receded from his pledges, would not assist her husband in pressing for their fulfilment, nor would she retrench her exorbitant expenditure. She contented herself with upbraiding Lord Everton for not

his estates in order to discharge such of their expenses as were in excess of his annual income, and for which they could not get credit. When pecuniary difficulties eventually made it incumbent on Lord Everton to point out to his imperious spouse that their affairs would assume a critical condition, Lady Everton avoided all responsibility, and protested that she would be amply provided for under her father's will. It was only after Hardcastle's death that Lady Everton realized her folly, and her husband's injury. The latter did not trouble her much, and the former only made her more impertinent and overbearing.

When Hardcastle's testamentary dispositions were investigated, it was found, not only that he had far less money than he had pretended, but that he had been induced by Falcon Small, Blooster, and their fraternity, to bequeath an unreasonable proportion of his property to various institutions with which those gentlemen were connected, and to certain remote relatives who were the personal friends, or the irresponsible tools, of the minister, and his accomplice. It is only fair to Hardcastle to say, that he did not make his unjust will without some qualms of conscience as to his obligation to provide for his own family in accordance with his various promises. But the crafty Blooster threw in his influence against it. "My dear sir," said he to him on one occasion, "if you make the provision which you talk of for Lord Everton, the world will say that you bribed him to marry your daughter."

"Yes," added silly Mrs. Hardcastle, still puffed out with pride, "and surely, as I have always said, the match is quite as good a thing for Lord Everton as for dear Victoria. Certainly Mr. Hardcastle's position in the city is as good as his."

The unjust man, therefore, made an unjust will. Two sons of his, most worthy young men, who had left home some years before to follow their profession as engineers in

"Don't you remember, sir," said Falcon Small, "how they scoffed at religious ways, and nearly broke your heart by their unfilial ridicule of our great work at the Church? Is it right that the riches which the Lord has given you, and for whose stewardship you must give an account, should be scattered by them in profligacy from Dan to Beersheba? Surely the Lord will not hold us guiltless by reason of mere consanguinity, if we divert into the paths of mammon the offerings which should be carried into the Temple of the Lord. The Lord will not hold him innocent who rewards those who have taken His blessed name in vain."

Hardcastle's fatherly emotions, which were never very strong, collapsed under this holy rebuke: his sons were not even mentioned in the will.

Mr. Bumpus, too, realized as he had never done before the grim meaning of the words which he had so often heard old Hardcastle sing, "Put not your trust in princes, nor in the sons of men." The unhappy youth, shortly after his marriage, advanced to his father-in-law a large sum of money for a business speculation. Like many conceited, pompous, inexperienced young persons, Bumpus thought that he knew the world well, and that he could trust his own unaided judgment as to the advisability of the transaction to which Hardcastle invited him. He knew nothing of the World of Cant, and thus he committed the absurdity of supposing that reliance could be placed upon the solemn word of honour of a friend, and deacon, of Falcon Small's. He learnt, too late, that the asseverations of such men are merely strings of falsehood. Hardcastle's will made no specific provision for the return to Bumpus of his money, and he was left to take his turn with ordinary creditors. Bumpus was thus brought, for the first time, into business contact with Blooster, and found to his amazement that he had to deal with an enemy. He could not account for Blooster's hostile attitude for a long time, but

from which it appeared that Blooster was nursing a virulent animosity against him for some playful remarks which he had made some four years previously about Blooster's bloated, gluttonous appearance.

"No, sir," said Blooster with insolent defiance, when one day Bumpus requested him to make arrangements for the repayment of the loan which he had advanced to Mr. Hardcastle. "I shall do nothing of the kind. You will prove upon the estate in the ordinary way, and I shall require strict evidence that the money has not been already repaid to you. I decline to have any altercation with you. I refer you to my solicitor, Mr. Scorpion. The position which I hold at Mr. Falcon Small's is a guarantee to the world that I shall act conscientiously, and fairly, to all parties."

The attitude which Blooster assumed, caused Bumpus all the embarrassment which it was intended to. The return of some of his money was of the utmost importance to him; but Blooster would not even pay the interest on the capital. Mr. Hardcastle's business had to be wound up before any satisfactory legal steps could be taken against Blooster. It was assumed that six months would be required for that purpose. After which the long vacation loomed in the future as a bar to even such redress as could be extorted from the dilatory Court of Chancery. In order to prevent himself from being in the meantime overtaken by actual impecuniosity, Bumpus was compelled to break up his home. Blooster's delight amounted almost to rapture. He felt sure that both this young man, and Lord Everton, saw through him, and despised him for his ignorance, his shamelessness, and his hypocrisy; and he rejoiced that it was in his power, under the guise of law and honesty, to injure and harass then, jointly and severally, without fear of exposure.

Blooster, at first, feared that Mrs. Hardcastle might be

were soon set at rest. She had no eye to penetrate his sophistical Cant, and no measure by which to gauge his tawdry professions of goodness. She had no instincts of honour which made her recoil from a base person, and as her feelings towards Bumpus were colder than even ordinary mother-in-law affection, she bore the sight of his persecution by Blooster with serene equanimity. She accepted the income provided for her by the will,—which Blooster took care to silence her tongue by paying punctually,—and left the other members of the family to settle their financial affairs with the holy executor as best they could.

Blooster's triumph was therefore complete. Elated with his success, he determined that he would use his newly acquired purse and power for the purpose of promoting some financial devices in the City. To this end, he held daily consultations with the knavish Mr. Scorpion, and matured two, or three, successful money plots.

Nor did his success end there. So dexterously did he, and his confederates in the City, use the fact of his being one of Hardcastle's executors to prove his honesty and wealth, that three respectable old tradesmen who had retired from business with ample means, were induced by Mr. Scorpion to stake their money in a bubble company which he and Blooster had projected long ago, but for want of credit and capital had been unable to launch.

Alas! in the very moment of triumph, Blooster's career came to an end. Mr. Scorpion and himself, being both gluttons, determined to celebrate the registration of their last and greatest Limited Liability Swindle by a feast. Their hilarity was immoderate; they chuckled over the gullibility of their dupes with a boisterous mirth which was altogether abnormal.

At the end of the repast, Falcon Small called at their dining room by appointment, to accompany Blooster to

Church. Mr. Falcon Small was in a hurry, according to his wont.

Blooster wished to start instantly, yet could not tear himself away from the luscious viands, and the champagne. He ate and drank to repletion with horrible celerity, until his bloated and purple face alarmed even the wily Scorpion, and the icy-hearted Small.

Presently he rose, staggered forwards in a fit towards the door, and fell down dead.

CHAPTER XLVII.

CANT, BLASPHEMY, PROFANATION, AND KNAVISHNESS. A PAIR OF LAWYERS.—MR. FALCON SMALL AS A TIME-SERVER.

FALCON SMALL, of course, delivered a funeral oration on the death of Blooster, and published it. His subject was, "The Instantaneous Transfiguration of the Christian Merchant;" and his text was, "Absent from the body, present with the Lord."

One passage of his sermon created quite a thrill of awe in the congregation. It was that one in which he described Blooster "rushing from the inexorable demands of commerce towards their Church to enjoy a holy hour of prayer, when the angelic hosts, unwilling to spare him any longer for the devotions of earth, summoned him to take his rightful place with a crown upon his head, and a harp within his hand, by the throne of God!"

Lord Everton and Mr. Bumpus, however, when they perused the printed discourse, were not able to dwell so admiringly on the sweet picture of Blooster as a crowned heavenly harpist as were Falcon Small and his flock. To them was left the painful and irksome duty of ascertaining how to rescue from Mr. Blooster's estate the money which belonged to them, and of which their families stood in need.

Their discovery of the state of affairs was appalling. They found that before taking his golden harp to Heaven, the celestial musician had misappropriated all their money. It was difficult for even an adroit accountant to detect, in the skilful confusion with which Blooster disguised his accounts, what money belonged to any one of a dozen different claimants. To make matters worse, Blooster had appointed as his executors Mr. Scorpion, and his "dear and trusted christian cousin, Oscar Crayford." The latter having renounced probate, on the ground that he required "all his time for the Lord," the whole trust estate passed into the hands of the nefarious Scorpion. In order to make a public show of honesty, he, though a solicitor, appointed another member of his profession, a tool of his own, solicitor to the estate, and professed to leave all matters of detail in his hands. This man's name was Krimes.

Scorpion's objects in making this appointment were, to increase his gains by multiplying costs, and to invent new excuses for delaying payments. Whenever these confederates were pressed by persons, claiming either under Hardcastle's will, or Blooster's, they protested, in defence, that they would throw the two estates into Chancery unless allowed to administer them in their own way. No creditor, and no *cestui que trust*, wished such a course to be pursued, and so the threat effectually warded off aggressive measures.

Mr. Bumpus, however, was not inactive. He felt that those who kept back the money which he had lent to Hardcastle, and which Hardcastle's estate could afford to repay, were doing him a cruel wrong. He inveighed, again and again, against the procrastinations and injustices which were practised towards him. But his efforts were unavailing.

In desperation he wrote to Falcon Small, setting out all the circumstances, and invoking his aid. Falcon Small had been paid legacies under both of the wills; and, under Hardcastle's will, had received £1000 for beautifying and adorning his Church. There had been no demur to the payment of those claims. Bumpus imagined that as the favoured divine had great influence with Scorpion, he would willingly use it in the interests of honesty and right. He was even credulous enough to suppose that Falcon Small would be indignant at the wickedness which his friend,

Mr. Scorpion, was practising towards the son-in-law of his old deacon, and would threaten him with a public exposure.

Nothing could surpass the amazement with which Mr. Bumpus received from Mr. Small the following evasive reply to the detailed, and specific charges, and statements, which he had made in his letter to him.

"Dear Christian Friend,—

"I deeply deplore that the afflicting hand of the Master has fallen upon you, but He chastens not willingly, nor does He in wrath rebuke the children of men. He sends you your trouble because He sees that you need it. If we bear no cross, we shall have no crown. These afflictions are sent to wean us from the world. We must be born again. Nothing but the blood of Christ can enable us to pass through the rugged ways of time and the opening gates of eternity. As a christian Minister the Master forbids me to enter into commerce, for He needs me to consecrate all my time to seeking out souls who shall gleam as jewels in His diadem. I must not, therefore, enter into any business matter between yourself and my dear and valued friend, Mr. Scorpion. I have no doubt, by the help of the Holy Spirit, you will have guidance, and that, in His own good time, God will make all clear which has become obscured by the untimely removal from our midst of our dear brethren, Mr. Hardcastle and Mr. Blooster. The Church militant could ill afford to spare such men, and weeps still for her loss, like Rachel mourning for her children. God grant that those who were related to them may press forward in our Church to fill up the vacant places. Ritualism is rife all around us. The Scarlet One of Rome is seeking to sap the foundations of our Protestantism. Truly these are times in which we should say with heart and voice, 'Jesus only.'

"Yours in the bonds of the Gospel,

"Falcon Small."

If Falcon Small had not been an exceedingly shrewd, well practised man of business, and thoroughly conversant with all the modes of motion in the commercial world, Mr. Bumpus would not have felt a pang of disappointment when he laid down this epistle. But, because he knew the keen, wily, mercantile capacity of the man, he was not only disappointed but disgusted.

He was conscious that Falcon Small quite comprehended the record of facts, figures, and allegations, which had been laid before him, and that his vague evasion, and fluent platitudes, were deliberately intended as a polite refusal to help an injured man.

Since his connection with the Hardcastle family, poor Bumpus had been compelled to learn awful lessons in the art and mystery of Cant, but this seemed to him the hardest of them all.

CHAPTER XLVIII

CANT PROTECTED BY CONVENTIONAL OPINION.—MR. CALEB FAITHFUL'S ONSLAUGHT.—MR. SCORPION AND MR. KRIMES BAFFLED.—LORD EVERTON'S EPISTOLARY CASTIGATION OF MR. FALCON SMALL.

"OUR grievance has no remedy," said Lord Everton one morning to Bumpus, who had called on him to ascertain whether any concerted action could be adopted against the maladministrators of the Hardcastle and Blooster estates. "If we throw the matter into Chancery, Mr. Scorpion and Mr. Krimes will devise such delays, and artifices, as will prevent our ever getting a decree excepting at a ruinous loss."

Lord Everton spoke on the authority of Mr. Truelight, an eminent Queen's counsel, who had been an intimate friend of the father of Isabel Landor, and who, at her solicitation, had given his careful attention to the complicated case.

"Dear Victoria," and Anastatia, had not been even ordinarily kind to their cousin when she lived with them; yet Isabel, immediately that she was made aware of their troubles, hastened to their assistance. After offering them a home in her beautiful residence, she made it her next duty to take counsel with those friends who by reason of their experience, acumen, and judgment, were competent to advise her. These included Mr. Lorraine, Mr. Melville, and Mr. Truelight. The result of their united deliberations was summarised in the dejected answer which Lord Everton gave to the disconsolate Bumpus.

It is a favourite piece of Cant with judicial platitudinarians that "there is no wrong without a remedy;" but any keen observer of the English legal system is aware that the phrase is merely one of those many tawdry wrappages with which well-paid conventional optimists cover over those corrupted, and festering forms of law, which leap about throughout the legal world, usurp the functions of Justice, and claim to be called by her name. We know, moreover, that many writs, indictments, and processes, may be merely acts of villainy licensed by authority, and that some judicial officials may fairly be described as petty tyrants by law established.

The reader will easily comprehend, that the position in which the Hardcastle claimants now stood was practically remediless by legal proceedings, and that nothing could be done until, by reason of effluxion of time, the respective executors should be deprived of all excuses for claiming further delay.

But just at the time when the Hardcastle funds seemed involved in a hopeless entanglement, and the gloom of despair was taking possession of the beneficiaries, a strange, unexpected sidelight, broke in upon the scene, and scared the wrong-doers, and all the regions of Cant around about them.

The storm clouds out of which this light came were generated in a public meeting in the " Romaine Mechanics' Institute," at which Mr. Krimes, Mr. Scorpion, Mr. Falcon Small, Mr. Caleb Faithful, and other gentlemen congregated. The immediate cause of explosion was, a much applauded proposal made by Mr. Falcon Small, that Mr. Scorpion should be elected one of the trustees of the institute. To this proposition, Mr. Caleb Faithful very bravely moved an amendment. He had heard something of Mr. Scorpion's professional dealings, and of his conduct in reference to the Hardcastle and Blooster properties, and he, in consequence, plainly denounced him as an unfit person for a post of trust and public honour. Appealed to by Mr. Falcon Small to withdraw his unchristian remarks, and audaciously challenged by Mr. Scorpion to make good his calumnious assertions, Mr. Caleb Faithful proceeded to verify, by reference to facts, every allegation which he had made. So completely did he sustain his objection to Mr. Scorpion's name, that Mr. Falcon Small's proposal had to be withdrawn from the meeting, amidst a scene of intense excitement.

Early in the following day, Mr. Caleb Faithful received a lawyer's letter from Mr. Krimes, demanding a written apology and a retractation of all the assertions which he had made respecting Mr. Scorpion's character. As Mr. Faithful treated the letter with contempt, a writ was served upon him, and he became defendant in an action for slander at the suit of Mr. Scorpion.

Until the very day of the trial Mr. Scorpion cherished the hope of being able, with the assistance of Mr. Krimes, to intimidate Mr. Caleb Faithful into a compromise. Mr. Falcon Small also officiously begged Mr. Caleb Faithful, as a christian gentleman, not to bring scandal on religion by appearing in court. But Mr. Krimes and Mr. Scorpion were mistaken in supposing that, by reason of his being a Dissenting Minister, Mr. Faithful was a man who would be terrified by them, and they misjudged him in assuming that he was a man who would succumb to the officious, servile wiles of Falcon Small.

Very vexed were they with each other when they found that the action at law, which they had only intended as a sham to frighten Mr. Faithful, had become a reality; and even their brazen audacity sustained a shock when, on the morning of the trial in Westminster Hall, Mr. Caleb Faithful stepped into the witness-box and specifically, and on oath, repeated all his allegations against Mr. Scorpion.

Nor was the comfort of the two worthy lawyers enhanced by the fact that the court during the trial was crowded with a hostile audience, composed of many of the clients whom Krimes and Scorpion had, at various times, injured,

which Mr. Truelight, Q.C., subjected the dastardly Scorpion. If anything were wanted to complete the discomfiture of Scorpion and Krimes, it was supplied by the verdict which the jury returned in favour of Mr. Faithful without a moment's hesitation, and in defiance of the misdirection of an "evangelical" judge.

Little did Mr. Caleb Faithful imagine, when he made his courageous stand at the "Romaine Mechanics' Institute," that the consequences would be fraught with blessings to persons in no way connected with the proceedings of that evening, or the affairs of the institution out of which the discussion in which he took part arose. Yet so it was. Undesignedly, Mr. Caleb Faithful was the deliverer of Mr. Scorpion's victims. His speech that night was reported by many newspapers. And, as the result, public attention was directed for the first time to the dishonest solicitor's conduct.

When the account of the trial was printed, of course Mr. Scorpion's shortcomings attained still greater publicity, and the verdict against him startled both his dupes and his confederates. The effect of all this was to weaken his professional position very seriously. He found himself compelled to alter his tactics completely for a time. The suspicions of clients having been aroused, they were no longer willing to be imposed upon by such of his old artifices as had been manfully exposed by Mr. Caleb Faithful.

Mr. Scorpion's conduct in reference to the administration of the Blooster and Hardcastle funds, became a notorious public scandal. As a mere means of self-preservation, he was obliged at last to recede from the fraudulent lines on which he had been regulating his arrangements in reference to them. And in order to allay the apprehensions of such clients as still employed him, and to silence the scornful sneers of his many enemies, he found it absolutely necessary at last to pay Lord Everton, Mr. Bumpus, and the other beneficiaries, the money which belonged to them.

But long before they received it, these gentlemen had learnt to conceive an intense abhorrence for that religious Cant which had brought so much misery into their lives, and that social Cant whereby society agrees to maintain, as long as possible, a public belief in mere conventional respectability.

Deep and lasting was their gratitude to, and their admiration for, Mr. Caleb Faithful, that chivalrous defender of public morality, for his disinterested opposition to the proposal whereby Falcon Small intended to add to the honours of one of the basest of men.

The most magnanimous reader will scarcely be surprised that Lord Everton, and Mr. Bumpus, eventually entertained for Mr. Falcon Small feelings of aversion. For, when that reverend gentleman had received all the benefits which accrued to him, and his institutions, under the respective wills of Blooster and Hardcastle, and became aware of the growing unpopularity of Mr. Scorpion, he awoke to an intense interest in all the affairs of the Hardcastle family. Directly he learned that Lord Everton, and Mr. Bumpus, had been paid the money which was due to them, and were consequently in a satisfactory pecuniary position, he hastened to offer them his fulsome congratulations; at the same time assuring Bumpus that he had never ceased to remember his letter, or to use "his influence with Mr. Scorpion to bring about the present consummation, for which he had been incessantly engaged in fervent intercessory prayer."

Falcon Small had always been a hunter after men of title, and he thought that the opportunity had arrived when he might turn Lord Everton to his purposes. He, therefore, wrote him a cringing letter, inviting him to preside at a meeting in one of the Church schoolrooms. The following reply from his lordship astounded him:—

"SIR,—

"I decline your invitation. When Mr. Hardcastle was alive you thought proper to pander to his prejudices by affecting to agree with him respecting the supposed unsoundness of my views in reference to what you coarsely designate the 'doctrine of the blood.' You created a breach between him and me in order to maintain your own ascendency over him. He has departed; but, in payment for your obsequiousness, he first made those equivocal tes tamentary dispositions which your perverted sense of justice suggested, and from which, directly and indirectly, you and one of your officials, have received no inconsiderable benefit. Those of us who had honest claims on his estate were, through the conduct of your own treasurer, and one of his mercantile minions, denied payment of even our just debts for a long time after Mr. Hardcastle's decease. Your influence was invoked on our behalf; yet, you not only refused to exert it, but publicly supported the shameless authors of our injuries, until the result of Mr. Caleb Faithful's trial had branded them. By way of disowning a connection which has ceased to be profitable, you now wish to identify yourself with the representatives of Mr. Hardcastle. As you have educated your followers in all the principles of toadyism and sycophancy, you think that I shall be an acceptable chairman to them because I have a title. In short, the meaning of your adulatory letter is that the time has arrived when you think you can make use of me to serve the selfish ends of Cant. Some years ago I should have fallen readily into your trap, but adversity has taught me many useful lessons, has opened my eyes, and strengthened my mind. Moreover, opportunities have, unfortunately, been thrust upon me for understanding you, your work, and the kind of moral influence which you exert upon your unhappy hearers. I am not now a cajolable subject. Let me add, as a man who retains his faith in the Scriptures, that I regard with horror the injury which is done to pure, and undefiled Christianity, by theatrical, popularity-hunting, sensation-loving pietists like yourself.

"Yours, etc., "EVERTON."

CHAPTER XLIX.

Cant and remunerative Philanthropy-mongering.—How a Religious Society is Incubated.—Mr. Tonkin Sappey and "The Salvation Mission to the Grades."—Mr. Adams, the great Subscription-list Maker.

WE must not lose sight of that promising young Evangelist who accompanied Dandy Filch on his London converting tour. Mr. Tonkin Sappey, like his friend, Mr. Dandy Filch, made the gospel pay him very well. He was one of those conceited young fellows who, by reason of their inaptitude for plodding and unostentatious work, are always disinclined to follow any legitimate business. The excuse which he made for not settling down methodically to any honest trade or profession was, that his zeal to help "the Master" forbade his devoting time to qualify himself for secular pursuits.

"Our dear Tonkin," said his mother, "will never be able to grovel in business. His mind is so occupied with the advancement of 'the cause of the Master!'"

The Sappey family were poor, very poor; theirs was what the world calls "genteel poverty," which is often compounded of presumption, false pride, and an ignorance of any useful handicraft. The Sappeys could not, therefore, afford to help "the Master," unless, at the same time, something was done to help them. At five-and-twenty years of age, the unremunerative and unremunerated Tonkin, found himself called on to solve, without further delay, the problem as to how best to advance at one and the same time "the cause of the Master" and the cause of the Sappeys. He had already enjoyed the notoriety which had followed his revivalistic, and evangelistic gyrations, and eagerly desired to continue them. But some financial inconveniences which threatened himself and his family, warned him loudly that the time had arrived when it was imperatively necessary for him to earn his livelihood.

It occupied Mr. Tonkin Sappey a long time to discover a plan whereby he could "carry on his work for the Lord" in a manner which would be pecuniarily profitable to himself. But heavenly light flashed on him one evening. It came, he said, "straight from the Master." "Mother," he exclaimed—for he was sitting at the family tea-table, and Mrs. Sappey was anxiously gazing at her pre-occupied son—"Mother," he exclaimed, "the 'Master' has found me a mission. I am to bear the story of the 'blood' to the grades. There is a wide field for the labour of your Tonkin."

Many a time was this tale told by Mrs. Sappey to her friends, of the circumstances under which her "dear Tonkin" suddenly received his commission from the "Master."

Tonkin rose from the tea-table, as he said, "to think, to pray, and to write." That very evening he sketched on paper an outline of his " Mission to the Grades."

The following morning he took his prospectus with him to his uncle, the Rev. Hamilton Carney, who had started upwards of a dozen societies, and was secretary to five of them. He desired the advice of this experienced speculator in philanthropy. The canny Scotchman was well pleased with his nephew's prospectus, and intimated that, with his help, a self-supporting society might be successfully floated. The uncle and nephew thereupon selected from their acquaintances certain gentlemen to form a pliant committee; and Mr. Tonkin Sappey returned home to prepare a suitable circular for their approval.

In the course of a few days the committee held a meeting. Offices were taken, and the "Society for Promoting the New Salvation Mission to the Grades" was incorporated;

Mr. Tonkin Sappey being appointed secretary with a salary of £300 a year. Mr. Tonkin Sappey's circular being duly approved, the society issued their manifesto as follows:—

"THE NEW SALVATION MISSION TO THE GRADES.

"It has long been felt by many earnest blood-redeemed workers for the Master, that a new effort should be made to help on His cause in England. Much has been done to promote His kingdom in heathen lands. Directed, and liberally supported by a christian government, the English army has exterminated entire tribes of foreign savages and unbelievers, and it is confidently expected that the distant countries which have been lately subjected to a baptism of fire and blood, will in future be inhabited by Christians in place of those extirpated heathen, who were, as we know, an abomination to our God. In view of the stupendous progress which the gospel may now be expected to make abroad, your committee, after a long season of earnest prayer, feel that the time has arrived when something equally energetic should be done to help the Master to gather in the elect at home. They have, therefore, resolved to invoke the aid of the departmental system, for the purpose of bringing into the fold such as should be saved. They conceive, that England should be converted to God, class by class, and kindred by kindred. They have consequently commenced the 'New Salvation Mission to the Grades.' They appeal for help to all evangelical Protestants.

"It is their intention to restore their fellow-men in detached groups to the Master. Also, to introduce the Master to their fellow-men according to their rank, and calling. In order to do this, special meetings, sermons, and lectures, will be held at stated times during the next few years, which will be arranged to suit the convenience of each grade of society. The Butchers will be invoked to

sweeps will be shown the 'fountain open for sin and uncleanness.' The Sailors will be told of 'those who go down to the sea in ships.' The Cab and Omnibus Drivers should be directed to the glorious 'New Jerusalem,' where they may land their passengers' souls, and their own too. The Bakers should be supplied with 'the Bread of life.' The Publicans should be acquainted with the 'stream from whence every thirsty soul may drink.' The Lamp-lighters should be introduced to the 'light which guides to Heaven.' The Milkmen might hear of the 'pure milk of the word' that can be obtained without money and without price. The Pork-butchers should listen to the tale of the swine 'that ran down a steep place into the sea.' The Fishmongers should hear of the 'great fish which swallowed the unbelieving Jonah.' The Tax-gatherers shall be shown the 'many mansions' that will know no taxing. The Organ-grinders shall be told of the celestial musicians before the throne of God, whose ranks they may one day join; and the Thieves of London shall find their way to the city where 'no thief can break through and steal.'"

In response to this circular the public soon remitted several sums of money to Mr. Tonkin Sappey. But the amounts were not large, and at the end of a month it was apparent that a vigorous effort would have to be made to get funds to pay the secretary's salary, and the office expenses. Mr. Tonkin Sappey, therefore, again took counsel with the Rev. Hamilton Carney.

"Yes," said Mr. Carney in answer to his nephew's inquiry, "I think I can help you in the matter. I will introduce you to my friend, Mr. Adams, the great subscription-list maker. He has floated no less than seven of my societies, and I do not see why he might not finance yours. We will go and see him."

Accordingly the two gentlemen set out together to the residence of Mr. Adams, in Wooleston Street, St. Daniel's Park.

The great subscription-list maker was at home, and without delay received them very courteously in his little library. He was a keen, quick-witted man. He had once held a good government appointment abroad, and he had seen and studied social life in all its forms. The causes which had led to his adoption of his present mode of living were somewhat obscure. But nothing could be clearer than the facts that he thoroughly understood his business, and was highly successful in it. He was a man of fluent speech, and of rapid judgment; and when the Rev. Hamilton Carney laid before him the case of the " New Salvation Mission to the Grades," he promptly but oracularly replied,—

"Your society will succeed, because it will enable the opulent classes, by means of the gospel, to attack the habits of the common people, and to assume a patronizing religious superiority over them. Your prospectus assumes that the upper classes are holy, and do not require preaching to, whilst the poorer grades all need to have a thorough crusade directed against their vices. This idea will be vastly acceptable in general society; and the upper, and middle classes, will be quite willing to forward the preaching of the gospel under conditions which, in the way you propose, will divert attention from their own sins, and fix it on those of the poor. I never act for societies which do not possess the elements of success. But I see that yours does possess those elements, and so I will act for you on my usual terms—thirty-five per cent. on all subscriptions, donations, and legacies, besides expenses out of pocket. All applications to the public for pecuniary aid to be sent out by me, but they will bear the address of your society, or, better still, the private address of your president. The note-paper, and envelopes, must be good, and must be embossed with your president's crest. Of course, my letters will be sent out in a gentleman's handwriting: letters in a clerk's kind of hand are never noticed by the better class of donors. I make another stipulation. All the replies which you receive are to be handed over to me directly they arrive."

"Could you not do the work a little cheaper, as it is for religious purposes?" suggested Mr. Tonkin Sappey.

Mr. Adams smiled, and shook his head.

"Are you sure you can get money for us?" was the next question of Mr. Tonkin Sappey, whose imagination hovered over the possibilities of his quarter's salary being in arrear.

"Perfectly sure," was the answer. "I have reduced philanthropy-mongering to an exact science. Give me any problem, I can tell you precisely how it will work out. Observe my official books; they are the result of prodigious experience. I have minutely analysed every subscription list which has been published by every society, and by every newspaper, for the last fifteen years. I apply to the public for subscriptions for twenty different societies. As a consequence, I procure a vast number of replies from men of all shades of opinion. By reason of this information, and with the assistance of what I derive from other sources, I know all the whims, foibles, and tastes, of the subscription-giving public. Look at my tabulated lists in these books, you will perceive how the donors are arranged. Class A.—Persons who only give in cases where royalty leads the way. Class B.—Persons who only give in cases of vast accidents by road or water. Class C.—Persons who only give when the names of donors are publicly advertised in the *Times* and elsewhere. Class D.—Persons who give in response to sensational details. Class E.—Persons who give only to Church objects. Class F.—Persons who only give when invited to become vice-presidents. I have upwards of a hundred different lists all arranged on this principle; and in each book is an arithmetical calculation, showing exactly what return in money will result from a thousand applications to any given class of men."

Mr. Hamilton Carney expressed, as he had often done

before, his admiration of the science of the great subscription-list maker, and Mr. Tonkin Sappey expressed in his face all the amazement which he felt.

When they rose to go, Mr. Adams added, "Permit me to give one word of advice. In order to make your appeal for subscriptions successful, you must add to your circular some statement about the personal advantages of beneficence. You see, you cannot flatter the vanity of your subscribers, by promising them that their names shall have much publicity, unless, indeed, you like to advertise each donation by special advertisement in the *Times*. Nor can you treat them to occasional meetings with dukes or earls, or any advantage of that kind, which fanatics and vulgar persons, such as we shall have to write to, would enjoy. You must, therefore, find some motive, or motives, to which you can appeal with a chance of success. My experience would suggest to me that, as you will have to address yourselves mainly to "religious" subscribers, and as this is a "religious" business, you cannot do better than appeal to their greediness, and their fear of Hell. Draw up some short statement, warning people not to disregard your application, and threatening them with consequences, in this world, and the next, if they do."

"No doubt your advice is valuable," replied the Rev. Hamilton Carney, "and we will act in part on the suggestion; but, as a Christian, I must protest against—"

"My dear sir," interrupted Mr. Adams, "pray don't do any professional deprecating here. You, and I, know one another. I am a man of business, and this is a matter of business; and when you are here, you are a man of business."

"Well, well," replied Mr. Carney, "we won't occupy your time with discussing our little differences; and as I think we all understand each other, we may take our leave."

Thereupon the interview ended.

On their way home, Mr. Hamilton Carney and Mr. Tonkin Sappey talked over Mr. Adams's suggested addition to the circular, and it was decided that Mr. Tonkin Sappey should prepare something suitable for submission to the next committee meeting. He did so, and as the committee highly approved the document which he laid before them, it was printed and sent out with the circular in the way which Mr. Adams had recommended. It read as follows :—

"ADVANTAGES OF BENEFICENCE.

"Some years ago a poor lad came to town in search of a situation as errand-boy. He made many unsuccessful applications, and was on the eve of returning to his parents, when a gentleman, prepossessed by his appearance, took him into his employment, and, after a few months, bound him apprentice. He so conducted himself during his apprenticeship as to gain the love and esteem of every one who knew him ; and, after he had served his time, his master advanced a capital for him to commence business with. He retired to his closet with a heart glowing with gratitude to God for His goodness, and solemnly vowed that he would devote a tenth part of his annual income to the cause of God. The first year his donation amounted to £10, which he gave cheerfully, and continued to do so till it amounted to £520 : he then thought that was a great deal of money to give, and that he need not be so particular as to the exact amount. That year he lost a ship and cargo, to the value of £10,000, by a storm. This caused him to repent, and he again commenced his contributions with a resolution never to retract. He was more successful every year, and at length retired. He still devoted a tenth part of his annual income for some years to the Master, till he became acquainted with *men of the world*, who by degrees drew him aside from God. He discontinued his donations, made large speculations, *lost everything*, and became almost as poor as when he came to town a starving errand-boy. Learn from this that God will not send you prosperity unless you present Him with substantial offerings in return."

Mr. Adams's efforts to make a subscription list for the "New Salvation Mission to the Grades" were highly successful. The paragraph about "the advantages of beneficence" roused numbers of people to give money, whom the first circular, when sent out by itself, had utterly failed to move.

As a consequence of the success of the society thus inaugurated, Mr. Tonkin Sappey received his salary regularly as secretary for many years, and Mr. Adams received his commission.

The cause of "the Master" was blasphemously paraded in a very vulgar fashion, by very vulgar people, in very vulgar places; but "the grades" refused altogether to become converts to the doctrines of the new Noodledom, although the society roared, and whined, and howled at them, with dismal pertinacity.

Artisans, and mechanics, whose robust intelligence and universal sympathies would have hailed with delight the gospel of "The Son of Man," turned away in loathing and indignation from the surfeit of drivelling twaddle which organized Cant, and remunerated inanity, substituted and recommended in its stead, under the auspices of "The Salvation Mission to the Grades."

CHAPTER L.

CANT AND CLERICAL OBSEQUIOUSNESS.—THE REV. SMALLMAN PETTY'S ASSIZE SERMON.—MR. JUSTICE HUMPLEBY.—TOM'S TRIAL AND SENTENCE.

WHILST the events recently related were transpiring, Tom still remained in jail awaiting his trial. At last the expected day arrived, and her Majesty's judges opened the county assizes at Cadley in a manner which delighted the eyes of those crowds who love to look at wigs, liveries, regimentals, powdered heads, cocked-hats, gay carriages, and troops of javelinmen and policemen, tramping to the sound of trumpets. The high sheriff of the county, who had to arrange the necessary inauguration details, was a very sensible little man, and kept the part which he had to play in the masquerade as free from ridiculous elements as circumstances would permit. But he afterwards got into trouble for this. The senior judge of the assize, an eminent Christian, threatened to fine him seventy pounds for appearing in court in ordinary black clothes. This embodiment of judicial wisdom insisted that a high sheriff, even though rheumatical and bandy-legged, should wear silk stockings, silver spangles, a court suit, and a toy sword dangling at his side.

According to immemorial custom, the judges, having opened the commission of assize, proceeded with their retinue and many of the barristers of the circuit to the Cathedral Church.

The assize sermon there was preached by the sheriff's Chaplain, the Rev. Smallman Petty, an obsequious looking man, about forty years of age, who had received an University education, and had enjoyed plenty of opportunities for acquiring that insight into Biblical truth of which he yet stood so much in need. In order to obtain a suitable text to suit his servile sermon he filched four words from their proper connection in the ninth verse of the 76th Psalm: "God arose to judgment." We should be chargeable with piracy of copyright if we reproduced here the ornate eloquence of that published and now popular sermon. We must, therefore, content ourselves with merely summarizing the leading divisions under which this great soul ranged his vast conceptions of the Divine justice. He tritely said, in the first place, that "God judges." In the second place, that "before God passes sentence on sinners, He listens to the Advocate whom He has specially appointed to plead with Himself on their behalf—Jesus Christ the righteous." He then drew a vivid parallel between the forensic performances of a barrister in court and the advocacy of Christ before the great Judge. Racket Raketown, the dashing but unscrupulous Old Bailey counsel, whilst he listened to this part of the discourse, evinced unmistakable signs of honest disgust at the impious analogy; but he was not long offended, for Mr. Smallman Petty, having completed his proofs of the resemblance between the two cases, passed on to his third argument. His proposition was, that "God judges the world by means of His chosen servants"—the chief of whom he intimated were her Majesty's judges. In the fourth place, he observed that God has special days for judgment, and the county assizes he inferred were the most important.

One of the members of the bar tittered just a little when the eloquent divine expatiated on the spiritual intimacy existing between God and the judges of Westminster Hall. Even the judges themselves, though naturally flattered, felt that the assertions with which the preacher backed up his argument were fulsome in the extreme. They wisely considered that, on the whole, it would be better for preachers to keep that kind of thing in abeyance until the good time coming, when elevation to the bench shall mean something more than mere success at the Old Bailey, or at Nisi Prius, or political party service in House of Commons squabbles. But still, the Chaplain's rhetorical effort, as a work of art, was admitted to be very effective; and, because the argument came from the pulpit, it did not occur to the congregation to be shocked at its blasphemy.

The fifth division, which prepared the way for a magniloquent peroration, marked that portion of the sermon which gave universal satisfaction. People in power like to have their self-importance encouraged; and the Chaplain now contrived to inspire every official connected with the business of the assizes, from the court-crier to the judges, with the idea that his vocation was of a heavenly nature. That important class of the community which believes that the great end of religion is to maintain all British institutions intact, unreformed, and unquestioned, was much gratified at the halo with which the assize preacher invested the judicial system. They felt that a man who could succeed in persuading a Cathedral audience that even the mechanical administration of English laws rested on Divine authority, was a most useful person to the state.

As the congregation broke up, a fox-hunting Tory squire, a tyrannical landlord, who represented his division of the county in Parliament, declared, with appropriate bucolic expletives, that he would appoint the preacher to his next vacant living. He did so. But though Mr. Smallman Petty secured the goodwill of the worthy patron, for which he had long been angling, it is questionable whether his assize sermon really did good to anybody but himself.

Many of his hearers were men dressed for the hour in a little brief authority, and flushed by a sense of power. He exerted pernicious influence on them when he defended their arrogant pretensions and pandered to their love of homage. It would have been more useful, it would have been more brave, it certainly would have been more Christ-like, if, in anticipation of the impending assize, he had counselled his hearers to do justice, love mercy, and walk humbly before God. For these very reasons he did not do so, for men of his type are never useful, never brave, never Christ-like.

Some similar reflections were passing through the mind of Mr. Melville when he left the Cathedral and wended his way towards the court, whither the judges and procession had already gone. On the road he was met by the solicitor and counsel whom he had retained to defend Tom. In their company he proceeded to the court.

A short time after their arrival in the Crown Court, Tom—the grand jury having found a true bill against him —was placed in the dock to take his trial before Mr. Justice Humpleby and a common, very common, jury.

The learned judge was a sleek, well-fed man, undersized in mind, heart, and body; but he had a great reputation as a staunch Churchman and a severe judge. It was his honest belief that humanity had no rights, duties, idiosyncrasies, or aspirations, which were not amply met, and provided for in, and by, the law-books.

The counsel for the prosecution was Mr. Babble, Q.C., a personal friend of Mr. Golding. As a bitter sectarian, who had gathered together his business by advertising himself at religious gatherings, anniversary services, and revivalistic demonstrations, he was much disliked by his brethren at the bar, who, whatever their faults may be, never descend to Cant.

Tom's counsel was Mr. Fairplay,—one of those men who by their nature exalt any profession to which they happen to belong. He was thorough in all his work, and learned, true, and fearless. Yet he did not succeed in his defence of Tom. Mr. Babble and Mr. Justice Humpleby gave him no chance.

But even before it became apparent that the judge was adverse to the prisoner, Mr. Fairplay intimated to Mr. Melville in court that there was no hope of Tom's acquittal. He had seen, he said, in the hands of the foreman of the jury, during the adjournment of the court, a newspaper called "The Christian's Nightlight in the tents of Moab." He knew the type of creatures who revelled in the putrescence of that spurious literature. He had always found them low, mawkish sentimentalists. As such they were like all their class: too callous to feel genuine sympathy for real suffering, and too stupid to comprehend any distinction between offences created by British statutes and crimes perpetrated against the laws of God. Mr. Fairplay was of opinion, that a jury presided over by a sentimentalist foreman would be more anxious to parade their conventional horror of sin than they would be to comprehend the mitigating circumstances which the sinner might urge.

The learned counsel's forecast was correct. The jury showed Tom no mercy. Although the indictment contained several minor counts, the jury ignored them all, and convicted him on the capital charge without even leaving the jury-box for consultation.

Upon their verdict being delivered, the crier of the court proclaimed a solemn silence. Civilization was about to perform one of her grandest feats: the first act in the tragedy of legalised murder was about to commence.

In order the better to mark the gravity of the occasion, Mr. Justice Humpleby placed a black cap on his head over his judicial wig. Then, addressing the prisoner, he lectured him on the inviolability of human life, told him that no man had any excuse for taking the life of another, and that in this case there was not a shadow of excuse for what he had done. He warned him "not to entertain any hope of mercy on earth," but advised him "to attend to the spiritual instructions of the Chaplain of the jail, and forthwith make his peace with God." In sonorous phrases he pointed out "that the crime committed was not only one against Walters,—that excellent servant, who bore an irreproachable character,—but also against society at large, whose sensibilities were extremely shocked at the occurrence, and whose laws were defied thereby." After prosing a little longer in the same strain, he pronounced the formal sentence of death by hanging.

When he had concluded, Tom, to the amazement of everybody, spoke thus, in calm quiet tones which held the crowded court spellbound :—

"My lord, nothing you can say can make me more sorry than I am for what I have done. But I did not mean to kill Walters. Whether I meant to, or not, seems to make no difference to you. You do not consider the motive. It appears that I ought to be killed all the same. Perhaps God will judge me by what I intended, and not by the accident I committed. As to the harm which you say I have done in hurting the feelings of society, I am sorry to tell you I don't mind that at all. Society never took any notice of my feelings from first to last, would not even let me have bread to eat, though I tried for it hard and honestly. No notice was taken of me at all until people thought I was a great murderer; then they began selling my likeness, writing in the papers about me, preaching sermons on me, and praying for me. Bad as I am, society has made plenty of use of me lately, one way and another, all for its own money profit. So it must bear up under the shock I have given to its feelings. My lord, if I had not had such a hard life, perhaps I should not think like this; but, as it is, I am quite ready to leave society and die."

The felon was then removed from the dock.

The judge, magistrates, Clergymen, Mr. Golding, and influential friends who occupied seats on the bench, all felt that the prisoner's words were an outrage, and if ever a villain deserved the gallows, he did.

CHAPTER LI.

CANT, OSTENTATION, AND COUNTERFEIT LIBERALITY. — MR. MELVILLE'S DISCOVERY. — MR. GOLDING AT BAY. — TOM IS HANGED.

IT is characteristic of the World of Cant that it always loves a notorious man. The knowledge of that fact raised the spirits of the Rev. Mr. Smallweed and the deacons of the Broadcray Baptist Chapel. It encouraged them to expect that at their annual meeting, which was to be held two days after Tom's trial, there would be a crowded audience to view the successful prosecutor. Mr. Golding, M.P., who was to occupy the chair. Their expectations were realized: the people came in crowds.

Mr. Golding made a grandiloquent speech, beseeching all his hearers to help the Lord by strengthening the cause of the Baptists throughout the world. Towards the further consolidation of his own popularity amongst these peculiar people, and for the purpose of assisting God in improving the spiritual condition of mankind, he announced, amidst deafening cheers, that he was about to subscribe a sum of £200 towards enlarging the Broadcray Baptist Chapel.

This munificence was overpowering. Golding's name was, during the rest of the evening, mentioned with high eulogy by all the little sectarians who addressed the assembly. There was not a speech delivered which did not contain loud-sounding praises to his name; and even the prayer, by which the Pastor brought the proceedings of the evening to a termination, minutely displayed, for the information of the Almighty, all the splendid virtues of this great Baptist light which Heaven, in the excess of its benevolence, had sent from the celestial spheres to irradiate at once the borough of Broadcray, the Baptist denomination, and the British House of Commons.

It was no wonder that Golding, after spending three hours at the meeting, in this atmosphere of Cant and adulation, returned to his home revelling in self-righteousness and vanity. The esteem in which he held himself was still further vastly inflated by an article in a local newspaper, which he found on his library table.

In that fulsome composition, one of his paid sycophants, a renegade Jew, who changed, and sold, his political principles according to a scale of prices, described Mr. Golding as one of the greatest thinkers of the age. It was Beelzebub flattering Judas; but it was delightful to Judas.

Flushed with joy at all his recent triumphs, Mr. Golding threw himself into his arm-chair, to smoke a cigar, and read for a third time the glowing article. His pleasure was brief. Though it was late, a visitor was announced whose business could not wait. He was Mr. Melville. No one could have been less welcome.

After apologising for the lateness of his visit, Melville said,—"I called respecting that unhappy lad who is now under sentence of death."

"A very righteous sentence, too," interrupted Mr. Golding.

"We will not debate a topic on which we are not likely to arrive at the same conclusion, Mr. Golding," said Melville, "because, with your permission, I wish to call your attention to something more practical and important. Will you be so good as to look at those letters?"

Golding did so, and soon grew tremulous and pale. The conversation which followed completed his embarrassment, despite all his artifices to conceal it. No wonder! The letters which Melville produced were the last links in a chain of evidence which he had discovered since the trial.

Mr. Golding had three sisters. One had committed suicide under the influence of religious monomania; the second had long resided with her husband in Australia; the third, when an impulsive girl of sixteen, had eloped from her childhood's home with a fascinating actor. Golding, and the other members of the bigoted and unrelenting Golding family, regarded her union with the actor, who did not long survive his imprudent marriage, as base in the extreme. In their eyes, a theatre was the most ungodly of institutions. In their estimate of men, an actor was a villain beyond the reach of God's grace. Florence Golding, on her marriage, was therefore anathematized. The Golding family told her she had disgraced herself and them, and that she was, therefore, never to see or write to them again. When her husband died she fell into dire poverty and distress. After years of bravely borne suffering, she applied to Golding for help. His letter in answer was stern, chilling, and cruel. He forbade her ever to write to him again. Stung to the quick by this rebuff, the indignant woman determined never to mention the name of her family any more. She kept her vow, and accordingly the name was not even known to her son. Yet she preserved the letters, and at her death they were part of the trifling little parcel of things of which Tom became the possessor. Of course, Tom was in ignorance of the import of these letters. It was by a remarkable series of coincidences that Mr. Melville was enabled, when he was looking at poor Tom's trifles, to understand their real meaning, and to follow up the clue which they gave him. Only a few hours had elapsed since Melville's inquiries had resulted in the discovery that Golding was the uncle of the doomed lad. Hence he paid Mr. Golding this visit. He besought him, under the circumstances, to add his signature to the requisition which was being numerously signed, praying for a respite of Tom's sentence. One of the letters which he placed in Mr. Golding's hands was the identical epistle which had been written by the prosperous Member of Parliament to his broken-hearted sister, long years before.

While Mr. Golding read it his self-composure left him, the colour faded from his cheeks, and, as he glanced at Melville, he inwardly groaned, "Hast thou found me, O mine enemy?" During a few minutes the shock, and surprise, seemed to conquer even the habitual audacity of the well-practised dissembler. But he soon rallied.

"How do you prove that this letter is not a forgery?" exclaimed he defiantly to Melville. "How can you prove it?"

"If I had no other proof," replied Melville, "the expression of your countenance is incontrovertible evidence that the document is genuine."

"Excuse me," returned Golding, "I cannot permit suggestions of that kind. If it be conceded that I ever wrote a peremptory letter to a member of my family, there is no proof that this is the letter. And if this be a document in my handwriting, there is nothing to show that it was not purloined from its rightful owner. A fellow like the prisoner is capable of anything. I will allow no insinuations or innuendoes. My reputation as a Christian, and public man, is not to be lightly spoken of; and if I hear any slanders respecting my alleged relationship to the murderer, I will instruct my legal advisers to institute proceedings against all parties implicated."

It was clear to Melville that the wily Baptist was inaccessible to the voice of mercy. Wholly regardless of the fate of his nephew, the uncle was solely anxious as to the best means of braving out his own false position.

"Your sister, sir," exclaimed Melville, "died in abject poverty in a London alley. Her son was an outcast, and you, without knowing the relationship, have been his relentless prosecutor on two occasions. As a result of your

facts before you. It rests with your conscience as to what you will do now that you know them."

But Golding was inexorable, evasive, and defensive; and Mr. Melville had to withdraw from his presence without having secured any benefit for Tom.

Golding, left by himself, relapsed into a wretchedness which contrasted strangely with the exultant mood in which he had passed the previous hours of the evening. The recollections of bygone years crowded upon him. The ghosts of long-buried deeds rose and scared him. He became agitated, yet neither pity, nor remorse, played any part in the emotional storm which made him tremble. The elements of that storm were nothing more than his own pride, arrogance, and selfishness. "How shall I save that poor boy?" was a question which failed to cause him even momentary solicitude. "How shall I uphold my own reputation?" was the problem the solution of which enlisted and stimulated all his faculties. The conclusion at which he arrived was that, at all hazards, he must continue to pursue the self-defensive policy which he had adopted during the interview with Mr. Melville. In the infinite littleness of his soul, he felt that he would be degraded if he acknowledged his relationship or put forth an effort to save, the starved, homeless poacher, who in a few days would die a felon's death. Accordingly he resolved that the facts should not be admitted by him even in conversation with his wife.

Mr. Melville was, therefore, left unaided by Golding in his efforts to get up a petition to the authorities for a commutation of Tom's sentence. The Home Secretary was known to Golding, and belonged to the same political party; the uncle's efforts, therefore, on behalf of the nephew might possibly have been of some service; but they were not forthcoming, and the prayer of Melville's numerously signed petition was refused.

Four days afterwards, civilization performed the final act

of her constantly called for, and ever popular, christian hanging tragedy.

It was very simple. First of all, Tom was provided with an unusually good prison breakfast. Then, the Chaplain ineffectually tried to induce him to say that he was "washed in the blood of the Lamb, and felt grateful to God." Soon afterwards the little sheriff, with his under-sheriff, various officials, the Chaplain, four newspaper reporters, and others,—altogether twelve persons,—came upon the scene.

A new interest was almost immediately added to the proceedings by the presence of the hangman, who, with his stalwart coadjutors, pinioned Tom. When their well-practised hands had reduced the emaciated and unresisting prisoner to a state of absolute helplessness, all the chivalrous little christian company marched compactly forward a few yards to that part of the prison where, in a private place, a gallows had been erected.

Here the hangman blinded his victim, put a rope round his neck, and without the slightest opposition, easily strangled him.

A black flag was hoisted over the jail to announce the splendid triumph of "christian" law over the felon.

Finally, an inquest was held over Tom's body, and the usual verdict was returned, that the deceased had been satisfactorily strangled in accordance with the enlightened laws of "the greatest of christian countries."

CHAPTER LII.

CANT A CURSE TO MANKIND.—RETROSPECT.—SUMMARY.—THE CRUSADE AGAINST CANT.

THE time has come when we must complete our record. Isabel Landor carried into practice the plan of life which, it will be remembered, she once propounded to her astonished aunt. She became celebrated as a scholar, a wit, and a philanthropist. Her home was the centre of beneficent, intellectual, and social influences. She reigned as a queen in a brilliant society, whose principle of cohesion was, love for culture, truth, purity, and rectitude.

Mr. Rainford eventually emerged from the shadows which shrouded his early manhood in The World of Cant. By the help of Melville, who never failed to sustain and encourage him, he grew brave and strong. In the land of common sense he found men of honest heart, and vigorous brain, who appreciated his teaching, and rejoiced in his aims. A congregation composed of such persons installed him as their Minister; and for the remainder of his days he was enabled to proclaim those grand truths of Christ which, though men of Cant decline to hear them, are essential to the progress and the welfare of the race.

Falcon Small lived to a cheerless old age. He died in Australia a very rich man; and, as he had been quite poor when he embarked in the ministry, the public came to the conclusion that he must have found the profession of a popular preacher exceedingly lucrative. He was soon forgotten. Standard English literature disdained to spare even a single niche wherein to preserve a paragraph, a sentence, or a phrase out of all of his many thousands of gushing effusions. The moral effects of his ministerial life were worthless, because he preached the death of Christ, not as an incentive to virtue, but as a substitute for it.

Lord Everton and Mr. Bumpus learned wisdom in the school of adversity; and in their mature years became useful members of society, and strong opponents of Cant.

Their wives never improved in character. The children of canting parents, they were by nature hard, deceitful, and shallow. They disregarded the truths which time reveals, and the lessons which experience teaches. They consecrated their lives to self-decoration, self-deception, and self-indulgence, and consequently their fussy existence was discontented and useless. To their husbands they were burdens; to men of thought they were a nuisance.

Mr. Krimes and Mr. Scorpion practised their honourable calling until by successful pillage each respectively made his fortune. When they eventually grew weary of the monotony of plundering widows and orphans, and retired from London into private suburban magnificence to enjoy their booty, conventional society cringed before their wealth like a Neapolitan rabble before a successful thief.

Mr. Caleb Faithful, by reason of his splendid faculties and heroic character, maintained his noble influence over his compeers during all the years of his life. His pigmy detractors failed to tarnish his glory, because it shone, where they had no entrance, in the warm affections of great souls whose capacities were called forth by the vigour of his grand intellect, the spirituality of his intuitions, and the tenderness of his heart.

Mrs. Tremlin-Charlesworthy renounced the Wesleyans and joined the Bible Christians. But neither Bibles nor Christians ever did her any good, for she remained steeped and saturated in Cant all her days. Her children became worthless characters; and she was wont in her old age to assert, with malign joy, that she was the only one of her family who was really "accepted in the Beloved."

Mr. Golding, towards the close of his life, lost his ascendency over the independent electors of his borough. They began to find out his true character, and refused to give him their suffrages. But the Conservatives—some of whom have a natural affection for a man who is false and unscrupulous—rallied round him, and secured his return to Parliament as a Liberal-Conservative; on condition that he would only very occasionally act the part of a Liberal in his speeches, and be an unfailing Conservative in his votes. At the time of his death, which happened long years ago, he was one of those shameless political bandits whose modern successors are designated, in derision of truth, "men of light and leading."

In connection with politics, it will be opportune to mention two other names—Sir Nicol Giltspur, and Mr. Agnew Mumm.

On the day after that on which Tom was executed, two parliamentary elections were brought to a termination. The borough of Pottledown returned as its member Sir Nicol Giltspur. The electors had enjoyed his beer and his bribes; and, led by the parsons of the State-paid Church, supported by game-preserving squires, by beer-kings, by roughs, and the jingo party generally, they decided, notwithstanding that their borough was teeming with all forms of pauperism, that the Tory principles which the civic knight professed were worthy of all acceptation.

So they sent him to St. Stephen's as the avowed enemy of all reform, and pledged to vote in favour of the maintenance of every British abuse.

The borough of Nobbington, at the same time, elected as its representative Agnew Mumm. The voters well knew that his poor thin lisping voice would never be heard in the House of Commons; and that he possessed neither the brains of a statesman nor the heart of a reformer. Yet they put him forward as their advocate and exponent. They could not allege that they were in love with the odd muddled political creed which he pleaded

The explanation of their conduct was found in the fact that he had systematically purchased the good-will of powerful sections of sectarians and crotchet-mongers, and by means of an elaborate administrative machinery had woven such an electoral net-work as precluded the successful approach into the borough of any rival candidate.

Both the honourable members ascended to St. Stephen's amidst a chorus of parliamentary hosannas. In the decline of life their own ambition, their wealth, and the public folly, secured for them two seats in Parliament which should have been given to men who had the eye to see, the heart to feel, and the courage to declare, the rights and the requirements of the over-taxed people of the realm.

Mr. Melville felt little interest in these elections. The lamentable end of Tom, the conduct of Golding, the apathy of doctrinal religionists to the claims of duty, the hollowness and insincerity of public men, and the servility of society, oppressed and saddened him. It is not to be inferred, however, that he at any time gave way to misanthropy; for, the fact is, that after the events related in this book, he exerted himself more energetically than ever in all good works.

He discussed his opinions freely with Mr. Lorraine, and carefully considered the causes which had produced England's social anomalies. Whilst he did so, the determination grew stronger within him every day to commence a crusade against the institutionalized iniquities of society.

His intellect, and his heart, alike revolted against the sycophancy, fanaticism, injustice, ignorance, and un-Christliness, which he beheld throughout the length and breadth of the land, organized for a variety of purposes into approved conventional systems, which displaced morality from politics, and divorced honesty from religion. He had long since grown weary of the jargon, and the din, of all that noble army of fashionable retainers who, in

dred blatant religio-commercial societies, are confederated for the purpose of proclaiming and defending—not the inherent rights and noble destiny of the human soul—but the gospel of technical respectability, the gospel of vapid inanity, the gospel of lachrymose dogmas, the gospel of vested interests, the gospel of dynastic supremacy, the gospel of hierarchic sovereignty, the gospel of silly ceremonies, the gospel of consolidated hypocrisy, the gospel according to Cant.

He felt that the hope of humanity must be sought in regions far beyond the English Religious Fogland. He was convinced that in the teaching, and in the spirit, of Jesus Christ, and nowhere else, was to be found that light which would guide mankind out of their selfishness, and sinfulness, into the paths of benevolence, and the virtues. Having the courage of his opinions, he, when his decision was ripe and his plans for action were mature, proclaimed to the world his conviction that conventional religiosity was a monstrous imposture. He asserted that the principles of Jesus Christ were practically ignored in modern English life—not only by the masses of this pharisaic, materialistic age, but notoriously by those who usurped their theological leadership and dominion, the priests, the charlatans, and the mountebanks. He protested that in his opinion England, with her Bloosters, her Goldings, her Falcon Smalls, and her Crayfords, was not worshipping Christ, but Cant.

Such utterances as these, from such a man, soon attracted extensive attention, and the various opulent virtue-monopolies of the country naturally, and at once, united against him in every demonstration of indignation which wounded vanity, rampant self-righteousness, and ecclesiastical rancour and virulence, could invent.

The entire tribe of professional theosophists, and all those paid and unpaid officials and high priests in the temple of Cant who profanely simulate the voice of God, and who impiously cajole mankind by delivering spurious judgments in His name, raised a multitudinous shout of angry execration.

But portentous clamour invented by the spite of mercenaries, and the frenzy of fanatics, possessed no power to appal a man who recognised the sound as being nothing but that mechanical stage thunder with which the strutting actors in the tinsel theatre of Cant are wont to delight their admirers, and intimidate clowns, and dupes.

With undisturbed serenity, and in company with his ever faithful friend Mr. Lorraine, he therefore pursued his daring course, inveighing against shams and falsehood, denouncing bigotry and oppression, pointing humanity to the True, the Beautiful, and the Good, and to the one Great Ideal.

Success to all who follow him in the heroic crusade against Cant, and to all who join him and his companions on their grand march!

May they everywhere overturn the false gods and images to which society is offering prayers! May they set Christianity free from those accursed bonds by which state-craft, priest-craft, and money-craft, have for centuries held her captive!

Success, again we say, to the revolt against modern Cant!

Humanity has endured its debasing tyranny far too long; the hour has struck when it should be dethroned for ever. It has polluted whatever it has touched. Its myriad subtle, sinister influences have forced their disease, mildew, blight, and venom, into the most holy scenes and associations!

Christianity is the purest of moral atmospheres; it invigorates the brain, and energizes the heart. Cant has emitted its filthy, putrescent, and deadly exhalations, into and throughout all those religious scenes where men go to seek that Divine atmosphere, so that unwarily they sicken, become delirious, languish, or die, even when searching for

Christianity is a spiritual garden, a paradise for the soul. Cant has violated its sacred precincts, destroyed the fairest fruits and flowers, and, in their place, has planted a rank and pestilent vegetation, reeking with poison for mankind. She has blasted all the landscape, and has hushed the jubilant voices of nature which resounded through the groves and bowers. Where she has located herself, no honest man is permitted an entrance; for the hissing Serpents of Slander are commissioned to guard the gate, and to attack with their deadly stings whosoever is unwilling to render to Omnipotent Cant, praise, glory, and gratitude, for the hideous desolation, and devastation which she has wrought.

Christianity is a fertilising river, impregnated with vitalising elements, and intended to be a blessing to the whole human race. In compliance with the vitiated taste of her votaries, Cant, like a demon, has been lurking at the spring, and, with the remains of corrupt theologies, has been poisoning the waters as they rise. She has delighted to construct narrow channels, stagnant pools, dirty ditches, baptisteries, fonts, and detestable barriers, for the purpose of intercepting the beneficent progress of the stream. She aims at empire, self-aggrandisement, and proprietorship, and, for her mercenary and tyrannical ends, would limit even the power of God. She abominates the freedom, the breadth, the vastness, and the grandeur of that "living" river, the waters whereof, in spite of villainy, will one day, by Heaven's decree, "make glad" all the nations of the world.

Success, then, to the crusade against Cant!

All hail! the dawning of that day which shall behold the final flight of the monster and her minions!

Published by Walter Scott.

Canterbury Poets, The. Cloth, Red Edges, 1s.;
Cloth, Uncut Edges, 1s.; Red Roan, Gilt Edges, 2s. 6d.
"Sunflower" Edition, 1s. 6d.; Roan, Gilt Edges, 2s. 6d.

American Humorous Verse. Edited by James Barr, of the *Detroit Free Press.*
> "An anthology of *American Humorous Verse*, by James Barr, is a work of rare excellence. Mr. Barr knows what he is about. His book is full of good pieces which are unfamiliar. There could be no higher praise."—*British Weekly.*

American Sonnets. Selected and edited by William Sharp.
> "Mr. Sharp's critical and explanatory introduction is good reading, and he deserves all praise for the rich literary dish he has provided."—*Birmingham Daily Gazette.*

Australian Ballads and Rhymes. Poems inspired by Life and Scenery in Australia and New Zealand. Selected and edited by Douglas B. W. Sladen, B.A., Oxon.
> "Mr. Douglas Sladen's pretty little volume is doubly welcome, not only as the first poetical anthology of the 'youngest born of Britain's great dominions,' but for its pleasant introduction of the singers whose songs have made it up, and for a valuable study of Henry Kendall as a bush poet."—*Academy.*

Ballades and Rondeaus, Chants Royal, Sestinas, Villanelles, etc. Selected, with chapter on the various forms, by J. Gleeson White.
> "Mr. Gleeson White's collection of *Ballades and Rondeaus* is a really delightful little book."—*Pall Mall Gazette.*

Beaumont and Fletcher's Plays. Selected, with an Introduction, by John S. Fletcher.
> "Any one who wishes to get some acquaintance of 'the sweets' of these dramatists without 'the bitters,' should give this little volume a place on their book-shelves."—*Oxford Review.*

Ben Jonson, Dramatic Works and Lyrics of. Selected, with Essay, Biographical and Critical, by John Addington Symonds.
> "A selection discreetly compounded and introduced by an admirable biographical and critical preface."—*Saturday Review.*

Béranger, Songs of. Translated and edited, with an Introduction, by William Toynbee. (*In preparation.*)

Blake, Poems and Specimens from the Prose Writings of. Edited, with Introductory Notice, by Joseph Skipsey.
> "It will delight every lover of Blake. The introductory sketch is one of the best we have read on the subject."—*Sheffield Independent.*

Alphabetical List of New Books and New Editions

Canterbury Poets—*continued.*

Border Ballads. Selected and Edited by Graham R. Tomson.
> "The best ballads are here given us out of a wide selection. The introductory note is scholarly and appreciative."—*Yorkshire Advertiser.*

Bowles, Lamb, and Hartley Coleridge. Selected, with Introduction, by William Tirebuck.
> "The work has been well and sensibly done, and the little volume ought to be welcomed as giving us the works of three poets too little known nowadays; the preface is extremely good."—*The Graphic.*

Burns.—Poems. With Biographical Sketch by Joseph Skipsey.

Burns.—Songs. With Critical Estimate by Joseph Skipsey.
> "The essays are valuable additions to Burns literature, and should be read by all who are admirers of the poet, and—for that matter—by all who are not."—*Derby Gazette.*

Byron. Vol. I.—Childe Harold and Don Juan. Selected, with Introduction, by Mathilde Blind.

Byron. Vol. II.—Miscellaneous.
> "A felicitous selection, prefaced by an appreciative biography of the poet."—*Oxford Times.*

Campbell. With Introductory Notice by John Hogben.
> "The introductory essay is all that such a notice should be. The little volume is a good one, and handy for the pocket."—*The Graphic.*

Cavalier and Courtier Lyrics. Edited, with an Introduction, by Will H. Dircks.

Chatterton. With Prefatory Notice, Biographical and Critical, by John Richmond.
> "The editor has done his work with care and skill, and the biographical and critical notice with which the volume opens is a model of what such articles should be."—*Glasgow Herald.*

Chaucer. Selected and Edited by Frederick Noël Paton.
> "The introduction gives a readable sketch of Chaucer's life, and the old English is so edited that a modern reader will find no difficulty in understanding it."—*Scotsman.*

Children of the Poets. An Anthology from English and American Writers of Three Centuries. Compiled by Eric S. Robertson.
> "A most delightful volume, the *best* of the series, which is saying a great deal."

Published by Walter Scott, London.

Canterbury Poets —*continued.*

Christian Year. Thoughts in Verse for the Sundays and Holy Days throughout the Year. By Rev. John Keble, M.A.

Coleridge. With Introduction by Joseph Skipsey.
"The volume is edited with diligent care, and in the arrangement of the poems capital judgment and good taste are displayed."—*To-day.*

Cowper. Selected, with Prefatory Notice, by Eva Hope.
"Miss Hope has done her work well and sympathetically, and the collection is welcome."—*Graphic.*

Crabbe. With Prefatory Notice, Biographical and Critical, by Edward Lamplough.
"The selection has been carefully made, and we do not doubt that, under his new appearance, the old poet will be to many a most welcome guest."—*Wales Observer.*

Days of the Year. A Poetic Calendar from the Works of Alfred Austin. Selected by A. S. With Introduction by William Sharp.
"To all who care for sweet thoughts sweetly expressed; to all who find melody and harmony in Nature, this daily remembrancer of the things that we delight in cannot fail to be a welcome companion."—*Standard.*

Dobell, Sydney. Selected, with Introductory Memoir, by Mrs. Dobell.
"The exuberant fancy, grace, and passion of the poet are well illustrated by the selections."—*Leeds Mercury.*

Early English Poetry. Selected, with Critical Introduction and Notes, by H. Macaulay Fitzgibbon.
"The work has been well done, and should be in the hands of all students of Early English Poetry."

Elfin Music. An Anthology of English Fairy Poetry. Selected and arranged, with an Introduction, by Arthur Edward Waite.
"This is a unique production, and abounds in gems of poetry, every great poet being placed under contribution. Mr. Waite's introduction is a careful historical treatment of the subject of fairy lore, which cannot fail to be of value to the student of literature."—*The Examiner.*

Emerson. With Prefatory Note by Walter Lewin.
"Readers may rest assured that no better, handier, or cheaper edition of the great essayist's poems—poems which, under all their rugged irregularities of form, are still brimful of deep and sincere thought—will ever be likely to come into market than that now lying before us in 'The Canterbury Poets.'"—*Dundee Advertiser.*

Alphabetical List of New Books and New Editions

Canterbury Poets—*continued.*

English Love Lyrics. Selected and edited by Percy Hulburd.

> "An attractive addition has just been made to Mr. Walter Scott's Canterbury Poets Series, in 'English Love Lyrics,' selected and edited, with an introduction, by Percy Hulburd."—*Graphic.*

German Ballads. Translated and edited, with an Introductory Note, by Elizabeth Craigmyle. (*In preparation.*)

Goethe's "Faust," with some of the Minor Poems. Edited by Elizabeth Craigmyle.

> "The essay by the editor is worthy of the subject; and the little volume is a choice and handy edition of the great poem."—*Newcastle Daily Journal.*

Goldsmith, The Plays and Poems of. With Introduction by William Tirebuck.

> "The introduction is a skilful piece of compressed biography, succinct, graphic, and faithful."—*Yorkshire Post.*

Great Odes: English and American. Selected and edited, with Introduction, by William Sharp.

> "The selection is a judicious one, and gives a good idea of the Great Odes of the English-speaking races."—*Oxford Review.*

Greek Anthology, Selections from. Edited by Graham R. Tomson.

> "Mrs. Arthur Tomson's delightful little volume of translations. . . . The introduction is exactly what it should be. It conveys a great deal of information, yet is sympathetic and picturesque in style from beginning to end."—*National Observer.*

Greenwell, Dora, Poems of. With a Biographical Introduction by William Dorling.

> "The selection before us is excellent in every way, and includes some of the best of her poetical pieces."—*Oxford Times.*

Heine, Heinrich. Selected, with Introduction, by Mrs. Kroeker.

> "Mrs. Freiligrath-Kroeker may be congratulated on her successful achievement, and we can heartily recommend her selections from Heine's poems to every English household where poetry is cherished."—*Literary World.*

Herbert's Poems, to which are added Selections from his Prose, and Walton's Life. With Introduction by Ernest Rhys.

> "The volume is altogether a delightful, comprehensive, and important one, and Mr. Scott has done well to issue it in his very valuable, neat, and cheap series."—*Brechin Advertiser.*

Published by Walter Scott, London.

Canterbury Poets—*continued.*

Herrick—Hesperides. With Notes by Herbert P. Horne.
> "A pretty edition, with some good notes."—*Athenæum.*

Hogg, James, the Ettrick Shepherd. Selected. Edited, with Introduction, by the Poet's Daughter, Mrs. Garden.
> "The reader may be assured that he has here the finest and most characteristic work of James Hogg."—*Oxford Times.*

Horace, Translations from. With Notes. By Sir Stephen E. De Vere, Bart.
> "This third edition is published in a cheap and handy form, and whatever verdict the public may pronounce on the translations themselves, no lover of Horace will refuse a grateful tribute of warm and well-merited praise to them, and to the admirable preface which sets them off so brilliantly."—*The Spectator.*

Hugo, Victor. Translated by Dean Carrington, with Introduction by Countess Martinengo-Cesaresco.
> "The translation is good, and I am reading the poems with much interest. I have no copy of them in the original, but there is a source of much enjoyment in the translation."—JOHN BRIGHT.

Humorous Poems of the Century. Edited by Ralph H. Caine.
> "Mr. Ralph H. Caine has got together a really amusing collection of humorous poems of the century to add to the Canterbury Poets."—*Manchester Guardian.*

Hunt and Hood, the Poetical Works of. Edited, with Introduction, by J. Harwood Panting.
> "The extracts are preceded by short biographical notices, and Mr. Panting, in his introduction, gives a careful estimate of the qualities and achievements of the two poets."—*Newcastle Daily Leader.*

Irish Minstrelsy. Being a selection of Irish Songs, Lyrics, and Ballads; Original and Translated. Edited, with Notes and Introduction, by H. Halliday Sparling.
> "It is such an anthology of Irish poetry up to the most recent date as will be a revelation of hitherto hidden wealth to most readers, and to experts will seem a triumph of competent editing."—*Truth.*

Jacobite Songs and Ballads. Selected, with Notes and Introduction, by G. S. Macquoid.
> "The selection is excellent, and the accompanying 'notes' exactly what is wanted in such a book."—*Arbroath Herald.*

Keats. With Introductory Sketch by John Hogben.
> "It is, like its fellows, a pleasant and convenient little volume."—

Alphabetical List of New Books and New Editions

Canterbury Poets—*continued.*

Lady of Lyons, The, and other Plays. By Lord Lytton. Edited, with an Introduction, by Farquharson Sharp.
"Many people will be glad to have the text of all three pieces in the neat and handy form in which they are here presented."—*Scottish Leader.*

Landor. Selected and edited by Ernest Radford.
"Altogether, we cannot speak too highly of this beautiful little volume of selections from Landor."—*Volunteer Service Gazette.*

Living Scottish Poets. Edited by Sir George Douglas, Bart. (*In preparation.*)

Longfellow. Selected, with Introduction, by Eva Hope.
"We have not seen yet so good a life of the poet as that which is included in this volume."—*Sunday School Times.*

Love-Letters of a Violinist, and other Poems. By Eric Mackay.
"He will probably be numbered with the choice few whose names are destined to live by the side of poets such as Keats, whom, as far as careful work, delicate feeling, and fiery tenderness go, he greatly resembles."—*Glasgow Herald.*

Marlowe, Selections from the Dramatic Works of. With Introduction by Percy E. Pinkerton.
"It gives us all that is best and most worthy of preservation in the poet's works in a compact and handy form."—*Literary World.*

Marston, Philip Bourke.—Song-Tide: Poems and Lyrics of Love's Joy and Sorrow. Edited, with Introductory Memoir, by William Sharp.
"Altogether, this volume is one for which we cannot offer Mr. Sharp gratitude too warm."—*Academy.*

Milton's Paradise Lost. Edited by J. Bradshaw, M.A., LL.D.
"All who desire to have the masterpiece of the great Puritan poet in a convenient and easily accessible form could not do better than become possessed of this issue."—*Dundee Advertiser.*

Moore, Poems of. Selected, with Introduction, by John Dorrian.
"The selections are judiciously made, and are conveniently grouped in appropriate classes; and the volume as a whole contains most of what the general reader would care to see of Moore."—*Aberdeen Free Press.*

Ossian. Poems of Ossian. Translated by James Macpherson, with an Introduction, Historical and Critical, by George Eyre-Todd.
"The poems of Ossian, as all scholars know, deserve a high place in the world of poetry, and in this edition will be found all that is of value in a translation at once able and characteristic."—*Barrow*

Published by Walter Scott, London.

Canterbury Poets—*continued.*

Owen Meredith (the Earl of Lytton), Poems of. Selected, with an Introduction, by M. Betham-Edwards.
"The selection is well made, and the selector's brief criticisms are adequate and to the point."—*Scotsman.*

Painter-Poets, The. Selected and Edited, with an Introduction and Notes, by Kineton Parkes.
"A good idea has been successfully carried out in this volume."—*Birmingham Daily Gazette.*

Paradise Regained, and Minor Poems. Edited by J. Bradshaw, M.A., LL.D.
"Mr. Bradshaw's selection ought to gain new readers for our noble Puritan poet among a generation that knows him too little."—*Northern Daily Telegraph.*

Poe. Poems, with Selections from the Prose. With Biographical Sketch by Joseph Skipsey.
"A choice edition, with a very good preface."

Pope. With Introductory Sketch by John Hogben.
"Mr. Hogben's selection and sketch are alike to be commended."

Praed. With Introductory Notice by Frederick Cooper.
"The first to give in convenient and cheap form a substantive selection of the work of one of the most charming of English verse-writers. His introduction is good."—*Saturday Review.*

Ramsay, Allan. With Biographical Sketch by J. Logie Robertson, M.A.
"The reading public have now what they had not before—a cheap and well-appointed edition of Ramsay, which gives all his best work and nothing but his best."—*Scotsman.*

Scott. Marmion, etc. Edited, with Prefatory Notice, by William Sharp.

Scott. Lady of the Lake, etc.
"A delightful prefatory notice."—*Derby Gazette.*

Scottish Minor Poets. From the Age of Ramsay to David Gray. Selected and Edited, with an Introduction, Glossary, and Notes, by Sir George Douglas, Bart.

Sea Music. An Anthology of Poems and Passages descriptive of the Sea. Edited by Mrs. Sharp.
"A volume for all lovers of the sea."

Shakespeare: Songs, Poems, and Sonnets. With Critical Introduction by William Sharp.
"The introductory note to this little volume of Shakespeare's Songs, Poems, and Sonnets is characterised by very sound common sense."—*Oxford Review.*

Canterbury Poets—*continued*.

Shelley. Lyrics and Minor Poems. With Introduction by Joseph Skipsey.
> "The very best and most characteristic of his work is represented."—*Cambridge Undergraduates' Journal.*

Songs of Labour. An Anthology. Selected and Edited by H. S. Salt. (*In preparation.*)

Sonnets of this Century. Edited by William Sharp.
> "The selection is very catholic and very complete, and we do not remember the name of any poet of the century whose work is worthy of consideration whom Mr. Sharp has failed to include."—*Spectator.*

Sonnets of Europe. A Volume of Translations. Selected and arranged, with Notes, by S. Waddington.
> "The present selection is in all ways an admirable one."—*The Academy.*

Southey. Selections from the Poems of Robert Southey. Edited, with Biographical and Critical Introduction, by Sidney R. Thompson.
> "The task of selection has been accomplished with insight and feeling. . . . Mr. Thompson also contributes a critical introduction, which is well written, shrewd, appreciative, and in every way competent."—*Notes and Queries.*

Spenser. Selected, with an Essay, Biographical and Critical, and Glossary, by Hon. Roden Noel.
> "The introductory essay is well done, and altogether the volume is a valuable addition to the series of 'Canterbury Poets.'"—*Cambridge Independent Press.*

Whitman, Walt. Leaves of Grass. Edited, with Introduction, by Ernest Rhys.

Whittier. Selected, with Introductory Notice, by Eva Hope.
> "Excellent, with a judicious memoir. It includes the poet's best work."—*Saturday Review.*

Wild Life, Poems of. Selected and edited by Charles G. D. Roberts.
> "The editing of this little volume has been executed with enthusiasm and yet also with care."—*Spectator.*

Women Poets of the Victorian Era. Selected and edited by Mrs. William Sharp.
> "Admirably done."—*Scottish Leader.*

Wordsworth. Selected and edited, with Introduction, Biographical and Critical, by A. J. Symington.
> "Every student of Wordsworth will be glad to have the poems in so small a compass, and prefaced with such an intelligent critical notice."—*Civil Service Gazette.*

Demy 8vo, Cloth, Gilt Edges, Price 5s. each.

Life of General Gordon.

WITH ILLUSTRATIONS.

By the Author of "Our Queen," &c., &c.

Heroes of the Great Republic.

ILLUSTRATED. LIVES OF

GENERAL GRANT, GENERAL LEE,
ABRAHAM LINCOLN, PRESIDENT GARFIELD,
AND LLOYD GARRISON.

By the Author of "Livingstone" and "Stanley."

Great Engineers.

WITH PORTRAITS AND ILLUSTRATIONS.

LIVES OF GEORGE AND ROBERT STEPHENSON,
TREVITHICK—HEDLEY—HACKWORTH—
I. K. BRUNEL—LORD ARMSTRONG—EIFFEL—
FOWLER—BAKER.

By J. F. LAYSON.

Life of John Wesley.

WITH PORTRAITS AND ILLUSTRATIONS.

By EDITH C. KENYON.

London: WALTER SCOTT, 24 Warwick Lane, Paternoster Row.

THE NOVELTY OF THE SEASON.

SELECTED THREE-VOL. SETS

IN NEW BROCADE BINDING.

6s. per Set, in Shell Case to match.

THE FOLLOWING SETS CAN BE OBTAINED—

POEMS OF

WORDSWORTH. KEATS. SHELLEY.	COLERIDGE. SOUTHEY. COWPER.	EARLY ENGLISH POETRY. CHAUCER. SPENSER.
LONGFELLOW. WHITTIER. EMERSON.	BORDER BALLADS. JACOBITE SONGS. OSSIAN.	HORACE. GREEK ANTHOLOGY. LANDOR.
HOGG. ALLAN RAMSAY. SCOTTISH MINOR POETS.	CAVALIER POETS. LOVE LYRICS. HERRICK.	GOLDSMITH. MOORE. IRISH MINSTRELSY.
SHAKESPEARE. BEN JONSON. MARLOWE.	CHRISTIAN YEAR. IMITATION OF CHRIST. HERBERT.	WOMEN POETS. CHILDREN OF POETS. SEA MUSIC.
SONNETS OF THIS CENTURY. SONNETS OF EUROPE. AMERICAN SONNETS.	AMERICAN HUMOROUS VERSE. ENGLISH HUMOROUS VERSE.	PRAED. HUNT AND HOOD. DOBELL.
HEINE. GOETHE. HUGO.	BALLADES AND RONDEAUS.	MEREDITH. MARSTON. LOVE LETTERS.

SELECTED TWO-VOLUME SETS

IN NEW BROCADE BINDING.

4s. per Set, in Shell Case to match.

SCOTT (Lady of the Lake, etc.). SCOTT (Marmion, etc.).	BYRON (Don Juan, etc.). BYRON (Miscellaneous).
BURNS (Songs). BURNS (Poems).	MILTON (Paradise Lost). MILTON (Paradise Regained, etc.).

London: WALTER SCOTT, 24 Warwick Lane, Paternoster Row.

SELECTED THREE-VOL. SETS

IN NEW BROCADE BINDING.

6s. per Set, in Shell Case to match.

O. W. HOLMES SERIES—

Autocrat of the Breakfast-Table.

The Professor at the Breakfast-Table.

The Poet at the Breakfast Table.

LANDOR SERIES—

Landor's Imaginary Conversations.

Pentameron.

Pericles and Aspasia.

THREE ENGLISH ESSAYISTS—

Essays of Elia.

Essays of Leigh Hunt.

Essays of William Hazlitt.

THREE CLASSICAL MORALISTS—

Meditations of Marcus Aurelius.

Teaching of Epictetus.

Morals of Seneca.

WALDEN SERIES—

Thoreau's Walden.

Thoreau's Week.

Thoreau's Essays.

FAMOUS LETTERS—

Letters of Burns.

Letters of Byron.

Letters of Shelley.

LOWELL SERIES—

My Study Windows.

The English Poets.

The Biglow Papers.

London: WALTER SCOTT, 24 Warwick Lane, Paternoster Row.

GREAT WRITERS.

A NEW SERIES OF CRITICAL BIOGRAPHIES.

Edited by Professor ERIC S. ROBERTSON, M.A.

MONTHLY SHILLING VOLUMES.

VOLUMES ALREADY ISSUED—

LIFE OF LONGFELLOW. By Prof. Eric S. Robertson.
"A most readable little work."—*Liverpool Mercury.*

LIFE OF COLERIDGE. By Hall Caine.
"Brief and vigorous, written throughout with spirit and great literary skill."—*Scotsman.*

LIFE OF DICKENS. By Frank T. Marzials.
"Notwithstanding the mass of matter that has been printed relating to Dickens and his works . . we should, until we came across this volume, have been at a loss to recommend any popular life of England's most popular novelist as being really satisfactory. The difficulty is removed by Mr. Marzials's little book."—*Athenæum.*

LIFE OF DANTE GABRIEL ROSSETTI. By J. Knight.
"Mr. Knight's picture of the great poet and painter is the fullest and best yet presented to the public."—*The Graphic.*

LIFE OF SAMUEL JOHNSON. By Colonel F. Grant.
"Colonel Grant has performed his task with diligence, sound judgment, good taste, and accuracy."—*Illustrated London News.*

LIFE OF DARWIN. By G. T. Bettany.
"Mr. G. T. Bettany's *Life of Darwin* is a sound and conscientious work."—*Saturday Review.*

LIFE OF CHARLOTTE BRONTË. By A. Birrell.
"Those who know much of Charlotte Brontë will learn more, and those who know nothing about her will find all that is best worth learning in Mr. Birrell's pleasant book."—*St. James' Gazette.*

LIFE OF THOMAS CARLYLE. By R. Garnett, LL.D.
"This is an admirable book. Nothing could be more felicitous and fairer than the way in which he takes us through Carlyle's life and works."—*Pall Mall Gazette.*

LIFE OF ADAM SMITH. By R. B. Haldane, M.P.
"Written with a perspicuity seldom exemplified when dealing with economic science."—*Scotsman.*

LIFE OF KEATS. By W. M. Rossetti.
"Valuable for the ample information which it contains."—*Cambridge Independent.*

LIFE OF SHELLEY. By William Sharp.
"The criticisms . . . entitle this capital monograph to be ranked with the best biographies of Shelley."—*Westminster Review.*

LIFE OF SMOLLETT. By David Hannay.
"A capable record of a writer who still remains one of the great masters of the English novel."—*Saturday Review.*

LIFE OF GOLDSMITH. By Austin Dobson.
"The story of his literary and social life in London, with all its humorous and pathetic vicissitudes, is here retold, as none could tell it better."—*Daily News.*

LIFE OF SCOTT. By Professor Yonge.
"This is a most enjoyable book."—*Aberdeen Free Press.*

LIFE OF BURNS. By Professor Blackie.
"The editor certainly made a hit when he persuaded Blackie to write about Burns."—*Pall Mall Gazette.*

LIFE OF VICTOR HUGO. By Frank T. Marzials.
"Mr. Marzials's volume presents to us, in a more handy form than any English or even French handbook gives, the summary of what is known about the life of the great poet."—*Saturday Review.*

LIFE OF EMERSON. By Richard Garnett, LL.D.
"No record of Emerson's life could be more desirable."—*Saturday Review.*

LIFE OF GOETHE. By James Sime.
"Mr. James Sime's competence as a biographer of Goethe is beyond question."—*Manchester Guardian.*

LIFE OF CONGREVE. By Edmund Gosse.
"Mr. Gosse has written an admirable biography."—*Academy.*

LIFE OF BUNYAN. By Canon Venables.
"A most intelligent, appreciative, and valuable memoir."—*Scotsman.*

LIFE OF CRABBE. By T. E. Kebbel.
"No English poet since Shakespeare has observed certain aspects of nature and of human life more closely."—*Athenæum.*

LIFE OF HEINE. By William Sharp.
"An admirable monograph . . . more fully written up to the level of recent knowledge and criticism than any other English work."—*Scotsman.*

LIFE OF MILL. By W. L. Courtney.
"A most sympathetic and discriminating memoir."—*Glasgow Herald.*

LIFE OF SCHILLER. By Henry W. Nevinson.
"Presents the poet's life in a neatly rounded picture."—*Scotsman.*

LIFE OF CAPTAIN MARRYAT. By David Hannay.
"We have nothing but praise for the manner in which Mr. Hannay has done justice to him."—*Saturday Review.*

LIFE OF LESSING. By T. W. Rolleston.
"One of the best books of the series."—*Manchester Guardian.*

LIFE OF MILTON. By Richard Garnett, LL.D.
"Has never been more charmingly or adequately told."—*Scottish Leader.*

LIFE OF BALZAC. By Frederick Wedmore.

LIFE OF GEORGE ELIOT. By Oscar Browning.

LIFE OF JANE AUSTEN. By Goldwin Smith.

LIFE OF BROWNING. By William Sharp.

LIFE OF BYRON. By Hon. Roden Noel.

LIFE OF HAWTHORNE. By Moncure Conway.

LIFE OF SCHOPENHAUER. By Professor Wallace.

LIFE OF SHERIDAN. By Lloyd Sanders.

LIFE OF THACKERAY. By Herman Merivale and Frank T. Marzials.

LIFE OF CERVANTES. By W. E. Watts.

Library Edition of "Great Writers," Demy 8vo, 2s. 6d.

London: WALTER SCOTT, 24 Warwick Lane, Paternoster Row.

Quarto, cloth elegant, gilt edges, emblematic design on cover, 6s.
May also be had in a variety of Fancy Bindings.

THE
MUSIC OF THE POETS:
A MUSICIANS' BIRTHDAY BOOK.

EDITED BY ELEONORE D'ESTERRE KEELING.

This is a unique Birthday Book. Against each date are given the names of musicians whose birthday it is, together with a verse-quotation appropriate to the character of their different compositions or performances. A special feature of the book consists in the reproduction in fac-simile of autographs, and autographic music, of living composers. The selections of verse (from before Chaucer to the present time) have been made with admirable critical insight. English verse is rich in utterances of the poets about music, and merely as a volume of poetry about music this book makes a charming anthology. Three sonnets by Mr. Theodore Watts, on the "Fausts" of Berlioz, Schumann, and Gounod, have been written specially for this volume. It is illustrated with designs of various musical instruments, etc.; autographs of Rubenstein, Dvorâk, Greig, Mackenzie, Villiers Stanford, etc., etc.

"To musical amateurs this will certainly prove the most attractive birthday book ever published."—*Manchester Guardian.*

"One of those happy ideas that seems to have been yearning for fulfilment. . . . The book ought to have a place on every music stand."—*Scottish Leader.*

London: WALTER SCOTT, 24 Warwick Lane, Paternoster Row.

Demy 8vo, Cloth, 420 Pages, Price 7s. 6d.

A SHORT HISTORY

OF

ANGLO-SAXON FREEDOM.

THE POLITY OF THE ENGLISH-SPEAKING RACE.

By JAMES K. HOSMER, Professor in Washington University; Author of "*A Life of Young Sir Harry Vane*," etc.

In this book an effort is made to compress a sketch of constitutional history for a period of nearly two thousand years, from the time of the Teutons of Cæsar and Tacitus to the British Empire and United States of 1890. Anglo-Saxon polity, in its long history, has shown adaptation to the needs of ever vaster multitudes and higher civilisations, manifold development and elaboration, one spirit, however, surviving throughout it all, apparent in the deliberations of the ancient folk-moots as in those of a modern Parliament. It is this unity which is traced in this highly interesting and brilliantly-written book.

"A volume in which Professor Hosmer ably propounds and justifies his well-known views. . . . The work might very properly be used in schools, but is also interesting to grown people, and may be strongly recommended to mechanics' institutes, workmen's clubs, and public libraries."—*Athenæum*.

London: WALTER SCOTT, 24 Warwick Lane, Paternoster Row.

COMPACT AND PRACTICAL.

In Limp Cloth; for the Pocket. Price One Shilling.

THE EUROPEAN
CONVERSATION BOOKS.

FRENCH	ITALIAN
SPANISH	GERMAN
NORWEGIAN	

CONTENTS.

Hints to Travellers—Everyday Expressions—Arriving at and Leaving a Railway Station—Custom House Enquiries—In a Train—At a Buffet and Restaurant—At an Hotel—Paying an Hotel Bill—Enquiries in a Town—On Board Ship—Embarking and Disembarking—Excursion by Carriage—Enquiries as to Diligences—Enquiries as to Boats—Engaging Apartments—Washing List and Days of Week—Restaurant Vocabulary—Telegrams and Letters, etc., etc.

The contents of these little handbooks are so arranged as to permit direct and immediate reference. All dialogues or enquiries not considered absolutely essential have been purposely excluded, nothing being introduced which might confuse the traveller rather than assist him. A few hints are given in the introduction which will be found valuable to those unaccustomed to foreign travel.

London: WALTER SCOTT, 24 Warwick Lane, Paternoster Row.

www.ingramcontent.com/pod-product-compliance
Lightning Source LLC
Chambersburg PA
CBHW051734300426
44115CB00007B/564